Political Ecology
across Spaces, Scales,
and Social Groups

Political Ecology across Spaces, Scales, and Social Groups

EDITED BY SUSAN PAULSON
AND LISA L. GEZON

RUTGERS UNIVERSITY PRESS

NEW BRUNSWICK, NEW JERSEY, AND LONDON

LIBRARY OF CONGRESS CATALOGING-IN-PUBLICATION DATA

Political ecology across spaces, scales, and social groups / edited by Susan Paulson and Lisa L. Gezon.

    p.   cm.

Includes bibliographical references and index.

ISBN 0–8135-3477-1 (hardcover : alk. paper) — ISBN 0-8135-3478-x (pbk : alk. paper)

    I. Political ecology—Case studies.   I. Paulson, Susan, 1961-   II. Gezon, Lisa L.

JA75.8.P627 2004

304.2—dc22

2004007499

A British Cataloging-in-Publication record for this book is available from the British Library

Manufactured in the United States of America

CONTENTS

Acknowledgments   *vii*

1   Place, Power, Difference: Multiscale Research at the Dawn
     of the Twenty-first Century   1
     LISA L. GEZON AND SUSAN PAULSON

2   Politics, Ecologies, Genealogies   17
     SUSAN PAULSON, LISA L. GEZON, AND MICHAEL WATTS

PART ONE
Policy and Environment

3   The Fight for the West: A Political Ecology of Land-Use
     Conflicts in Arizona   41
     METTE J. BROGDEN AND JAMES B. GREENBERG

4   Whose Water? Political Ecology of Water Reform
     in Zimbabwe   61
     ANNE FERGUSON AND BILL DERMAN

5   The New Calculus of Bedouin Pastoralism
     in the Kingdom of Saudi Arabia   76
     ANDREW GARDNER

6   Land Tenure and Biodiversity: An Exploration
     in the Political Ecology of Murang'a District, Kenya   94
     A. FIONA D. MACKENZIE

7   The Political Ecology of Consumption:
     Beyond Greed and Guilt   113
     JOSIAH McC. HEYMAN

PART TWO

Social Hierarchies in Local-Global Relationships

8   Finding the Global in the Local: Environmental Struggles
     in Northern Madagascar   135
       LISA L. GEZON

9   Symbolic Action and Soil Fertility: Political Ecology and the
     Transformation of Space and Place in Tonga   154
       CHARLES J. STEVENS

10   Gendered Practices and Landscapes in the Andes:
     The Shape of Asymmetrical Exchanges   174
       SUSAN PAULSON

11   Undermining Modernity: Protecting Landscapes and
     Meanings among the Mi'kmaq of Nova Scotia   196
       ALF HORNBORG

PART THREE

Forest Visions

12   Shade: Throwing Light on Politics and Ecology
     in Contemporary Pakistan   217
       MICHAEL R. DOVE

13   A Global Political Ecology of Bioprospecting   239
       HANNE SVARSTAD

14   The Emergence of Collective Ethnic Identities
     and Alternative Political Ecologies in the
     Colombian Pacific Rainforest   257
       ARTURO ESCOBAR AND SUSAN PAULSON

     Notes on Contributors   279
     Index   283

ACKNOWLEDGMENTS

Five years ago, as we planned an invited session at the ninety-ninth annual meeting of the American Anthropological Association, we began the conversations that led to the collaborative production of this book. Most of the contributors were present at that double session, held in San Francisco in November 2000, as either presenters or participants in the ensuing discussions. Andrew Vayda, who had provided important stimulus in his 1999 co-authored article "Against Political Ecology," used his role as discussant to pose a series of key challenges for ongoing work.

Our shared enthusiasm to address those challenges and continue to explore the methodological and theoretical possibilities of political ecology evolved into a special issue of *Human Organization* (vol. 62, no. 3, fall 2003) called "Locating the Political in Political Ecology." Thanks go to Don Stull, editor of *Human Organization*, for offering excellent editorial support, obtaining serious and comprehensive peer reviews, and guiding us in ways that made our message accessible and valuable to a wider audience. Six articles from that special issue—those by Mette J. Brogden and James B. Greenberg, Anne Ferguson and Bill Derman, Michael R. Dove, Andrew Gardner, Susan Paulson, and A. Fiona D. Mackenzie—were adapted as chapters for this book, where they are complemented by eight new chapters. While the book builds on concepts and challenges outlined in the introduction to that special issue, its broadened scope of interest is manifest in the reshaping of specific analyses and the incorporation of a variety of new topics and types of study.

We are grateful for the sincere commitment of the thirteen scholars from several disciplines who contributed so enthusiastically to this book. We also want to acknowledge other scholars who have been valuable contributors to our ongoing discussions about political ecology, its applications, and its possibilities since the inception of this project. The intellectual participation of Janice Harper and Dianne Rocheleau, who presented valuable papers related to these themes at the 2000 and 2001 American Anthropology Association meetings and engaged in fruitful exchanges with both editors, enhanced the book's development. Their work in applying political ecology to urban settings is advancing the frontiers of the field in exciting ways. Other key interlocutors include Gene Anderson, Tom McGuire, Susan Lees, Terre Satterfield, and Brad Walters. We thank all of them for their contributions to the conceptual and methodological discussions advanced here. And we thank those who have made this project practically feasible, including Kristi Long, our editor at Rutgers University Press; Adi Hovav, editorial assistant at Rutgers; Jessica Cook, undergraduate assistant to Lisa L. Gezon at the State University of West Georgia; and Andrew Gardner, who did a careful job compiling the index.

We would like to acknowledge intellectual debts to mentors who wakened us to themes vital to this book and motivated us to explore them as graduate students and beyond. Lisa L. Gezon would like to acknowledge Conrad Kottak, who has been a constant source of encouragement and intellectual clarity, and Roy Rappaport, who inspired new ways of thinking about how humans interact with the material world around them. Susan Paulson would like to recognize Paul Friedrich for his inspiring innovations in ethnography, poetics, and politics, and Terry Turner, whose enduring work with Marxian theory in anthropology and with indigenous movements for sociocultural and territorial autonomy is echoed throughout this book.

Finally, we would like to emphasize that this project should not be read as a collection of distinct papers, each written by a single scientist representing his or her own research and analysis. This has been a participatory and collaborative project from the beginning, and the result is a book conceived and constructed as a whole, in which each part communicates a key dimension of the message and demonstrates unique applications of the shared approach. Lisa L. Gezon and Susan Paulson wrote or co-authored three and four chapters, respectively, and both engaged extensively in shaping and editing all fourteen chapters. We hope that the resulting book does credit to those participants mentioned here as well as the many others colleagues whose ideas and questions have helped to shape this collaborative project. We have worked to present key concepts, methods, and applications that characterize the dynamic field of political ecology today. This book does not aim, however, to establish an authoritative definition of political ecology. Rather, we intend to provide ideas and tools to motivate and support diverse researchers, scholars, students, and actors to understand and address human-environmental issues in ways we have not yet dreamed of.

SUSAN PAULSON AND LISA L. GEZON

Political Ecology
across Spaces, Scales,
and Social Groups

1

Place, Power, Difference

Multiscale Research at the Dawn of the Twenty-first Century

LISA L. GEZON AND SUSAN PAULSON

Innovations and debates within political ecology, as well as critiques of the approach as a whole, have motivated serious reflection about the methods, concepts, and studies that make up this relatively new field. As environmental issues become increasingly prominent in local struggles, national debates, and international policies, scholars are paying more attention to conventional politics and to more broadly defined relations of power and difference in interactions among human groups and their biophysical environments. This move has generated questions about the role of politics in environmental scholarship and practice as well as concerns that ardent attention to political phenomena may leave ecological detail in the shadows. In efforts to work more closely with political, economic, *and* ecological concerns and phenomena, political ecologists have pursued several promising paths: they have looked beyond the local community to explain natural resource use, explored power dynamics in everyday interactions and formal policy arenas, and paid increasing attention to the environmental interests, knowledge, and practices of social groups differentiated by race, ethnicity, gender, or other factors.

The innovative approaches and analyses brought together in this book are representative of a new wave of research that is highly conscious of these issues. The book may be viewed as a tool kit of vital concepts in political ecology, providing a set of research models and analytic frameworks as examples for beginning researchers and more seasoned researchers and practitioners who are interested in expanding their work to encompass diverse spaces, develop multiscale analyses, and increase sensitivity to social differences.

During the past two decades, various disciplines, including anthropology, sociology, geography, biology, and political science, have embraced political ecology as an approach that addresses the concerns of both political economy and cultural ecology. In their seminal work on the social dynamics of land degradation,

1

Piers Blaikie and Harold Brookfield (1987) defined the field: "the phrase 'political ecology' combines the concerns of ecology and a broadly defined political economy. Together this encompasses the constantly shifting dialectic between society and land-based resources, and also within classes and groups within society itself" (17). By focusing on factors that shape relations of power among human groups and link local biosocial landscapes to global processes, this work has led to results that challenge dominant interpretations of the causes of environmental degradation and contest prevalent prescriptions for solving such problems.

Early political ecology developed around a set of core concepts. First is the idea that resource use is organized and transmitted through social relations that may result in the imposition of excessive pressure of production on the environment (Watts 1983). Second is the recognition of a plurality of positions, perceptions, interests, and rationalities in relation to the environment (Blaikie 1985, 16) such that one person's profit may be another's toxic dump. Third is the idea of a global connectedness through which extralocal political economic processes shape and are influenced by local spaces. And fourth is a refined concept of marginality, in which political, economic, and ecological expressions may be mutually reinforcing: "land degradation is both a result and a cause of social marginalization" (Blaikie and Brookfield 1987, 23). More recent inquiry and action have generated debate over political ecology's conceptual apparatuses, research methods, and internal logic and led to discussions and scholarship that work to strengthen the field and enhance its ability to wrestle with new issues and problems.

The studies in this book apply concepts of environment that encompass biophysical phenomena, social practice, and cultural meaning. They investigate political dimensions of the environment in a world that is interconnected by increasingly powerful communication and transportation technologies yet situated within and reliant upon widely varied geophysical locations. As a whole, the book demonstrates that a serious analysis of political phenomena and forces does not merely add another dimension to an already complicated interdisciplinary field but vitalizes environmental study and practice in crucial ways.

The Book

The studies in this book are all grounded in the political ecology framework just sketched, yet each applies distinct concepts to address specific issues and resources in a unique ecological and geographical context. Taken together, the chapters describe the use and contestation of resources such as land, water, soil, trees, biodiversity, money, knowledge, and information. They consider wideranging ecological settings, including deserts, coasts, rainforests, high mountains, and the modern metropolis; and they explore sites around the world, from Canada to Tonga.

Each chapter presents, defines, and applies selected key concepts, including those with long histories as well as recently developed ones. The ideas developed include commodification, commodity fetishism, complexity theory, consumption, discourse, empowerment and disempowerment, ethnicity, gender, globalization, identity politics, land tenure regimes, land-water reforms, modernity, modes of production, narrative, neoliberal economic policies, scarcity, stakeholders, territorialization, and webs or chains of causality. In addition to explaining their own uses of these concepts, the authors demonstrate how differently situated social and interest groups vary in their understanding and use of ideas such as biodiversity, nature, territory, and value.

Chapter 2, "Politics, Ecologies, Genealogies," traces some of the rich traditions of thought, research, and practice that have led up to current approaches to political ecology. It selectively reviews a long history of debate about relations between humans and the biophysical environment as carried on in ecological anthropology and cultural ecology, political economy and theories of global connectedness, and geography and disaster research. The chapter ends by considering some challenges faced by political ecology at the dawn of the twenty-first century, as diverse scholars continue to draw on and reinterpret these traditions, bringing them together in innovative ways with methods, ideas, and analytic turns from a range of new theoretical currents.

Part 1: Policy and Environment

This theoretical chapter is followed by three sets of cases that focus respectively on how politics and institutions affect access and use regimes, the dynamics of social differentiation in the production of globally connected local landscapes, and the ways in which diverse visions of the environment represent, negotiate, and shape landscapes and actions within them. In chapter 3, "The Fight for the West," Mette J. Brogden and James B. Greenberg explore the formidable challenges that state territorialization practices and the commodification of natural resources present for the sustainable use of natural resources. Specifically, they analyze land-use trends in Arizona, focusing on growing conflicts over the use of land for ranching and real estate development. In one such case, disputing stakeholders came together in a political initiative that fostered collaboration and knowledge sharing. In the context of this collaboration, a study of land degradation revealed that the loss of grazing land could actually be detrimental to biodiversity—a finding that was contrary to the expectations of urban-based environmentalists. The authors use this case to argue that difficult environmental problems may require innovative political approaches that rest on models of cooperation rather than competition.

In chapter 4, "Whose Water?" Anne Ferguson and William Derman examine contestations over water in Zimbabwe. From the vantage points of different social groups, water is conceptualized as a human right, a scarce commodity, and a tool for social transformation and equity. The authors' methods and analysis challenge ecological concepts that isolate nature (or environment-minus-humans) from the power-knowledge dynamics that shape human manipulations of the material world. This chapter underscores the need for environmental scholars and practitioners to engage with environmental phenomena from multiple points of entry, including those that illuminate relations of power, knowledge, and resistance and those that reveal social-racial differentiation of access and control over resources such as water.

In chapter 5, "The New Calculus of Bedouin Pastoralism," Andrew Gardner works with rapid appraisal activities among Bedouin herders in Saudi Arabia but also examines extralocal institutions and government policies and analyzes regional climate and other environmental trends. Gardner's investigation of increasing disease and mortality among herds kept by Bedouins in the wake of the Gulf War starts with the popular hypothesis that smoke from oil fires caused the declines. Yet his study identifies additional contributing factors, including changes in border policies, governmental price supports for barley, the expanded use of pickups and water trucks, the growth of a cheap expatriate labor force, and a decade-long drought. Gardner argues that narrowly focusing analysis on specific environmental events such as the Kuwaiti oil fires limits understanding of the complex webs of determination and the interlinked processes that account for outcomes such as desertification.

Like Gardner, Fiona D. Mackenzie, in chapter 6, "Land Tenure and Biodiversity," rejects research models that circumscribe inquiry to the local level and principally seek proximal causes. In an innovative analytical move, she brings together literature on land tenure and biodiversity, examining the effect of various land tenure regimes and related agricultural processes on the presence of biodiversity. In her study of the Murang'a District in Kenya, she analyzes the exercise of power in gendered struggles to access and control land in highly complex situations of legal plurality and considers how these struggles interrelate with productive practices to affect conditions of biodiversity. In this programmatic piece, Mackenzie identifies both various kinds of land tenure and a series of questions one needs to ask to uncover what each form of tenure might imply for biodiversity. The chapter implicitly critiques biodiversity studies that focus on forests, ignoring the importance of biodiversity in agriculture.

In chapter 7, "The Political Ecology of Consumption," Josiah McC. Heyman moves us to an urban setting, studying patterns of consumption on the U.S.-Mexican border. He contrasts concerns about excessive consumption on the part of scientists, environmental activists, and prosperous people of the world with concerns of the working poor, who worry about not being able to consume enough. In a political ecology analysis of consumption, he explores historical processes by which people became consumers of mass manufactured goods and resource-energy inputs, politics of credit and wages, changes in the arrangement of space and time, and larger dynamics of national debt, currency exchange values, and the North American Free Trade Agreement (NAFTA). This chapter reveals the limits of typical policy approaches (such as price incentives and moral suasion) to ameliorating the environmental effects of consumption and brings to the fore alternative approaches centered on shared learning between experts and populaces.

Part 2: Social Hierarchies in Local-Global Relations

Intensive local enthnologies of farming, fishing, and other livelihood activities demonstrate ways in which social differences between commoners and royalty, men and women, or Native Americans and white ones are expressed. In chapter 8, "Finding the Global in the Local," Lisa L. Gezon investigates two cases of conflict over rights to resource access in northern Madagascar, analyzing how parties with various sources of political legitimacy interact to challenge and negotiate access to the region's land and forest resources. International conservation movements, international aid and loan restructuring, and neoliberal economic emphasis on land privatization provide a global framework within which people negotiate access to land at the local level. Conflicts among various actors and groups, including people living locally, an indigenous political-religious leader, a council of royal elders, and personnel from a conservation and development project expose tensions among identities, cultural logics, and discourses of rights and responsibilities concerning the environment. This analysis reveals a situated, performed, and locally embedded globalism, one that exists and evolves in human interactions shaped by social difference.

By bringing together ethnography, ecology, and history in the kingdom of Tonga, Charles J. Stevens seeks to understand, in chapter 9, "Symbolic Action and Soil Fertility," the ongoing transformation from a millennial agroforestry system into an increasingly capital-intensive production system oriented toward both market and subsistence activities. Both interpretation of public ritual and scientific analysis of soil fertility are important in understanding the transformation of agriculture in the kingdom. Recent changes in agricultural organization are linked to political and social changes that began in nineteenth-century efforts to consolidate power and unify the island archipelago. One unintended consequence of recent changes has been growing economic independence among Tongan commoners, who are now asserting a greater political voice and using land for personal economic gain as well as to fulfill social and ritual obligations.

In chapter 10, "Gendered Practices and Landscapes in the Andes," Susan Paulson also examines a sustained political push toward agricultural modernization and the unintended consequences of that push as she traces changes in gendered organization of labor and the social construction of landscape in the Bolivian Andes. The chapter looks at the degradation of steep slopes and the reduced productivity and social value of women who manage these slopes for small livestock grazing and fuelwood collection. Starting with an ethnographic exploration of local productive practices and relations, Paulson widens her scope to encompass asymmetrical relations of exchange at play in markets, migrations, and development projects. Simultaneously, she considers political decisions and policies that contribute to the uneven terrain on which these exchanges take place. The chapter presents methodological options for approaching environmental problems as integrally social and ecological and for considering these problems in multiscale frames of reference that allow us to examine links among local phenomena and regional or global processes.

In chapter 11, "Undermining Modernity," Alf Hornborg studies how Mi'kmaq Native Americans in Nova Scotia resist forces of economic modernization as they struggle to prevent a sacred mountain from being turned into a giant granite quarry. Hornborg argues that the decontextualizing cosmology of modern economics, which aspires to engulf all local systems of meaning, functions to open local communities and ecosystems to outside exploitation. Against this background, both the Mi'kmaq traditionalists and proponents of a biocentric "deep ecology" have revolted against mainstream economic discourse. By evoking the mountain's sanctity and drawing on warrior images and threats of violent resistance, the Mi'kmaq activists managed to transform the terms of environmental discourse and negotiation to advance a vision in which cultural, existential, and political dimensions of environmental engagement are intermeshed in the lives of different social groups.

Part 3: Forest Visions

Analyses carried out on levels ranging from local epistemology to global policy show that competing representations of and discourses about nature can have powerful impacts on environments and the people who live in them. In chapter 12, "Shade," Michael R. Dove considers relationships between Pakistani farmers and the National Forest Department by focusing on conceptions of tree shade, a topic that does not initially appear to have much to do with politics. Dove shows how farmers' complex system of beliefs about shade (as an emission characterized by density, temperature, taste, and size) underlies local strategies of on-farm tree cultivation and contradicts government foresters' beliefs that farmers are hostile to the presence of trees on farms. He argues that the farmers' belief system collapses the dichotomies between tree and crop, forest and farm, forest department and farmer, and indeed nature and culture that serve the interests of the National Forest Department. Dove's work underscores the importance of approaching environmental issues as struggles over not only material resources but also the social construction of environmental knowledge and representations.

The bioprospectors studied by Hanne Svarstad in chapter 13, "A Global Political Ecology of Bioprospecting," see the forest as a mine hiding financially lucrative secrets. In this case study on bioprospecting in rural Tanzania by the U.S. company Shaman Pharmaceuticals, Svarstad argues for a multipronged analysis. She begins by situating the case within a historicized political economy and then identifies competing global discourses of bioprospecting (for example, as biopiracy or a win-win scenario) and examines perceptions and actions of local actors in relation to dominant global processes and discourses as well as at a critical distance from them. Finally, she contextualizes the competing discourses within broader ideological and political frameworks—of populism in the case of biopiracy and neoliberal economics in the case of the win-win scenario— in constructing her own analysis of bioprospecting. In Svarstad's view, while skepticism about the effects of global capitalist economics has been warranted, it does not necessarily follow that patenting (a cornerstone of the win-win, neoliberal approach) has been detrimental to local concerns about safeguarding access to plant resources.

Working at the intersection of political ecology theory and concepts and practices emerging from a social movement of black communities in the Pacific rainforest of Colombia, Arturo Escobar and Susan Paulson lay the groundwork in chapter 14, "The Emergence of Collective Ethnic Identities," for rethinking the appropriation and conservation of biological diversity from the perspective of social movements. The authors concentrate in particular on those movements that have emerged recently in biodiversity-rich regions. Current debates on biodiversity have begun to embrace the importance of local knowledge and traditional production systems for managing the planet's genetic resources. Escobar and Paulson address the less-known phenomenon of social movements that are crafting their own conceptualizations of biodiversity and their own strategies for its appropriation and conservation. They suggest that the conceptual approach emerging in one Colombian movement can offer a valid political ecology framework for analysis and practice that is distinct from (although related to) those developed by other prominent actors, such as academics, progressive intellectuals, and nongovernmental organizations.

Space, Scale, and Local-Global Links

In a world where people are sharply divided by differentials of power, prestige, and wealth, the decisions and actions of some carry more weight than others; and some people benefit more than others from given assumptions and representations. Vital to the work in this book are critical ideas about space and scale, themes that traverse all the chapters. A focus on identifying proximate causes of ecological degradation rather than analyzing structural factors, institutional dynamics, or global forces has often led to placing responsibility for change on impoverished minority communities or poor populations in the developing world rather than on more globally powerful societies and economies (Sachs

1993). Recent scholarship has challenged that focus. In their analysis of western African landscapes, for example, James Fairhead and Melissa Leach (1996) found that colonial stereotypes of the destructive native land manager had long guided the formulation of research questions and the interpretation of findings. In Madagascar, Lucy Jarosz (1993) demonstrated that deforestation that had been physically perpetrated by local populations (and blamed on them) was actually linked to colonial land appropriations and forced labor campaigns that resulted in mass flights of people into the fragile rainforest areas along the east coast (see also Gezon and Freed 1999).

At a time when scholars in the social and natural sciences are seeking ways to study phenomena across scales, political ecology has criticized tendencies among government and development agencies to address ecological problems with immediate technical solutions and ignore ways in which nonlocal policies and capital flows influence and perpetuate resource-use patterns at local levels. In response, political ecologists have sought to expand the scale of analysis to address national and global processes that transcend geographically separable locales.

To this end, previous work on the ecology of complex societies and global economies has been revived and retheorized. Julian Steward (1972) devoted the final two chapters of his seminal work, *Theory of Culture Change*, originally published in 1955, to examining the processes of state formation and the effects of industrialization, urbanization, and a cash crop–plantation economy on local subsistence practices. It makes sense, then, that one of Steward's students, Eric Wolf, went on to develop a powerful analytic framework linking ecological with political-economic phenomena across diverse scales of action and analysis. In an early exploration of property issues, Wolf (1972, 202) emphasized the importance of studying regional dynamics as well as their influence on the battleground of contending material, legal, and ideological forces on which local land struggles are played out. Later, he strove to explain systematic privilege and marginality in different parts of an increasingly connected world through the study of colonialism and world system dynamics (Wolf 1982).

Current political ecologists engage in broad experimentation and ardent debate around questions of how to prioritize and link together studies and analyses ranging in scale from a single household garden to the whole earth and its atmosphere. Some important currents of thought on ecological sustainability and biodiversity conservation have privileged the global and moved attention away from studying local biophysical processes (for example, studies of global warming and deforestation on aggregate levels) as well as the sociopolitical practices and knowledges involved therein. (See Bradnock and Saunders 2000 and Horta 2000 for more extended critiques.) Studies of political and economic globalization through flows of capital and information have also tended to ignore local contexts and the dynamics of production and meaning found there. Yet

Arjun Appadurai argues that the local remains analytically critical for global studies despite the expanding reach and homogenizing effects of what he calls financescapes and mediascapes. He argues that dynamic interaction between technologies, ideologies, ecologies, and culturally linked communities render the specific local effects of global capital and idea flows unique and unpredictable (Appadurai 1996, 33–36). Although localities are affected by global decision making, political ecologists such as Ramachandra Guha and Joan Martínez-Alier (1997) point out that they are not passive recipients; rather, local struggles engage globally prominent ideas in ways that often have larger effects. Chapters 11 (Hornborg) and 14 (Escobar and Paulson), for example, analyze cases in which traditional rural people engage with globally powerful environmental discourses and processes in ways that are both innovative and transformative.

Questions about the nature of scale allow for creative investigations into what defines place and landscape. Do *local* and *traditional* have tangible physicality, while *global* and *modern* refer to placeless flows of capital and anonymous people? In her study of the urban service sector, Saskia Sassen (2000) suggests otherwise: delivery persons, secretaries, and custodians are deeply rooted in physical space, although in ways that may differ from the physicality of Pakistani or Bolivian farmers. Studies on commodity chains and consumption, including the one in chapter 7 (Heyman), provide valuable insight into physical and meaningful connections between sites of production, distribution, and consumption (see also Bernstein 1996, Collins 2000, Ribot 1998). The understanding that global flows are necessarily embedded in local processes prompts a consideration of place not merely as an isolatable physical space but as a dimension of historical and contemporary connections. As Hugh Raffles (2002) argues, "place, as much as race, class, and gender, [is] itself a social relationship" (46). Because of their simultaneous focus on the materiality and meaning of place, this book's studies in environmental anthropology and social geography promise to help demystify the relationships between local sites of research and more distant locales with which they are connected.

In political ecology, place has often referred to rural, agricultural spaces. As Heyman's contribution in chapter 7 shows, recent work in political ecology increasingly explores ecologies of urban spaces. In her study of Santiago, capital of the Dominican Republic, Dianne Rocheleau (2002) explores the creation of new material and symbolic ecologies of urbanization and "glocalization" in unfolding encounters between biological communities, livelihoods, landscapes, technologies, and social relations. Within the municipality of Santiago, one can find species from the now-decimated forests and savannas of the region, along with new species that have arrived from forests, fields, and factories across the planet. Rocheleau's socioecological study of this evolving biodiversity links particular groups of people and specific ecological properties and species in complex ecologies shaped by urbanization, *zona franca* (free trade zone) factories, twenty-four-hour supermarkets, a tourist highway and ring road, the decline of tobacco production, and a recent explosion of sport utility vehicles. She relates this biological diversity to the collective ecological imagination in Santiago, which is fueled by visiting migrants from New York City; the "tele-visions" of Miami, Los Angeles, Caracas, and Rio beamed into private homes; the dreams of birdwatchers in distant North American cities; and memories of an agrarian past. The webs of relations identified in two peri-urban watershed communities reveal the prospects for and vulnerabilities of *convivencia*—a viable cohabitation of culture and nature based on local experiences, choices, and relationships.

The work of Janice Harper (2002) on asthma among poor minorities in Houston follows in the tradition of environmental justice scholarship (for example, Bryant 1995, Merchant 1994) and advances the frontiers of political ecology into the study of industrialized urban environments. Although Houston is a global power center whose harbor hosts an extraordinary flow of petroleum and money, Harper demonstrates that it is also a polluted place inhabited by people with little access to that power associated with those resources. By integrating political ecology with critical medical anthropology, she explores the ways in which environment intersects with health and the differing social responses to environmental practices that affect human health. Her research suggests that local understandings of respiratory health often contradict public health concepts of environmental health and, in turn, shape people's interactions with the environment.

Ultimately, these studies move away from a reified concept of global and local as separate but sometimes intersecting scales of analysis. Rather, the global is conceived as one aspect of a localized site, to the extent that people in any given zone of interaction act within the parameters of policies, authorities, and material conditions that have sources outside the reach of immediate local networks. This understanding of local-global relationships points to the importance of studying the local not only through rural or marginal spaces but also through spaces in which powerful decisions are made, such as corporate boardrooms, legislatures, and cyberspaces, where virtual communities negotiate decisions that affect people in material locales.

Power and Social Difference

Efforts to operationalize the theoretical and philosophical concerns of political ecology in field research and analysis have raised challenging questions. How can we explore the circulation of power in different contexts? How can we identify and study differences and relations among actors? How do our goals for social and environmental justice influence our research designs and questions?

The contributors to this book find that people exercise political ideas and actions related to production and resource use in diverse arenas, infusing them with cultural knowledge and values that vary remarkably across interest and social groups. Each chapter identifies specific contexts in which power operates and within which people communicate by means of discourses and representations of the environment. The authors identify regimes of knowledge in a world where not all knowledges or technologies enjoy equal power, raising questions about how and why particular interests and values predominate and how power circulates in ways that influence biophysical or social outcomes.

Awareness of the deep and complex ways in which dynamics of unequal social and political power affect ecological systems informs the dual commitment of political ecology to both understanding and action. As Karl S. Zimmerer (2000) says, "Political ecology seeks to contribute *both* to sound environmental management (including nature conservation) and to the empowerment of disadvantaged social groups" (357). In *Liberation Ecologies*, editors Richard Peet and Michael Watts (1996) are also explicitly concerned about a more equitable distribution of resource risks and benefits, highlighting the "liberatory or emancipatory potential of current political activity around environment and resources" (2). In a similar vein, Dianne Rocheleau, Barbara Thomas-Slayter, and Esther Wangari (1996) note the importance of a heightened sense of agency and empowerment resulting from women's increased involvement in environmental issues, management, and conflicts worldwide (18).

Chapter 4 (Ferguson and Derman) in this book analyzes political and bureaucratic strategies in Zimbabwe that influence situations in which water resources have long been developed to benefit powerful commercial farmers, a white minority. The study reveals ironic contradictions resulting from the fact that new policies designed to promote greater racial and gender equity and participation were developed exclusively by high-level bureaucrats who appropriated trendy discourses of stakeholder participation to attract international donors. In her aptly titled *Who Pays the Price?* editor Barbara Johnston (1994) and her contributors point out the importance of analyzing power as socially differentiated and relational. Specifically, they demonstrate that certain actions aiming to provide a higher standard of living for one group of people often jeopardize the well-being of others. Access to gold and copper for people in the United States, for example, has resulted in the death of the Ok Tedi River (and devastation to those whose livelihoods depend on it) in Papua New Guinea (Johnston and Jorgensen 1994).

In chapter 10, on relationships between gendered labor and changing landscapes in the Andes, Paulson analyzes relations of power that link local and nonlocal spaces. She examines a watershed in which environmental spaces and resources controlled and managed by men from wealthier families have been taking on greater prominence, while those managed primarily by women and poorer families have been reduced and degraded in greater proportion. But as Paulson scales up to wider relations of power and difference, it becomes clear that national markets discriminate against and exploit the labor and produce of indigenous men in ways that contribute to the impoverishment and social devaluation of rural men, as well as women and resources, while they in some ways benefit national and international business interests.

The social relations revealed in these studies are never simple cases of the powerful dominating the weak, and they reveal power as negotiated and shifting. In chapter 8, Gezon shows that the power of any actor can shift, presenting a case in which a Malagasy indigenous leader who enjoyed the support of the local people in his opposition to a nongovernmental conservation organization's imposed prohibition on entering a protected forest later met with resistance when he tried to stop people from cutting down trees for construction wood. In another analysis of conflict (chapter 3), Brogden and Greenberg describe territory contests between two powerful interest groups in Arizona: ranchers and middle-class suburbanites, many of whom embrace an environmentalist ideology. Their analysis suggests that both groups may lose when environmentalist politics marginalize ranchers, which could result in ranch land being sold and parceled into new subdivisions.

In contrast, Hornborg (chapter 11) finds positive possibilities in the complex symbiosis that has been developing between environmental and indigenous movements in many parts of the world. His case study in Nova Scotia traces unexpected alliances that emerged between the Mi'kmaq Indians, who were resisting a proposal for building a mega-quarry that would damage sacred sites vital to their spiritual identity, and an environmentalist coalition that was interested in protecting coastal habitats. These cases reveal that environmental marginalization is not a simple question of the rich taking resources from the poor but an analytically complex, historically contingent, and often elusive process enacted by people who are differentiated in multiple ways.

In sum, the investigation of environmental issues in diverse spaces and on different scales, together with methodological attention to relations of difference and power within and among spheres, presents possibilities for more complex understandings of the causal connections among factors at play. Each author in this collection establishes links between multiple sites and forces—links that may be multidirectional and dialectical, not simply linear. These models address two vital questions: where and how do we look for causes, and where should we work on solutions?

New Research Models and Analytic Frameworks

In addition to pursuing analytical questions about relationships between people and places, this book explores ways of gathering information relevant for understanding those relationships. It considers the application of multiscale research models that bring together selected ecological phenomena; local cultural and political spaces; and global flows of policies, capital, personnel, and discourse. Attention is also paid to the place of the hallmark ethnographic method, participant observation, within such a multiscale model. Early political ecologists sought to demonstrate links between land-tenure regimes or social marginalization and environmental changes such as soil erosion and deforestation. What they failed to do, however, was explore the complex and overlapping ways in which the landscapes are negotiated and affected by actions in diverse arenas such as the household, the workplace, the community, and the state. At the same time, they underestimated the extent to which meaningful constructions of the world—in other words, cultural contexts—influenced action. Current research continues to seek better methods to learn about and from these arenas and also to investigate the workings of knowledge, discourse, and practice within social movements, international financial and policy institutions, national and global governments, and other spaces.

The scholars contributing to this book explore not only class but also ethnic, gender, and religious dynamics and movements, applying research questions and tools that help to open up and disaggregate formerly opaque categories of resource users labeled "farmers," "tribesmen," "business," or "authorities." In her study of biodiversity (chapter 6), for example, Mackenzie brings together colonial writings, institutional documents, and contemporary narratives to reveal a complex field of discourse and action in which distinct voices and visions interact to shape evolving landscapes and social practices in Africa.

In the inaugural issue of the *Journal of Political Ecology*, James B. Greenberg and Thomas K. Park (1994) emphasize research and action focused on real people and places; and they credit Marx for foregrounding "the dialectic between individuals, their productive activity in human society, and nature that political ecology seeks to address by his insistence that one must begin not with abstract premises or dogmas (Marx and Engels 1970 [1846], 42) but with the productive activities of real individuals" (1). In a critique of political ecology, Andrew Vayda and Bradley Walters (1999) argue for an even more materialist model in which we "begin research with a focus on the environmental events or changes that we want to explain" (169). In the present book, however, Ferguson and Derman (chapter 4) question the universal appropriateness of anchoring our research models in specific environmental changes circumscribed in time and space. They argue that we should sometimes begin research by analyzing environment-related policy and planning, which can be relevant long before any consequences may be observed or documented in the biophysical environment.

Differences also arise among strategies developed to contextualize tangible people, practices, and biophysical phenomena in larger historical and ecological processes and among the criteria used to identify causes underlying the phenomena in question. Vayda and Walters (1999) propose to "work backward in time and outward in space so as to enable us to construct chains of causes and effects leading to those events or changes" (169). Yet other scholars are questioning conventional notions of linear time, proximal space, and causal chains. In chapter 5, Gardner interweaves multiple conceptions of space and time in order to understand the high mortality rate of sheep and goats in Saudi Arabia after the Gulf War. He first considers the hypothesis that pollution from the oil fires caused the problem. Upon collecting more data, however, he moves beyond a simple linear model of causation to explore multidimensional dynamics of kinship and labor, historical shifts in territorial boundaries and state policies, migration patterns, and technological changes (such as the introduction of Jeeps and water trucks) that have dramatically transformed Bedouin use and perception of space-time in ways that significantly influence herd ecology.

The question of where to start and how to move between scales—in research and in analysis—is particularly tricky for political ecologists, who are acutely aware of how cognitive models of scale carry deeply embedded assumptions about space, time, history, and causality. Recent critical studies reveal some of the practical, and political implications of models of scale used to organize and interpret information (Brosius 1999, Brown 2002, Levin 1992). As Anna L. Tsing (2000) argues, scale is not something "out there" to be discovered by the careful scientist. Rather, it is constantly made, negotiated, and transformed as people interact in specific times and places.

While new technologies ranging from DNA analysis to global imaging systems (Moran and Brondizio 1998) allow for work on increasingly minute and expansive scales, ethnography remains central to the study of global processes as they play out in specific locales. Indeed, ethnography remains central to all the chapters in this volume. George E. Marcus (1995) defines *ethnography* as "research predicated upon attention to the everyday, an intimate knowledge of face-to-face communities and groups" (99). Evaluating local-level studies, he writes, "Any ethnography of a cultural formation in the world system is also an ethnography of the world system" (99). Both Marcus and Michael Burawoy (2000) encourage a research strategy aimed at understanding time and space from the perspective of the people being studied.

In chapter 13, Svarstad argues that movement in a hermeneutic circle between global, regional, and local scales and perspectives benefits analysis on all levels: the ways in which an issue is shaped in global discourses and policies provides important context for interpreting specific cases on the local level, while specific local experiences influence and shed light on global trends and processes. The case studies in this book combine ethnographic methods such as participative observation in farming, housework, and social movements with biological analyses of soils, cultivars, and trees. They include discourse analyses of texts, policies, and legislation; examination of archival and other historical records; and sociological analyses of complex institutions. Some study globally powerful corporations, economic trends, and discourses. Svarstad points out that the challenge of implementing so many diverse research methods in such disparate spaces can seem overwhelming to the individual researcher; and she makes a case for doing long-term, multiperson, interdisciplinary studies in which links among materials, spaces, and levels of analysis are developed in a cumulative and collaborative process. This book, developed through multiyear conversations and interactions, contributes to building the kind of collaborative community necessary to carry out that vision.

REFERENCES

Appadurai, Arjun. 1996. *Modernity at Large: Cultural Dimensions of Globalization*. Minneapolis: University of Minnesota Press.

Bernstein, Henry. 1996. "The Political Economy of the Maize Filière." *Journal of Peasant Studies* 23, nos. 2 and 3: 120–45.

Blaikie, Piers. 1985. *Political Economy of Soil Erosion in Developing Countries*. London: Longman.

Blaikie, Piers, and Harold Brookfield. 1987. *Land Degradation and Society*. London: Methuen.

Bradnock, Robert W., and Patricia L. Saunders. 2000. "Sea-Level Rise, Subsidence and Submergence: The Political Ecology of Environmental Change in the Bengal Delta." In *Political Ecology: Science, Myth, and Power*, edited by Philip Stott and Sian Sullivan, 66–90. London: Arnold.

Brosius, J. Peter. 1999. "Analyses and Interventions: Anthropological Engagements with Environmentalism." *Current Anthropology* 40, no. 3: 277–309.

Brown, J. Christopher. 2002. "Politics of Scale and Construction of 'The Local' in Amazonian Sustainable Development Programs." Paper presented at the Conference on Globalization and Geographies of Conservation, University of Wisconsin, Madison, April.

Bryant, Bunyan, ed. 1995. *Environmental Justice: Issues, Policies, and Solutions*. Washington, D.C.: Island.

Burawoy, Michael. 2000. *Global Ethnography: Forces, Connections, and Imaginations in a Postmodern World*. Berkeley: University of California Press.

Collins, Jane. 2000. "Tracing Social Relations in Commodity Chains: The Case of Grapes in Brazil." In *Commodities and Globalization: Anthropological Perspectives*, edited by A. Haugerud, M. Priscilla Stone, and Peter D. Little, 97–109. New York: Rowman and Littlefield.

Fairhead, James, and Melissa Leach. 1996. *Misreading the African Landscape: Society and Ecology in a Forest-Savanna Mosaic*. Cambridge: Cambridge University Press.

Gezon, Lisa L., and Benjamin Z. Freed. 1999. "Agroforestry and Conservation in Northern Madagascar: Hopes and Hindrances." *African Studies Quarterly*. 3, no. 1: 8–29.

Greenberg, James B., and Thomas K. Park. 1994. "Political Ecology." *Journal of Political Ecology* 1, no. 1: 1–12.

Guha, Ramachandra, and Joan Martínez-Alier, eds. 1997. *Varieties of Environmentalism: Essays North and South*. London: Earthscan.

Harper, Janice. 2002. "Breathless in Houston: An Ethnography of Asthma." Paper presented at the sixty-second annual meeting of the Society for Applied Anthropology, Atlanta, March 8.

Horta, Korinna. 2000. "Rainforest: Biodiversity Conservation and the Political Economy of

International Financial Institutions." In *Political Ecology: Science, Myth, and Power*, edited by Philip Stott and Sian Sullivan, 179–202. London: Arnold.

Jarosz, Lucy. 1993. "Defining and Explaining Tropical Deforestation: Shifting Cultivation and Population Growth in Colonial Madagascar (1896–1940)." *Economic Geography* 69, no. 4: 366–79.

Johnston, Barbara, ed. 1994. *Who Pays the Price? The Sociocultural Context of Environmental Crisis*. Washington, D.C.: Island.

Johnston, Barbara, and Daniel Jorgensen. 2994. "Mineral Development, Environmental Degradation, and Human Rights: The Ok Tedi Mine, Papua New Guinea." In *Who Pays the Price? The Sociocultural Context of Environmental Crisis*. edited by Barbara Johnston, 86–98. Washington, D.C.: Island.

Levin, Simon A. 1992. "The Problem of Pattern and Scale in Ecology." *Ecology* 73. no. 6: 1943–67.

Marcus, George E. 1995. "Ethnography in/of the World System: The Emergence of Multi-Sited Ethnography." *Annual Review in Anthropology* 24, no. 1: 95–117.

Marx, Karl, and Friedrich Engels. 1970 [1846]. *The German Ideology*. New York: International.

Merchant, Carolyn, ed. 1994. *Ecology: Key Concepts in Critical Theory*. Atlantic Highlands, N.J.: Humanities Press.

Moran, Emilio F., and Eduardo Brondizio. 1998. "Land-Use Change after Deforestation in Amazonia." In *People and Pixels: Linking Remote Sensing and Social Science*, edited by Diana Livermann, Emilio F. Moran, Ronald R. Rindfuss, and Paul C. Stern, 94–120. Washington, D.C.: National Academy Press.

Peet, Richard, and Michael Watts. 1996. *Liberation Ecologies: Environment, Development, Social Movements*. New York: Routledge.

Raffles, Hugh. 2002. *In Amazonia: A Natural History*. Princeton, N.J.: Princeton University Press.

Ribot, Jesse C. 1998. "Theorizing Access: Forest Profits along Senegal's Charcoal Commodity Chain." *Development and Change* 29: 307–41.

Rocheleau, Dianne. 2002. "Cyborg Forest, Garden City: Culture, Nature, and Webs of Power in Santiago, Dominican Republic." Paper presented at the 101st annual meeting of the American Anthropological Association, New Orleans.

Rocheleau, Dianne, Barbara Thomas-Slayter, and Esther Wangari, eds. 1996. *Feminist Political Ecology: Global Issues and Local Experiences*. London: Routledge.

Sachs, Wolfgang, ed. 1993. *Global Ecology: A New Arena of Political Conflict*. London: Zed.

Sassen, Saskia. 2000. Cities in a World Economy. Thousand Oaks, Calif.: Pine Forge.

Steward, Julian. 1972 [1955]. *Theory of Culture Change: The Methodology of Multilinear Evolution*. Urbana: University of Illinois Press.

Tsing, Anna L. 2000. "The Global Situation." *Cultural Anthropology* 15, no. 3: 327–60.

Vayda, Andrew, and Bradley Walters. 1999. "Against Political Ecology." *Human Ecology* 27, no. 1: 167–79.

Watts, Michael. 1983. *Silent Violence*. Berkeley: University of California Press.

Wolf, Eric. 1972. "Ownership and Political Ecology." *Anthropological Quarterly* 45, no. 3: 201–5.

———. 1982. *Europe and the People without History*. Berkeley: University of California Press.

Zimmerer, Karl S. 2000. "The Reworking of Conservation Geographies: Nonequilibrium Landscapes and Nature-Society Hybrids." *Annals of the Association of American Geographers* 90, no. 2: 356–69.

2

Politics, Ecologies, Genealogies

SUSAN PAULSON, LISA L. GEZON, AND MICHAEL WATTS

During the past two decades, the field of political ecology has advanced through research, analysis, and applied practice across disciplines that include anthropology, biology, geography, philosophy of science, and political science. Scholars working with political ecology approaches have challenged dominant interpretations of the causes of environmental degradation and contested prevalent prescriptions for responding to such problems. The intellectual and political origins of the term *political ecology* date to the 1970s, when a variety of rather different commentators, including anthropologist Eric Wolf, journalist Alexander Cockburn, and environmental scientist Grahame Beakhurst, coined it as a way of conceptualizing the relations between political economy and ecology in the context of a burgeoning environmental movement (Keil and Faucett 1998, Watts 1983a). Current working definitions of political ecology include Dianne Rocheleau's (1999) specific focus on intersections between "the social relations of power and the formation and functioning of ecologies and landscapes" (22) and Arturo Escobar's (1999) broad "study of the manifold articulations of history and biology and the cultural mediations through which such articulations are necessarily established" (3). Chapter 1 discussed visions and applications that are vitalizing the field at the dawn of the twenty-first century; and in chapter 2, we explore the intellectual genealogy leading up to the present and some new challenges that lie ahead.

Political ecology's originality and ambition arise from its efforts to link social and physical sciences to address environmental changes, conflicts, and problems. In this initiative, analyses of social relations of production and questions of access and control over resources—the basic tool kit of political economy—are applied in order to understand forms of environmental disturbance and degradation and to develop prospects and models for environmental rehabilitation and conservation, as well as environmentally sustainable alternatives.

From the beginning, then, political ecology has been analytical, normative, and applied, a unity confirmed by the 1989 founding of the policy-oriented journal *Land Degradation and Rehabilitation* by Piers Blaikie and others. From early on, political ecology theory and practice have also been shaped by concerns for marginal social groups and issues of social justice, concerns that have taken the forefront in recent publications such as *Liberation Ecologies* (Peet and Watts 1996) and *The Environmentalism of the Poor* (Martínez-Alier 2002).

Several long traditions of scholarly effort to understand relations between culture and environment coalesced into what we know as political ecology amid a surprisingly diverse array of theoretical developments. These included changing applications of evolutionary biology, a resurgence of interest in Marxist concepts and analyses, efforts to reconceive relations between materialist and symbolic theories, and the emergence of new sciences of ecosystems and cybernetics. Global affairs and world historic events also influenced the scene. The growing visibility of peasantries in the developing world (notably, China and Vietnam), together with the socio-psychological and scientific consequences of the cold war and the threat of nuclear warfare, highlighted concerns about the inequitable distribution of global resources and risks and the possibility that global conflict might lead to unfathomable environmental disaster.

Intellectual Genealogies

In this section we provide a brief account of the confluence among these sets of ideas and historical processes. Our decision to highlight certain strands of the field's history reflects our own trajectories and interests and necessarily represents only a partial view of the complex heritage, multiplicity of issues, and diversity of positions that energize political ecology.

Ecological Anthropology and Cultural Ecology

Interest in the relationships between people and their material environments has a long and rich history in anthropology. Vital debates running through more than a century of anthropological scholarship center on the value of holistic interpretations of unique human and environmental situations versus the value of comparative universal frameworks, on the importance of materialist versus culturalist explanations, and on the type of field and analytical methods needed to understand a topic of study that is always both biophysical and culturally meaningful. At the turn of the twenty-first century, political ecologists are influencing these ongoing conversations by problematizing the nature-versus-culture dichotomy underlying much early debate and developing research frameworks that link local ethnographic and ecological research with mezzo-level institutional and historical studies and global political and economic analyses.

 Nineteenth-century theorists used subsistence strategies and technologies as criteria to categorize groups on an upward continuum from "savage" to "barbarian" to "civilized" (Morgan 1877). This comparative ranking approach, based primarily on readings of travelers' and missionaries' accounts and government reports, resonated with and contributed to popular ideas about social evolution. Although Lewis H. Morgan (1877) believed that the technology used to appropriate natural resources determined other facets of social life, he explained the evolution of technology itself as an inevitable progression through universal stages; neither cultural nor environmental factors were given much causal relevance.

In reaction to this evolutionary school of thought, American anthropologists including Clark Wissler (1940, Wissler and Weitzner 1922) and Alfred Kroeber (1963 [1939]) developed the culture-area perspective, which emphasized the creative role of culture in shaping ways in which people manipulate and conceptualize the material environment. Culture-area theorists embraced the idea of *possibilism*, stating that while the biophysical environment narrows the range of possible cultural forms, culture is what begets culture. In Kroeber's words, "environment does not produce a culture, but stabilizes it" (6). C. Daryll Forde (1963) further critiqued the idea that environment or technology significantly determines cultural forms, explaining that "religious concepts may deeply affect economic and social development and may limit or even prevent adaptations that are obviously possible" (vi). These debates over the relative powers of culture and ecology met up with parallel scholarship in geography, and Kroeber and Forde had strong links to geography at Berkeley and University College, London.

During the 1920s and 1930s, the processes through which cultural knowledge and practice are diffused across space and time were explored through massive surveys aiming to inventory thousands of cultural traits or objects across geographical regions of North America. The culture-area perspective opened up the possibility of seeing culture as influenced, but not determined, by material parameters and recognized that cultural beliefs and practices also affect the material environment and human interactions with it. This new respect for the generative power of culture, together with the dialectical understanding of culture-environment relationships, formed a vital foundation for political ecology approaches. This era, sometimes called the golden age of anthropology (Stocking 1992), also ushered in the kind of intense, multifaceted, on-the-ground ethnographic research that would define cultural anthropology for the rest of the twentieth century and that continues to play an essential role in the multisited and multiscale research strategies developed by political ecologists today.

In the mid-twentieth century, anthropologist Julian Steward (1972 [1955]) forged a new kind of comparative analysis of human-environment relationships with an approach he called cultural ecology, whose central objective was to explain cultural similarities in light of similar environments, subsistence patterns, and economic arrangements (37). In Steward's words, "The problem is to ascertain whether the adjustments of human societies to their environments require particular modes of behavior or whether they permit latitude for a certain range of possible behavior patterns" (36). Steward made culture-environment relations a point of departure for explaining cultural types: "constellations of core features which arise out of environmental adaptations and which represent similar levels of integration" (42). Perhaps the best known is the exogamous patrilineal band, hypothesized to exist where there is sparse population and scattered nonmigratory game and where transportation is limited to human carriers. Steward's central research goal of understanding how people living in sociocultural groups survive within particular environments has endured long after many scholars have written off the materialist explanations, emphasis on synchronic studies, and ignorance of social differentiation and power that characterized this school of work.

In a move that defined cultural ecology in the 1960s and 1970s, Andrew Vayda and Roy Rappaport (1967) argued that human ecology should not follow Steward's model of using cultures as units of analysis. Instead, in what came to be known as the Columbia school of ecological anthropology, they developed an ecosystems model that treated human populations as one of a number of interacting species and physical components. In anthropology and geography, this school of thought provided a sophisticated body of theory and research to demonstrate how subsistence people in isolated regions maintained adaptive structures with respect to their environments. In Rappaport's (1968) terms, "cognized models" of the environment—embodied in various ritual, symbolic, and religious practices—were cultural mechanisms for the kind of environmental adaptation that interested students of western ecological sciences and evolutionary theory. Thus, for example, ritual pig killing among Tsembaga Maring of highland Papua New Guinea functioned as a thermostatic device that prevented pig overpopulation and maintained some sort of balance in the fragile tropical ecology. The Columbia school of cultural ecology made a lasting methodological impact because of its emphasis on intensive empirical investigation of sociocultural phenomena and physical environmental processes such as nutrient flows, caloric intake, and productivity. Its theoretical focus on explaining cultural forms in terms of their functional value in adapting to material environments has been much more widely debated. In response to critiques by anthropologists such as Jonathan Friedman (1979), who saw in cultural ecology the worst excesses of functionalism, Rappaport (1984) later developed a more sophisticated approach to adaptation, drawing upon the work of Gregory Bateson (1972), cybernetics, and information theory.

As scholarly paradigms evolved in the latter half of the twentieth century, cultural ecology research, including that done by ethnobotanists (Berlin et al. 1974, Conklin 1954), was criticized for underestimating the role of cultural meaning, ignoring social power and inequality, and focusing too narrowly on the local to the exclusion of the dynamics of colonialism and the encroachment of a global capitalist economy (Peet and Watts 1993).[1] In retrospect, however, Michael R. Dove (1999) argues, "In the context of the then-prevailing deprecation of indigenous societies under the aegis of high-modernist development theory, the detailed descriptions of vernacular technology and knowledge central to early ecological anthropology can now be read as politically empowering counterdiscourses" (290).

Cultural Geography and the Environmental Turn

In geography, another genealogy emerged from rather different intellectual sources, which were at times linked directly to anthropology. One line was associated with the Berkeley School of Cultural Geography and Carl Sauer (1952). Sauer was interested in the historical transformation of the landscape, patterns of environmental and cultural diffusion, and the domestication of plants and animals. His own thinking intersected with Kroeber's while they were both at Berkeley, but their legacies diverged. Sauer's emphasis on the morphology of landscape was a forerunner of what in the 1950s became a move toward understanding human transformation of the earth (Thomas 1956).

Another trajectory of geographical thought and research that contributed to the field of political ecology was associated with Berkeley alumnus William M. Denevan, who with a group of students at the University of Wisconsin, Madison, proffered a significant rethinking of the environmental history of the Maya, Amazonia, and the Andes (Turner 1983, Nietschmann 1973). Central to this work and its concerns was the deployment of the new systems ecology to analyze flows of energy and materials within pre-Columbian systems of agriculture and trade. This group of scholars asked how Amerindian populations could exploit the delicate tropical ecosystems and support surprisingly large population densities through raised field agriculture, intensive swiddening, aquaculture and other social-technological systems. Here, geography intersected with anthropology, especially in the extensive work of Betty Meggers, who applied cultural ecology approaches in archaeological and prehistorical studies of Amazonian and Andean production systems and collaborated in the East Africa project of the late 1960s and early 1970s that brought together geographers and anthropologists (see Porter 1965). This line of work has contributed directly to current political ecology concerns about sustainable production systems, local knowledge systems, and indigenous communities.

James J. Parsons's pathbreaking work on raised fields in Bolivia and Colombia made central contributions (Denevan 1989), and Denevan's student Bernard Nietschmann (1973) provided a sophisticated cultural ecological account of the Miskito Coast in which he documented how communities had adapted to local niches and orchestrated marine and land-based microenvironments in their livelihood systems as well as how this adaptive capacity was being undermined by the growth of commercial turtle exploitation. Much of Nietschmann's work was directly shaped by the ideas of Roy Rappaport and Kent Flannery at the University of Michigan, where all three were located in the early 1970s. In this context, Nietschmann took cultural ecology to a point at which the questions he asked required a sophisticated grasp of political economy.

This tradition of cultural ecology has continued in geography, sometimes in a tense relationship with the political ecology approaches that developed in its wake (see Turner 1983, Mortimore 1998). Much of the tension turns on debates about the extent to which the language of adaptation should be retained in analysis, the role played by population and technology as driving forces, and the centrality of the social relations of production and the accumulation process emphasized by political economy. The key book in geography that pushed beyond (and irrevocably broke with) more conventional approaches to cultural ecology and hazards was Kenneth Hewitt's (1983) *Interpretations of Calamity*, which proved to be an important bridge to political ecology and paved the way for critical work that was to follow (Blaikie et al. 1994, Zimmerer and Bassett 2003). Paul Richards, who was trained as a geographer and moved to anthropology, was also a key bridging figure; and his *Indigenous Agricultural Revolution* (1985) represented an important shift toward a more critically engaged link among culture, power, and ecology.

Disaster Research and Environment As Hazard

Paralleling these explorations in cultural ecology, interest developed across various disciplines in exploring human and cultural responses to hazards and disasters. Geographers Gilbert F. White, Ian Burton, and Robert W. Kates were at the forefront of this work in the 1950s and 1960s (see Watts 2000 for a review), focusing on differing sorts of natural perturbation—tornadoes, earthquakes, floods—in the United States and on the perceptions and behaviors of threatened communities and households. Centers for disaster studies appeared around the country, notably at Ohio State University and the University of Colorado, Boulder, as sociologists and geographers schooled in survey research, cognitive studies, and behavioralism sought to understand why individuals misperceived, ignored, or responded in diverse ways to environmental threats. As the cold war deepened, attention turned toward not-so-natural hazards and disasters—notably, the immediate threat of atomic disaster, which generated a number of government-funded studies on perceptions of and responses to environmental threats.

By the 1970s, centers for hazard or disaster research (often with financial backing from the real estate industry, insurance companies, and the federal government) had made a substantial impact in the area of domestic policy (see White 1974, Burton et al. 1978). Much of this work drew on organic analogies of adaptation and response but was also sensitive to cultural perceptions and questions of organizational capacity and access and availability of information. Systems thinking and organization theory were central to the intellectual architecture of this body of scholarship (Watts 1983b), and interdisciplinary research led scholars to realize that disaster prevention, preparations for it, and responses to it were highly political. Much of this work focused on U.S. domestic issues such as perceptions of earthquake hazards or responses to tornadoes, but a growing body of work in the 1960s and early 1970s turned to the developing world. Topics explored included the social organization of responses to floods and drought in the semi-arid tropics, and work on the perception of environmental variability among developing-world peoples intersected with anthropological work on ethnobotany (see Porter 1965, Scott 1979).

Interdisciplinary studies of human responses to hazards and disasters, together with environmental anthropology and cultural geography, were informed by new research into cybernetics, organization theory, and systems theories, which derived from theory of machines and artificial intelligence developed particularly during World War II. Central figures here were Gregory Bateson (1972) and Howard T. Odum (1971), who, while very different in intellectual orientation, provided languages and concepts for thinking about humans in ecosystems and living systems as well as the flows of matter, information, and energy that coursed through human-environment practice and interaction. Some of this tradition has continued in the recent work of Jeanne X. Kasperson and Roger Kasperson (2001) on global environmental risks and managing hazards related to modern technology.

Political Economy

Impulses that reinvigorated the analytic tradition of political economy and motivated new applications to environmental issues came from two related sources in the 1960s and 1970s. First was the proliferation of peasant studies (Shanin 1970, Wolf 1969) and critiques of colonialism (Asad 1973) that brought to the fore questions of social differentiation, exploitation, and the impact of international markets on the rural poor in the developing world. Second was a vital resurgence of Marxism in social sciences and development studies (Bryant 1998) in a variety of guises, including world systems theory, dependency theory, structural Marxism, and Marxist feminism, that advanced concepts of control and access to resources, marginalization, relations of production, surplus appropriation, and power.

These two tendencies confronted cultural ecology by going beyond the study of isolated or subsistence communities in putative equilibrium with their physical environment to examine the impact of markets, social inequalities, and political conflicts and to analyze forms of social and cultural disintegration associated with the incorporation of local communities into a modern world system. In the context of broader shifts in scientific paradigms toward stances of nonequilibrium, attention to maladaptation and disruption took precedence over a previous focus on adaptation, self-regulation, and homeostatis (see also Biersack 1999, Rappaport 1993).[2]

In this era of vigorous debate and change across the social sciences, numerous scholars were motivated to reread Karl Marx and Marxisms and identify
points of potential convergence between political economy and cultural ecology.[3] Howard L. Parsons (1977) notes that, from the Middle Ages until the Industrial Revolution, western concepts of nature were dominated by the static
hierarchical trope of the great chain of being. "In the nineteenth century, the
concept took on the notion of strife, interpenetration, and transformation
among things," in that new context Marx and Friedrich Engels developed "their
appreciation of the dialectical power in human history and society and their
grasp of the dialectical effects of social practice upon the world of external
nature" (8).

Starting in the 1920s, members of the Frankfurt school had drawn on Marx
and Engels's perceptions of the ecological and human costs of capitalist modes
of production to develop a multidisciplinary critique of dominant social theory,
science, and technology. While building on Marx's political economy framework,
Max Horkheimer and Theodor W. Adorno (1976 [1945]) critiqued his faith in the
Enlightenment myth of progress via the domination of nature and his belief that
cultural change necessarily led to betterment. Carolyn Merchant (1994) portrays
the Frankfurt school's skepticism: "Rather than seeing the progressive aspects of
modernity in which science, technology, and capitalism increasingly improve on
the human condition, they emphasized modernity's dehumanizing tendencies,
its destruction of the environment, its potential for totalitarian politics, and its
inability to control technology" (1–2).

The dialectical interaction of the material and the social, so vital in Marx
and the Frankfurt school, gave way in mid-twentieth-century anthropology to
polarized antagonism between those who privileged material explanations and
those who privileged symbolic meaning and social explanations.[4] Sherry Ortner
(1984) describes anthropology in the 1960s as torn by acrimonious debate.
"Whereas the cultural ecologists considered the symbolic anthropologists to be
fuzzy-headed mentalists involved in unscientific and unverifiable flights of subjective interpretation, the symbolic anthropologists considered cultural ecology
to be involved with mindless and sterile scientism, counting calories and meas-
uring rainfall while willfully ignoring the one truth that anthropology had presum-
ably established by that time: that culture mediates all human behavior" (134).[5]

In a work that helped to launch political ecology, Eric Wolf (1982) sought to
transcend the paralyzing dichotomy between the material and the meaningful
by working with the two axiomatic understandings of the human condition on
which Marx's theory of production rests. The first is that *Homo sapiens* is part of
physical nature. The second is that we are a social species; that is, humans are
linked to other humans, and to other aspects of nature, through social relations.
Wolf resuscitated Marx's concept of production to refer to the mutually dependent relations among nature, human labor, and social organization, together with

his concept of modes of production, understood as historically specific sets of social relations, knowledge, and technologies through which labor is employed to wrest energy from nature (73). Jonathan Friedman's (1975) Marxist-inspired analysis of swidden production and the relationship between farmers and the state provides an excellent example of early political ecological writing, and his critical work was key in moving some currents of ecological anthropology toward political ecology.

The political economy work of Wolf, Friedman, and others, together with parallel advances in structuralism, practice theory, structural Marxism, and feminist and postcolonial theories, significantly transformed social science in the late twentieth century. Political ecology in the 1990s was marked by creative cross-fertilization among these diverse approaches and by the interrogation of assumptions in intellectual traditions that were institutionalized in nineteenth-century science. Key among these received assumptions are the dichotomy between physical nature and meaningful culture, the adequacy and naturalness of academia's disciplinary structure, and the putatively value-free status of western scientific concepts.

questioning assumptions

Current Conversations in Political Ecology

Today, at the dawn of the twenty-first century, diverse scholars continue to draw on and reinterpret concepts from ecological anthropology, cultural geography, and political economy, bringing them together in innovative ways with methods, concepts, and analytic turns from a wide range of theoretical currents. Two vital questions lie at the heart of contemporary political ecology. How can we frame, carry out, and analyze research that stretches across different spaces, scales, and social groups? And how can we better conceptualize the political in studies of environmental changes, problems, and issues?

Place and Scale

By locating their environmental studies in the context of political economic systems and relations, political ecologists opened the possibility of bringing into the analysis social relations and places that are not necessarily proximal to the ecological phenomena of interest. This move distanced them from conventions of human and cultural ecology that tended to situate causes of and solutions to environmental crises in local-based problems such as overpopulation, poor land management, or inappropriate technology. In one landmark study, Susanna Hecht and Alexander Cockburn (1989) anchored the causal dynamics of rapid deforestation in eastern Amazonia in national and international factors that motivated those who cleared tropical rainforests to create pasture for cattle ranching that was, in fact, both economically inefficient and environmentally destructive. The authors found that macrolevel political-economic forces, not the least of which were the rents and subsidies generated by the Brazilian junta and successive democratic governments, created conditions of high profitability that influenced varied social forces acting on the environment, including ranchers, peasants, workers, and transnational companies.

The kind of multiscale approaches presented in this book are evident in Andrew Gardner's investigation (chapter 5) of increasing disease and mortality among Bedouin herds in Saudi Arabia in the wake of the Gulf War. On the ground among the herders, Gardner used rapid appraisal activities simultaneously with ethnographic observation of practices such as labor arrangements and the use of pickups and water trucks. He examined national policies such as governmental price supports for barley and changes in border policies and patrols. On a regional level, he considered smoke from oil fires during the war, political economic conditions in neighboring nations that led to the growth of a cheap expatriate labor force in Saudi Arabia, documentation of regional climate, and environmental trends including a decade-long drought.

Relations of Social Difference

Other significant advances arise from the use of concepts and tools that illuminate differences in knowledge, interest, practice, and power among social groups differentiated by class, race, ethnicity, gender, and other sociocultural systems. Early studies in political ecology tended to focus on land managers, considering their relationship to nature in a "historical, political and economic context" (Blaikie and Brookfield 1987, 239). Yet the land managers who were scrutinized were overwhelmingly male, rural subjects from the developing world and, rather curiously, appeared to be quite apolitical. In Piers Blaikie's (1985) study of soil erosion, for example, and Michael Watts's (1983a) discussion of pastoralism in West Africa, there is almost no consideration of peasant resistance or gender and household dynamics in association with soil problems.

Political ecologists have since then paid increasing attention to the ethnic identities, gender roles and relations, multiform institutions, governance apparatuses, political involvements, and other social factors that condition the knowledge, decisions, and actions of diverse land managers. Notable here are feminist insights into the gendered character of environmental knowledge and practice (Braidotti et al. 1994, Carney 1996, Gezon 2002, Mackenzie 1995, Paulson 1998, Schroeder 1993, Shiva 1988, Rocheleau et al. 1996), concern about indigenous rights and territorial autonomy (Bassett 1988, Beckett and Mato 1996, Jones 1995), and critical analyses of development processes informed by movements for social and environmental justice (Bryant 2002, Guha 1994, Peet and Watts 1996, Zimmerer 2000). From the start, political ecology was firmly grounded in class analysis; now it is developing a more comprehensive social theory that allows for identification and analysis of dynamics among multiple, overlapping dimensions of identity.

In this book, for example, Josiah McC. Heyman (chapter 7) contrasts the concerns and discourses about consumption advanced by environmentalists in overdeveloped societies with those of working-class consumers on Mexico's border, who worry about not being able to consume enough. By bringing together the analysis of historical processes by which people became consumers of mass-manufactured goods and resource-energy inputs with an in-depth ethno-graphic study of the immediate politics of consumption, such as protests over electricity-rate increases, Heyman illuminates the importance on various scales of social differentiation in terms of nationality, ethnicity, gender, generation, and socioeconomic class.

Politics

A central question has emerged in both political ecology and critiques of it: how do we conceptualize the political? Significant debate has arisen around methods and concepts used to address the political in political ecology. The first generation of political ecology work was criticized for lacking a consistent treatment of politics and having an abstract conceptualization of political economy (Peet and Watts 1993). Later scholars have been accused of assigning too much importance to political control over natural resources, being driven by populist political agendas, and prioritizing politics to the point of abandoning ecology altogether (Vayda and Walters 1999). At the heart of this issue are questions about what constitutes politics and how political phenomena interrelate with ecological ones.

Early political ecology made the key theoretical move of replacing the "human" in human ecology with a Marxist-inflected political economy. This move meant shifting emphasis from biophysical characteristics of human life, analyzed through theories of evolution and adaptation, toward the study of social and cultural dimensions of human life embedded in historical contexts. Applications that followed from Piers Blaikie and Harold Brookfield's (1987) broadly defined political economy were certainly not of a theoretical piece. For Watts (1983b), political economy drew upon a Marxian vision of social relations of production as an arena of possibility and constraint. For Blaikie and Brookfield (1987) it meant a concern with effects "on people, as well as on their productive activities, of on-going changes within society at local and global levels" (21). And for Martínez-Alier, political economy became synonymous with economic and ecological distributional conflicts (Guha and Martínez-Alier 1997).

Other valuable takes on the political have included analyses of conventional geopolitics and the history of unequal power relations between northern and southern nations (Escobar 1995, Grossman 1998, Sachs 1993), grassroots and academic engagement with environmental issues (Brosius 1999, Posey 1983), and red-green political activism (Atkinson 1991), so named for the links it forged between movements for social and environmental justice and emancipation.

Finally, studies such as those brought together in this book emphasize the importance of ethnographically based research on practices and negotiations of power relations both among resource users and between resource-using communities and outside holders of power.

In sum, political ecology's underspecification of political economy and the political, its sometimes vague use of these terms to refer to exogenous forces and systems, together with a surge of creative applications that locate politics in all kinds of unsuspected places have led to uncertainty and debate about the nature and place of politics in environmental analysis. At this point, a more explicit conceptualization of power and politics is needed to better operationalize research on environmental changes and conflicts and develop improved ways of addressing practical problems of resource degradation and social marginalization.

Toward a Conceptualization of the Political

In this book, *political* is used to designate the practices and processes through which power, in its multiple forms, is wielded and negotiated. In line with Alf Hornborg's (2001) definition of *power* as "a social relation built on an asymmetrical distribution of resources and risks" (1), we explore ways in which power circulates among and between different social groups, resources, and spaces. In his chapter "Facing Power" Wolf (2001) urges scholars to continue thinking about diverse articulations of power and defines several types, including power as a personal attribute, the ability of an individual to impose his or her will on another, and the power to control settings in which people may act and interact. Wolf identifies as most powerful the type of power that not only acts willfully within and controls other action in settings or domains but also constructs and orchestrates those settings and specifies the distribution and direction of energy flows within them (384). In short, this is the power to shape environments for human action and interaction.

The studies in this book demonstrate that all kinds of human relationships have political elements, often manifest in the strategic use of position, knowledge, or representations to gain differential access to resources. "The political" therefore encompasses not only formal politics but all kinds of everyday interactions as well. Judith Butler (1997) goes further to locate power in the ways in which people, resources, and places are constituted: "We are used to thinking about power as what presses on the subject from the outside, as what subordinates. . . . This is surely a fair description of what power does. But if, following Foucault, we understand power as forming the subject as well, as providing the very condition of its existence and the trajectory of its desire, then power is not simply what we oppose but also, in a strong sense, what we depend on for our existence" (2).

Many political ecologists have drawn from Butler and other poststructural feminist and practice theorists (such as Bourdieu 1977, Giddens 1984, Ortner

1989) to approach politics more broadly as power relations that shape and pervade all human interactions, are characterized by challenge and negotiation, and are infused with symbolic and discursive meaning. As political ecologists develop more sophisticated understandings of the ways in which power and politics influence culture-environment interactions, they consistently emphasize the importance of studying social dynamics together with material dimensions of the environment. Researchers including Karl S. Zimmerer (1996) and Matt Tur-ner (1999) provide important models for successfully merging rigorous ecological methods for studying biophysical events and phenomena with social science methods for analyzing diverse political, social, and economic facets of these events and phenomena.

Knowledge, Discourse, and Environmental Politics

A growing focus on the politics of discourse has raised serious questions about the way in which nature is conceived and represented in western scholarship as well as in policy, legislation, and media (Adger et al. 2001). Essentialist conceptualizations of nature as a category of reality that exists independently of human thought and action have been challenged by a growing conviction that the idea and experience of nature are "always constructed by our meaning-giving and discursive processes, so that what we perceive as natural is also cultural and social" (Escobar 1999, 2). Sharp debates have arisen in environmental anthropology and geography about the extent to which research and analytic methods should include the examination of pertinent environmental discourses (a move sometimes precipitously relegated as postmodern) and the extent to which they should focus on collecting biophysical data (a strategy sometimes speciously distinguished from the previous one as "empirical"). Attempting to bridge these antagonistic positions, Arturo Escobar (1999) entreats constructivist postmodernists and realist empiricists to recognize both the biophysical basis of reality and the historical and discursive contexts in which knowledge of it is gathered (3).

When culturally situated knowledges and discourses (including those of the scientists themselves) are ignored or excluded from research models, the environment is sometimes treated as an unproblematic universal category, an arena of natural laws. By critically examining the putatively objective and neutral domains of empirical science, political ecologists and others have drawn to the surface a series of embedded assumptions that reflect the cultural, colonial, gender, religious, and class characteristics and interests that underlie various scientific projects. Geographer Piers Blaikie (1985) has urged scholars as well as policymakers to recognize that "even a position of so-called neutrality rests upon partisan assumptions" (1). With Brookfield, he has questioned the heavy focus on technological fixes that regularly characterize the response of the scientific community and governmental agencies to environmental problems. Instead, they encourage an approach that represents environmental degradation as both a social problem and a biophysical condition: "while the physical reasons why land becomes degraded belong mainly in the realm of natural science, the reasons why adequate steps are not taken to counter the effects of degradation lie squarely within the realm of social science" (Blaikie and Brookfield 1987, 2).

Since publication of these seminal works, scholars have formulated a broad critique of the modern western conception of the world as two qualitatively distinct realms, each appropriately studied by either natural or social sciences (Painter and Durham 1995, Paulson 1998). David Harvey (1998, 332) proposes that we examine the current physical world not as pristine nature but as a set of "radically different environments that have been created under several centuries of capitalism" in which "the circulation of money is a prime ecological variable" (see also Haraway 1989, Escobar 1999). Contributors to Philippe Descola and Gísli Pàlsson's (1996) collection encourage greater attention to ethno-epistemologies that provide alternative means of conceptualizing the ways in which humans live within a material environment.

Philip Stott and Sian Sullivan's (2000) edited book explores implications of conventional representations of nature and science through case studies that demonstrate how scientific research designs and data presentations are guided by unexamined assumptions about how to ask questions and which methods to apply in investigating them. They argue that such assumptions contribute to results of scientific studies that may (consciously or not) legitimize the interests of certain social groups over others, thereby entering the political arena.

Reflecting and Acting with Political Ecology

The studies of environmental degradation and conflict brought together in this book lead to implicit (if not explicit) recommendations for action, and many political ecologists are purposefully engaged in such action. Indeed, "new ecological anthropology" in general has been as much about finding practical solutions to environmental problems as about building new methodological and theoretical approaches to study those phenomena (Kottak 1999, 23). At the 1996 founding of the Anthropology and Environment Section of the American Anthropological Association, Carole L. Crumley (2001) wrote that anthropologists "must enter current debates over environmental issues by as many avenues as possible, on our own behalf as well as that of those whose lives and circumstances we study" (ix). And in Nancy Peluso and Michael Watts's (2001) *Violent Environments*, scholars from numerous disciplines engage to analyze and explore practical solutions to ominous environmental problems and threats.

The means that political ecologists employ for collecting, analyzing, and using data overlap in vital ways with those of applied anthropology in general. Shared elements include attention to and mutual collaboration with various kinds of social groups and social movements; interest in documenting the distribution of benefits, together with their costs and risks on various scales; concern about environmental decision making and conflict resolution; and investigation of the environmental and social consequences of development models and discourses. Within this field of shared concerns, political ecologists have insisted that attention to practical engagement with different stakeholders and the search for practical solutions to social-environmental problems be part of a methodological commitment to understanding how the environmental uses and conditions in question are affected by larger economic and political systems as well as by discursive and cultural constructions of the environment. Barbara Johnston has tirelessly promoted stronger relationships among research, practice, and activism: forging models for understanding the social context of environmental decision making in the edited book *Who Pays the Price?* (1994), elaborating concepts of environmental justice within a human rights framework in *Life and Death Matters* (1997), and encouraging anthropologists to become involved in policymaking and debate.

A vital international movement in political ecology has promoted political action toward a more equitable distribution of economic and ecological resources and risks. The journal *Capitalism, Nature, Socialism* was established in 1988 at the Center for Political Ecology in Santa Cruz, California, and continues to embrace a red-green scholarly and activist stance. In 1990, the companion journal *Ecología Política* was founded in Barcelona under the direction of Joan Martínez-Alier, with the express goal of bringing together scholarship on social conflict in resource management with analysis of green political actions and visions.

Enrique Leff (1999, 15) argues that this intimate tie among theory, practice and politics pushes all of us, even privileged scholars, to include our own positions and actions in the frame of analysis. And recent efforts of political ecologists to understand and participate in the ensemble of forces linking social change, environment, and development are giving rise to new questions. For example, how do we situate ourselves in the circuits of power, knowledge, and practice that we seek to understand? As scholars and as those who influence policy, we are becoming increasingly aware of the power relationships that link certain ways of knowing and communicating with greater access to social and physical resources. This awareness has encouraged the development of participatory (Chambers 1992), collaborative (Zimmerman 2001), or reflexive research methods that aim to translate the knowledge of marginal or subaltern people into power, respect, and rights. It has also motivated environmental scholars to seek various ways of advocating for the groups with whom they work.

THE INTELLECTUAL GENEALOGIES discussed in this chapter have led up to current approaches to working across spaces, scales, and social groups and to new ways of conceptualizing and applying ideas of the political in political ecology. New multiscale approaches are helping us to understand relations between local cultural-environmental changes and global economic and political forces and processes, while sensitivity to social differentiation and marginalization are generating insights into dynamics of knowledge and decision on multiple levels.

Increasing sensitivity to political dimensions of environmental phenomena has led to all kinds of new questions and results. We do not place these political issues outside of, or even adjacent to, the domain of the material but see them as inextricable dimensions of it. We argue that studies that document erosion and those that analyze tenure policies are equally political in nature (insofar as they all use categories and questions grounded in certain visions and interests) and equally ecological (insofar as they all seek to understand the interrelationships between organisms and their environments). As a whole, this book makes a strong argument for bringing both kinds of studies into the same field of analysis. In our own research, as well as in the chapters collected here, we seek to incorporate political dynamics into environmental analyses in ways that do not dilute the study of the ecological but strengthen our ability to understand and contribute to the dialectical processes through which humans appropriate, contest, and manipulate the world around them. Vital conversations about our role as environmental scholars and practitioners—questions that are deeply political—resonate throughout this book. These discussions are part of a quest to ask questions and gather information in ways that facilitate struggles for greater social and environmental justice and lead to the development of fruitful applications for the new information and vision obtained through this scholarship.

NOTES

1. Later work in ethnobotany and symbolic ecology has taken greater care to note the political and economic context of local understandings and practices in relation to the biophysical environment. See, for example, Descola and Pàlsson (1996), Nazarea (1999), Kempton (2001), and Balée (1999).

   Within ecological anthropology there have also been critiques of an overemphasis on bounded local analyses. In a retrospective assessment of his study of the Betsileo of Madagascar in the 1970s, Kottak (1980) noted that Rappaport's model did not allow for an understanding of "the role of stratification and the state in determining differential access to strategic and socially valued resources" (Kottak 1999, 24).

2. Some scholars who continued to embrace the language of ecology turned to analyses like those of Botkin (1990), who rejected homeostasis in favor of dynamic and discordant harmonies, focusing on patterns that were recognizable yet continuously and unpredictably changing.

3. Bryant and Bailey (1997) provide a good assessment of ways in which scholars explored applications of historical materialism to environmental issues during this period.

4. Meanwhile, debates among materialists over whether to locate key determinative forces in the harnessing of energy (White 1949), the mode of production and reproduction (Harris 1979), technology (Sahlins and Service 1960), or specific structures of social relations (Friedman 1974, 1976) led to a renewed interest in understanding bio-

physical dynamics in the context of social-political organization of production and cultural-ideological systems.

5. A related dichotomy pitted those who embraced scientific methods in the pursuit of objective studies against those who privileged analyses informed by the social sciences and humanities. A recent manifestation of this particular division was seen in the establishment of the Society for Anthropological Sciences and its first meeting, entitled the "Salon des Récusés," occurring simultaneously with the 2002 annual meeting of the American Anthropological Association in New Orleans.

REFERENCES

Adger, Neil, Tor Benjaminsen, Katrina Brown, and Hanne Svarstad. 2001. "Advancing a Political Ecology of Global Environmental Discourses." *Development and Change* 32: 681–715.

Asad, Talal. 1973. *Anthropology and the Colonial Encounter.* New York: Humanity Books.

Atkinson, A. 1991. *Principles of Political Ecology.* London: Bellhaven.

Balée, William, ed. 1998. *Advances in Historical Ecology.* New York: Columbia University Press.

Bassett, Thomas. 1988. "Political Ecology of Peasant-Herder Conflicts in the Northern Ivory Coast." *Annals of the Association of American Geographers* 78, no. 3: 453–72.

Bateson, Gregory. 1972. *Steps to an Ecology of Mind.* New York: Ballantine.

Beckett, Jeremy, and Daniel Motto, guest eds. 1996. *Indigenous Peoples/Global Terrains.* Special issue of *Identities* 3, nos. 1 and 2.

Berlin, Brent, Dennis E. Breedlove, and Peter H. Raven. 1974. *Principles of Tzeltal Plant Classification: An Introduction to the Botanical Ethnography of a Mayan Speaking People of Highland Chiapas.* New York: Academic Press.

Biersack, Aletta. 1999. "Introduction: From the 'New Ecology' to the New Ecologies." *American Anthropologist* 101, no. 1: 5–18.

Blaikie, Piers. 1985. *Political Economy of Soil Erosion in Developing Countries.* London: Longman.

Blaikie, Piers, and Harold Brookfield. 1987. *Land Degradation and Society.* London: Methuen.

Blaikie, Piers, ed., with Terry Cannon, Ian Davis, and Ben Wisner. 1994. *At Risk: Natural Hazards, People's Vulnerability, and Disasters.* London: Routledge.

Botkin, Daniel B. 1990. *Discordant Harmonies.* New York: Oxford University Press.

Bourdieu, Pierre. 1977. *Outline of a Theory of Practice.* New York: Cambridge University Press.

Braidotti, Rosi, Ewa Charkiewics, Sabine Hausler, and Saskia Wieringa. 1994. *Women, the Environment, and Sustainable Development: Towards a Theoretical Synthesis.* London: Zed.

Brosius, J. Peter. 1999. "Analyses and Interventions: Anthropological Engagements with Environmentalism." *Current Anthropology* 40, no. 3: 277–309.

Bryant, Raymond. 1998. "Power, Knowledge, and Political Ecology in the Third World." *Progress in Physical Geography* 22, no. 1: 79–94.

———. 2002. "False Prophets? Mutant NGOs and Philippine Environmentalism." *Society and Natural Resources* 15, no. 7: 629–40.

Bryant, Raymond L., and Sinead Bailey. 1997. *Third World Political Ecology.* New York: Routledge.

Burton, Ian, Robert W. Kates, and Gilbert F. White. 1978. *The Environment As Hazard.* New York: Oxford University Press.

Butler, Judith. 1997. *The Psychic Life of Power.* Stanford, Calif.: Stanford University Press.

Carney, Judith A. 1996. "Converting the Wetlands, Engendering the Environment: The Intersection of Gender with Agrarian Change in Gambia." In *Liberation Ecologies*, edited by Richard Peet and Michael Watts, 165–87. New York: Routledge.

Chambers, Robert. 1992. "Rural Appraisal: Rapid, Relaxed and Participatory." Discussion paper, no. 311. Institute of Development Studies. Unpublished.

Conklin, H. C. 1954. "An Ethnoecological Approach to Shifting Agriculture." *Transactions of the New York Academy of Sciences* 17: 133–42.

Crumley, Carole L. 2001. "Introduction." In *New Directions in Anthropology and Environment*, edited by Carole L. Crumley. Walnut Creek, Calif.: Altamira.

Denevan, William M. *Hispanic Lands and Peoples: Selected Writings of James J. Parsons*. Boulder, Colo.: Westview.

Descola, Philippe, and Gísli Pàlsson, eds. 1996. Nature and Society: *Anthropological Perspectives*. New York: Routledge.

Dove, Michael R. 1999. "Comments on Peter Brosius' Analysis and Interventions. Anthropological Engagements with Environmentalism." *Current Anthropology* 40, no. 3: 290–91.

Escobar, Arturo. 1995. *Encountering Development: The Making and Unmaking of the Third World*. Princeton, N.J.: Princeton University Press.

———. 1999. "After Nature: Steps to an Antiessentialist Political Ecology." *Current Anthropology* 40, no. 1: 1–30.

Forde, C. Daryll. 1963. *Habitat, Economy, and Society*. New York: Dutton.

Friedman, Jonathan. 1974. "Marxism, Structuralism, and Vulgar Materialism." *Man* 9, no. 3, new series: 444–69.

———. 1975. "Tribes, States, and Transformations." In *Marxist Analyses and Social Anthropology*, edited by Maurice Bloch, 161–202. London: Malaby.

———. 1976. "Marxist Theory and Systems of Total Reproduction." *Critique of Anthropology* 7: 3–16.

———. 1979. "Hegelian Ecology." In *Social and Ecological Systems*, edited by P. Burnham and R. Ellen, 253–79. New York: Academic Press.

Gezon, Lisa L. 2002. "Marriage, Kin, and Compensation: A Socio-Political Ecology of Gender in Ankarana, Madagascar." *Anthropological Quarterly* 75, no. 4: 675–706.

Giddens, Anthony. 1984. *The Constitution of Society: Outline of the Theory of Structuralism*. Berkeley: University of California Press.

Grossman, Lawrence S. 1998. *The Political Ecology of Bananas: Contract Farming, Peasants, and Agricultural Change in the Eastern Caribbean*. Chapel Hill: University of North Carolina Press.

Guha, Ramachandra. 1994. "Radical Environmentalism: A Third-World Critique." In *Ecology: Key Concepts in Critical Theory*, edited by Carolyn Merchant, 281–89. Atlantic Highlands, N.J.: Humanities Press.

Guha, Ramachandra, and Joan Martínez-Alier, eds. 1997. *Varieties of Environmentalism: Essays North and South*. London: Earthscan.

Haraway, Donna Jeanne. 1989. *Primate Visions: Gender, Race, and Nature in the World of Modern Science*. New York: Routledge.

Harris, Marvin. 1979. *Cultural Materialism*. New York: Random House.

Harvey, David. 1998. "What's Green and Makes the Environment Go Round?" In *The Cultures of Globalization*, edited by Fredric Jameson and Masao Miyoshi, 327–55. Durham, N.C.: Duke University Press.

Hecht, Susanna, and Alexander Cockburn. 1989. *The Fate of the Forest*. London: Verso.

Hewitt, Kenneth, ed. 1983. *Interpretations of Calamity from the Viewpoint of Human Ecology*. Boston: Allen and Unwin.

Horkheimer, Max, and Theodor W. Adorno. 1976 [1945]. *Dialectic of Enlightenment*, translated by John Cumming. New York: Continuum.

Hornborg, Alf. 2001. *The Power of the Machine: Global Inequalities of Economy, Technology, and Environment*. Walnut Creek, Calif.: Altamira.

Johnston, Barbara, ed. 1994. *Who Pays the Price? The Sociocultural Context of Environmental Crisis*. Washington, D.C.: Island.

———. 1997. *Life and Death Matters: Human Rights and the Environment at the End of the Millennium*. Walnut Creek, Calif.: Altamira.

Jones, James. 1995. "Environmental Destruction, Ethnic Discrimination, and International Aid in Bolivia." In *The Social Causes of Environmental Destruction in Latin America*, edited by Michael Painter and William Durham, 169–216. Ann Arbor: University of Michigan Press.

Kasperson, Jeanne X., and Roger Kasperson. 2001. *Global Environmental Risk*. Tokyo: United Nations Press/Earthscan.

Keil, Roger, and Leesa Faucett, eds. 1998. *Political Ecology: Global and Local*. London: Routledge.

Kempton, Willett. 2001. "Cognitive Anthropology and the Environment." In *New Directions in Anthropology and Environment*, edited by Carole L. Crumley, 49–71. Walnut Creek, Calif.: Altamira.

Kottak, Conrad. 1980. *The Past in the Present: History, Ecology, and Cultural Variation in Highland Madagascar*. Ann Arbor: University of Michigan Press.

———. 1999. "The New Ecological Anthropology." *American Anthropologist* 101, no. 1: 23–35.

———. 2003. *Anthropology: The Exploration of Human Diversity*. 9th ed. New York: McGraw-Hill.

Kroeber, Alfred L. 1963 [1939]. *Cultural and Natural Areas of Native North America*. Berkeley: University of California Press.

Leff, Enrique. 1999. "Comments on Steps to an Antiessentialist Political Ecology by Arturo Escobar." *Current Anthropology* 40, no. 1: 20–21.

Mackenzie, A. Fiona D. 1995. "'A Farm Is Like a Child Who Cannot Be Left Unguarded': Gender, Land, and Labour in Central Province, Kenya." *Institute of Developmental Studies Bulletin* 26, no. 1: 17–23.

Martínez-Alier, Joan. 2002. *The Environmentalism of the Poor: A Study of Ecological Conflicts and Valuation*. Northampton, Mass.: Elgar.

Merchant, Carolyn. 1994. *Ecology: Key Concepts in Critical Theory*. Atlantic Highlands, N.J.: Humanities Press.

Morgan, Lewis H. 1877. *Ancient Society*. Chicago: Kerr.

Mortimore, M. 1998. *Adapting to Drought*. Cambridge: Cambridge University Press.

Nazarea, Virginia. 1999. *Ethnoecology: Situated Knowledge/Located Lives*. Tucson: University of Arizona Press.

Nietschmann, Bernard. 1973. *Between Land and Water: The Subsistence Ecology of the Miskito Indians, Eastern Nicaragua*. New York: Seminar Press.

Odum, Howard T. 1971. *Environment, Power, and Society*. New York: Wiley-Interscience.

Ortner, Sherry. 1984. "Theory of Anthropology Since the Sixties." *Comparative Studies in Society and History* 126, no. 1: 126–66.

———. 1989. *High Religion: A Cultural and Political History of Sherpa Buddhism*. Princeton, N.J.: Princeton University Press.

Painter, Michael, and William H. Durham, eds. 1995. *The Social Causes of Environmental Destruction in Latin America*. Ann Arbor: University of Michigan Press.

Parsons, Howard L. 1977. *Marx and Engels on Ecology*. Westport, Conn.: Greenwood.

Paulson, Susan. 1998. *Desigualdad social y degradación ambiental en América Latina*. Quito, Ecuador: Abya Yala.

Peet, Richard, and Michael Watts. 1993. "Production: Development Theory and Environment in an Age of Market Triumphalism." *Economic Geography* 69, no. 3: 227–53.

———. 1996. *Liberation Ecologies: Environment, Development, Social Movements*. New York: Routledge.

Peluso, Nancy, and Michael Watts, eds. 2001. *Violent Environments*. Ithaca, N.Y.: Cornell University Press.

Porter, Philip W. 1965. Environmental Potential and Economic Opportunities—A Background for Cultural Adaptation." *American Anthropologist* 67, no. 2: 409–20.

Posey, Darrell A. 1983. "Indigenous Ecological Knowledge and Development of the Amazon." In *The Dilemma of Amazonian Development*, edited by E. F. Moran. Boulder, Colo.: Westview.

Rappaport, Roy. 1968. *Pigs for the Ancestors: Ritual in the Ecology of a New Guinea People*. New Haven, Conn.: Yale University Press.

———. 1984. *Pigs for the Ancestors: Ritual in the Ecology of a New Guinea People*. 2d ed. New Haven, Conn.: Yale University Press.

———. 1993. "The Anthropology of Trouble." *American Anthropologist* 95: 295–303.

Richards, Paul. 1985. *Indigenous Agricultural Revolution: Ecology and Food Production in West Africa*. Boulder, Colo.: Westview.

Rocheleau, Dianne. 1999. "Commentary on 'After Nature: Steps to an Anti-Essentialist Political Ecology,' by Arturo Escobar." *Current Anthropology* 40, no. 1: 22–23.

Rocheleau, Dianne, Barbara Thomas-Slayter, and Esther Wangari, eds. 1996. *Feminist Political Ecology: Global Issues and Local Experiences*. London: Routledge.

Sachs, Wolfgang, ed. 1993. *Global Ecology: A New Arena of Political Conflict*. London: Zed.

Sahlins, Marshall D., and Elman R. Service. 1960. *Evolution and Culture*. Ann Arbor: University of Michigan Press.

Sauer, Carl. 1952. *Agricultural Origins and Dispersals*. New York: American Geographical Society.

Schroeder, Richard A. 1993. "Shady Practice: Gender and the Political Ecology of Resource Stabilization in Gambian Gardens/Orchards." *Economic Geography* 69, no. 4: 349–65.

Scott, Earl P. 1979. "Land Use Change in the Harsh Lands of West Africa." *African Studies Review* 22, no. 1: 1–24.

Shanin, Teodor, ed. 1970. *Peasants*. London: Penguin.

Shiva, Vandana. 1988. *Staying Alive: Women, Ecology, and Development*. London: Zed.

Steward, Julian. 1972 [1955]. *Theory of Culture Change: The Methodology of Multilinear Evolution*. Urbana: University of Illinois Press.

Stocking, George. 1992. *The Ethnographer's Magic and Other Essays in the History of Anthropology*. Madison: University of Wisconsin Press.

Stott, Philip, and Sian Sullivan, eds. 2000. *Political Ecology: Science, Myth and Power*. London: Arnold.

Thomas, William L. 1956. *Man's Role in Changing the Face of the Earth*. Chicago: University of Chicago Press.

Turner, B. L. 1983. *Once Beneath the Forest: Prehistoric Terracing in the Rio Bec Region of the Maya Lowlands*. Boulder, Colo.: Westview.

Turner, Matt. 1999. "Conflict, Environmental Change, and Social Institutions in Dryland Africa." *Society and Natural Resources* 12, no. 2: 134–56.

Vayda, Andrew, and Roy Rappaport. 1967. "Ecology, Cultural and Noncultural." In *Introduction to Cultural Anthropology*, edited by J. Clifton, 477–97. Boston: Houghton Mifflin.

Vayda, Andrew, and Bradley Walters. 1999. "Against Political Ecology." *Human Ecology* 27, no. 1: 167–79.

Watts, Michael. 1983a. "The Poverty of Theory." In *Interpretations of Calamity*, edited by K. Hewitt. London: Allen and Unwin.

———. 1983b. *Silent Violence.* Berkeley: University of California Press.

———. 2000. *Struggles over Geography: Violence, Freedom, and Development.* Heidelberg, Germany: University of Heidelberg, Department of Geography.

White, Gilbert F. 1974. *Natural Hazards, Local, National, Global.* New York: Oxford University Press.

White, Leslie. 1949. *The Science of Culture.* New York: Grove.

Wissler, Clark. 1940. *Indians of the United States: Four Centuries of Their History and Culture.* New York: Doubleday, Doran.

Wissler, Clark, and Bella Weitzner. 1922. *The American Indian: An Introduction to the Anthropology of the New World.* New York: Oxford University Press.

Wolf, Eric. 1969. *Peasant Wars of the Twentieth Century.* New York: Harper Torch.

———. 1982. *Europe and the People without History.* Berkeley: University of California Press.

———. 2001. *Pathways of Power: Building an Anthropology of the Modern World.* Berkeley: University of California Press.

Zimmerer, Karl S. 1996. "Discourses on Soil Loss in Bolivia: Sustainability and the Search for Socioenvironmental 'Middle Ground.'" In *Liberation Ecologies: Environment, Development, Social Movements*, edited by Richard Peet and Michael Watts, 110–24. London: Routledge.

———. 2000. "The Reworking of Conservation Geographies: Nonequilibrium Landscapes and Nature-Society Hybrids." *Annals of the Association of American Geographers* 90, no. 2: 356–69.

Zimmerer, Karl S., and Thomas J. Bassett, eds. 2003. *Political Ecology: An Integrative Approach to Geography and Environment-Development Studies.* New York: Guilford.

Zimmerman, Larry. 2001. "A New and Different Archaeology? With a Postscript on the Impact of the Kennewick Dispute." In *Reappropriation Reader: Who Owns Indian Remains?* edited by D. Mihesua. Lincoln: University of Nebraska Press.

PART ONE

Policy and Environment

3

The Fight for the West

A Political Ecology of Land-Use Conflicts in Arizona

METTE J. BROGDEN AND JAMES B. GREENBERG

In the global economy, the commodification of nature and the territorialization practices of nation-states pose formidable challenges to sustainable uses of natural resources. Certain environmental problems such as growth management and residential sprawl have proved to be intractable issues in our existing political processes. This case study of grazing and growth conflicts in Arizona demonstrates that intractable environmental problems may actually be emergent properties of complex systems, requiring new political approaches that foster collaboration and knowledge sharing between disputing stakeholders. One such multi-stakeholder collaboration in Arizona revealed that attempts to remove grazing from Arizona landscapes could actually be detrimental to biodiversity, contrary to the expectations of grazing critics.[1]

Since World War II, there has been a dramatic increase in migration to western states. In recent years, this has produced residential sprawl and created conflicts between urban and rural populations over land use on millions of acres of public land. The issues are far more complex than public debates and proposed solutions would indicate (Sheridan 2001). At stake in these conflicts are not just the values of these interest groups but ultimately how humans can inhabit landscapes and use natural resources sustainably.

In this chapter we tap the fields of political ecology, environmental conflict resolution (ECR), and the science of complexity to frame the problem of sustainability and to understand the issues surrounding land-use conflicts in Arizona. These approaches may also help us to reintegrate the ecological, economic, and sociopolitical aspects of systems that have been the special purview of narrow disciplines and so open a space for building more effective understandings and solutions to broad-scale environmental problems.

The Problem of Sustainability

Ecological systems evolve logics of interaction and production based on processes such as nutrient cycling, energy flows, and water cycles. Ecological regions or zones may be characterized by their specific elements (such as soil types, geomorphology, elevation, climate) that together create the potential for biotic production at an identifiable level and diversity, even given their stochastic nature (Brogden n.d.).[2] Overextraction of natural resources can degrade or significantly alter elements of an ecosystem, tipping it beyond its ability to sustain the same degree of biotic productivity and diversity or to recover from the external perturbation.[3] In theory, sustainable natural resource use implies (1) that extractive activities do not outstrip a resource in the short term and (2) that the ecological system in which it is embedded maintains the ability to regenerate the resource over the long term.

By contrast, economic systems evolve logics of interaction and production based on prices, markets, and costs that are quite different from those governing ecological systems. The economic sustainability of an enterprise or a household merely requires that income should exceed expenditures by a sufficient margin to meet enterprise or household needs over time. The problem for policymakers is how to reconcile these very different rationalities.

To create a sustainable intersection between economic and ecological functioning, governance structures and social institutions must enable resource users to accommodate—and even benefit from—the temporal and spatial variability of natural resources. At the same time, these institutions must successfully mediate (1) competing claims to resources and (2) the different outcome time scales associated with economic decision making and ecological functioning. Ideally, mechanisms are available to resolve conflicts over competing claims in peaceful and stable ways and to balance levels of extraction needed to support households and business enterprises against recovery rates of exploited natural resources.

In a classic subsistence economy (an admittedly ideal type), producers deal directly with nature and make limited demands on a variety of natural system elements. Because nature provides feedback and payoffs in the form of increasing or decreasing biotic productivity, human populations may evolve sustainable practices. By contrast, in modern industrialized economies, producers and consumers are often far apart; and extensive external inputs may even decouple economic actors from dependence on their own locale. Nature no longer provides direct payoffs and feedback. Natural resource users-consumers converse with markets instead of nature and work to maximize profit by sourcing elements of ecological systems from all over the globe rather than making the most of a local ecological system's biotic productivity over time. In a global market, demands for resources seem infinite. However, sustainable use of natural systems and their elements ultimately depends on a local logic. This logic requires an integrative approach to the management and regulation of identifiable ecological units—such as watersheds or ecological regions—that respects the dynamics of the particular ecological system. But at least three macrolevel forces work against such management: global economic integration, specialized academic disciplines, and the territorialization practices of nation-states, which divide ecosystems into spatially and conceptually fractured jurisdictions.

Commodifying certain elements within natural systems subjects them to a different logic—the market's, where decisions regarding resources are severed from an understanding of their role within ecological system functioning. Nature is stripped of local meaning that may serve a necessary mediatory role and becomes merely an array of commodities. Globalization exacerbates these effects. Decisions occur in global markets and boardrooms far distant from local ecological systems (Greenberg 1998). Moreover, global markets and multinational corporations source natural elements from all over the planet, driving prices down and setting up conditions in which, to sustain themselves, local producers must extract more of a resource to make up for the reduction in price. Finally, since economic processes transcend the boundaries of nation-states, these centers of economic decision making can exert enormous pressure on governments for favorable decisions in ongoing contests over territorialization of resources, making the challenges to sustainable human use of natural resources formidable indeed.

When land is commodified as real estate rather than being seen as an integral part of ecosystems, it becomes, to some degree, a good that may be bought and sold like any other (Godelier 1977, Greenberg 1998, Marx 1977 [1867], Taussig 1980). Yet because land is spatially fixed, its commodification takes on somewhat different dynamics as compared to mobile resources so that, even in complex contemporary societies, what happens to land inextricably remains tied to local contexts, even if ownership is not.

Currently, sprawling residential development challenges the sustainable use of natural resources. Nonetheless, in the spatial fixedness of land and its inexorable relation to local communities, we do spy a kind of hope. Where competing groups are able to understand how their interests in landscapes might intersect, they may join forces and press for integrative approaches to the management of landscapes and the associated ecological systems they support. In fact, a number of these experiments are underway across the west as community-based collaborative (CBC) groups have formed to resolve local conflicts over resources and implement more holistic resource management. But unless CBC participants can extend their purview and influence to the policy level, where resource territorializations are defined and contested, they are likely not to succeed.

Territorialization: Setting the Rules of Human Engagement
with the Natural World

The absence of sociopolitical institutions that regulate resource use and owner-ship sets up an incentive for individuals to rapidly degrade a resource because, as Garrett Hardin's (1968) concept of tragedy predicts, if an individual does not make use of the resource, someone else will, and the opportunity for use will be lost. Hardin mistakenly described this dynamic as the "tragedy of the commons," a notion that has been critiqued (McCay and Acherson 1987, Netting 1993) because he applied his argument to communally owned resources under the assumption that they lacked rules of access. What he actually described was an open access regime in which resource degradation indeed occurs because no rules of access and use exist, leading to what is more properly called a "tragedy of open access." The enduring challenge for sustainable human engagement with the environment is to establish and enforce rules of engagement that enable resource users and managers to respond flexibly to changing systems and new information while providing the stability of access that enables planning.

Contemporary nation-states generate numerous structural obstacles to the development of flexible frameworks. They carve up the natural world into both physical spaces that define territorial units and their boundaries and conceptual spaces through which jurisdiction over particular resources is divided among bureaucratic structures. In the United States, for example, forests are the respon-sibility of the U.S. Department of Agriculture's Forest Service, while wildlife is managed by state wildlife agencies and, in cases of species endangerment, the U.S. Department of the Interior's Fish and Wildlife Service. These physical and conceptual territorializations of resources set the rules of production, control, and access (Greenberg 1998; Heyman 1994, 13–14; Mann 1993, 44–91), although they usually make virtually no sense from an ecological standpoint. Further-more, since bureaucratic structures are set up to simplify and regularize decision making, their responsiveness to local variance and ability to mediate competing claims to resources are limited as the rules of access and use become inscribed in law and administrative procedures.

As the state defines spaces and organizes resources by setting up jurisdic-tions and administrative rules, these arrangements in turn draw the social and political fault lines along which further disputes develop. It is important to understand that territorializations are historical products of contestation and negotiation for access and control over natural resources among competing groups, interests, and classes (Greenberg 1998). As such, they embed certain environmental values, which become part of the political idiom through which territorializations are justified or contested. Conflicts develop on the ground as well as in political arenas, where competing interests seek to influence or gain control over the agencies, laws, and regulations that govern natural resources. In the United States, territorializations are contested through political lobbying in Congress and state legislatures, elections, organized public input or appeals to administrative rule making, litigation, and grassroots activism. Thus, political organizing and disputing are ways for civil society to communicate with the state, and interest groups press arguments through the politics of pluralism.

In this interface between state and civil society, some actors achieve voice and some do not. Pluralistic politics leave out actors and interest groups who are too small or powerless to be effective as lobbyists or too scattered politically to be able to elect representatives. Globalization may move the interests of marginalized groups and local communities even further off stage. Fairness would insist that these groups find an effective voice. But as our case study will show, fairness is not the only reason why it is important for them to find a voice.

Reterritorialization: When Existing Tenure Arrangements Are Successfully Contested

Reterritorialization occurs when there is a reassignment of resource access rights to a different population or interest group (Greenberg 1998). Perhaps different users now have access to the same natural resource elements. Alternatively, an interest group may redefine commodity values and achieve the power to rearrange access rights to a natural system so that previous commodity values become obsolete and unprivileged. An example of this more complex reterritorialization process can be seen in the American southwest. Here, livestock grazing on public lands is being challenged by urban-based environmentalists, who are not only seeking to protect wilderness and its wildlife but also looking for recreational spaces where they can commune with nature.

When a new value conflicts with the old, and power shifts enough so that the new commodity value achieves a plurality, reterritorialization results in previous users' loss of access to territories supporting earlier commodity values. Territories and agency policies may then be redrawn to maximize production of the new resource value. Predictable discursive strategies assist this process, often vilifying the historical user personally or culturally or because that user has degraded the natural system.

Vilifying discourses become particularly salient in democratic electoral processes in which voters have a slew of issues and candidates to decide on and neither the time, the expertise, nor the inclination to study each issue in its complexity. Well-honed, catchy messages disseminated through media sound bytes and local reporting appeal to popular values and ideologies, thereby mystifying the fact that these disputes are actually competing claims between interest groups rather than clear moral imperatives. Furthermore, these arguments may have nothing whatsoever to do with fostering sustainable resource use, even when their proponents are utterly convinced that they do. For example, the case study in this chapter shows that simply getting cows off public lands will not preserve wildlife values. It also shows how contesting groups often exhibit, at one and the same time, excellent intentions toward the resource (such as wanting it to persist into the future) and self-interest (such as wanting something from it). While these values usually do not coincide completely, the pursuit of self-interest is not necessarily bad but must be viewed clearly. Existing uses or practices may indeed be detrimental to an ecological system and need to be changed. But in the contemporary era, as we suggest in this chapter, it is highly unlikely that any single interest group really knows what changes may be needed to allow ecological systems to recover. Complex systems encompass a web of causality and relations and require, at the least, exchanging information among actors to achieve an understanding of the system's complexity; co-constructing potential solutions among competitors; and making arrangements for adjusting the solution as circumstances, knowledge, and the environment change.

When ecological problems arise, they often entail multifaceted legal and political disputes that may involve a host of local, state, and national bureaucracies. Again, in such disputes, local communities and users, who often are the actors most dependent on and most knowledgeable about the resource, have difficulty finding a voice. Even when governmental policies and regulatory efforts attempt to strike a balance between the conservation of natural resources and the interests of various groups, these efforts are frequently either poorly coordinated or have contradictory effects on the ecosystem. As a result, years may pass before any solution or agreement is reached. In the meantime, irreversible environmental damage may continue (Rappaport 1994).

Reterritorialization in the American Southwest: A Case Study

We turn now to a case study of reterritorialization processes in Arizona. Data for this case study came from five years of participant-observation research of conflicts over land use in Arizona, including more than one hundred formal and informal interviews with ranchers, conservation and environmental nongovernmental (NGO) representatives, ranchette owners, federal and state agency representatives, and other public officials. Some interviews were conducted as we researched the transition from ranching to real estate development in one Arizona community. Others were conducted as part of research on the negotiation process of the Arizona Growing Smarter Commission and during the political implementation of its results in the following legislative session. Interviews were also completed in preparation for a conference about growth management initiatives on the 2000 ballot in Arizona. In addition, co-author Mette J. Brogden observed public meetings of the Sonoita Valley Planning Partnership and the Diablo Trust, two CBC groups in Arizona, as well as public meetings of the Arizona Growing Smarter Commission in 1999 and sessions of the 2000 Arizona legislature. Participant-observation data were also obtained in the course of Brogden's facilitation of stakeholder dialogue at the Arizona Common Ground Roundtable.

After World War II, a significant reterritorialization process began in the western and southwestern United States. It has accelerated in the past two decades, propelled largely by demographic pressure as migrants from the east, the midwest, and California have moved to the intermountain west in search of, among other things, lifestyles with more elbow room, better weather, and gorgeous views.

Actually, two reterritorializations are occurring, following two different but related commodifications of the landscape. The first is taking place on public lands, where urban dwellers value the landscape as a context for recreational experience that includes seeing abundant wildlife and communing with nature. To the extent that domestic livestock compete for forage with wildlife as well as leave cow pies on hiking trails, grazing and the new recreational values seem to be at odds, and conflict has ensued. Over time, urban environmentalists have elaborated a discourse that has painted a picture of morally deficient ranchers degrading the public's resources on public lands while eating at the public trough.

Their assertion of resource degradation has some foundation. In certain areas, overgrazing and overstocking has resulted in environmental degradation—some of it quite serious—although the worst occurred near the turn of the twentieth century, during the tragedy of open access, before limitations on access to rangeland commons were instituted (Sayer 1999, Sheridan 2001). So when environmentalists have looked at the condition of rangelands, they have found a basis in fact for their complaints. Less widely known is the fact that, at the turn of the twentieth century, ranchers themselves were insisting that regulation was needed and were highly impatient because it was not happening quickly enough (Diana Hadley, personal communication, June 2001).[4] This information should give us pause: social institutions that mediate resource access and use do not come into being overnight.

Urban-based environmentalists have sought to use the Endangered Species Act of 1973 to challenge ranching because they see grazing as the major culprit in the endangerment of species in the southwest. According to James H. Brown, biologist and past president of the Ecological Society of America, however, "Far more habitat has been destroyed to provide water to cities, subdivisions, and irrigated agriculture than by even the heaviest grazing pressure" (Clifford 1998, A33). And ranched areas are often the primary—or even the only—areas where species of concern are now found.[5] Perhaps it should surprise no one that urban environmentalists' most successful battles to preserve some of these species are being fought in rural areas against a ranching subculture with small numbers of people (read: votes).

Urban environmentalists have also been on the front lines in their own immediate settings, trying to gain some control over real estate development. Indeed, they are well aware that the pressure on ecological systems is tied to the commodification of landscape for residential development. Time and again in areas of population growth, developers seem to get exactly what they want in rezonings, zoning protection of rights to develop, legislation, and land purchases. In pursuing their business, they carve up more and more of the landscape surrounding cities, even though city inhabitants would prefer to preserve that land as open space. It seems not to matter that polls show that a super-majority of the public wishes the surrounding area to be left undeveloped (74 percent in a January 2000 Greater Phoenix Leadership poll). Endangered species lawsuits are virtually the only tools enabling environmentalists to get some political leverage in the fight to control development.

Sprawl—the second reterritorialization in the southwest—is happening despite the fact that almost all concerned (even developers) do not want it and each interest group is actually complicit in its occurrence.[6] The phenomenon proceeds through a combination of "If we build it, they will come," and the existence of a plethora of individuals who are making myriad individual decisions about where to live (read: in pretty natural areas). Newcomers in one desirable rural area rationalized their decision to build there with comments such as "It's just one small parcel," or "If I don't do it, someone else will," or "If I thought for one minute that my moving back into an urban area would stop development in this area, I'd do it," or "Why should I restrain myself when no one else does?"[7] Such comments evince the dynamics of an open-access regime.

The two reterritorializations—one apparently wanted by the environmentalist community, one apparently not—are connected because of how ranching evolved in Arizona. Ranching is a land-extensive activity in the semi-arid southwest. It requires access to significant acreages of forage to be economically viable. The homesteading model of 160 acres that worked in the midwest was woefully inadequate in Arizona; even increasing the homestead allocation to 640 acres proved to be insufficient. Consequently, land-tenure arrangements developed over time, providing ranchers with access to forage on federal and state trust lands but not concentrating land ownership in the hands of a very few. Thus, ranch units in Arizona are overwhelmingly comprised of a deeded portion owned outright by the rancher and forage leases on public lands (Sayer 1999, Sheridan 2001). This system of tenure rights has been institutionalized at the federal level within administrative policies of the Forest Service and the U.S. Department of the Interior's Bureau of Land Management and at the state level in Arizona State Land Department policies. The system is now being challenged through lawsuits as part of the reterritorialization process that is underway.

The system has had some interesting advantages. First, land ownership patterns in some parts of Arizona are highly checkered because of the way in which lands were selected to go into the school trust as state trust lands and because of how the early settlers selected homestead acreages. The deeded portions of ranches in Arizona—and elsewhere in the west—contain the most productive, water-rich, and biodiverse areas of the region. Land remaining in federal and state ownership surrounds private lands. If lands and resources had been individually managed on the scale of the mosaic pieces evident on an Arizona land ownership map, the landscape could have ended up quite fragmented. Thus, the tenure system that evolved to help assure economic viability also helped assure that larger areas of land would be managed together, enabling ranchers to move herds in rotation systems that allow for the regeneration of forage plants.

Second, federal ownership protects a significant portion of Arizona lands from development. But the private lands in the state that can be sold and converted for residential and ranchette development are exactly those with the most biodiversity along streams and fertile bottomlands. Residential development is much more of a threat to species (in most cases) than ranching is, especially as real estate development turns into sprawl (Sheridan 2001). So despite the landscape effects of livestock grazing in Arizona, in some important respects it has actually worked to conserve ecological values over time.

Ranching in the arid southwest, however, has always been a bit of a place-holding venture. Since the southwest is subject to drought, most land is marginal for agricultural production without irrigation. Ranching has been a way for some to earn a living from the land until it can appreciate in value enough to be sold and used for some other purpose, either commercial or residential development. Like other agriculturalists across the country, ranchers are usually land-rich and cash-poor. Therefore, they hold two somewhat competing interests at the same time:

- Ranchers want to use the land for ranching and maintain their rural livelihood strategy because they have built up their expertise, their herds, and their unique, embodied funds of knowledge of the land and food production over time, knowledge that has been hard won and that few urban dwellers have.
- They hope that their land will appreciate in value because if the ranching enterprise fails, they can sell the land and secure the financial future of themselves and their heirs.

While ranchers feel compelled to try to protect both those interests (Arizona Common Ground Roundtable discussion, April 1998), the latter interest assumes priority in the following cases (Brogden n.d., Sheridan 2001):

- Access arrangements on public lands become too tenuous.
- Ranch economics (because of globalization of agricultural commodities markets) are unfavorable.
- Land prices skyrocket.

Thus, reterritorialization on public lands becomes tied to reterritorialization on private lands, and urban dwellers and ranchers become locked in a dance toward urban sprawl and rural fragmentation from ranchette development that neither side really wants to see happen.

Complexity and the Intractability of Emergent Systemic Problems

The dynamics of residential sprawl reveal, ironically, that the most open-access regime going is based on the market. Contrary to Hardin's expectations that privatizing the commons would halt resource degradation, private property sold through an open-access land market is driving urban sprawl and the piecemeal fracturing of rural landscapes that threatens biodiversity. What this implies is that to create effective stewardship of resources, rules must be developed to govern what lands may be turned into commodities. But a question remains: how should this happen in a legal system highly elaborated around private property and its attendant rights?

An even more fundamental question is, why in a democratic society are such problems so intractable? If no one wants sprawl and loss of open space, why are these outcomes so difficult to stop? The new science of complexity may offer a key understanding of why such problems arise and become intractable.[8] One of the most useful concepts deriving from complexity theory is that of emergence in self-organizing systems. *Emergence* refers to a persistent observable pattern that results from local interactions of individuals but is not available to or producible by any single individual or single interaction. Emergent properties of systems develop in the absence of a centralized governance structure or plan.

Stuart A. Kauffman (1995, 56) illustrates the phenomenon of emergence in the following way: suppose a set of buttons is scattered on a table, and someone randomly picks up two buttons, connects them with a thread, and then sets them down. Then he picks up two more, connects them with another thread, and sets them down; and he continues to follow this pattern. After a while he will begin to lift a few additional buttons with the two he has selected because they are also connected to the two selected. But at a certain point, when he goes to pick up two buttons, so much connectivity will have developed that he will observe what's called a *phase transition*. That is, he will pick up a whole web of threads and buttons along with the two buttons he has chosen. That web is an emergent property of a system that self-organized from the simple repeated act of connecting two buttons with a single thread.

Applied to social or ecological systems, emergence results from local interactions of individuals, but an individual interaction cannot produce the emergent structure. The whole, in other words, is more than the sum of its parts. Local customs, rules, and desires may give rise to systemic outcomes that are not expected, intended, or even wanted by individual actors.

Sprawl is happening partly because increasing wealth and migration help create the market for the commodification of landscape. That explanation, however, captures only part of the systemic issue. Sprawl is fundamentally an emergent outcome fueled by a multiplicity of actions taken by individuals moving about the landscape, making their individual decisions to inhabit, purchase, develop, vilify each other, ranch, litigate, or sell land—all without a central plan. It is complex and multifaceted and cannot be reduced to blaming any single interest group. The situation would be much easier to handle if it were easy to blame someone because then we could simply eliminate one class of behaviors and fix the problem. Indeed, a desire for that type of solution renders us susceptible to vilifying arguments.

Since no single activity is responsible for undesired emergent properties of complex systems, such problems are intractable in our pluralistic political processes. Pluralistic politics are rarely about seeking to see the whole system; rather, they are about resolving competing claims to resources. In pluralistic politics, groups bump up against each other, form coalitions, and compromise to try to leverage power and votes. Political actors hope that, in the course of this rough-and-tumble process, views will coalesce into a majority view that prevails and results in wise policy. But groups try to knock each other's viewpoints out because they see each other as competitors. Thus, policy proposals are not the results of a process in which a variety of groups worked to perceive systemic problems and develop appropriate systemic solutions. Instead, they are based on the view from one or two vantage points. Politicking groups get absorbed in positional bargaining—compromising and chipping away at other positions to find a bottom line. And there is hardly ever time in the fast pace of legislative decision making to go back and rediagnose problems and then recast policy solutions that are based on a more complex understanding of phenomena.[9]

Environmental Conflict Resolution: Resolving Complex Environmental Issues through a Mutual Gains Strategy

During the past thirty years, new sociopolitical methods for addressing environmental problems and disputes have evolved. Subsumed under the rubric of environmental conflict resolution (ECR), this new field broadly encompasses a multiplicity of efforts to build consensus or foster collaboration among disparate interest groups in the development of environmental policy and settlement of conflicts (Bingham 1986, Carpenter and Kennedy 1988, Fisher and Ury 1981, Moore 1996, Susskind 1999). ECR processes operate quite differently from pluralistic political processes and judicial rulings that heretofore have set the rules of human engagement with the environment. Whereas judicial rulings and majority-rule legislative processes have tended to create winners and losers, ECR processes encourage stakeholders to take a mutual gains approach, recognizing that most disputes are not zero-sum.

ECR processes in the United States often engage a professional neutral party to mediate or facilitate discussions. A cadre of professionals, drawn largely from the fields of law and psychology, now practice in the ECR field. Their theories of practice suggest that to construct solutions around areas of common interest, stakeholders must educate each other about their interests and their individually held knowledge about the resource as well as the decision parameters and incentive structures that frame their actions. As stakeholders pool their knowledge, they begin to understand the complexity of the system and how the emergent problem is being produced. In theory, this opens a space for them to develop management approaches and policy incentive structures that encourage new individual decision making so that the system becomes reorganized toward a different emergent outcome. Multi-stakeholder approaches characterizing ECR processes thus may have the potential to handle unwanted emergent patterns more effectively than pluralistic politics can, which seek to suppress voices and achieve outright wins.

In Arizona and other western states, multi-stakeholder dialogues have been occurring in what many refer to as community-based collaborative groups. Most CBCs have been initiated by stakeholders (who may include agencies) to resolve conflicts over the use and management of specific watersheds or local landscapes. As they develop a better understanding of what is occurring in the system, they begin to create ongoing, adaptive-management plans that they hope will better handle the naturally occurring fluctuations in ecological processes as well as correct poor landscape outcomes of management regimes. These groups have been in existence for close to ten years, and researchers are in the beginning stages of trying to assess their environmental outcomes and answer meta-questions concerning their development.[10]

There are many such groups in Arizona. The Malpai Borderlands group organized to reintroduce fire into a grassland system. The Diablo Trust organized to address grazing issues on public lands. The Sonoita Valley Planning Partnership involved stakeholders in a discussion of an allotment management plan for the Empire-Cienega Natural Resource Area. The Altar Valley Conservation Alliance formed to document resource conditions across this large ranching valley. There are also watershed groups working to restore and maintain healthy watershed functions. In all cases of which the authors are aware, CBC groups become involved in managing the entire ecological system—a resource that doesn't move—rather than maintain a focus on one or two individual elements of the system.

Multi-stakeholder Collaborative Policy Dialogues

State and national multi-stakeholder policy dialogues extend the CBC trend, but they differ in that they are not tied to a specific landscape. Instead, they attempt to address the many arenas in which the broad-based conflicts over land use are happening, including policy and institutional arrangements at the state and national levels. Of more recent origin than CBCs, policy-focused efforts seem a logical and necessary next stage of systemic reorganization around natural resources, for at least two reasons.

First, the purview of many CBC groups extends onto federal lands (and in Arizona, state trust lands), and their work is bound by federal regulations that are not specific to a locale. Many of these regulations are keyed to focus on particular resources within ecological systems rather than address the system as a whole. For example, the Endangered Species Act has a single-species focus and can lead to management conundrums in which two or more endangered species are trying to occupy the same area but have incompatible habitat requirements. If regulations or administrative policies constrict actions that the group sees as critical to the effective management of the whole system, it must find a way to address the federal regulations. As we've noted, however, it is very difficult for a local group to address national policy.

Second, conditions threatening a local ecological system may not be under the control of a local group. A local CBC group can institute watershed restoration projects, but the most significant threats may involve (for example) decisions to allocate water outside of watersheds.

Given these issues, local groups must find a way to gain a voice at regional, state, and national levels; and multi-stakeholder policy dialogues offer such a possibility. But the challenges to creating effective collaborative policy dialogues are quite different from those at the local CBC level. Policy-focused dialogues operate more directly and more recognizably in the political arena, working across ecological system types to address broad-based conflicts that pit environmental values and ideologies against each other. These conflicts are fought out in a bewildering array of jurisdictions and systemic levels. Challenges to grazing, for example, occur during individual Bureau of Land Management or Forest Service allotment management planning, during national forest planning, through litigation that forces agencies to comply with provisions of the Endangered Species Act, in political lobbying at state and federal levels during legislative and budget processes, in legal challenges to Arizona State Land Department leasing policies, in local and state elections, in municipal or county planning processes such as the development of Pima County's Sonoran Desert Conservation Plan, in state wildlife department administrative policymaking and planning, and likely in other arenas of which we are not yet aware. Thus, political ecologists must investigate a variety of arenas to understand the ecology of politics around natural resource use.

ECR policy dialogues are sociocultural innovations that address political complexity by gathering competing interests into a single dialogic process. The conflict analysis that ECR practitioners complete before initiation of a dialogue includes identifying the stakeholders, intervening legal structures, and jurisdictional

procedures and understanding the history of conflicts. Once a process is convened, stakeholders continue to map this ecology as well as their disparate behaviors and decision parameters under existing administrative environments.

An Example of a Collaborative Policy Dialogue: The Arizona Common Ground Roundtable

The Arizona Common Ground Roundtable is a statewide policy dialogue that
grew out of an initial conversation between the Nature Conservancy, three ranching families, and anthropologist and ranch historian Tom Sheridan in an effort
to move beyond the polarized debate around public lands grazing. Convened
and facilitated by staff from the Udall Center's ECR program, in several months'
time the group came to understand a great deal about the political, social, economic, and ecological environments that ranchers were facing that might lead to
decisions to sell their ranches for real estate development.

When it became clear to participants that the reterritorialization process on
public land was related to sale of ranches for real estate development, they began
to focus on how to build solutions based on a common interest of preserving
open space. Conservationists wanted to achieve landscape preservation that
could keep ecological units intact and support biodiversity, while ranchers
wanted both to keep ranching and to protect their financial investment in land
in case the economic viability of the ranch enterprise failed. The group adopted
a strategy of looking for policy solutions that would achieve landscape conservation by keeping ranchers ranching and using ecologically sensitive practices.
This proved difficult for a variety of reasons.

Conservationists, for example, either had to overcome salient beliefs that
ranching was responsible for massive degradation to landscapes or decide to
proceed despite this belief, with the rationale that ranching was the lesser of two
evils. For their part, ranchers saw themselves as producing a public good (food);
and when in their course of discussion they heard the conservation side continuing to characterize ranching as the lesser of two evils, they became even more
mistrustful of the conservationists' support of various proposals.

Indeed, the many arenas in which the reterritorialization battles were
occurring fostered ongoing difficulties with trust, especially on the part of ranchers. Ranchers are trying to protect four types of land-tenure arrangements in Arizona: private property, Forest Service allotments, Bureau of Land Management
allotments, and state trust land leases. Political maneuverings and litigation
continued in each of these arenas while the group worked and resulted in participants' reluctance to commit to supporting policy recommendations throughout the legislative process.

For example, participants proposed interesting ideas for how to protect private property rights and prevent "takings" of property value without compensa-

tion through the purchase of development rights (PDR). This proposal partially responds to the question of how society can avert the tragedy of open access associated with land markets. PDR involves the sale of a conservation easement on a piece of private property. The easement restricts the ability to convert the land for residential development, while allowing existing uses (such as ranching) to continue. It is a way for ranchers to cash out the development value of their land without having to actually develop it, so it addresses both their interests: continuing to ranch and protecting their investment in the land. On the conservation side, programs that have been set up elsewhere in the country to facilitate execution of PDRs establish priorities for use of funds to purchase development rights, thereby enabling the targeting of limited funding to areas of ecological concern.

In Arizona, reterritorialization challenges to land-tenure arrangements on public and state trust lands worked against the acceptance of PDR as a solution. If a rancher sells a conservation easement and then loses access to a forage allotment, he or she will lose the ability to maintain a viable ranch operation. The rancher then potentially loses the remaining value of the privately owned portion of the ranch that is associated with the ability to ranch. Therefore, until ranchers can be assured of retaining the value of their land as a working landscape or be compensated for its loss, they may not be disposed to sell an easement as a way of protecting the land from development. This issue was not resolved during roundtable discussions.

For multi-stakeholder policy dialogues to achieve an effective collaboration, stakeholders—who have cut their political teeth in pluralistic political processes—need time to develop negotiation skills that foster collaboration. This was evident, for example, during the initial stages of roundtable discussions, when instead of taking the time needed to build mutual trust, interest groups rushed to present policy solutions before gathering enough information to fully understand the complexity of the problem. Many played their cards close to their chests because they viewed themselves as taking part in a competitive bargaining situation rather than educating each other about interests so they could think outside the box together. Others initially wanted to prevent differences of opinion from surfacing for fear they would obscure common ground rather than seeing the importance of understanding those differences before diagnosing the problem and constructing effective solutions.

It may take several years to develop the trust and interest-based bargaining skills that are critical for effective collaboration. Indeed, this has been the experience of CBC groups (Mandy Metzger, president of Diablo Trust, personal communication October 1998).

We expect this task to be even more difficult in policy dialogues, where the number of stakeholders and interests may be huge. For even if a dialogue group is convened and spends the lengthy time necessary for participants to acquire new political reflexes that match the collaborative mode, diagnoses the problem, and finally arrives at collaboratively developed recommendations, participants must return to existing policymaking arenas that operate through pluralistic politics. This implies that participants in collaborative policy dialogues cannot jettison their pluralistic political skills in favor of collaboration and consensus; they will have to acquire new skills, pivot between skill sets, and figure out when and how to use each.

A Need for Hybrid Politics

To reiterate, new sociopolitical methods for addressing environmental problems and disputes are needed to handle unwanted emergent environmental patterns that seem intractable within the framework of usual pluralistic politics. We are not suggesting, however, that pluralistic political methods should be marginalized or eliminated. Pluralism has an extremely important place in the face of unwanted emergent patterns such as sprawl. Regulatory and administrative structures ossify around the privileging of one commodity value and control by groups with access rights. Where power is too concentrated and bureaucratic structures too deaf and blind, pluralist activism is critical to the achievement of change. Activism enables conflicts to reach a critical state that forces powerful parties both to respond to changing public values and to see and address problems that they would otherwise be inclined to externalize. The Tucson-based Center for Biological Diversity, among other activist groups, has been so successful in pursuing a lawsuit strategy using the Endangered Species Act that ranchers—the traditional power holders in the west—are being forced to come to terms with the new values entering the region.[11] Indeed, in one roundtable meeting a rancher expressed gratitude to the center because it had forced attention on a number of important environmental and economic issues that otherwise might have emerged so gradually as to be imperceptible until it became too late to turn back the tide.[12]

Pluralistic politics enable activists to speak truth to power when power is concentrated in one interest group or coalition and to bring power to the table. Collaborative approaches enable effective conversation among stakeholders when power is diffuse and help them to understand the truth about emergent patterns so they can construct a more sustainable path to the future. Pluralism backstops collaboration. It keeps collaboration honest because, if key interests are not adequately addressed, proposals will become the subject of oppositional activism.

Conclusion

Land-use conflicts in Arizona illustrate that the tragedy of open access is not just about environmental degradation. It is also about individuals having to choose between their good intentions and sentiments and protection of their economic interests. Their dilemma creates an opening for the vilification of interest groups in reterritorialization contests, which, in the current globalizing context and without the benefit of collaboration, will most likely lead to unintended environmental degradation of an even greater degree because all stakeholders do not recognize what is creating an emergent problem. Our example shows this dynamic in Arizona, where ranchers have been vilified to the possible detriment of biodiversity.

The public has needed a way to create more sustainable solutions to complex environmental disputes. Economic globalization and territorialization processes of nation-states foster conditions leading to ecological system degradation through commodification of natural resource elements. Contests over resources that are fought as win-lose propositions will not solve the problem because they narrow the question to something that is resolvable as an allocation dispute. The sustainability problem is more than one of allocation. It requires both that competing claims to resources be resolved and that institutions successfully mediate between the different time scales of economic and ecological functioning.

Sustainable paths to the future can seem elusive. We do not know enough about natural system processes. We need time to develop new political skills. The pace of environmental change appears to be quickening with global warming, and the international political system seems much less stable in the era since September 11, 2001. War is rarely good for either the ecological systems or the local human communities in its path.

But we see hope because new means are being created for taking more holistic approaches to systemic problems, focusing attention on resources that do not move—that are the "ground" of ecological processes and communities. In the natural and social sciences, complexity theory and political ecology approaches offer new frameworks for understanding complex environmental issues. Community-based collaborative groups are gaining some political leverage by focusing attention holistically on landscapes or watersheds. Their work is gradually extending into institutions and policy arenas through multi-stakeholder policy dialogues that follow the collaborative and consensus-building precepts of the maturing field of environmental conflict resolution. Whether these efforts can effectively counterbalance the forces of economic globalization and political instability depends at least on the following: development of effective hybrid politics pursued at many levels (including internationally), clear-eyed assessment of interests, collaborative efforts toward development of resource-use strategies that enable the present generation to meet its needs without compromising the ability of future generations to do the same, and environmental justice for all who depend on the use of a resource at a given point in time.

NOTES

1. Mette J. Brogden is an anthropologist, an environmental conflict resolution practitioner, a researcher, and program manager of the Environmental and Public Policy Conflict Resolution program at the University of Arizona's Udall Center for Studies in Public Policy, 803 East First Street, Tucson, Arizona 85719; e-mail: *metteb@u.arizona.edu*. James B. Greenberg is a research professor and associate director of the Bureau of Applied Research in Anthropology, University of Arizona, P.O. Box 210030, Tucson, Arizona 85721-0030; e-mail: *jgreenbe@u.arizona.edu*. Research on the transition of an Arizona rural area from ranching to real estate development was partially supported by the Udall Center through a grant from the Morris K. Udall Foundation. We wish to thank the many ranchers, conservationists, agency personnel, public officials, and scientists who were interviewed for study. Thanks also to participants in the Arizona Common Ground Roundtable for their contributions to understanding land-tenure systems and stakeholder interests in Arizona. Earlier versions of this chapter were presented at the Political Ecology Society meetings in San Francisco (March 2000) and at American Anthropological Association meetings in San Francisco (November 2000).

2. *Sustainability* as a construct has been extensively critiqued (see, for example, Sachs 1993, 17–20, and Stott and Sullivan 2000). Likewise, *nature, biodiversity, ecological systems*, and other constructs to which we refer have been hotly debated (see Escobar 1999). In general, we agree with Escobar's distinction between "the belief in the existence of pristine Nature outside of history and human context" and "the existence of a biophysical reality—pre-discursive and pre-social if you wish—with structures and processes of its own which the life sciences try to understand (1–2). We follow the latter usage in all references to *nature, natural processes,* and *ecological systems*.

3. See Brogden (n.d.) for a discussion of the progression of theory in understanding change within rangeland ecological systems. We mean here to resist ideas of system homeostasis while acknowledging tendencies for ecological communities to exhibit characteristic production and complexity.

4. For a review of grazing history and the progression of its regulatory framework, see Hadley's (2001) case study of one district in the Coronado National Forest.

5. In Pima County, for example, the endangered cactus ferruginous pygmy owl is predominantly found in Altar Valley, a ranching area, although its habitat reportedly extends through the greater Tucson area.

6. Developers do not set out to create sprawl; rather, they set out to create a profit by doing what they know how to do to meet the demand for homes and home sites. Indeed, a critical finding from interviews with stakeholders before a conference on growth management in Phoenix (October 6, 2000) was that developers found sprawl to be a serious quality-of-life problem that had long-term negative effects on their business, and they wanted effective growth management measures instituted by government.

7. These quotations are from Brogden's 1996–97 interviews with twenty rural ranchette owners (residents for less than fifteen years) in an area of Arizona undergoing conversion from ranching to residential development.

8. A number of fields are taking up and elaborating complexity theory, notably biology but also economics, social theory, and ecology (Waldrop 1992).

9. Comments on pluralistic politics are based on data obtained through observation of interest-group negotiations during the 1999 Arizona Governor's Growing Smarter Commission process, the subsequent special session of the 2000 Arizona legislature convened by Governor Jane Dee Hull to pass Growing Smarter legislation, and both for-

mal and informal interviews with representatives of key interest groups conducted within two months following passage of the legislation.

10. The Community-Based Collaboratives Research Consortium's interesting web site may be viewed at *http://www.cbcrc.org.*

11. Although we cannot do justice to the story in a brief note, the Center for Biological Diversity targets land uses that it believes endanger species and develops litigation strategies that interfere with the targeted land use. Ranching has been viewed by environmental groups as highly detrimental to species survival; this assertion is quite contested and the subject of a great deal of research. Many now accept, however, that year-round livestock access to riparian areas is detrimental to these systems; and ranchers and other range managers have developed special management strategies for riparian areas that allow those regions to revert to earlier stream morphology configurations and rebound in vegetation productivity. The center has focused a great deal of effort on the issue of riparian area protection, and it would be hard to ignore the contribution their activism has made to restoration and protection of these areas of rich biodiversity.

12. Ranch economics have been difficult for a number of reasons, but commodity markets in an era of globalization have kept prices unchanged while costs of production (land, fencing, and insurance, for example) have increased. The problem becomes clear only gradually since ranch profits seem to cycle up and down in ten-year stretches (Brogden n.d.).

REFERENCES

Bingham, Gail. 1986. *Resolving Environmental Disputes: A Decade of Experience.* Washington, D.C.: Conservation Foundation.

Brogden, Mette, ed. n.d. "Bridging the Urban-Rural Divide: A Framework for Sustainable Ranching." In *Arizona.* Report of the Sustainable Ranching Study Committee to the Core Working Group of the Arizona Common Ground Roundtable. Tucson: Udall Center for Studies in Public Policy.

Carpenter, Susan L., and W.J.D. Kennedy. 1988. *Managing Public Disputes: A Practical Guide to Handling Conflict and Reaching Agreements.* San Francisco: Jossey-Bass.

Clifford, Frank. 1998. "Home on the Eco-Range." *Los Angeles Times*, August 2, pp. A1, A32–33.

Escobar, Arturo. 1999. "After Nature: Steps to an Antiessentialist Political Ecology." *Current Anthropology* 40, no. 1: 1–30.

Fisher, Roger, and William Ury. 1981. *Getting to Yes: Negotiating Agreement without Giving In.* Boston: Houghton Mifflin.

Godelier, Maurice. 1977. *Perspectives in Marxist Anthropology.* Cambridge: Cambridge University Press.

Greenberg, James B. 1998. "The Tragedy of Commoditization: Political Ecology of the Colorado River Delta's Destruction." *Research in Economic Anthropology* 19: 133–49.

Hadley, Diana. 2001. "Grazing the Southwest Borderlands." In *Forests under Fire: A Century of Ecosystem Mismanagement in the Southwest*, edited by Christopher J. Huggard and Arthur R. Gomez. Tucson: University of Arizona Press.

Hardin, Garrett. 1968. "The Tragedy of the Commons." *Science* 162: 1243–48.

Heyman, Josiah McC. 1994. "The Mexico–United States Border in Anthropology: A Critique and Reformulation." *Journal of Political Ecology* 1: 41–65.

Kauffman, Stuart A. 1995. *At Home in the Universe: The Search for Laws of Self-Organization and Complexity.* New York: Oxford University Press.

Mann, Michael. 1993. *The Sources of Social Power*. Vol. 2, *The Rise of Classes and Nation-States, 1760–1914*. Cambridge: Cambridge University Press.

Marx, Karl. 1977 [1867]. *Capital*, translated by Ben Fowkes. Vols. 1–3. New York: Vintage.

McCay, Bonnie J., and James M. Acherson. 1987. *The Question of the Commons: The Culture and Ecology of Communal Resources*. Tucson: University of Arizona Press.

Moore, Christopher W. 1996. *The Mediation Process: Practical Strategies for Resolving Conflicts*. 2d ed. San Francisco: Jossey-Bass.

Netting, Robert McC. 1993. *Smallholders, Householders: Farm Families in the Ecology of Intensive, Sustainable Agriculture*. Stanford: Stanford University Press.

Rappaport, Roy. 1994. "Disorders of Our Own." In *Diagnosing America: Anthropology and Public Engagement*, edited by Shepard Forman, 235–94. Ann Arbor: University of Michigan Press,

Sachs, Wolfgang. 1993. "Global Ecology and the Shadow of Development." In *Global Ecology: A New Arena of Political Conflict*, edited by Wolfgang Sachs, 3–21. London: Zed.

Sayer, Nathan. 1999. "Species of Capital: An Anthropological Investigation of the Buenos Aires Ranch (Pima County, Arizona) and Its Transformation into a National Wildlife Refuge." Ph.D. diss., Anthropology Department, University of Chicago.

Sheridan, Thomas E. 2001. "Cows, Condos, and the Contested Commons: The Political Ecology of Ranching in the Arizona-Sonora Borderlands." *Human Organization* 60, no. 2: 141.

Stott, Philip, and Sian Sullivan, eds. 2000 *Political Ecology: Science, Myth, and Power*. London: Arnold.

Susskind, Lawrence, Sarah McKearnan, and Jennifer Thomas-Larmer. 1999. *The Consensus Building Handbook: A Comprehensive Guide to Reaching Agreement*. Thousand Oaks, Calif.: Sage.

Taussig, Michael. 1980. *The Devil and Commodity Fetishism in South America*. Chapel Hill: University of North Carolina Press.

Waldrop, M. Mitchell. 1992. *Complexity: the Emerging Science at the Edge of Order and Chaos*. New York: Simon and Schuster.

4

Whose Water?

Political Ecology of Water Reform in Zimbabwe

ANNE FERGUSON AND BILL DERMAN

At the September 2002 World Conference on Sustainable Development, held in Johannesburg, South Africa, water was the center of contestation and debate. It was variously characterized as a scarce resource, an economic good, a human right, a matter of national and international security, and an environmental right. In this chapter, we examine the process of water reform underway in Zimbabwe. The complex interplay of environmental, economic, social, and rights-based discourses and practices related to this essential natural resource provides a point from which to consider current debates surrounding how the political is conceptualized in political ecology. We draw on Alberto Arce and Norman Long's (2000) concept of counter-development as a way of illustrating how local understandings are used to comprehend and reshape global discourses and how, in turn and less frequently, the local influences global discourses.

Political Ecology: Research Issues and Methods

The study was an interdisciplinary, collaborative, and comparative project involving faculty and graduate students at the Center for Applied Social Sciences at the University of Zimbabwe and ourselves at Michigan State University.[1] Given the interdisciplinary nature of the research, political ecology offered a shared analytical framework that encompassed the issues and methods familiar to the anthropologists and resource economists engaged in the study. Researchers agreed on the following conceptual framework derived from the works of Piers Blaikie (1996, 1999), Blaikie and Harold Brookfield (1987), Philip Stott and Sian Sullivan (2000) and other political ecologists:

1. The central concern of political ecology is understanding the relationship between social and environmental change. Political ecology draws on insights from a variety of environmentally related disciplines in the social and environmental sciences.

2. The outcomes of environmental change are often felt unevenly by different social groups. Explaining why and how this unevenness is generated links political ecology to political economy and makes conflict and contestation over resources central to most analyses.

3. Power is a central focus of the political in political ecology. Increasingly, a concern with power relations extends beyond the local level and decenters and problematizes unidimensional treatments of the state, donor groups, nongovernmental organizations, and their related discourses.

4. In contrast to earlier approaches, which assumed that ecological systems tended toward equilibrium, political ecology recognizes that resource use patterns may be ecologically degrading while being socially profitable or functional, at least in the short term, for some actors.

5. Ecosystems and social systems are regarded as mutually constituted. In theory, the goal is to develop modes of analysis that encompass and relate social and ecological variables, although there is an increasing tendency to focus analysis on social and political factors and pay less attention to dimensions and agency drawn from the environmental sciences.

6. Political ecology combines and relates different levels of analysis. Conceptualization of these levels requires new styles of analyses since much of the local is permeated by and can mirror and refract the global. Similar complexities exist in linking micro-habitats, bioregions, and so on to global environmental change and social factors operating on different scales.

7. Political ecologists usually study the complex interactions between a changing environment and changing society within the context of local histories and ecologies.

8. Many political ecologists share a concern about policy formation, social justice, and the linking of research to action.

Although most countries in southern Africa are undergoing similar transformations in their water sectors, Zimbabwe was selected for study because the reform was further along in implementation than it was in many other countries in the region. The overall research goals were to examine whether or not the new water reform broadened disadvantaged groups' and women's access to water and increased their voice in the new water-related institutions and laws. More specifically, would the new water laws and policy help raise the poor's standard of living? Would black and white farmers be able to work together as members of the new water institutions to achieve new goals? Would new patterns of democratic decision making be created outside the rigid party structure of the ZANU-PF, which until 2000 had been the dominant political party and virtually the only party in rural areas? In short, we placed the political at the center of our study with a deep concern for social justice in policy formation and implementation. We adopted a proactive stance in the research process and provided a continual flow of recommendations for increasing marginalized groups' participation in the newly instituted catchment and subcatchment councils and other management bodies.

The Political Ecology of Water Reform in Zimbabwe

We began the research by focusing on the social, political, and policy dimensions of Zimbabwe's water reform, with the goal of later examining the reform's social and environmental consequences. Although the political was foregrounded, this was not because we were downplaying the importance of environmental change. Instead, our choice reflected the fact that reform is in its early stages and to date has had little environmental impact. Waiting to begin study until the environmental consequences are evident at the local level casts political ecologists in the role of carrying out analyses of impacts and negates their part in guiding policy and practice. In the nexus between the social and the ecological (in this case, with priority given to the political), we can begin to understand why Zimbabwe's water reform is constituted as it is and what its probable social and environmental consequences may be. This perspective permits examination of the interplay of the varied conceptualizations of the value of water and the different understandings of water reform at the international, national, and local levels among the actors involved.

Hegemonic versus Multiple Discourses

Much political ecology literature emphasizes the hegemonic nature of global capitalism. While recognizing capitalism's centrality, there is reason to problematize and deconstruct it. We first identified competing ideological frameworks, or ways of valuing water in Zimbabwe and southern Africa. While it is tempting to present them as independent of one another and subsumed by an ascendant global capitalism espoused by institutions such as the World Bank, what existed was more complex. Various actors in Zimbabwe's water reform made use of these frameworks in different ways as they attempted to shape the new policy document, laws, and practices to serve their interests.

At the international level, the Dublin Principles are widely recognized axioms for water reform (Solanes and Gonzalez-Villarreal 1999), and the thinking behind them has been incorporated into policy documents authored by the World Bank and other donor organizations (FAO 1995, 2000; World Bank 1993, 2002). The four principles are (1) freshwater is a finite and vulnerable resource, essential to sustain life, development, and the environment; (2) water development and management should be based on a participatory approach involving users, planners, and policymakers at all levels; (3) women play a central part in the provision, management, and safeguarding of water; and (4) water has an economic value in all its competing uses and should be recognized as an economic good. Like all international documents, the Dublin Principles were shaped by the varied interests of the policy drafters. For example, the water policy advisor for NORAD (the Norwegian development agency) was instructed to ensure that water was treated as an economic good as well as to recognize women's roles as water managers.

Other international documents reflect competing discourses on the value of water that, if not yet dominant, may become so. Peter Gleick (1999) adopts a human-rights approach. He views water as different from other commodities and argues that, with growing global water scarcity, a right to water should be recognized to protect the poor and vulnerable from having an essential ingredient of life priced beyond their means. In a previous article, we also proposed some human-rights–based approaches to water reform (Ferguson and Derman 1999). Using the framework of the Convention on the Elimination of All Forms of Discrimination against Women, Anne Hellum (2001) suggests ways for water planners to legally recognize women's rights to water and include them in planning and policymaking. With the growing importance of a human-rights approach to development, it is conceivable that a rights-based approach to water will ultimately rival a commodity-focused one.[2]

Another important orientation to water draws on the metaphors of scarcity and security. Security issues can be soft (environmentally focused) or hard, with an emphasis on the role of water scarcity in war and conflict. This approach is reflected in a Food and Agriculture Organization of the United Nations (FAO) document (2000) that develops the concept of freshwater security (Falkenmark and Lundqvist 1995), and Marq de Villiers's (1999) focus on the prevention of war. Finally, water use and conservation principles are found in international policy-setting environmental documents linking water to the global agenda for sustainable development, such as the chapter on water resources in Agenda 21 and various policy statements emerging from the 2002 environmental summit in Johannesburg, South Africa (Derman and Ferguson 1999).

Those who provide water as well as those who use it are engaged in struggles to redefine rights of access to the resource. This is reflected in shifting conceptualizations underlying the rural water and sanitation programs in Africa. Frances Cleaver (1998a, 1998b), Cleaver and Diane Elson (1995), and Anne Ferguson (1998) have documented this change in approach and explored its ramifications for women's control over water resources. Water is now frequently conceptualized as either productive or primary, with greatest importance in most policy documents given to its productive uses. A similar change in thinking about potable water has occurred in the public health domain and in water management circles (Nicol 2000).[3]

The point is that these various discourses all coexist in differing combinations from country to country and institution to institution and among different actors within the same country or institution. Many are informed by neoliberal economic thinking, but others respond to counter-discourses and histories. States in southern Africa are constructing their national water laws and water management administration, often drawing on multiple (and sometimes contradictory) frameworks. Actors in these countries use these various frameworks to further specific political and personal agendas, as described in this chapter.

Zimbabwe's Water Reform in Global and Local Context

How are these various conceptualizations of water—as a scarce commodity, a human right, and a tool for social transformation and greater participation and equity—being used in Zimbabwe? How do different actors use these international frameworks and more locally derived ones to attempt to shape and benefit from the water reform process? As part of the process of selective incorporation and use of discourses, we consider how certain actors seek to avoid the application of particular international principles or to refashion them to suit other ends.

Zimbabwe's newly enacted water reform policy and laws contain and sustain contradictory principles and agendas. For example, the concept of primary water was incorporated into these documents, thereby acknowledging that people have a right to use water for drinking, cooking, washing, watering livestock, making bricks for houses, and other noncommercial purposes. These same instruments, however, embrace the key neoliberal concepts of water demand management and cost recovery espoused in the Dublin Principles, by the World Bank, and by other large international lending and donor institutions. Left out of Zimbabwe's new policy and laws but debated at the local levels are other perspectives on water. One widespread discourse throughout southern Africa is the close relationship thought to exist between ancestral spirits, the state of society, and rainfall. Conceptualizations of water embodied in the new laws and policy do not include consideration of ancestors' agency in producing rain based on their evaluation of the moral state of civil society. Nonetheless, these struggles over meaning can be just as important as the struggles over the resources themselves (Derman and Hellum 2002; Moore 1996, 128).

Competing discourses include assumptions about the nature of water; the hydrological cycle; a changing environment and economy; the relationship among water quality, people, and disease; and so on. Embedded in the different perspectives are assumptions about the monetary, political, social, and ecological value of water. To account for this complex set of competing understandings within an ecological framework, which privileges environmental effects over a more inclusive and iterative approach to human-environmental interactions, or to suggest that the discourse and practice related to capitalism and neoliberal economic values are the prevailing ones, inadequately represents the current state of affairs and obscures people's agency.

Finally, the current political situation in Zimbabwe calls attention to the importance of the wider political, economic, and social context in understanding how the water reform process evolves. Implementation of the new water acts and policy is caught up in, and cannot be considered separately from, the current crises involving the new fast-track land reform. Since the failed constitutional referendum in 2000, most white-owned commercial farms in Zimbabwe have been resettled under the fast-track land reform program. *Fast track* is best characterized as land confiscation or appropriation by the national government for political ends. It was one of ZANU-PF's and President Robert Mugabe's strategies to win the March 2002 presidential elections and maintain power. The implications of these developments for the water reform process are explored later in the chapter.

The New Water Laws and Administrative Structures

Zimbabwe's reform incorporates two key components of international neoliberal capitalist thinking about water. Notions of existing or impending water scarcity underlie the global rationale for reform, while decentralized stakeholder management is regarded as central to improved resource use and conservation. These two concepts intersect with Zimbabwe's colonial history and racialized present as reflected in government land and water policies.

The motivations for water reform in Zimbabwe reflect an interplay among international forces, including the World Bank, United Nations organizations (especially the FAO), international environmental organizations, and different elements within the government. Central actors in national government are the Department of Water Development; the Ministry of Agriculture, Finance, and Planning; and the President's Office. New water policies and laws represent high-level Zimbabwean bureaucrats' efforts to use international principles to forge a national strategy to attract funding from the World Bank, the FAO, and other national donors in line with their political, social, and personal agendas.[4] Following extensive consultation with the World Bank, internal meetings of stakeholders in Zimbabwe, and the report of Zimbabwe's Land Tenure Commission (Rukuni 1994a, 1994b), which indicated that water distribution and use had the same inequitable allocation patterns as land did, the government of Zimbabwe decided to restructure the water sector. The changes are embodied in two acts: the Water Act of 1998 and the National Water Authority Act of 1998. Historically, one primary mission of the Departments of Water Development and Hydrology was to provide water to users. In the past, the Department of Water Development constructed reservoirs throughout the country in a manner that overwhelmingly favored the white residents of the (at that time) colony of southern Rhodesia who occupied the most productive lands. Because of periodic droughts, southern Rhodesia was viewed as water scarce, requiring an extensive system of dams and reservoirs to ensure water supply for cities, mines, and farms.

The 1998 water legislation transferred national planning functions to a new parastatal agency, the Zimbabwe National Water Authority (ZINWA), which has become the owner of public dams that store more than 5,000 megaliters of water. ZINWA is to be funded primarily through the sale of water behind government dams, provision of water to cities, and levying of water to large-scale users. It will draft master plans for the development of Zimbabwe's waters and for the protection of its environment and will work with each of the seven catchment councils established as a result of the reform to develop catchment outline plans, which include basic demographic, hydrological, and economic information to permit efficient water management, use, and development.

Localizing Water Reform in Zimbabwe

The research focused on how three national concepts have been refashioned as a result of the reform: the notion of scarcity, the concept of stakeholder participation, and the user-pays principle. Stakeholder participation and the user-pays principle are discussed here.

STAKEHOLDER PARTICIPATION. The assumption that users will manage water more effectively if they are engaged in the institutions of water management is a central feature of the Dublin Principles and of Zimbabwe's water reform. The way in which the Dublin Principles are applied varies from country to country; no formulas exist that identify who should be included in the new management institutions. In July 1997, two pilot catchment projects were launched in Zimbabwe—the Mupfure and the Mazowe—to study different models of stakeholder participation to determine which should serve as the model for the country as a whole.

The Mupfure Catchment experiment was donor-funded and government-supported, while the Mazowe Catchment Council was privately initiated and organized. The Mazowe Project was strongly pro-business. It opposed heavy reliance on government on two grounds: the first related to government's lack of accountability; the second stemmed from the council's belief that ultimately people had to rely on their own skills, abilities, and resources if the reform were to succeed. Mazowe Project planners tended to minimize the resource differentials among different stakeholder groups in their catchment, including those between white commercial farmers and communal-area farmers. The Mupfure Project, in contrast, was far more government-oriented and prone to making claims about how the water reform would result in greater prosperity and access to water. It relied heavily on donor funds to underwrite activities and draw support, thus reinforcing an attitude of dependence on government. The Mupfure Project sought to engage communal-area farmers through meetings and locally based development projects, although donor support for these local-level initiatives was short-lived.

In addition to these basic differences in philosophy, other key differences between the Mazowe and Mupfure models rested in the definition of stakeholders and the proposed systems of representation. The Mazowe Catchment developed a bottom-up management approach. It instituted water user boards (WUBs) as the third and lowest administrative tier and the location from which all decision making would originate. WUBs were composed of fifteen members—eight elected by users and seven nominated to represent the most important economic sectors.[5] The Mupfure, in contrast, did not have this third-level administrative tier and recognized only the catchment and subcatchment councils.

In the end, the government did not await the outcome of this experiment in representation and instead opted to impose its own structure and system of representation on all catchments. The motivation was Zimbabwe's deepening political and economic crisis, necessitating a rapid shift of the financial costs of water management from central government to the new parastatal, ZINWA, via reliance on the user-pays principle. Thus, ironically, centralized government chose the decentralized model to follow in the catchments established as a result of the new legislation.

LOCALIZED DEFINITIONS OF STAKEHOLDER PARTICIPATION. Perhaps even more significant than the transfer of authority to ZINWA is the creation of catchment councils and subcatchment councils as major management entities composed of representative stakeholder groups. Zimbabwe has been divided into seven catchments: ecologically derived administrative divisions that do not correspond to other existing political boundaries and create jurisdictional conflicts. Provincial governors and administrators, for example, do not feel ownership for catchments because many catchments transcend provincial boundaries.

According to the (Subcatchment Councils) Water Regulations of 2000, the following stakeholder groups are to elect representatives of the subcatchment councils: rural district councils, communal-area farmers, resettlement farmers, small-scale commercial farmers, large-scale commercial farmers, indigenous commercial farmers, urban authorities, large-scale miners, small-scale miners, industry, and any other stakeholder group the catchment or subcatchment councils may identify. The number of members on subcatchment councils is not fixed by legislation nor are the procedures for how stakeholders are to be selected from within their constituent groups. To date, no subcatchment council we are familiar with is actually composed of representatives from all the just-listed stakeholder groups.

Catchment councils are made up of the chairpersons of subcatchment councils and other members. In practice, unlike what is called for in the statutory regulations, each subcatchment council sends two officers to the catchment council. There are no provisions for representation by stakeholder group on the catchment councils themselves. The assumption is that stakeholders are represented at the subcatchment council level. Catchment council responsibilities include collaborating with ZINWA in preparing and updating catchment plans, deciding on and enforcing all water allocation and reallocation, developing and supervising programs for catchment protection, issuing and overseeing permits for water use, establishing and maintaining a data base and information system (with ZINWA), and overseeing operations and functions of subcatchment councils. Subcatchment councils are to monitor the allocation of water permits, water flows, and use. They also are to assist in pollution control, catchment protection, and data gathering and collect fees that will be used for the performance of their duties.

Race is an important element in participation. As noted, a central aim was to broaden stakeholder representation beyond white commercial farmers by including black communal-area farmers on the catchment and subcatchment councils. While black communal-area farmers are now represented on councils, significant disparities remain between the number of stakeholders and the number of stakeholder representatives. The largest number of water users by far are communal-area farmers. Yet they have the same number of representatives on councils as, for example, large-scale indigenous farmers, whose numbers are very small in comparison. If there is to be a significant change in access to water, then representation patterns will have to be made more equitable.

While greater racial equity has been a centerpiece of the reform, gender equity, featured in the Dublin Principles and many other international documents and strongly promoted by international donors, has received little local support. This is true despite women's heavy involvement in agricultural production and household water provisioning. Neither in the laws nor in the statutory instruments implementing the water reform has any mention been made of how to incorporate women more fully into water management and development. Observations at catchment council meetings indicate that the few women present are usually either technocrats or secretaries. Few women have been elected to councils.

Finally, our surveys indicate that key stakeholders identified at the village level are not represented on councils. Seventy-five percent of rural Zimbabweans interviewed believe that customary authorities—chiefs and spirit mediums—should regulate water. Yet they have no formal representation on stakeholder bodies.

In general, our observations suggest that there were no clear-cut divisions observed between black and white participants on catchment councils. The commercial farmers and the government technocrats often speak a common technical language. They are familiar with concepts such as water rights, permits, flows, storage rights, and so on. But the white farmers are very suspicious of the government and do not trust that monies collected will be used for the stated purposes. They share a belief that the national government has been highly corrupt. (While discussing such issues, the white farmers usually take care to assure the government officials present that they are not part of the problem.) The white commercial farmers and members representing communal areas both have an intense skepticism of government capacity. They often agree that concerns of communal-area residents are ignored by government.

USER-PAYS PRINCIPLE. The concept of user pays is central to the functioning of the new administrative structures. User pays has become a rallying point used by various actors to garner support for their versions of water reform. The concept derives authority from the Dublin Principles, although the drafters might not recognize it in such bald, free-marketeer form. While capturing the reductionist philosophy of those seeking to make water quantity allocations and quality characteristics reducible to market forces, the application of this principle in Zimbabwe indicates the need to move beyond international texts to discover how the principle is shaped by various actors. Thus, research reveals the more complicated national and local agendas behind the international economistic perspectives advocated by the World Bank and other major lenders and seemingly adopted whole face by the government of Zimbabwe. Similar to many other policies, this one is negotiated, reworked, and presented differently to different national constituencies.

The vast majority of Zimbabweans does not have water rights in the legal sense of the term and is not likely to gain them as a result of the new laws. What most people have are primary-use rights, which enable them to use water without payment for drinking, washing, watering livestock, and tending small gardens, as previously described. The principle of user pays applies only to the small number of consumers (mostly large-scale irrigated farms and mining operations) who use water for commercial purposes. These commercial users, while few in number, nonetheless consume most of Zimbabwe's water. Although the number of commercial users is not great in comparison with the total population, neither ZINWA nor the catchment councils have the capacity to monitor and enforce the user-pays principle even among members of this small group.

In emphasizing the principle of user pays, the water reform goes against how Zimbabweans view and value water. In village-level surveys in three catchments, we found that more than 90 percent of those interviewed did not think they should pay for water used for commercial purposes. When payment is involved, the consensus was that it should be for irrigation, canals, pumps, and other infrastructure, not for water per se. In short, user pays is not a principle accepted by most rural dwellers.

ZINWA and the catchment councils are further handicapped because there is no mechanism to determine what constitutes either a sound economic price for water or a socially acceptable one. Despite this situation, these new administrative bodies are to be funded through the sale of water and levies on water permit holders. For the moment, ZINWA has set new prices for water in an effort to generate the needed revenue. Great uncertainty exists, however, concerning commercial farmers' abilities or willingness to pay because most large-scale commercial farmers either have been forced off the land or are refusing to pay for water because of threats against their farms. As we write, discussions with those sent out to collect payments and levies from the new settlers (those now living on what had been commercial farms) indicate that either they are not farming or they are not willing to pay for water. It is not clear how ZINWA will survive, given these conditions. Clearly, the link between land and water reforms is evident, even though to date there has been little effort to relate or coordinate these reforms involving Zimbabwe's most fundamental natural resources.

Another contentious feature hampering water reform is that the former staff of the Department of Water (engineers, hydrologists, accountants, planners, secretaries, drivers, and so on) all remain employed, now by ZINWA instead of the department. They have been transferred to and now serve as the catchment manager's staff. One catchment alone has sixty-two employees. The funding implications of this transfer of personnel (amounting essentially to the creation of seven miniature water departments), along with the issue of the emerging working relationships between designated experts and stakeholders, constitute part of our ongoing research. Indeed, the placement of large numbers of government employees and technocrats in stakeholder organizations indicates government's suspicion of the newly created stakeholder organizations.

A central concern of commercial farmers and others is, what will we get in services for our monies? This is a potentially divisive issue between commercial and communal areas in catchments because those not holding water permits may not be entitled to any services. Some commercial farmers assumed that since they were paying for permits, they should be the ones reaping the benefits. In the end, however, some commercial farmers and others argued that unless water reform had a developmental dimension benefiting communal-area farmers as well, there was no point in carrying it out.

A fundamental divide remains in how water is valued. Catchment and subcatchment council members have learned that, without the user-pays principle, they will not have the resources to function. On the other hand, communal-area farmers who have not had to pay for water in the past continue to resist notions of paying for it. Communal-area farmers surveyed were divided evenly over the issue of whether water should be regulated at all. They were almost unanimously opposed to paying for water for primary purposes (drinking, watering livestock, and brick making). While the new water management institutions may be comfortable valuing water monetarily, most small-scale farmers continue to resist this approach.[6]

Conclusion

These issues must be considered within the wider context of the implosion of the government budget and the economy as a whole since 2000. Zimbabwe's economy is in free fall—characterized by soaring inflation, lack of external investment funds, exceptionally high internal rates of interest driven up by the government's borrowing, a foreign exchange shortage, and unappropriated expenses to raise salary levels for potential supporters of the president. The crisis has been intensified by the withdrawal of major lending and donor organizations, notably the World Bank, the European Union, and the government of Denmark. Those donors who remain supportive are shifting their emphasis to supplying food for an increasingly impoverished and hungry nation. With the exception of the Dutch government, which continues to support two catchment councils (the Sanyati and the Mzingwane) and the creation of an Association of Catchment Councils, donor support for water reform has all but disappeared.

The current drought means that there are growing shortages of water while the capacity to manage water has been diminished due to the financial crisis. Thus, water shortages now pose a national crisis. The proposed solutions are to continue to shift water management away from government to catchment councils, subcatchment councils, and a self-funded ZINWA, despite lack of potential revenues at the local level. The existing climate of violence and land occupations renders the prospect of successful water reform highly unlikely.

To summarize, using illustrations from Zimbabwe, we have raised issue with notions of hegemonic discourses popular in some recent scholarship by drawing attention to the multiple ways in which water is valued in international and national contexts and how these different dialogues are used by actors to position themselves and their interests. In the Zimbabwean cases as well, the supposedly emancipatory rhetoric and potentials of the reform are not as straightforward as one might think. While ostensibly aiming to increase racial equity by providing black communal-area farmers with greater access to water resources, the emerging realities on the ground are quite different. As with the fast-track land reform program, it appears that the major beneficiaries of water reform are likely to be middle- or upper-class black entrepreneurs and political supporters of ZANU-PF rather than black land- and water-short communal-area farmers. The notion of *people* is a highly problematic category in Zimbabwe, where the government and the party claim to speak for the people while excluding all those identified as whites, all members of the opposition political party, and almost anyone who disagrees with ZANU-PF's program and President Mugabe.[7]

Arce and Long (2000) contend that modernity has multiple faces consisting of different types of representations, practices, discourses, performances, and organizational forms. In their view, counter-development constitutes a "balancing act between introduced bureaucratic procedures and local practices" (19).

Our many years of experience in working with development in diverse contexts in Africa leads us to share this perspective, at least in its broad outlines (Ferguson and Derman 1999). Political ecologists using this framework would inquire into how local understandings, or in Joan Martínez-Alier's (2002) words, "languages of valuation," are used to comprehend, reshape, or resist these global processes, much as we have illustrated in this chapter.

Water reform has taken back stage (for the moment) to national politics in Zimbabwe; but given the reappearance of serious drought, contestations over water will again intensify among users in different economic sectors, the environment, and aquatic ecosystems as well as among the neighboring states. We would like to see the power balances in those contestations altered so that the vast majority of water users have greater say and greater access to the new water-related institutions. Thus, in the complex world of water reform, multilateral banks and institutions, national water departments, engineers, large-scale farmers, women irrigators, and so on, finding social and environmental policies that work remains a challenge. A large-scale experimentation in the water sector is well underway throughout southern Africa, and it is difficult to predict the possible social or environmental outcomes. Political ecologists, with their focus on the dynamics of human environmental interactions, their concern with power relations, and their linking of theory and practice, are well situated to study this process and provide recommendations for the way ahead.

NOTES

1. Bill Derman has been supported in related research by a Fulbright-Hays Research Grant, a Wenner-Gren Foundation Grant for Anthropological Research, and the BASIS Collaborative Research Support Program for water and land research in southern Africa. Anne Ferguson has been supported by a Fulbright-Hays Research Grant and the BASIS Collaborative Research Support Program. We wish to thank the CASS Water Research Team, comprised of Dr. Francis Gonese, Mrs. Claudious Chikozho, Jim Latham, Steven Mandivengerei, and Pinnie Sithole.

2. On November 27, 2002, the United Nations Committee on Economic, Social, and Cultural Rights adopted the following General Comment on water: "The human right to drinking water is fundamental for life and health. Sufficient and safe drinking water is a precondition for the realization of all human rights." This is a major step in the international recognition of a right to drinking water.

3. Productive water is used to produce goods for sale. Primary water is used for household domestic needs. Cleaver (1998a, 1998b) has an excellent critique of trying to render water used for drinking, bathing children, and so on as nonproductive. Nicol (2000) also reflects this shift as he places in doubt the relationship between water supply and disease.

4. Although local groups were not involved in the initial phases of the reform design process, key stakeholder groups were identified as a result of this process. These were large-scale commercial farmers represented by the Commercial Farmers Union, mining companies, cities, the Agricultural Rural and Development Authority (a parastatal that owns multiple farms throughout Zimbabwe), and government itself.

5. It is clear that the planners had little experience with communal areas where the economic sectors of mines, industry, and large-scale farmers were generally absent but nonetheless represented on the councils.

6. We carried out surveys in 521 households in six subcatchments in 2001. One set of questions addressed issues of water regulations and paying for water.

7. The white commercial farmers have been driven off their farms by the fast-track land reform begun in March 2000. Of the former 4,500 white farmers, fewer than 500 are left on their farms, and many are not farming. For an examination of the intersection of land and water, see Derman and Gonese (2003).

REFERENCES

Arce, Alberto, and Norman Long. 2000. "Reconfiguring Modernity and Development from an Anthropological Perspective." In *Anthropology, Development and Modernities: Exploring Discourses, Counter-Tendencies and Violence*, edited by Alberto Arce and Norman Long, 1–31. London: Routledge.

Blaikie, Piers. 1996. "Post-Modernism and Global Environmental Change." *Global Environmental Change* 6, no. 2: 81–85.

———. 1999. "Development, Post-, Anti-, and Populist: A Critical Review." *Environment and Planning* 32: 1033–50.

Blaikie, Piers, and Harold Brookfield. 1987. *Land Degradation and Society*. London: Methuen.

Cleaver, Frances. 1998a. "Choice, Complexity and Change: Gendered Livelihoods and the Management of Water." *Agriculture and Human Values* 15, no. 4: 293–99.

———. 1998b. "Incentives and Informal Institutions: Gender and the Management of Water." *Agriculture and Human Values* 15, no. 4: 347–60.

Cleaver, Frances, and Diane Elson. 1995. *Women and Water Resources: Continued Marginalisation and New Policies*. Gatekeeper Series, no. 49. London: International Institute for Environment and Development.

Derman, Bill, and Anne Ferguson. 1999. "Water and the Environment in the Water Reform Process in Zimbabwe: Contested Practices and Understandings." In *Water Policy: Security Issues, International Review of Comparative Public Policy*, edited by Scott Winter and Scott Whiteford, 11: 207–28. Stamford, Conn.: JAI.

Derman, Bill, and Francis Gonese. 2003. "Water Reform: Its Multiple Interfaces with Land *Reform and Resettlement.*" In *Delivering Land and Securing Livelihood: Post-Independence Land Reform and Resettlement in Zimbabwe*, 287–307. Harare: University of Zimbabwe, Centre for Applied Social Sciences; Madison: University of Wisconsin, Land Tenure Center.

Derman, Bill, and Anne Hellum. 2002. "Neither Tragedy nor Enclosure: Are There Inherent Human Rights in Water Management in Zimbabwe's Communal Lands?" *European Journal of Development Research* 14, no. 2: 31–50.

de Villiers, Marq. 1999. *Water Wars: Is the World's Water Running Out?* London: Weidenfield and Nicolson.

Falkenmark, Malin, and Jan Lundqvist. 1995. "Looming Water Crises: New Approaches Are Inevitable." In *Hydropolitics: Conflicts over Water As a Development Constraint*, edited by Leif Ohlsson, 178–212. London: Zed.

Ferguson, Anne. 1998. "Water Reforms in Zimbabwe: Gender Equity Dimensions." Paper presented at the annual meeting of the American Anthropological Association, Philadelphia, December.

Ferguson, Anne, and Bill Derman. 1999. "Water Rights vs. Right to Water: Reflections on Zimbabwe's Water Reforms from a Human Rights Perspective." Paper presented at the annual meeting of the American Anthropological Association, Chicago, November.

Food and Agriculture Organization of the United Nations (FAO). 1995. "Water Sector Policy Review and Strategy Formulation: General Framework." FAO Land and Water Policy Bulletin. Rome.

———. 2000. "New Dimensions in Water Security." Document no. AGL/MISC/25/2000. Rome.

Gleick, Peter. 1999. "The Human Right to Water." *Water Policy* 1, no. 5: 487–503.

Hellum, Anne. 2001. "Towards a Human Rights Based Development Approach: The Case of Women in the Water Reform Process in Zimbabwe." *Law, Social Justice and Global Development* (http://elj.warwick.ac.uk/global/issue/2001–1/hellum.html).

Martínez-Alier, Joan. 2002. *The Environmentalism of the Poor: A Study of Ecological Conflicts and Valuation.* Northampton, Mass.: Elgar.

Moore, Donald. 1996. "Marxism, Culture, and Political Ecology: Environmental Struggles in Zimbabwe's Eastern Highlands." In *Liberation Ecologies: Environment, Development, and Social Movements*, edited by Richard Peet and Michael Watts, 125–47. New York: Routledge.

Nicol, Alan. 2000. "Adopting a Sustainable Livelihoods Approach to Water Projects: Implications for Policy and Practice." Working paper, no. 133. London: Overseas Development Institute.

Rukuni, Mandivamba. 1994a. "Report of the Commission of Inquiry into Appropriate Agricultural Land Tenure Systems." In *Main Report.* Vol. 1. Harare: Government of Zimbabwe Printers.

———. 1994b. "Report of the Commission of Inquiry into Appropriate Agricultural Land Tenure Systems." *Technical Reports.* Vol. 2. Harare: Government of Zimbabwe Printers.

Solanes, Miguel, and Fernando Gonzalez-Villarreal. 1999. "The Dublin Principles for Water As Reflected in a Comparative Assessment of Institutional and Legal Arrangements for Integrated Water Resources Management." Santiago, Chile: Global Water Partnership.

Stott, Philip, and Sian Sullivan. 2000. "Introduction." In *Political Ecology: Science, Myth and Power*, edited by Philip Stott and Sian Sullivan, 1–14. London: Arnold.

World Bank. 1993. "Water Resources Management: A World Bank Policy Paper." Washington, D.C.

———. 2002. "Water Resources Sector Strategy: Strategic Directions for World Bank Engagement." Draft for discussion. Washington, D.C., March 25.

5

The New Calculus of Bedouin Pastoralism in the Kingdom of Saudi Arabia

ANDREW GARDNER

From a promontory in the deserts of the kingdom of Saudi Arabia, it would not be uncommon to spot two, three, or more herds of sheep roaming in the gentle valleys below. Hardscrabble land, dusty plains, or the smooth lines of sand dunes —all are accustomed to use, and those who use them are undeterred by the seeming lack of vegetation. From that same promontory, one might spot a Bedouin camp on the horizon, perhaps fifteen or twenty miles distant, signaled by a collection of two or three tents, a handful of pickup trucks, and a larger water truck that even at great distances can catch the eye. By navigating the web of converging and diverging tracks that connect all points in the great northern deserts, one might approach the Bedouin camp. The open vistas of the desert announce your arrival well in advance, and should men appear outside the tent, they will certainly invite you inside.

Bedouin hospitality is legendary, and for good reason. Coffee and tea are served, and dates, whose pedigree is often announced, are passed around in a bowl. Camel's milk is proffered, and the head of the household will insist a lamb be killed for dinner to commemorate the visit. As ethnographic encounters, the sessions are unusual, for the roles frequently reverse: visitors are plied for information, not only of their purpose and intent, but for news of rain, political events, the condition of distant rangelands, the scores of recent football games, and, in my case, the availability of the American drug Viagra. Over the course of an hour or two, the constellation of men in the public area of the tent changes as relatives and friends arrive and depart.

In the two months our small research group spent roaming the deserts of northern Arabia, our conversations with Bedouin pastoralists yielded a portrait of a people enmeshed in a complex and evolving relationship with the landscape on which they have traditionally depended. In this chapter, I trace the complexity and change in this relationship to a host of factors in the social, political, and economic context that marks contemporary pastoralism in the kingdom. Unraveling the interplay of these factors would require a detailed ethnographic portrait, not only to update Donald P. Cole's (1975) seminal work but also to provide a glimpse into the lives of an understudied people, for the Bedouin, like all Saudi nationals, live under a regime that has little interest in the ruminations of western social scientists. Nevertheless, because of the short duration of our fieldwork, producing such an ethnographic portrait would be impossible. Instead, by combining the data produced in our rapid appraisal with an examination of the social, political, and economic forces in which the kingdom's Bedouin are now enmeshed, I use this chapter to address key questions and critiques concerning the future of political ecology, particularly those posed by Andrew Vayda and his associates (Vayda and Walters 1999, Vayda 1983, Vayda et al. 1991, McCay 2000).[1]

Vayda's attack on political ecology is multistranded, but of concern here are the following. First, he suggests that political ecology brings a highly structured a priorism to the exploration of the human-environmental nexus—one that inevitably uncovers various political and economic factors at the root of causality and does so at the expense of other potential factors. Second, he argues that political ecology has abandoned ecology and with it the need for empirical, ecologically driven evidence to support explicit chains of causality. He contends that an event-oriented approach provides a more useful methodological framework for describing the complexities of the human-environmental nexus, and he terms this approach *event* (or *evenemental*) ecology. This proposal emerges from a line of arguments often framed as calls for problem-driven research and, in more theoretical form, as contentions against an anthropological tendency toward unfocused holism and the vagaries of processualism (McCay 2000).

Critics have used evenemental approaches and the methodological prescription for working outward in scope and backward in time to attack the recurring importance of political factors in much contemporary work produced under the banner of political ecology. In working through the details of the case study presented here, I seek to demonstrate that even as a "self-styled political ecologist" (to use Vayda's and Walter's [1999, 168] terminology), my a priori assumptions are less about the primacy of political causes than about a concern for a methodological holism—in essence, with avoiding an a priorism concerning any particular cause, political or not. Moreover, I argue that, in the hands of many practitioners, event ecology and progressive contextualization themselves manifest a causal a priorism that leads away from the principal strengths of anthropological inquiry. In other words, for anthropologists concerned with environmental policy and, more generally, with political ecology, the focus on singular events and unilinear causation obscures the complex and contingent interplay of the forces driving environmental change.

The Kuwait Oil Fires As Event

As part of a project funded by the Meteorology and Environmental Protection Agency (MEPA) of the kingdom of Saudi Arabia, I spent two months in the late spring of 1999 in the deserts of northern Saudi Arabia and in Jeddah, the cosmopolitan hub of the kingdom. Our research team, comprising Dr. Timothy Finan, myself, and four researchers from MEPA, conducted a total of twenty-seven interviews. Thirteen were conducted with extended Bedouin families from seven different tribes (Shammar, Beni Murrah, Muhtair, Harb, Sabeer, Osman, and Al Sudah). The remaining interviews consist of both individual and group interviews with herders, health administrators and doctors, veterinarians, and other officials with specific or general knowledge of the Bedouin people, their animals, the rangeland, and the history of its use.

Our research team faced two distinct tasks. First, we were commissioned to provide an ethnographic context for the hypothesized impact of the Kuwaiti oilfield fires on Saudi Bedouin livelihood. This task, we learned, was part of the kingdom's effort to seek reparations for the 1990–91 Iraqi incursions into Kuwait.[2] Second, we were to ascertain the potential utility to the Bedouin people of government-generated climate information and provide the kingdom with recommendations for tailoring that information to the needs of contemporary Bedouin pastoralists. Although the second research question resulted in a variety of interesting conclusions, this chapter focuses largely on the perceived impact of the Kuwaiti oilfield fires. These fires, set by retreating Iraqi forces, sent plumes of soot high into the atmosphere. Traces were measured as far away as Japan and Hawaii, and major plumes of soot from the fires hung over the northeastern region of Saudi Arabia for months. According to the Bedouin pastoralists, day became night; white clothes turned black after only hours of wear; and plants, sand, and sheep were covered in an oily film.

The short-term effects of both the war and the oil fires were the primary focus of attention in the period after the 1991 Gulf War. In regions proximate to the burning oil wells, the environment withstood a variety of effects. Beyond the impact of the fires themselves, oil spills, abandoned military encampments, chemical dumping, and spent munitions resulted in a variety of environmental problems. The range and intensity of these localized impacts have been well documented by climatologists and rangeland specialists (Omar et al. 1998), but these assessments were mostly confined to the region in and around the battlefield itself and therefore well north of the grazing lands of northern Saudi Arabia. For the larger region, early predictions suggested that soot clouds from Kuwait might instigate a "nuclear winter" with vast effects on the global climate (Marshall 1991). Further research documented episodic events of smog and rain linked to the soot cloud (Browning et al. 1991). But long-term effects of soot deposition have not been identified; and more specifically, no causal link between soot deposition and the condition of rangelands has been established.

Outside the circle of the scientific debate are the experiences of the thousands of Bedouin nomads who endured both wartime and postwar disruptions of their livelihood. Their accounts of the soot clouds provide an ethnographic glimpse that documents a different facet of the social and environmental impact of the Gulf War and its aftermath. Bedouin nomads—and for that matter, anyone in the northeastern region of the kingdom at the time of the war—remember the plume of soot from the Kuwaiti oil fires. Most participants could vividly describe the event: "We have been in this region for thirty or forty years, and we were here during the war. After the smoke, the vegetation died and is only now becoming green again. The smoke was overhead for a year; we had to change clothes every day because clothes that were white would become black by nightfall."[3]

Another Bedouin participant noted: "The smoke was thick here for one day and then here for fifteen days on and off. It came on a Tuesday night. . . . oil covered the water, and the sky was dark on Wednesday." One of the most memorable environmental events in recent times, the plume from the Kuwaiti oil fires recurs in Bedouin discussions as a point of chronological demarcation. Historical discussions and descriptions often began with "before the smoke" or "before the war," and most of the participants could name their precise location on the day the plume first arrived.

The Bedouin participants' vivid descriptions of the cloud of soot were frequently accompanied by descriptions of increasing animal mortality. Contemporary Bedouin herds are plagued by a host of maladies, some of which are capable of decimating an entire herd in a few short days. Participants articulated these conditions and, with some frequency, linked them and the condition of the rangeland to soot from the oil fires: "A lot of animals died here after the war. Animals would stop eating until they just died. They were weak and had problems with their throats, like tumors. These impacts showed up just after the war and continue today. The animals become weak and their stomach and intestines swell. Then they just die."

These snippets of discussion might suggest that we were affirming the hypothetical link between the oilfield fires and problems on the contemporary rangeland. In the terminology of event ecology, we had taken a problem-specific approach to the research question and thereby contextualized the assumed causal events with ethnographic data, providing some support for the link between two environmental events: the soot cloud from the Kuwaiti oil fires and the rampant animal mortality reported by participants. To end with such a conclusion, however, would be a disservice to the ethnographic data derived from our work there. Furthermore, while some political ecologists suggest that we corral the practice of holistic (and therefore unfocused) ethnographic inquiry (see McCay 2000), the principal strength of ethnography is its rich and varied content.

So what had been omitted in this simple causal conclusion concerning the relationship between the Kuwaiti oil fires and ruminant mortality? In reexamining the data, numerous alternative causal explanations rose to the surface. The Bedouin noted, for example, that they had begun to face competition from villagers and townsfolk, many of whom now maintain their own herds of sheep. They noted that the average herd size had grown exponentially over the past several decades. They lamented that the borders to Kuwait and Iraq, once permeable, were now closed to travel. They described how inexpensive migrant laborers from the poorest quarters of the globe had become widely available in Saudi Arabia and were now an integral component of the Bedouin livelihood. And we noted that nearly all of the Bedouin families interviewed had pickup trucks, and most had a water truck as well. Finally, precipitation data for the northern regions of the desert indicate that rainfall was extremely low in the years surrounding the Gulf War. Together these factors build a basis for alternative explanations. Small clues direct the conclusion away from a simple causal chain of events connecting the Kuwaiti oil fires to diminishing rangeland conditions—away from unilinear treatments of causality—to considerations that drift in a multitude of directions and depend on a variety of anthropology's analytic tools and perspectives.

This leads me to the principal contention of this chapter: that an approach focusing on the event of the 1991 Gulf War oil fires diverts attention from the confluence of processes driving environmental change in the desert. In the following sections, I describe other fields of causation, better conceived as processes. These processes overlap and intertwine. Several are contingent upon others, and several belong to an entirely different order. Rather than a product of this anthropologist's muddled descriptions and wandering interests, the multiplicity of causal domains is a key aspect of the data. By reframing the dilemmas of the Saudi Bedouin people in these varied causal domains, I argue for holistic approaches to anthropological inquiry.

Diverging Class Structure

Saudi oil reserves are the largest in the world. By recent estimates, the reserves constitute one-fourth of the world's supply of petroleum (EIA 2001). The wealth generated by these natural riches is largely controlled by the Al-Saud family and a handful of others in the family's inner circle (MacFarquhar 2001). The royal family's legitimacy is partly construed by their control and custodianship of the holy cities of Mecca and Medina, partly by the money that courses through an economy that they significantly control. On the one hand, these funds fuel mechanisms of direct control: Saudi military forces, combined with internal security forces, are the United States' largest customers for military hardware (Curtiss 1995). On the other hand, their legitimacy is buttressed by a complex social contract in which the royal family, as patron, trades a generous welfare state for political quiescence (Champion 1999).

While the victory of allied forces over the Iraqi army was widely touted in the western media, these reports often elided the mercenary underpinnings of the Gulf War. Assistance to the Kuwaitis and, by extension, to Saudi Arabia was enacted only through a series of agreements in which Saudi Arabia essentially agreed to foot the bill for the war. In the final accounting, the war cost nearly $55 billion, representing nearly the entire savings of the Saudi government (Curtiss 1995). In the years after the war, the Saudi government enacted a series of austerity measures that scaled back the social services constructed in decades past.

The effects of these austerity measures exacerbated existing class divisions. In my discussions with project participants, the Saudi citizenry was frequently described as three distinct classes: the ruling elite, the urban middle class, and the predominately rural lower middle class. These taxonomies typically omitted the massive expatriate underclass (forming one-fourth of the nation's total population). While no precise figures are available, there is little evidence of belt-tightening in the royal family and their elite beneficiaries, who, as a group, are estimated to directly control 40 percent of petroleum revenues (Shaoul 2000). The multifaceted welfare state (including but not limited to free health care, free universities, stipends for students, agricultural price supports, and regulated utility rates) benefited both the urban and rural classes. As the government scaled back these benefits, however, it also eroded the traditional social contract between the royal elite and the underclasses, instigating a period of social and economic unrest (Champion 1999).

Our discussions with the Bedouin participants uncovered two contradictory trends at work in these historic currents. Individuals, not necessarily Bedouin, able to negotiate these changing conditions and successfully amass wealth (particularly people in the smaller towns and villages scattered throughout the northern deserts) capitalized on growing inequities by hiring expatriate herders to build and manage herds of goats, sheep, and camels. For the wealthiest townsfolk, a Bedouin-style tent and a herd of animals near town represented not just a new, productive investment but also a possession of symbolic importance tied to the history of the Saudi Arabs and their emergence from the desert, analogous to the trophy ranches maintained by wealthy Americans in the cattle country of the west.

For other townsfolk, austerity measures enacted by the government meant an increase in costs and, for legions of civil servants, decreases in their relative income. For these people, establishing small herds of goats, camels, and sheep was a coping strategy—a second source of income created by adding a new component to their livelihood. The move was buttressed by the availability of cheap expatriate labor and premised on the decades-earlier breakdown of tribal control of grazing lands (discussed later in the chapter). In conjunction with increasing rates of unemployment (Champion 1999), our Bedouin respondents reported dramatic increases in the number of non-Bedouin herds on the range in the postwar period.

The impact of these processes was twofold. First, in a tragedy-of-the-commons scenario, the growing number of animals on the range increased pressure on the rangeland environment, particularly in the environs surrounding the villages and towns of the northern deserts. Second, dramatic increases in the number of animals on the range—specifically, the increased density of herds near towns and villages—intensified the prevalence of communicable disease within and among herds. Originating in the complexities of the global political economy of petroleum and further articulated through the political particularities of the Saudi nation-state, these effects were borne by non-Bedouin and Bedouin pastoralists alike.

Impermeable Borders

The Bedouin people of Saudi Arabia, like their brethren in the other desert regions of the Middle East and northern Africa, were thoroughly accustomed to the hardships imposed by land and climate, for the bounties of the desert are scattered and ephemeral. Historically, the Bedouin have been mobile people. It is problematic, however, to speak of Bedouin migration as a coping strategy for times of hardship. Indeed, their livelihood was constructed in an environment of nearly constant environmental and climatic hardship. Migration, rather than a temporary strategy, was a way of life.

The national boundaries of Saudi Arabia and the surrounding countries were imposed over a more fluid set of cultural groups. Tribes and tribal allegiances spanned these borders; and when relations between nations remained positive, the flow of Bedouin migration continued unabated. One Bedouin participant recalled the days before the introduction of barley: "When the drought would come, we would move sometimes as far as Syria. At the time I had many fewer animals." Other participants noted moving toward Iran or north to the verdant rangelands of Iraq. Conversely, Bedouin pastoralists from the surrounding countries also used the rangelands of the kingdom.

The Gulf War ended these historic migration routes, at least for the time being. Not only did enforcement of national boundaries block traditional migratory corridors to better northern pastures, but the safety offered by the relative stability of the Saudi government—as protector of the rangelands—also attracted Bedouin from Kuwait, Iraq, and other gulf states. Our research team encountered several Iraqi encampments during our travels in the northern deserts. Although their legal status on Saudi soil is questionable, the laws are vague and rarely enforced; and the plateaus, valleys, and sand dunes of the northern desert offer ample refuge for those of indeterminate status.

Saudi Bedouin now find themselves grazing herds among Bedouin from nearby states as well as among herds belonging to non-Bedouin Saudis. This change has resulted in the effects described above: more animals on the grazing lands and a subsequent increase in communicable disease through animal proximity. But as several Bedouin participants reported, it has also resulted in foreigners' introduction of new sheep and goat species. Many Bedouin participants believed these sheep and goat varieties are an additional cause of the increasing prevalence of ruminant disease in the region because, in the participants' view, they are poorly adapted to the specific rigors of the Saudi desert.

The Introduction of an Underclass

The wealth generated by the nation's oil reserves and the government's active pursuit of foreign labor to meet market demands have fostered a vast expatriate underclass in the kingdom. Despite the combined forces of what is known as *Saudiization* (the government's recent program for encouraging Saudi nationals to take jobs traditionally reserved for expatriate labor) and a rapidly falling per capita income, estimated at less than half of what it was twenty years ago, the expatriate labor force still makes up great majority of the Saudi work force (Kostiner 1997).

A traveler in the kingdom can hardly overlook the presence of this vast work force. Filipinos work as concierges in large hotels and are prized as domestic servants in private homes. Saudi families unable to afford a Filipino house worker, I was told, opt for a less expensive Sri Lankan. Expatriates from the Indian subcontinent staff stores, Bengalis cut hair in countless barbershops, and groups of Somali youth offer to wash cars at busy urban parking lots. Lebanese and Turks prepare food in restaurants in cities large and small, and the Nepalese (one of the newest ethnic work forces in the kingdom) pump gas.

In the class structure described previously, the expatriate work force benefits the urban middle class, providing an able work force in the numerous occupations considered beneath the station of Saudi nationals.[4] Even in our travels through the northern environs, however, the presence of these expatriate laborers was nearly ubiquitous; and further investigation suggested that it has influenced Bedouin livelihood in several important and distinct ways.

First, the presence and availability of inexpensive expatriate labor has encouraged non-Bedouin pastoralism. By sponsoring individuals from northern India, Pakistan, Sudan, and other poor countries with a pastoral heritage, urban and village-dwelling Saudis have been able to tap an experienced reservoir of labor to manage ruminant herds that, as described, are an economic strategy for coping with declining income from small business ventures, minor professional occupations, and poorly paid civil posts. In numerous visits to encampments in the northern deserts we encountered such enterprises: after a series of introductions, our research team would discover that the herd's owner was not present but lived in a nearby town, typically visiting the encampment on the weekend to check on his investment.

Second, the introduction of inexpensive foreign labor has allowed Bedouin pastoralists to contract expatriate laborers and thereby increase the size of ruminant herds. This strategy has been used to replace family labor sources: sons, who in the past would have helped manage the herd, are now commonly sent to Riyadh or elsewhere for university training. Moreover, in combination with factors such as introduction of the truck and an increasing reliance on foreign barley, an expatriate labor force has helped to shift the underlying logic of Bedouin pastoralism from an environmental calculation to an economic one.

Although I will discuss these issues in more detail later in the chapter, suffice it to say here that, by enabling competition from non-Bedouin Saudi nationals and providing a mechanism for increasing the size of Bedouin herds, expatriate labor has encouraged dramatic increases in the number of animals on the rangeland. As one Bedouin participant noted, "There are lots more animals on the range now because people have more money, and there's barley, and it's easy and affordable to bring in someone to care for the animals."

Barley Supplements and Rainfed Rangeland

Before the end of the twentieth century, Bedouin pastoralism functioned according to an environmental calculation that encompassed traditional migratory patterns developed over centuries, a vast communicative network entwined with complex familial and social relations, and a detailed knowledge of the desert and its flora. Travel over great distances was a necessity. Hence, the camel, used for transportation, meat, and milk, was the keystone of Bedouin livelihood. Its continued symbolic importance to both Bedouin and non-Bedouin Saudis is beyond question. In the last decades of the twentieth century, however, with the shift to a livelihood based on markets rather than the ecology of the rangeland, herd typology shifted from one based upon camels to one based upon sheep. One factor that encouraged this process was the introduction of barley into the pastoral livelihood.

The immense social net put into place by the Al-Saud family, made possible by the wealth generated from petroleum sales, included price supports for barley. People who identify themselves as Bedouin occupy a distinct and complex position in the kingdom's cultural milieu; for while they are often disdained as uneducated, provincial, and irreverent, they at the same time occupy a mythic location in the kingdom's cultural constellation. For many Saudi, the Bedouin's perceived resilience and fierce independence inspire pride and admiration. But general assessments suggest that, as a socioeconomic class, they benefited the least from the rapid development and concomitant social services established in the kingdom (Finan and Al-Haratini 1996, 1997; Finan et al. 1995). Nevertheless, even minor government assistance has provoked wholesale changes in the Bedouin livelihood.

Beginning in 1973, the government forged strong subsidies for barley sup-plements with the idea of providing a security net for pastoral Bedouin in times of drought. This policy represented part of the aforementioned social contract between the royal family and its subjects. Hindsight reveals a host of unintended consequences associated with the introduction of inexpensive barley supple-ments, foremost of which was the construction of a formidable buffer to Bedouin vulnerability to climate variability. The concept of vulnerability buffering has been explored elsewhere (Finan et al. 2002, Gardner 1999). For Bedouin pas-toralists, inexpensive barley supplements provided a ready strategy for coping with drought by mitigating the necessity to move great distances in search of rangeland and thus encouraged the expansion of marketable sheep herds.

As part of recent austerity measures, the Saudi government abandoned these price supports, resulting in additional widespread trauma to the Bedouin livelihood as barley prices rose to meet market levels. In previous decades, Bedouin reliance on barley supplements had become all encompassing; and Saudi Arabia remains the largest importer of barley in the world, principally from the European Union but also from Australia, Canada, and other nations (Lau 1999). Our fieldwork, completed in a fairly dry year, revealed the scope of this dependency. As one Bedouin participant noted, "There was no time this year I went without barley. The rangeland was bad all year, and if there's no food, the animals die. Barley goes for SAR 27 [just over seven dollars] a bag, and I feed my animals twenty-six bags every other day." Another respondent contextualized the barley issue in contemporary Bedouin life:

> I've not gone a single day this year without barley. Life is becoming very difficult. I'm buying twenty bags of barley a day, and I have to buy gas and fix my truck, and I have installment payments for the truck too. I don't know if my sons will follow in my footsteps. . . . I have relatives and friends that graduated from high school, but there's nothing for them to do. I guess my sons will do this, as there's no other alternative.

The impact of increasing Bedouin reliance on barley supplements has had several effects on their livelihood. First, it has fostered the tendency to keep larger ruminant herds and removed the culling impact of severe droughts. Sec-ond, barley supplements, in tandem with multiple other factors discussed in this chapter, have made it possible for non-Bedouin Saudi with no indigenous knowl-edge of the rangeland or climate of the region to successfully own and manage their own herds of animals. Together, these factors have led to increases in the prevalence of animal disease and mortality as well as increased pressure on the fragile rangelands of the northern deserts. Furthermore, the Bedouin herders' increasing dependency on imported barley has enmeshed them in a political economy driven by both regional and global dynamics.

The Breakdown of Tribal Land Tenure

While no longer ubiquitous among the citizenry of the kingdom, tribal affiliation remains central to the identity of urban and rural Saudis alike. For the Bedouin peoples of the kingdom, however, tribal affiliation signifies more than identity. In centuries past, tribal affiliation conferred land tenure on the Bedouin individual. Each tribe had a homeland in the desert—a *dirah*—over which he and his tribe had rights. While the vague spatial boundaries of these dirah formed an indigenous set of parishes in the desert environs of Saudi Arabia, the practical foci of ownership were water sources, keystones in the social geography of the region.

Migration patterns often traversed multiple *diyar* (the plural form of dirah); and in times of drought, tribesmen found themselves forced to move beyond the confines of their dirah. Both types of movements, seasonal and strategic, relied on the nuances of intertribal relations. These relations formed not only the basis from which the nation-state of Saudi Arabia emerged but also a complex social mechanism for governing rangeland resources because entry into the dirah, even in times of abundance, was limited.

By royal decree, this system of land tenure was abolished in the early 1950s (Cole 1982). Tribal affiliation nevertheless remains central to Bedouin identity; and Bedouin tribes continue to be strongly associated with their home dirah, a situation reinforced by royal appointments of tribal leaders to local government positions. But underlying this continuity is a fundamental change in the land tenure system—a change that has not only allowed the free flow of Bedouin to more verdant pastures but also permitted non-Bedouin to begin grazing herds on the land. As one participant noted, "This is the dirah of the Harb, but many tribes come here now. . . . in the old times, you couldn't just go anywhere you wanted."

The impact of modernity, while changing the cast of pastoralists who are utilizing the rangeland, has done little to diminish the scope of Bedouin communicative networks. Information about rain travels quickly by word of mouth, often faster than the government-sponsored climate information system and its daily radio reports. As one Bedouin participant described, "I hear about other places from other Bedouin. We always see each other and we talk. We are Bedouin, and we're always looking for good rangeland. If it rains anywhere in the kingdom, people start to move, and we are always asking each other about the land. When I get there, even if it's crowded, I take my place among the others."

As the reader might suspect, the breakdown of traditional tenure systems has contributed to increases in the number of animals on the range and thereby the increased prevalence of communicable disease in animal herds—all of which fits neatly into revisions of the tragedy-of-the-commons literature (McCay and Acheson 1987, Monbiot 1994). But as the Bedouin just quoted has noted, freedom of movement has resulted in more than just a generalized increase in rangeland use. The Bedouin community is well aware of locations of rain and pasturage; government-sponsored climate reports inform non-Bedouin pastoralists and town-based herders, who rapidly learn of new pasture. As a result, Allah's bounty is quickly consumed.

Some researchers have an additional concern. The traditional tenure system, combined with difficult terrain and the limitations of camel-based transportation, meant that inaccessible reaches in the northern deserts remained pockets of biodiversity (Finan and Al-Haratini 1996, 1997; Finan et al. 1995). These areas, too, have been opened by the breakdown in tribal land tenure.

Trucks, Roads, and Water

Nearly thirty years ago, in his two years of fieldwork in the Rub' al-Khali, Cole (1975) noted the growing presence of the truck. Dawn Chatty (1996) revisited this dimension of modernization in her analysis of contemporary Bedouin livelihoods. I confirm their observations. The truck is the foundation of contemporary Bedouin livelihoods and, as such, intertwines with the other processes of modernization described in this chapter. All the Bedouin camps we visited possessed at least one small pickup truck, and many maintained multiple vehicles. With these vehicles, Bedouin scout for distant pastures, visit friends and family, carry animals to market, and transport barley back to camp.

In addition to playing these specific roles in the contemporary pastoralist livelihood, the truck has instigated a series of much deeper changes in Bedouin life. The journey to town—perhaps once a day, perhaps less frequently—has reshaped the social landscape of Bedouin life, moving the hub of communication outside the tent and into the marketplaces of villages and towns. While meetings of family and guests in the main tent of the Bedouin encampment still play an important role, the transfer of vital political, social, and climatic information often takes place in town at the markets where barley is purchased and animals sold. In this context, the Bedouin meets a larger cross-section of individuals with whom information is exchanged—a cross-section less mediated by the intricacies of tribal relations and one in which information is drawn from a much larger geographical domain.

Similarly, the truck has facilitated the shift from camel-based herds to sheep- and goat-based herds. Sheep and goats are much less resilient to the hardships of the arid desert and require water almost daily. So in addition to pickup trucks, all the Bedouin camps we contacted possessed a larger water truck, essential for maintaining sheep and goat herds. Water trucks provide an additional buffer against the arid ecology of the region, allowing the Bedouin to keep large herds of animals on land with little or no water resources by freely drawing water from government-constructed wells.

Finally, one must note the physical infrastructure of the region as a factor in these processual changes. With the wealth of the oilfields in government coffers, Saudi agencies have embarked on a significant set of infrastructural improvements in the northern regions of the kingdom. New roads, like thin strips of black duct tape on the sands of the northern deserts, connect all major towns and a host of minor agricultural regions, villages, and waypoints. With these roads in place (and no apparent speed limits to slow travel), Bedouin pastoralists are able to move water, animals, and camps quickly to new locations.

In general, the Bedouin are happy to have such freedom of movement. As one participant remarked, "In the old days, there was no truck to get around in— we had to go by camel. The truck is a good thing, for I can go and scout new pasture when I hear about it." At the same time, the pickup truck, the water truck, and the freedom of movement granted by improvements to physical infrastructure and the breakdown of traditional tenure systems put untold stress on the rangeland. Not only do these factors facilitate barley-based herd management, but they have also opened new desert regions to grazing. Their impact becomes obvious in times of rain. One Bedouin participant described the effects of truck-based pastoralism: "I remember one time when there was a lot of rain here, and a bunch of people came from the north, paying SAR 2000 [approximately 530 dollars] to make the journey. Soon the whole area was overgrazed. There wasn't enough for everyone, so most of them moved on." In the end, the introduction of trucks to the Bedouin livelihood has removed geographical limits on the Bedouin grazing strategy. Again, the result is clear: these changes have increased pressure on the rangeland and, at the same time, foster the spread of communicable diseases in overcrowded herds.

Climate and Rangeland

Historic rainfall data specific to the northern regions are lacking. Since 1980, however, MEPA has maintained a series of weather stations in all parts of the nation. While the data generated by these stations do little to portray long-term climatic cycles, the data from the five weather stations proximate to our study area, although incomplete, reveal the span of the most recent drought (see fig. 5.1). According to all five stations, the drought could be traced back into the 1980s, well before the climatic effects of the Gulf War and its aftermath.

My purpose here is not to argue that the Gulf War had no impact on the climate or the rangelands of northern Saudi Arabia. Rather, these data merely identify a climatic pattern distinct from the Gulf War and its aftermath. The decade-long drought, beginning somewhere near 1984 and reaching a critical low in 1990 (just as the Gulf War began), indicates a line of causality beginning with the climatic cycles of the region and ending with the current conditions of the rangeland.

At the same time, these climatic issues must be contextualized in the larger processes described in this chapter, including the closure of traditional migra-

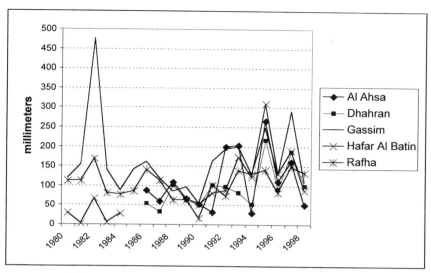

FIGURE 5-1. Annual rainfall from regional weather stations.

tory routes in and through Iraq (a historical strategy for coping with periodic droughts) as well as the introduction of barley supplements, thus allowing the Bedouin to persevere in spite of poor climatic conditions. Through this contextualization, climate emerges as another contributing factor in the panoply of difficulties noted in the contemporary Bedouin livelihood.

Event and Process

Andrew Vayda's and Bradley Walters's (1999) critique of political ecology is linked to a call for a problem-driven approach to anthropological research that focuses on particular events and their causes—an evenemental hub from which lines of causation stretch outward in scope and backward in time (Vayda et al. 1991, Vayda and Walters 1999). In the environmental history of the Arabian rangelands, the aftermath of the Gulf War (smoke in the air for months, an oily film on the landscape) looms large as such an event. Moreover, this event figured prominently in our discussions with those who use the rangeland: the cloud of soot from the Kuwaiti oil fires represents a singular and catastrophic event in the social memory of the Bedouin people. But as a causal isolate of environmental change, the smoke and soot of the Kuwaiti oil fires is a poor choice for an event to represent the complexities of the human-environmental nexus, for it eclipses the numerous other causes underlying environmental change in the northern deserts of the kingdom.

In the hands of some practitioners, Vayda's progressive contextualization is used to simplify the complex and contingent nature of causation, to presuppose an internal order to that causation (see Walters 2000, for example). At the center is the environmental event (the a priori assumption of the event ecologist) and, from it, radiating outward in scope and backward in time, are chains of causation, some political, some not. The strength of this model is its ability to organize causal factors into a comprehensible structure. Yet the multiple causes affecting the Saudi Bedouin do not fit into neat valences of event ecology, nor do they extend outward from a single environmental event.

Rather, the environmental impacts described here—and I have consciously switched between rangeland degradation, ruminant mortality, and the event of the Gulf War itself—are nodes in a complex web of causation, one that has overdetermined the observable, environmental results of the present day (Althusser 1965).[5] On the one hand, I have tried to show that if one adopts these environmental effects as the problem to be explained (and thereby concedes to the a priorism of event ecology), causation stems from a variety of sources of a different order. These environmental impacts can be traced to processes of a global order, including the machinations of the global political economy of the petroleum industry as well as globalization of the grain and labor markets. One can also trace the end results to processes at a national level: to the specificities of the political-religious leadership structure of the kingdom and the tripartite class structure described by our Saudi contacts. At the local level, one can see how these global processes articulate in the Bedouin livelihood. The Bedouins adapted to the introduction of the truck, the availability of barley, the breakdown of the traditional system of rangeland tenure, and countless other events by making adjustments to their livelihood, incorporating new technologies, practices, and strategies into their daily lives. Children leave for college, trucks replace camels, and conversations move from the tent to the market.

On the other hand, the hub-and-spokes model promoted by some practitioners of event ecology fails to fully explore the mechanics of causality. The strands of causation forming this web interact with one another in time: there is a diachronic and contingent aspect to causation that must be accounted for. In the driest years of the 1970s, Bedouin nomads began to use barley supplements to feed their herds. Market relations of a global scope were built over time but were accelerated by the shift in herd typology from the rugged camel to the more precarious sheep. The shift to sheep, however, was only achieved because of the increasing availability and prevalence of the truck. Financing the purchase of the truck, however, required increased herd size and a more developed local market. Increased herd size in part resulted from the importation of an expatriate labor force. And so on. The links among these events connect each with the others in a conceptual morass, and only by ignoring the interconnections can one fit these causal processes into the neat valences of progressive contextualization.

Here I argue with Fernand Braudel (1972) that events are "crests of foam that the tides of history carry on their strong backs" (21). Analyses of process yield a diachronic tapestry to which singular events can be attached and contextual-ized—a "time oriented perspective on continuity and change" (Moore 1987, 729) and one attentive to the "order, antiorder, and nonorder" of the causal relations (730). In the case of the Bedouin in northern Saudi Arabia, causal forces shaping their lives only become sensible when contextualized amid the historical processes that make up change.

In the end, I hope this case study demonstrates the need for an open-ended ethnographic investigation that transcends a simple, problem-driven approach. I argue that ethnography, whether under the banner of political ecology or not, is by definition holistic and open-ended; the knowledge it derives pushes beyond the confines of simple causal links. The result is a complex, intercon-nected, and diachronic description of causality. The job of the political ecologist becomes one of placing environmental results in this processual web—in essence, contextualizing environmental events, policies, and decisions in the processes uncovered through ethnographic research. Processual analysis, as a counterpart to a holistic ethnographic approach, provides a framework for connecting these local events to larger historical processes. At the same time, it provides a frame-work for comparison, a set of templates by which the parallels or differences revealed by ethnography can be compared.

No single event, nor any single chain of events, encapsulates the complexi-ties of the forces driving environmental change in the lives of Saudi Bedouins. The current condition of the rangelands was overdetermined by a complex web of factors, all in interaction with one another, in which environmental factors were just one component. Yet the forces at work at global, national, and local lev-els, as well as the decisions and strategies through which the Bedouin have adapted to these forces, become sensible under the rubrics of processes such as moderniza-tion and globalization. Via processual analysis, we can see how Saudi Bedouin lives become connected to lives in faraway places described by other anthropologists.

NOTES

1. The centerpiece of this corrective is Vayda and Walters (1999). I also, however, include Vayda's (1983) article on progressive contextualization as an early manifestation of this debate, as well as Vayda et al. (1991). The meta-history of this debate in political ecology has been further clarified in McCay (2000).

2. The United Nations Compensation Commission managed these claims.

3. The quotations in this chapter are from individuals interviewed in the course of the project, often translated by interpreters during interviews. Typically, Timothy Finan or I would ask a question from a topical outline constructed before our arrival. Many non-Bedouin participants spoke English. When we were interviewing Bedouin men, how-ever, the questions and responses were translated by our Saudi counterparts.

4. Champion (1999) has described this attitude as the *mudir* syndrome, using the Arabic word for "director." Despite government efforts to shift unemployed youth into a vari-ety of semi-menial positions, he perceives a durable and historic attitude in which nothing less than a position of authority is palatable to a Saudi national.

5. Althusser's notion of overdetermination has been described to me as the causal condition in which, as a result of the multiplicity of causal factors, the removal or negation
   of any single causal strand does not alter the final outcome (personal communication,
   Thomas K. Park, October 29, 2002).

REFERENCES

Althusser, Louis. 1965. *For Marx*, translated by Ben Brewster. New York: Pantheon.
Braudel, Fernand. 1972. *The Mediterranean and the Mediterranean World in the Age of Philip II.* Vol. 1. New York: Harper and Row.
Browning, K. A., R. J. Allam, S. P. Ballard, R.T.H. Barnes, D. A. Bennetts, R. H. Maryon, P. J. Mason, D. McKenna, J.F.B. Mitchell, C. A. Senior, A. Slingo, and F. B. Smith. 1991. "Environmental Effects from Burning Oil Wells in Kuwait." *Nature* 351: 363–71.
Champion, Daryl. 1999. "The Kingdom of Saudi Arabia: Elements of Instability within Stability." *Middle East Review of International Affairs* 3, no. 4: 49–73.
Chatty, Dawn. 1996. *Mobile Pastoralists: Development Planning and Social Change in Oman.* New York: Columbia University Press.
Cole, Donald P. 1975. *Nomads of the Nomads: The *Al Murrah Bedouin of the Empty Quarter.* Chicago: Aldine.
———. 1982. "Tribal and Non-Tribal Structures among the Bedouin of Saudi Arabia." *Al-Abhath* 30: 77–93.
Curtiss, Richard H. 1995. "Four Years after Massive War Expenses Saudi Arabia Gets Its Second Wind." *Washington Report on Middle East Affairs* (September): 48–49.
Energy Information Administration (EIA). 2001. "Saudi Arabia." Retrieved November 14, 2002 (http://www.eia.doe.gov/emeu/cabs/saudi.html).
Finan, Timothy J., and Eisa R. al-Haratini. 1996. *Modern Bedouins: The Transformation of Traditional Nomad Society in Al-Taysiyah Region of Saudi Arabia.* Tucson, Ariz.: Bureau of Applied Research in Anthropology.
———. 1997. *The Impacts of Current Natural Resource Management Practices among Saudi Arabian Bedouins: A Case Study from the At-Taysiyah Region.* Tucson, Ariz.: Bureau of Applied Research in Anthropology.
Finan, Timothy J., Eisa R. Al-Haratani, Abdulaziz Al-Eisa, Khalid Amin, Siraj Miriki, Mohammed Habib, and Adel Gusti. 1995. *Impacts of Modernization on Saudi Arabian Bedouin Groups: An Anthropological Study.* Tucson, Ariz.: Bureau of Applied Research in Anthropology.
Finan, Timothy J., Colin T. West, Diane Austin, and Thomas McGuire. 2002. "Processes of Adaptation to Climate Variability: A Case Study from the U.S. Southwest." *Climate Research* 12, no. 21: 299–310.
Gardner, Andrew. 1999. "Land Use and Land Tenure in the Middle San Pedro River Valley." In *An Assessment of Climate Vulnerability in the Middle San Pedro River Valley,* edited by Timothy J. Finan and Colin West. Tucson, Ariz.: ISPE/CLIMAS.
Kostiner, Joseph. 1997. "State, Islam and Opposition in Saudi Arabia." *Middle East Review of International Affairs* 1, no. 2: 85–96.
Lau, Beth. 1999. "Market Analysis Division, Policy Branch, Adaptation and Grain Policy Directorate, Agriculture and Agri-Food Canada." *Bi-Weekly Bulletin* 12, no. 15: 3.
MacFarquhar, Neil. 2001. "A Nation Challenged: Saudi Arabia." *New York Times*, November 18, p. B5.
Marshall, Eliot. 1991. "'Nuclear Winter' from the Gulf War Discounted." *Science* 251: 372.
McCay, Bonnie J. 2000. "An Event Ecology of Ecologies in Anthropology." Paper presented at

the annual meeting of the American Anthropological Association, San Francisco, November 18.

McCay, Bonnie J., and James M. Acheson. 1987. *The Question of the Commons.* Tucson: University of Arizona Press.

Monbiot, George. 1994. "The Tragedy of the Enclosure." *Scientific American* (January): 159.

Moore, Sally Falk. 1987. "Explaining the Present: Theoretical Dilemmas in Processual Ethnography." *American Ethnologist* 14, no. 4: 727–36.

Omar, Samira A. S., E. Briskey, Raafat Misak, and Adel A.S.O. Asem. 1998. "The Gulf War Impact on Terrestrial Environment of Kuwait: An Overview." Paper presented at the First International Conference on Addressing Environmental Consequences of War: Legal, Economic, and Scientific Perspectives, Washington D.C., June 10–12.

Shaoul, Jean. 2000. "Amnesty International Reports Widespread Human Rights Abuses in Saudi Arabia." Retrieved April 26, 2000 (http://www.wsws.org/articles/2000/apr2000/saud-a26.shtml).

Vayda, Andrew P. 1983. "Progressive Contextualization: Methods and Research in Human Ecology." *Human Ecology* 11, no. 3: 265–81.

Vayda, Andrew P., Bonnie J. McCay, and Christina Eghenter. 1991. "Concepts of Process in Social Science Explanations." *Philosophy of the Social Sciences* 21, no. 3: 318–31.

Vayda, Andrew P., and Bradley Walters. 1999. "Against Political Ecology." *Human Ecology* 27, no. 1: 167–79.

Walters, Bradley. 2000. "Political and Non-political Influences on the Ecology of Philippine Mangrove Forests." Paper presented at the annual meeting of the American Anthropological Association, San Francisco, November 18.

6

Land Tenure and Biodiversity

An Exploration in the Political Ecology of Murang'a District, Kenya

A. FIONA D. MACKENZIE

Since the 1992 signing of the United Nations Convention on Biological Diversity, biodiversity has become a salient component of international discourse and, as such, a key means through which power relations at the global level are redrawn (Escobar 1996). The struggle over intellectual property rights and plant breeders' patents is one dimension of this discourse and the focus of substantial research (Mooney 1996). In the contest to establish whose knowledge counts and the effort to promote the conservation of biodiversity globally, those people who depend on the maintenance of biodiversity for their livelihoods are increasingly recognized as central players. Yet despite global recognition of the need for local-level research on biodiversity, study of the relationship between tenurial rights to agricultural land and biodiversity has been neglected (Howard-Borgas and Cuijpers 2002).[1]

In sub-Saharan Africa, land tenure has been debated particularly with respect to the efficient use of land. Yet early studies frequently failed to recognize the complex sets of rights and responsibilities of individuals and collectives through which tenure issues were defined. Recently, research in sub-Saharan Africa has recognized that small-scale farmers, who may often produce for subsistence as well as exchange, are responsible for maintaining the genetic diversity of their crops; but such studies have generally ignored the part played by property rights. In particular, research has not considered how people who are differentiated, for example, by class, gender, generation, marital status, race, and ethnicity negotiate rights of access and control of resources and land use in order to foster or undermine plant genetic diversity.

This chapter suggests ideas for conceptualizing the relationship between land-based property rights and biodiversity, drawing primarily on fieldwork conducted in Kenya in the mid-1980s and literature pertaining to sub-Saharan Africa. I focus on relations between the political and the ecological at the local level but argue that research into the relationship between tenurial practice and land use, and thus biodiversity, must engage iteratively with the complex intersection of the local and the global. Local promotion (or otherwise) of genetic diversity is entwined with social, economic, and political relations at far larger scales of inquiry.

The theoretical ground for this proposal is informed by poststructural political ecology. Recognizing both the advances and limitations of work such as that of Piers Blaikie and Harold Brookfield (1987), more recent research, inspired in part by postcolonial and feminist theorization of difference and discourse theory, has extended previous work in political ecology by exploring relations of power/knowledge as articulated through discourse in the relationship between people and land/economy and by examining the construction of nature in social struggle (Braun and Castree 1998, Escobar 1996, Neumann 1998, Peet and Watts 1996). In common with previous work, the approach recognizes in this chapter that how people relate to each other and the environment affects and is affected by their relationship to the means of production, including land, forests, and livestock. It also recognizes that such relationships are historically constituted and connected to other geographical scales of analysis. This approach suggests, further, that the relationship between people and, for example, land may be understood not only through the analysis of material relations of production but also through the view that the materiality of such relations is bound up with the symbolic resources or frameworks of meaning through which people define and legitimate their rights to land and through which they resist others' attempts to appropriate it. The approach explores the ways in which "nature" is socially constructed as people negotiate rights to land collectively or as individuals. Methodologically, I draw on a case study carried out in Murang'a District, Kenya, and other work that, in large measure, involves in-depth qualitative research. In many cases, this research parallels Michael Burawoy et al.'s (2000) global ethnography, which sees local cases as integrally interconnected with circuits of global capital. In Murang'a, I carried out field research over a five-year period in the 1980s. My work included participant observation and the collection of personal narratives from elderly Kikuyu women and men. People who were interested in recalling their agricultural histories were chosen from a range of socioeconomic strata. They were identified through purposive sampling involving a network that extended outward from the family of the interpreter with whom I worked. Given the political sensitivity of the research, I was cautioned that there was no alternative to this procedure.

My research was supplemented at the local level by analyses of the land register, coffee cooperative documents, and key interviews—for example, with local government officials and members of women's groups. To extend the research historically and connect it with the "global," I consulted archives in Nairobi,

Edinburgh, Oxford, and London. Documents included colonial records, government documents, records of the Church of Scotland Mission, and anthropological treatises.

The methodology adopted was one of discourse analysis, juxtaposing different accounts and sources of information, thereby teasing out the silences or
making visible the contradictions. By this means, I explored processes through
which the relationship between the political and the ecological can be created
and analyzed connections between power-resistance and power-knowledge.
People's experiential ecological knowledge and land-use practices vary according to political positionings, and this approach allowed for the investigation of
complex social relations in which people are differently positioned vis-à-vis the
land in terms (for example) of gender, class, age, or marital status.

This chapter examines, in turn, biodiversity, rights to land, and rights to
labor and its product to draw out conceptual issues germane to examining the
relationship between land tenure and biodiversity. The penultimate section of
the paper attempts to move research forward through a series of questions concerning land to which individualized rights are claimed, land where common
property rights are held, and places where there are collective rights to land
under individual control.

Whose Biodiversity?

Recognizing that small-scale farmers have nurtured plant genetic resources for
millennia, I begin an exploration of the relationship between biodiversity and
land tenure by examining the concept of local ecological knowledge and then
consider how such knowledge relates to global discourses of biodiversity, conservation, and sustainability. Variously accorded such names as *metis* (Scott 1998)
or "local traditional knowledge" (Ingold and Kurttila 1999), the concept is contrasted
with what is generally referred to as "scientific explanation" (Scott 1998, 323–28).

Common to these conceptualizations is the view that such knowledge is better defined in terms of skills and experience than as a set of identifiable facts or
principles. James Scott (1998), for example, defines *metis* as "a wide array of practical skills and acquired intelligence in responding to a constantly changing natural and human environment" (313). Such skills are learnt through practice and
applied with subtlety in particular situations. For Tim Ingold and Tehri Kurttila
(1999), local traditional knowledge is "generated in the practices of locality"; it is
"inseparable from actual practices of inhabiting the land" (2, 6). Such knowledge
consists of skills "regrown in each generation through training and experience
in the performance of particular tasks" (Ingold 2000, 5) rather than being a stock
of knowledge or an unchanging cultural heritage passed down intact from one
generation to the next—an artifact that can be separated from the context of its
production.

Ingold and Kurtilla (1999) distinguish this conception of local knowledge from "modern traditional knowledge," defined as knowledge that may claim to be traditional but is "enframed in the discourse of modernity" (17). For Arturo Escobar (1996, 56), it is through this second way of conceptualizing local knowledge that nature is capitalized in its postmodern form. In contrast to the capitalization of nature in its modern form, where nature is "defined and treated as an external, exploitable domain," a process that proceeds through the use of "expert," "scientific" discourses of modernity, the postmodern form of ecological capital has to do with "a new process of capitalization, effected primarily by a shift in representation [whereby] previously uncapitalized aspects of nature and society become internal to capital" (47). This second form of ecological capital proceeds not only through "the symbolic conquest of nature" (for example, through the establishment of biodiversity reserves and recognition of local communities as stewards of nature) but also through "the semiotic conquest of local knowledge" (56). In other words, local knowledge is valued but only to the extent that it has utilitarian value (57).

In this construction of local knowledge, people and communities are clearly recognized as "the source and creators of value—not merely as labor or raw material" (Escobar 1996, 57), a process achieved through discourses such as those of sustainable development and biodiversity (63). In contrast to the modern and exploitative form of ecological capital, the postmodern form is conservationist. It recognizes that production of local knowledge is critical for ensuring the sustainability of biodiversity, and local people in communities are seen as stewards of the land and its biological diversity. But in this conceptualization, local knowledge is extracted from the environ- ment in which it is created. It is not conceived to be part of "a complex cultural construction, involving movements and events profoundly historical and relational" (57). Nature becomes something "out there" that may be collected—in Escobar's words, "reinvented as environment so that capital, not nature and culture, may be sustained" (49).

Before considering tenurial conditions through which biodiversity is supported, it is necessary to consider what *local* means when local knowledge is referred to and ideals of biodemocracy invoked. All too frequently, the notion remains unproblematized. Where, as in sub-Saharan Africa, there is gender-differentiated responsibility for agricultural production in smallholding systems, it is vital to recognize women's primary responsibility for supporting genetic diversity (Leach and Fairhead 1995; Opole 1993; Rocheleau 1991, 1995; Worede and Mekbib 1993). It is also essential to recognize that local agricultural systems and communities are cross-cut by other axes of social differentiation—class, age, ethnicity—and that such differences, multiple and shifting, "fractured and fracturing" (Laurie et al. 1999, 26) as they are, affect people's experiential knowledge and thus land-use practices, which in turn affect plant genetic diversity. Dianne E. Rocheleau (1991, 1995), for example, has shown, not only the degree to which

women and men in Kathama, Machakos District, Kenya, have distinct environmental knowledge and the degree to which there has been "a feminization of
rural environmental science" (Rocheleau 1995, 13) with increased rates of male
migration to urban centers but also how, in times of drought, poor women rely
not just on their deep agricultural knowledge but also their political and social
skills in obtaining access to resources—private plots or public lands controlled
by men. Local knowledge of biodiversity, like global discourse, does not exist
beyond the purview of politics. It is parlayed into existence through the play of
social relations.

Struggles over Land: The Case of Murang'a District, Kenya

A key finding of Rocheleau's research is that women's rights of access and control of land frequently are not commensurate with their responsibilities for agricultural production or ecological sustainability. In this context, a central concern
in under- standing the relationship between tenure regime and biodiversity is to
ask not simply what set of property rights promotes biodiversity but whose
rights are secure under which system of tenure and how this, in turn, influences
land-use practices that maintain plant genetic diversity.

Land tenure in sub-Saharan Africa is more usefully conceptualized in terms
of rights of access and control than of ownership. The notion of ownership, as
H.W.O. Okoth-Ogendo (1978) has demonstrated, reflects Eurocentric values and
practices and exists only where there is exclusive control of land and where land
has, basically, sole value as a commodity. Property rights in Africa, he suggests,
are more accurately understood as complex systems of interlocking rights, each
right reflecting the power allocated to individuals for a particular purpose. Each
person holds a "bundle of rights" related to specific functions such as cultivation, grazing, or the collection of firewood. Each function carries with it "varying
degrees of control exercised at different levels of social organization" (63).

Distinguishing between rights of access and control and recognizing the complexity, elasticity, and overlapping nature of such rights leads to a more nuanced
understanding of the relationship to a land of people differently positioned with
respect (for example) to gender, age, wealth, or ethnicity. This distinction is also
vital in understanding how women's proprietary right in many societies was recognized under customary land law. The separation between rights of access (use
rights) and the right to allocate (understood by the right of control), and the sub-
ordination of the latter right to the economic functions of the former, secured
women's "proprietary position" (Okoth-Ogendo 1978, 508) in economies that
depend heavily on their labor.

The distinction is also critical in exploring questions of security of tenure
that, particularly where customary law prevails, rest on the resolution not only of
rights of access and control within the household but also of latent tension

between interests of the collective and the individual. Tenurial rights frequently concern both the rights of individuals to particular parcels of land and also rights to land held in common—that is, land that falls within the territorial jurisdiction of the kin group. These categories of rights may change seasonally or over time as agricultural land reverts to fallow or bush (Leach 1994). Rights to common land may also change through individual tenure-building practices. Thus, for example, rights to gather nontimber forest products to which the collective has use rights may be altered by bringing specific trees or wild food and medicinal plants under individual control (149–53). Further, in understanding tenure relations, it may be necessary to recognize that farmers differentiate between land and tree tenure and that there are frequently sanctions against women planting trees where those trees are considered to be territorial markers.

These rights may be customary, but that does not mean they are beyond the realm of political struggle. Deep historical analyses of customary law in Africa offer incontrovertible evidence of the degree to which custom provided the symbolic resource, or the discursive means, through which people struggled for control of land under colonial rule. People differentiated by class and gender claimed custom as a strategic and symbolic resource in the local struggle over land as this contest interrelated with the colonial state's efforts to legitimate its rule (Chanock 1985). My research in Murang'a District, an area of smallholdings in Central Province, Kenya (Mackenzie 1998), illustrates how customary law before and during colonial rule was part and parcel of social change and political struggle.

Before colonialism, security of tenure in Murang'a depended on the resolution of two sets of tensions. The first was between individual and collective rights to land of the (male) kinship group; the second was between women (as wives and producers but nonmembers of the kin collective) and men (non-producers, as far as basic crop production was concerned, yet members). Rights to land were, in both situations, subject to negotiation. Under colonial rule, customary law provided the means through which individuals or groups, differentiated by race, class, and gender, negotiated access to and control of land. Contradictory re-creations of customary law allowed, on the one hand, the state to alienate African land for settler agriculture. Here, customary law became an "ideological screen of continuity," a "language of legitimation" (Chanock 1985, 59, 4). On the other hand, it provided the political space through which Africans resisted colonial rule and reworked customary land law that privileged (male) rights to allocate land and the individual interests of wealthier men. As use rights were silenced in this dominant discourse of customary tenure, poorer men lost out, as did women. Their use rights became increasingly invisible in the growing conflict defined by race and class. It was not a matter of women's or poorer men's total exclusion from rights sanctioned by custom; but their tenurial security decreased, and customary land law then provided the symbolic means through which they constructed a discourse of resistance defined in terms of gender and class. Customary law was and remains a means through which people differentiated (among other things) by race, class, gender, or age assert, or attempt to assert, rights to land. Rights to land under such law are malleable and can be manipulated and are continuously re-created in the resolution of conflict (Mackenzie 1998).

Customary land law does not simply disappear with the introduction of freehold tenure or the establishment of contract production regimes. Research in Murang'a demonstrates that the new system of tenure—the consolidation of land and then its registration in individual freehold title, imposed by a colonial regime in the 1950s—does not preempt existing rights. Rather, what emerges is a complex picture in which people contest rights to land by drawing, as exigency demands or financial resources dictate, on whichever legal resource they can. And while it may indeed be the case that women's tenurial security is compromised in situations of legal plurality, and that even where they hold a title deed, they may not be able to exercise tenurial rights to land they own, women are highly resourceful in securing their rights (Mackenzie 1990).

Two instances, drawn from personal narratives collected in Murang'a in the 1980s, indicate something of the complexity of the struggle. In the first, Wacheke and her dying husband recognized her vulnerability in maintaining rights to the land when only their three daughters and no son had survived childhood. Her husband's stepbrother, Bibia, had sold his inheritance soon after land reform and wanted to acquire this land for his son. He was ready to claim it, on his step-brother's death, on the grounds of customary practice—that is, of ensuring that the land remained in the patriliny. To prevent Bibia from snatching the land, Wacheke and her husband decided that she should marry a woman with sons. An elderly man explained the political import of this practice of becoming a female husband: "If, for example, Kamande's mother [my wife], doesn't have a son, but only you, a daughter, who will marry and go away, that will be the end of our name. If we wish to retain our name, we can marry a girl and have her here and she can bear children with whomever she wishes. After our death, she would keep everything. Nobody could get this from her. Or a woman could marry a girl after the death of her husband."

Wacheke thus evoked a customary idiom, that of a female husband, to counter the maneuvering of her brother-in-law to gain control of the land to which, after her husband's death, she held the title deed. She explained that, after her husband had died, despite marrying a woman with sons and retaining the title deed in her name, she faced a constant struggle. She had managed to retain rights to the land but had been unable to give land to a married daughter, Nyambura, who lives in Ukambani but lacks land. Such a gift was promised by Wacheke's husband, but Wacheke dared not give Bibia grounds for further claim to the land, in this case because the gift would be construed as a loss of kin territory.

In a second instance, Wanjiku, a woman then in her early forties and a school principal, wanted to invest some of her savings in land registered in her name. She and her husband had previously combined their earnings to purchase 4.45 hectares to add to the 3.6 hectares that had been allocated to her husband by her parents on his marriage. Her husband had insisted that the land purchased from their joint savings be registered in his name alone. With persistence on her part, and after much dispute, he agreed that 0.1 hectares would be registered jointly in both names. Although she has (relatively) well-paid employment and two sons as well as three daughters, Wanjiku is conscious of her insecurity; with savings invested in land registered in her husband's name, she would have no recourse to this asset in the event of divorce. Thus, in 1982, she negotiated with a (female) friend to purchase 1.2 hectares of land on her behalf at some distance from her home. It had been difficult to save for this purchase because her husband insisted that she disclose all her finances to him, without reciprocation. Unfortunately, her husband learnt of the proposed purchase and warned her against engaging in such dealings again.

With respect to rights to land where contract farming has been introduced, research again suggests that women's security of tenure is threatened. In one dramatic example of the extension of irrigation in Jahaly-Pacharr swamps, the Gambia, women were unable to exercise their rights to the rice harvest even when, after their protests, irrigated land was registered in their names. As Judith Carney and Michael Watts (1990) show, men were able to turn customary rights pertaining to the distinction between individual and household land and labor to their advantage through their manipulation of specific customary idioms, thus taking control of the products of women's labor—rice. With respect to the sustainability of production, at issue in these cases are not only secure rights to land, although these are clearly central to the renegotiation of the conjugal contract, but also rights to labor and control of the product of labor expended on that land. I turn now to examine these issues in order to develop the argument that questions of maintenance of plant genetic diversity are integrally bound up in the complexity and diversity of social relationships.

Rights to Land, Labor, and the Product of Labor

Analysis of the politics of labor in the production of coffee in Murang'a District reveals the degree to which the household has become a deeply contested site in which rights to land, labor, and the product of labor are constantly subject to negotiation. On the basis of evidence that documents the insecurity women face with respect to these rights, particularly those women from poorer households, which are in the majority, and evidence that this insecurity is played out in terms of land use and management, I argue that it is essential to connect these issues to those of practices associated with the maintenance of biological diversity to understand how the maintenance of biodiversity is implicated in these political relationships.

Coffee was introduced in Murang'a as part of the 1954 Swynnerton Plan, and colonial agricultural officers targeted its production toward men. Nevertheless, officials noted that within a few years women formed the majority of coffee growers, numbering 16,000 of the total 26,000 growers, a proportion that has increased substantially in recent years, with rates of male outmigration reaching 75 percent in some areas. A crisis in the early 1980s, caused by the continuing drop in the quality of coffee exported from the district, made visible the fact that a lack of secure remuneration for women had led them to decide against prioritizing the harvesting of coffee on their own holdings.

The problem centered on the way in which coffee processing and marketing are organized through sixteen coffee societies, each a member of the Murang'a District Farmers' Cooperative Union (MDFCU). Because membership in the cooperative is based on title to the land, men are in the great majority of official members, constituting 89.9 percent of members in the case of the Njora Coffee Growers' Cooperative Society (total membership 5,784 in 1984) and 83.2 percent in the case of Irati (total membership 3,221 in 1984). It is they who received payments for coffee delivered to the societies; and as became clear, they frequently did not pass on money to their wives, who had labored on the crop.

Women's response to the lack of remuneration for their labor, in a situation where they generally held sole responsibility for meeting daily household needs, was to withdraw their labor. This withdrawal became more acute as the effects of structural adjustment programs (undertaken by the state after agreements with the World Bank) were felt at the local level. With an increased emphasis on export earnings from coffee, costs were shifted from the paid to the unpaid economy, and social relations became increasingly polarized (Elson 1994, Gladwin 1991). Women from resource-poor households who did not receive adequate compensation for their labor on coffee were particularly vulnerable. Resistance was both individual and collective. At the individual or family level, women and children could be seen boarding trucks in great numbers during the picking season for the short journey to coffee estates in Kandara and Makuyu divisions of Murang'a or to Kiambu District. By working for wages on the estates, rather than tending coffee on their husbands' land, they were able to secure remuneration for their labor.

Women also renegotiated the conjugal contract by invoking the customary idiom of *ngwatio*, a practice that in the past had centered on reciprocal labor arrangements—for example, working as a group in turn on each others' farms during peak labor periods. But now the groups sold their labor power for a wage, able to command a higher wage by picking coffee collectively than would otherwise have been possible. In more formal *mabati* (literally, metal roof) groups, which had begun as rotating savings and loans societies in the late 1960s, women in the 1980s also turned increasingly to activities designed to earn an income that they, as individuals, could control (Mackenzie 1987).

The response of the MDFCU to the decline in coffee quality in the early 1980s was to encourage members to change from individual (male) accounts to joint (spousal) accounts at the four savings and credit sections (SCS) of the union. The success of this initiative may be gauged from the fact that, between 1982 and 1984, 40.8 percent of the accounts at the one SCS where research was conducted, Maragua SCS, had changed from individual (male) accounts to joint accounts. The senior savings clerk explained the wide discrepancy in the percentage of joint accounts among the six coffee societies belonging to this SCS (from 17.1 percent in the case of Njora to 55.4 percent and 79.2 percent, respectively, for Irati and Thanga-ini) on the grounds of far higher rates of male outmigration in the latter two areas. Although these figures do not in themselves guarantee that women will be able to exercise the control they need over the proceeds of their labor, they do suggest at least a degree of success in reconstituting gender relations in their favor by negotiating the politics of coffee production.

Together with research such as that of Judith Carney and Michael Watts (1990) and Richard Schroeder (1999) in the Gambia, and Catherine S. Dolan (2001) in Meru, Kenya, the Murang'a study demonstrates the complexity and negotiability of rights and responsibilities when economic survival is at stake. Yet none of this research explores the implications of intensified conflict over local resources for issues concerning biodiversity. It is not difficult to draw out the possible implications of intensified crop production for the market, a deepening of intra-household struggle that accompanies this action, frequently accompanied by the growing casualization of women's labor, and the increased demands on women's labor time under structural adjustment programs, for issues of ecological significance.

At the conceptual level, a brief discussion of the politics of soil management practices suggests ways in which research that focuses on ecological issues, specifically biodiversity, may be taken forward. Research carried out in Murang'a (Mackenzie 1995) suggested that sustainable management of the soil was bound up not only with the level of wealth or poverty of the household but also with how successfully women (with primary, and often exclusive, responsibility for agricultural production) were able to secure rights to land and labor. The research suggested that the option value (Blaikie 1989) of maintaining the soil through labor-intensive practices such as mulching or green manuring may decline with lowered security and that women may compromise their knowledge as farmers in the effort to meet immediate household responsibilities. Their deep and ecologically precise knowledge of particular places and practices that support genetic diversity may be threatened as a result of such choices. It may also be threatened as genetically uniform crops such as hybrid or composite maizes displace those crops that they have bred for ecological specificity, and as there is a decline in "the spaces between" (Rocheleau 1995, 12): hedgerows, the edges of paths or roads, or areas of woodland or grass found among the cultivated plots, where women used to gather wild foods. Ritu Verma's (2001) recent research supports these observations, showing unequivocally how politically embedded are the everyday practices of soil management. In the context of Maragoli, Western Kenya, she deepens the analysis by demonstrating how people differentiated by gender, class, age, marital status, and life-cycle position, negotiate rights to land, labor (on the farm and off the farm), and the product of labor and how struggles concerning these rights, caught up themselves in processes of macroeconomic change, play out with respect to land use and management practices.

Toward a Framework for Research

The relationship between land tenure and biodiversity cannot be divorced from the broader political economy.[2] With reference to that relationship and the more general issue of whose rights are secure under which tenurial regimes and how this influences land-use practices associated with plant genetic diversity, I propose the following questions, both to move research forward and to conceptualize relationships among people, land rights, and biodiversity. For heuristic purposes, I divide the questions into three sections: (1) land to which individualized rights are claimed, (2) land to which rights are held in common, and (3) land under individual control to which there are collective rights.

Land to Which Individual Rights Are Claimed

A key question emerges from research in Murang'a District, where tenure is increasingly individualized: to what extent have people differentiated, among other things, by gender, class, age, or marital status changed practices of land use that may previously have ensured the maintenance of crop genetic diversity? A second question follows: to what extent do new practices contribute to enhancing crop biodiversity? Further questions follow: in attempts to exert individual rights to land, what tenure building practices are employed? Who can employ them—women? men? differentiated by age and stage of life cycle? migrants compared to long-term residents or others? For example, to what extent is the planting of specific crops or trees part of a strategy of tenure building? On what symbolic resources do people rely in trying to assert these rights? What are the implications of such measures for increasing biodiversity in a particular area? In situations where the state promotes the expansion of a crop such as coffee for export, or where the production of a crop such as rice or maize is singled out as a priority for meeting urban food requirements, what strategies do people (differentiated by class, gender, age, or social position in terms of their tenurial rights) choose to minimize risks? Do these strategies affect practices that previously ensured the maintenance of biodiversity?

Research by Robert McC. Netting and M. Priscilla Stone (1996) shows that by producing for both subsistence and the market, Kofyar farmers in Nigeria "necessarily discourage specialisation and propagate agro-diversity under circumstances of increasing resource scarcity and higher population pressure" because it reduces risk, provides a measure of insurance, contributes to long-term resource productivity, and allows for the optimal use of available labor (53). Jane Guyer (1996) and H.B.S. Kandeh and Paul Richards (1996) also provide evidence of benefits with respect to biodiversity under situations of social and economic change, including intensification of production associated with commodification and an increase in population.

Recent research in the cotton zone of southwest Burkina Faso, although not explicitly addressing the issue of biodiversity, supports the view that intensification of production, associated with an increase in population, leads to soil building (Gray and Kevane 2001). Leslie C. Gray and Michael Kevane also argue that soil building is linked to tenure building although, interestingly, they claim that tenurial status has little bearing on a farmer's choice to invest in soil quality. Their evidence suggests that farmers with less secure access to land invest in the soil through practices such as manuring, crop rotation, and leaving trees in fields to improve their tenurial rights. Research by Eve L. Crowley and Simon E. Carter (2000) draws attention to the need for precise investigation into soil management practices that vary in time and space and to relate changes in practice to changes in people's access to land, labor, and capital and to the ecological specificity of their knowledge, to crop preference, and to the market. Questions that arise from this work and that of Gray and Kevane (2001) concern the complex interrelationships among intensification of production, land tenure, social differentiation, soil management, and plant genetic diversity. For example, is it women or men from poorer households (who have previously had less reliance on the market in terms of obtaining seeds) who have been the principal custodians of genetic variety? If so, to what extent have recent changes in production, soil management regime, and land tenure affected their practices associated with ensuring the maintenance of biodiversity?

Where contract farming has been introduced, what effect does such production have for the negotiation of intra-household rights to land, and what are the implications for plant genetic diversity? Catherine S. Dolan's (2001) study of the production of French beans in Meru as part of a strategy promoted by the World Bank to diversify agriculture in Kenya shows how horticulture, previously a domain in which women could exercise control in the production of local vegetables for household use and for sale in local markets, has been "rapidly intensified, commoditised and, in many cases, appropriated by men" (40). What are the implications for local biodiversity when local vegetables that were previously more widely grown are increasingly displaced by beans of genetic uniformity for export outside the country?

From the research identified here, it is clear that, given the specificity not only of ecological issues but their deep embeddedness in matters of politics—of household, community, state, and global trade regime—that future research must engage in not only locally precise questions but also questions about how very local matters are interconnected with those at wider scales of inquiry.

Land Subject to Common Property Regimes

A critical question concerning land where common property regimes are the basis of production is how are rights to land managed as tenure becomes increasingly individualized? Other questions follow: are collective regulatory procedures under threat because of changes in the local or broader political economy (for example, extension of hectarages for the production of crops for the market)? What types of regulatory procedures stimulate conservation of biodiversity?

With reference to these questions, it is useful to refer to Margaret A. McKean's (2000) list of attributes or principles that are critical for the success of common property regimes. They include the right of user groups to organize without interference, distinct boundaries of the resource in question, clear and enforceable rules, a fair rather than egalitarian distribution of decision-making rights, and a devolved authority structure that permits flexibility at the most local level (43–48). Critical of this "bureaucratic model of common property resource management," Frances Cleaver (2000) proposes a "moral ecological framework" in which institutions are conceived as "embodiments of social process," negotiated through cultural meanings, symbols, and values in any particular context (365). Drawing on research in Zimbabwe, she argues that institutions that manage common property resources are "partial, intermittent and indeed often invisible, being located in the daily interactions of ordinary lives." Collective action "is as often organized around reproductive as productive activities, is frequently ad hoc, variable and not necessarily output-optimizing" (381). As I have mentioned, such observations imply that deeply ethnographic research is needed to capture the meanings and values attached to common property.

Such an approach is also needed to address other specific questions. Is land held in common gaining in significance in terms of maintaining plant genetic diversity in places where agricultural land is under individual control and there is increased production for the market? What are the tenurial rights (for example, of gathering) to extensive areas held in common and the places between cultivated fields or along the sides of streams or roads? Does the significance of in-between spaces increase as larger areas of common property (for example, forests) decline? How are rights to common property, including gathering rights, differentiated, for example, by gender, age, wealth, marital, or "insider" versus "outsider" status? How are such rights legitimized? How do these rights vary according to the type of resource? In what ways have they changed with a decrease of forest land or other land held in common? What are the implications of these changes for biodiversity? Joann McGregor's (1995) work in Shurugwi, one of Zimbabwe's most deforested communal areas, is useful in demonstrating the degree of precision needed in research of these questions. She shows how tenurial rights may vary, for example, with respect to indigenous fruit and rights to naturally regenerating trees (which local people may view as common property even when they are located on privatized land); rights to indigenous fruit on planted trees (in which labor has clearly been invested), in contrast, are seen as individual.

Under what conditions do people engage actively in building rights to common property and by so doing increase biodiversity? In this context, Fairhead and Leach (1996) provide dramatic evidence from the forest-savanna transition zone of the Republic of Guinea of an increase in forest cover (taking the form of "forest islands") associated with increases in population, contradicting the narratives of "experts" from the days of colonial rule to the present. The authors demonstrate the degree to which people here are actively engaged in supporting biodiversity.

Finally, what is the role of the state in the management of common property? If relations between a body such as a forestry commission and local people are adversarial, what forms do acts of resistance take, and do they lead to misuse of the forest so that genetic diversity is negatively affected? Frank M. Matose's (1994) research in the Mafungautsi Forest Area of northwest Zimbabwe, for example, identifies several means through which, in a situation of political conflict, certain groups of people who had lost rights to land resisted the efforts of the forestry commission to exert control by gathering prohibited forest and non-forest products in defiance of regulations. Research is needed to assess the impact of these actions on biodiversity.

Land under Individual Control to Which There Are Collective Rights

Research by Lisa Leimar Price (1997) suggests a need to examine the relationship between land tenure and biodiversity not only in situations of individualized tenure or common property regimes but also where collective rights may be exercised over land under individual control. Her insightful study of wild plants in Northeast Thailand focuses on the changing and socially intricate relationship between rights to plants and land tenure in a matrilineal and matrilocal society in which land under women's control has become increasingly privatized. Her research suggests that, in this context, an individual's right to harvest wild plant food is related to both local concepts of tenure (the negotiability of collective gathering rights to privately held land) and how a plant species is ranked with respect to taste, market value, and rarity (217). She sees social consensus at the community level as critical for protecting collective gathering rights on privately owned agricultural land and, with state law, for restricting rights to gather wild plants for the market and sometimes household consumption when a wild plant is recognized as rare.

In this system, women own the agricultural land and, as gatherers, managers, and marketers of wild food plants, possess knowledge of the status of particular species and the authority gained over time, through practices of matrilocality, to build consensus around restrictions to gathering as well as support usufruct rights to land under private tenure. As Price (2001) notes, we do not know "how such species level systems of increasing protection and privatization function in contexts where women are lacking the authority over agricultural land, long term social networks, and female kinship networks." Nor do we know "the different valuations men versus women place on selected species and where conflict and cooperation may emerge" (19).

Her work suggests that research is needed into social processes that sanction collective rights to gather wild plant foods from agricultural land under individual control. Are such institutions socially inclusive? How do collective rights vary according to the type of resource gathered or whether the plant is to be used for household consumption or the market? Finally, in what ways and under what conditions does the exercise of such rights, and production for the market as well as for consumption, support or undermine genetic diversity?

Conclusion

In this chapter, I make a case for research that explores the relationship between land-based property rights and biodiversity, recognizing that this field has been much neglected. I have viewed the relationship through the lens of poststructural political ecology and primarily in the context of sub-Saharan Africa, drawing on my own research in Murang'a District, Kenya, and the related work of other researchers concerning relationships between people and the land. A poststructural political ecology approach demonstrates the political embeddedness of the relationship between people and land and recognizes that this relationship is bound up with not only material relations of production but also the frameworks of meaning through which land rights are negotiated. Although the chapter focuses principally on the local level, it also makes clear that the local does not exist in isolation from the global but is co-produced with it.

This last point is clearest in my discussion of "whose biodiversity?" which argues that notions of biodiversity and local knowledge must be problematized. First, the discussion shows how local knowledge of genetic diversity may be caught up in what Escobar (1996) has referred to as modern and postmodern forms of ecological capital through discourses of development and sustainability. Second, it indicates how local experiential knowledge must be contextualized within the complexity of political relations that inform rights to land, specifically axes of social differentiation such as gender, class, and age. These, in turn, are related, among other things, to structural adjustment programs that may demand an increase in genetically uniform crops for the export market.

The argument concerning the political embeddedness of the issue of biodiversity can be extended by drawing on poststructural political ecology to demonstrate the complexity of people's rights to land. Evidence from Murang'a shows that this complexity centers on how people, differentiated by gender and class, claim rights to land through different legal resources, whether these resources are defined by custom or by the state. Legal resources are malleable and manipulable and provide legitimizing frameworks through which control over land is both exerted and resisted.

Recognizing that people's relationship to the land is defined not only by tenurial rights, I consider how rights to labor and the product of that labor influence land-use practices. Research conducted in Murang'a does not allow this argument to be extended as far as the question of maintaining biodiversity, but it does show clearly how land-use practices associated with the soil are part of a nexus of political relationships within the family and the broader political economy. Rocheleau's (1995) work in Machakos District, Kenya, makes explicit this connection with genetic diversity.

Near the end of the chapter, I posed a series of questions to move the research agenda concerning the political embeddedness of biodiversity and its relationship to land use and land tenure, distinguishing between land to which individual rights are claimed, land to which rights are held in common, and land under individual control to which collective rights are negotiated.

Certain methodological implications follow directly from this discussion. First, given the intricacy of the relationship between the political and the ecological and the complexity of rights to land, locally precise work is needed. It must focus on not only material processes associated with people's rights to the land but also the meanings and values through which people define themselves in terms of the land, including the much neglected area of spiritual connection to the land. In-depth ethnographic methods, including personal narratives and participant observation, are thus called for. But although this argumentation implies a case study approach, my previous discussion makes it clear that case studies cannot exist in a vacuum. Poststructural political ecology theorizing has shown how intricately connected the local is with the global. In this context, Burawoy et al.'s (2000) concept of global ethnography is particularly insightful. Here, the challenge for research into land and biodiversity is to explore the ways through which the locally specific is interconnected with extralocal social, political, and economic domains, often evidenced through discourses such as those of sustainability and biodiversity.

NOTES

1. I would like to thank the International Development Research Centre, Ottawa, which gave me a sabbaticant award supporting research on which this chapter is based. My particular thanks go to Kathleen Flynn Dapaah and Sheri Arnot for assistance in identifying key literature.

2. With respect to questions of security of tenure and long-term agricultural sustainability, I have not addressed the issue of HIV/AIDS. Research is urgently needed into the question of security of tenure in areas where death rates are high and acute loss of local ecological knowledge may be occurring and into subsequent effects of this situation on the maintenance of crop genetic diversity.

REFERENCES

Blaikie, Piers. 1989. "Environment and Access to Resources in Africa." *Africa* 59, no. 1: 18–40.

Blaikie, Piers, and Harold Brookfield. 1987. *Land Degradation and Society.* London: Methuen.

Braun, Bruce, and Noel Castree, eds. 1998. *Remaking Reality: Nature at the Millenium.* London: Routledge.

Burawoy, Michael, Joseph Blum, Sheba George, Zsusa Gille, Teresa Gowan, Lynne Haney, Maren Klawiter, Steven Lopez, Seán Ó Riain, and Millie Thayer. 2000. *Global Ethnography.* Los Angeles: University of California Press.

Carney, Judith, and Michael Watts. 1990. "Manufacturing Dissent: Work, Gender, and the Politics of Meaning in a Peasant Society." *Africa* 60, no. 2: 207–40.

Chanock, Martin. 1985. *Law, Custom and Social Order: The Colonial Experience in Malawi and Zambia.* Cambridge: Cambridge University Press.

Cleaver, Frances. 2000. "Moral Ecological Rationality, Institutions, and the Management of Common Property Resources." *Development and Change* 31, no. 2: 361–83.

Crowley, Eve L., and Simon E. Carter. 2000. "Agrarian Change and the Changing Relationships between Toil and Soil in Maragoli, Western Kenya (1900–1994)." *Human Ecology* 28, no. 3: 383–414.

Dolan, Catherine S. 2001. "The 'Good Wife': Struggles over Resources in the Kenyan Horticultural Sector." *Journal of Development Studies* 37, no. 3: 39–70.

Elson, Diane. 1994. "Micro, Meso, Macro: Gender and Economic Analysis in the Context of Policy Reform." In *The Strategic Silence: Gender and Economic Policy,* edited by Isabella Bakker, 33–45. London: Zed.

Escobar, Arturo. 1996. "Constructing Nature: Elements for a Poststructural Political Ecology." In *Liberation Ecologies,* edited by Richard Peet and Michael Watts, 46–68. London: Routledge.

Fairhead, James, and Melissa Leach. 1996. *Misreading the African Landscape: Society and Ecology in a Forest-Savanna Mosaic.* Cambridge: Cambridge University Press.

Gladwin, Christina H., ed. 1991. *Structural Adjustment and African Women Farmers.* Gainesville: University of Florida Press.

Gray, Leslie C., and Michael Kevane. 2001. "Evolving Tenure Rights and Agricultural Intensification in Southwestern Burkina Faso." *World Development* 29, no. 4: 573–87.

Guyer, Jane. 1996. "Diversity at Different Levels: Farm and Community in Western Nigeria." *Africa* 66, no. 1: 71–89.

Howard-Borgas, P. L., and W. Cuijpers. 2002. "Gender Relations in Local Plant Genetic Resource Management and Conservation." In *Encyclopedia of Life Support Systems.* Oxford: UNESCO.

Ingold, Tim. 2000. *The Perception of the Environment: Essays in Livelihood, Dwelling, and Skill.* London: Routledge.

Ingold, Tim, and Tehri Kurttila. 1999. "Perceiving the Environment in Finnish Lapland." Manchester, England: University of Manchester, Department of Anthropology. Unpublished paper.

Kandeh, H.B.S., and Paul Richards. 1996. "Rural People As Conservationists: Querying Neo-Malthusian Assumptions about Biodiversity in Sierra Leone." *Africa 66*, no. 1: 90–103.

Laurie, Nina, Claire Dwyer, Sarah Holloway, and Fiona Smith. 1999. *Geographies of New Femininities.* Harlow, England: Longman.

Leach, Melissa. 1994. *Rainforest Relations: Gender and Resource Use among the Mende of Gola, Sierra Leone.* Edinburgh: Edinburgh University Press.

Leach, Melissa, and James Fairhead. 1995. "Ruined Settlements and New Gardens: Gender and Soil-Ripening among Kuranko Farmers in the Forest-Savanna Transition Zone." *IDS Bulletin 26*, no. 1: 24–32.

Mackenzie, A. Fiona D. 1987. "Local Organization: Confronting Contradiction in a Small-Holding District of Kenya." *Cahiers de Géographie du Québec 31*, no. 83: 273–86.

———. 1990. "Gender and Land Rights in Murang'a District, Kenya." *Journal of Peasant Studies 17*, no. 4: 609–43.

———. 1995. "'A Farm Is Like a Child Who Cannot Be Left Unguarded': Gender, Land and Labour in Central Province, Kenya." *IDS Bulletin 26*, no. 1: 17–23.

———. 1998. *Land, Ecology and Resistance in Kenya, 1880–1952.* Edinburgh: Edinburgh University Press.

Matose, Frank M. 1994. "Local People's Uses and Perceptions of Forest Resources: An Analysis of a State Property Regime in Zimbabwe." Master's thesis, University of Alberta.

McGregor, Joann. 1994. "Gathering Produce in Zimbabwe's Communal Areas: Changing Resource Availability and Use." *Ecology of Food and Nutrition. 33*: 163–93.

McKean, Margaret A. 2000. "Common Property: What Is It, What Is It Good for, and What Makes It Work." In *People and Forests: Communities, Institutions, and Governance*, edited by Clark C. Gibson, Margaret A. McKean, and Elinor Ostrom, 27–55. Cambridge, Mass.: MIT Press.

Mooney, Pat R. 1996. "The Parts of Life: Agricultural Biodiversity, Indigenous Knowledge, and the Role of the Third System." *Development Dialogue 1–2*: 7–183.

Netting, Robert McC., and M. Priscilla Stone. 1994. "Agro-Diversity on a Farming Frontier: Kofyar Smallholders on the Benue Plains of Central Nigeria." *Africa 66*, no. 1: 52–70.

Neumann, Roderick. 1998. *Imposing Wilderness: Struggles over Livelihood and Nature Preservation in Africa.* Berkeley: University of California Press.

Okoth-Ogendo, H.W.O. 1978. "The Political Economy of Land Law: An Essay in the Legal Organization of Underdevelopment in Kenya, 1895–1974." Ph.D. diss., Yale University.

Opole, Monica. 1993. "Revalidating Women's Knowledge on Indigenous Vegetables: Implications for Policy." In *Cultivating Knowledge*, edited by Walter de Boef, Kojo Amanor, and Kate Wellard, with Anthony Bebbington, 157–64. London: Intermediate Technology Publications.

Peet, Richard, and Michael Watts, eds. 1996. *Liberation Ecologies.* London: Routledge.

Price, Lisa Leimar. 1997. "Wild Plant Food in Agricultural Environments: A Study of Occurrence, Management, and Gathering Rights in Northeast Thailand." *Human Organization 56*, no. 2: 209–21.

———. 2001. "Women at the Center: 'Wild' Plant Food Use, Gathering Rights, and Management in Disturbed Farming Environments." Paper prepared for the Workshop on Comparing and Contrasting Different Approaches on Uncultivated Plant Foods, Harare, Zimbabwe, September 4–6.

Rocheleau, Dianne E. 1991. "Gender, Ecology, and the Science of Survival: Stories and Lessons from Kenya." *Agricultural and Human Values* (winter–spring): 156–65.

———. 1995. "Gender and Biodiversity: A Feminist Political Ecology Perspective." *IDS Bulletin* 26, no. 1: 9–16.

Schroeder, Richard A. 1999. *Shady Practices: Agroforestry and Gender Politics in the Gambia.* Berkeley: University of California Press.

Scott, James. 1994. *Seeing Like a State: How Certain Schemes to Improve the Human Condition Have Failed.* New Haven, Conn.: Yale University Press.

Verma, Ritu. 2001. *Gender, Land, and Livelihoods in East Africa: Through Farmers' Eyes.* Ottawa: International Development Research Centre.

Worede, Melaku, and Hailu Mekbib. 1993. "Linking Genetic Resource Conservation to Farmers in Ethiopia." In *Cultivating Knowledge*, edited by Walter de Boef, Kojo Amanor, and Kate Wellard, with Anthony Bebbington, 78–84. London: Intermediate Technology Publications.

7

The Political Ecology of Consumption

Beyond Greed and Guilt

JOSIAH McC. HEYMAN

The Politics of Perspective

Students, scientists, and activists are increasingly concerned about how modern consumption affects the environment.[1] There are good reasons for this concern. Mathis Wackernagel and William E. Rees's (1996) ecological footprint method shows how consumption of final goods (like food), services (like travel), and supplies (like electricity) directly and indirectly use and degrade a significant portion of the earth's resources. Appropriately, concern about consumption is growing among the prosperous people of the world—in both overdeveloped and underdeveloped societies—as they anxiously contemplate their use of energy and materials. Such worries are well expressed in the title and content of Alan Durning's (1992) activist book, *How Much Is Enough?* Two assumptions undergird the thinking of Durning and similar critics. One is that consumption is a matter of desire and volition: I *want* this car. The other is that it is a matter of personal choice: *I* want this car. Over many years of teaching about wealth and poverty, development, material goods, and the environment, I have found that students alternate between greed and guilt about consumption precisely as a result of thinking within those confining assumptions. These assumptions have other effects also: they draw our attention to items about which we make conscious choices, such as clothes or fast food; and they render invisible less individualistic kinds of consumption such as houses, transportation, water, sewage, energy, education, and so on. (See Carrier and Heyman 1997 for a more thorough discussion of these issues.)

The working poor of Agua Prieta, Sonora, Mexico (a small city on the U.S.-Mexico border) offer an illuminating contrast. They are just as concerned with consumption but from an opposite perspective: they worry about not being able to consume enough. Between 1982 and 1986, purchasing power in Mexico fell by nearly one-half due to the nation's massive debt to U.S. banks and the extreme austerity measures imposed so that debt payments could be extracted from the

Mexican people. Purchasing power has risen and fallen since then, but the situation remains essentially the same as it was in 1984 to 1986, when I lived in Agua Prieta. People there worried constantly about consumption, but not just because they were deprived and wanted more stuff. It was because they relied on key purchased goods, services, and inputs (a good example being electricity) as an inescapable part of their way of life, and they faced difficulties in meeting those needs. Another reason they were so aware of consumption is that many of them worked in *maquiladoras* (factories) making goods (such as shirts and televisions) for the visibly wealthier U.S. market just across the boundary. Comparisons to the materialist colossus of the north were unavoidable. Precisely because Aguapretense were preoccupied with survival as consumers, they talked about consumption frequently and in heartfelt ways so that I follow their lead in studying and writing about this subject.[2]

In this chapter, I discuss three politics of consumption: the politics of perspective and knowledge, political ecology, and immediate political struggles over goods and services. The first topic is raised by comparing environmentalist and Aguapretense viewpoints. In the former perspective, consumption can be understood as personal but also troubling; in the latter perspective, it can be seen as a largely external force but also good. This is not to say that there is no objective ground to our discussion. Importantly, the tiny consumer actions of working-class Mexicans do have significant ecological effects when added up by the thousands and millions. A good example is beef consumption, which significantly increased when people migrated to the city from rural Sonoran villages (where ironically they raise but rarely eat cattle) and which in turn is linked to degradation of arid pasturelands (Sheridan 1988; Heyman 2001b, 148). These processes cannot be erased by declaring them simply matters of meaning and point of view. But inequalities in formulating knowledge and perspective are crucial to how facts are recognized and connected together and how policy (collective social action) is decided and implemented on ostensibly factual bases. In particular, anxieties about environmental damage in overdeveloped nations—indeed, I would say the projection of guilt from the self onto others—helps nongovernmental environmental organizations raise money and frame conservation policy in the underdeveloped world (Carrier in press).

The dominant politics of perspective on consumption favor two consumption policies. One, moral suasion, plays on people's environmental awareness and guilt to bring about conscious efforts at ameliorating environmental damage. Recycling is an excellent example because it is easy to make people aware of what they personally discard and recycling fits the emotional, personal, and volitional biases of our characteristic politics of ecological knowledge. The moral values embedded in everyday consumption, however, are internally complex and differ from setting to setting, specifically between working-class Mexicans and middle-class U.S. residents. The other policy is price incentives. Important resources, such as fossil fuel energy, sometimes have artificially low prices that encourage their excess use. Even were the full market price to be charged, it does not take into account the full cost of environmental effects, such as global warming and smog. Under the "I want this car" assumption, changing the price structure should motivate people to use resources more appropriately and conservatively. But this assumes that prosperous consumers have a good deal of discretion and flexibility and can respond to price incentives by changing consumption intensities. As we shall see, raising resource prices amounts to a punitive tax for poor working people whose historically sedimented, intricately organized way of life does not permit them to cut back significantly on use of water, electricity, propane, and so on. Both moral suasion and price incentives have their place, but this chapter proposes that we widen our vision of politics to include popular involvement in making and learning environmental knowledge about consumption and that we also consider how to increase the capabilities of poor consumers to act on that knowledge.

Consumption As Human, Consumption As Capitalist

I learned about consumption in Agua Prieta from middle-aged to elderly women, the veritable masters of this craft. Not only had they spent many years doing laundry, cooking, cleaning, drawing water, and so on; but they actively monitored relative prices in two nations (Mexico and the United States); transmitted and received gossip about good deals on used furniture, appliances, and other consumer durables; and managed the blended income from their daughters' factory jobs, their husbands' day labors, their sons' undocumented work in the United States, and their own microscopic house-front stores. I also spent considerable time hanging out in small mechanical and welding shops, where I witnessed the equivalent male world centered on cars, trucks, and repairable appliance motors and mechanisms. Encountering consumption from this grassroots, ethnographic perspective, one is struck by the craft, intelligence, toil, meaning, and nurturing love for family members and friends encapsulated in consumption (Miller 2001). A good example of this at the border was Mexicans shopping in the United States, especially before the severe peso devaluations of the 1980s made it more expensive to buy things in dollars. Women's skill in knowing which groceries (chicken, fresh milk, diapers) were cheaper in the United States embodied both their dedication to the well-being of their families and their intellectual mastery of the complicated opportunities of border economics. And for housewives, getting out of the house was sheer pleasure. Prosperous working men told similar stories of shopping for used construction materials, welding supplies, car parts, and tools.

Consumption is indeed a rich, rewarding, and deeply human activity. Although cultures differ enormously in economic relations and material items, there is no situation devoid of activities we can conceive of as consumption. Consumption is not just using up goods. Not only is there final consumption, such as eating food (and, of course, even what is referred to as final consumption produces waste products); but there are many activities of productive consumption, such as the unpaid and often unrecognized labors of housewives cooking food. At the same time, people conduct these life-renewing and life-affirming activities within specific ecological and social relations. The politics of who could get a local visa to shop in the United States (Heyman 2001a), the economics of purchasing mass-manufactured commodities, and the ecology of drawing on resources (for example, agro-industrial chicken) transferred from significantly different habitats all matter greatly. The different arrangements of this human fundamental, then, constitute our second politics of consumption and ecology, which we will approach through the prism of political ecology. An example of this level of analysis is the conversion of natural flows and substances into objects (commodities) that can be sold and consumed according to a metric (money) that differs in crucial ways from the transfer of energy and nutrients in nature (Greenberg 1998, Hornborg 2001). Another inquiry concerns the effects of capitalist relations on the organization of time and space, especially within the work of consumption. Important questions of perspective and policy on consumption and environment, then, cannot be understood without intellectual work at the level of political ecology.[3]

Political ecology of this sort, however, can be dauntingly abstract. It is hard to envision how one would concretely recognize it or go about studying it. Allow me, then, to digress briefly on how I studied consumption in Agua Prieta. I drew on four methods: participant observation, inventories of household material belongings, open-ended interviews focused on the histories of specific appliances, and contextualizing of ethnographic material with historical documentation. As mentioned, through participant observation (visiting people's houses, small stores, workshops, and so on), I was immersed in the daily life of consumption. With time, I applied more systematic methods to the subject. First, I collected a set of information about the material items in a family's house and yard; I also included the house itself and its components.[4] Questions included when and how acquired (given, purchased, and so on), from what person or store, for how much, whether or not the purchase involved credit or time payments, whether it was new or used when purchased, who it was considered to belong to, what it was used for (and if it worked), where in the house it was located, what was its quality and status, and so forth. The volume of goods (such as clothes and utensils) belonging even to a relatively poor border Mexican household is surprisingly large, and asking a robust set of questions about each and every item taxed the patience of my hosts and myself. I focused on items belonging to two sets. One was to inventory all the major tools of productive consumption: house, vehicles, major appliances, furniture, televisions, radios, and stereos. Then, to be sure I had captured personal and collective meanings (not just practical chores), I selected ten items that were visibly decorative or that people volunteered to me as personally significant.

A second method stemmed from the first one, illustrating directly how to address political-ecological questions in an ethnographic way. This method consisted of long, open-ended interviews in which I systematically traced the history of houses, major appliances, and vehicles for eight households, going over some of the questions just listed (how acquired, when, and so on) but this time locating them in the more ample context of extended family histories collected at the same time. And I did this not just for the immediate item at hand (say, a propane stove) but for all previous items of the same kind or past technological equivalents: cast-iron woodstoves and, before that, shaped clay ovens. Importantly, my informants enjoyed appliance histories; and they readily and effectively made connections between key appliance dates and important events in their lives, such as marriage or moving from a peasant farm to a mining town or border city.

To contextualize these appliance histories, I drew on primary and secondary historical sources on northern Mexico and the western United States. The historical material enabled me to trace dates and places in major patterns of political, economic, and ecological change that had taken place in the region during the previous century and connect those patterns to the specifics of appliance histories. For example, one could identify times and places when typical Mexican goods that had been made either by consumers-users themselves or purchased from regional craftspeople were replaced by mass-manufactured commodities brought from the United States, either by returning migrant workers or by North American–owned mine company stores, and observe how this pattern had persisted to the present day in the Mexican border city (although today more goods are made in Mexico).

The analytic framework of this study brings together information and experience from multiple sources and analyzes dynamics at different scales, ranging from contemporary household economics to regional history. The approach illuminates connections between the geographic penetration of capitalism into Mexico, the commoditization of paid wage labor, the commoditization of unpaid labor (productive consumption), and the technological-ecological connection of consumers to fossil fuels and other commoditized natural inputs (water, electricity, propane, gasoline, and so on). It also pays attention to the personal meaning of these transformations. For example, Francisco, as a young man in the 1940s, learned to drive and repair a truck for a high country sawmill. Mechanical work became his lifelong occupation and fascination, which he passed along to his son, as I discovered when I visited their small workshop. He had used a new commodity, for a period had become a commodity himself (a laborer), yet remained a full human being alive with craft and intelligence.

Findings from this research, as well as in-depth discussions of the interpretation and analyses of the material, have been published elsewhere, forming
the basis for the analytical generalizations that follow (see especially Heyman
1994a, 1994b, 1990, 1991, 1997, 2001b; Carrier and Heyman 1997). A key pattern
that emerged was consumer proletarianization (Heyman 1994b, 180). *Proletarianization* is a social science term (originally from Karl Marx) that refers to the historical process by which people lose control of the means of production—land,
tools, resources, and so on. Once people become proletarians, they have to work
for the capitalists who own those means of production, thus bringing widespread wage labor into being. By imperfect analogy, consumer proletarianization
refers to householders and localities that lose the traditional devices, raw materials, skills, and social relations needed to produce their daily existence: to heat
their houses, cook their food, cover their roofs, and so on. In the consumer
proletarianization case, the product (everyday goods and services) goes to individuals and families; but having lost the main means of self-provisioning, consumers must purchase commodity inputs from the capitalist economy—
appliances, construction materials, grocery store food, manufactured clothing,
and so on.

Classic Marxist literature focused specifically on paid labor outside the
home and unconsciously embodied a male-gendered vision of proletarianization.
Consumption, especially the unpaid labor and technology of household work,
were slighted because of their association with women. Likewise, the separation
of industrial production from household production and consumption isolates
domestic labor from monetary market value and hence from the economy as
narrowly defined by economists. I take my cue instead from the feminist revision
of Marxist thought, especially Rayna Rapp's (1983) important concept of proletarianization from the household out. Studying this process answers the question "how did people become consumers?" at least in the contemporary sense of
consumer. Fortunately, for northern Sonora, Mexico, I was able to trace almost
all the changes that were involved.

Among the items that mark this process, stoves are particularly illuminating. Before the importation of U.S. household technologies began in the 1880s,
Sonorans cooked on a variety of platforms using firewood. *Hornillas*, ovens made
of unfired clay, were made and maintained locally (although the technology
itself was Spanish in origin). Women made the ovens and replastered their sides
as walls cracked or shed patches. Women and children harvested firewood locally.
Cast-iron stoves replaced hornillas as early as 1900 in towns and by the 1950s and
1960s in the countryside. Such stoves also burned firewood but probably were
more fuel-efficient than the older technology was. During the past three
decades, gas ranges substantially replaced woodstoves, although many people
retained woodstoves for times when the forty-five-kilogram cylindrical tanks of
propane could not be refilled. Through this century-long sequence of technolog-

ical change, both the cooking device and the fuel shifted from being locally supplied to being externally purchased, industrially produced commodities; local roles at most consisted of small mechanical workshops where ranges were repaired.

Initially, I interpreted the causes of this change to be demographic and ecological shifts involving the movement of people into cities, where firewood was scarcer and more expensive, and denudation of timber by lumbermills, railroads (for railroad ties), and mine companies (for mine posts and to fuel roasters and smelters) (Heyman 1994b, 199–201). In other words, I hypothesized that consumer change happened when people were constrained from using the old technology. Jason Antrosio (2002), building on my work, offers a more sophisticated model for the adoption of stoves in Latin America, including their attractive qualities and meanings such as being modern, clean, and efficient. Stoves in this sense provide a means for women to provide supposedly better care for the family. Likewise, family members who earn money can pool resources to buy stoves, thereby showing dedication to the mutual family enterprise and especially the women (mothers and wives) who conduct it. This accords with the Sonoran evidence and suggests that consumer proletarianization occurs through attractions as well as constraints. For either reason, it is truly proletarianization since purchasers are no longer able to make the technologies themselves nor provide the main inputs; they are forced to consume. Once key skills (making and maintaining clay hornillas) disappear by not being transmitted to a younger generation, they are effectively lost forever. Thus, the political ecological perspective reveals that consumption practices are shaped by the technologies and practices available in particular historical and social contexts and that we cannot expect people to disengage from their existing ecological practices (such as burning propane or firewood) unless some other technology or mode of activity becomes available to them. The practice of household and community-regional self-sufficiency, while possible with a great deal of idealistic effort, becomes in practical terms increasingly unlikely, even unthinkable.

The political ecological perspective also encourages us to examine how capitalist consumption comes from and brings about changes in culturally organized time and space. A woman who grew up in a small farming community near Agua Prieta had moved to the border city to work in a shirt factory. Once she had woken with the dawn to collect water and wood and heat tortillas; now, as she bitterly recounted, her life was ruled by the alarm clock. The change was not a matter of sheer time; she probably arose earlier on the farm. Rather, it was the strict rigidity of schedule and the transfer of control from self to external device to conform to a factory work schedule. One could hardly find a better example to support the thesis of historian E. P. Thompson (1967), who argued that linked transformations in "time, work-discipline, and industrial capitalism" drastically changed the world view of proletarianized peoples. Were we to look further, however, we might find that scheduling and time-space conceptions are also increasingly shaped by formal schooling. Not only do schoolchildren leave and reappear at set times, but the increasingly isolated housewife is deprived of their companionship and assistance in minding smaller children, lugging water, running errands, and so on. In conjunction with this increasingly rigid (and often complex) set of schedules, the demand for clean clothes increases as well as meals for hungry children and husbands returning to the home.

These time demands refract into the work routines and technologies of the household. Women coped with changing patterns of time and volume of material possessions by using blenders for chile sauces and refried beans, washing machines for cleaning clothes, and faucets and pipes to deliver water. (Lest it be thought that I impose an analysis on this material, women provided me with exactly this interpretation of blenders and washing machines.)

Let us focus on one particular technology, electric lights, that clearly alters the format of the day. As noted, the traditional rhythm of the day was set by dawn, dusk, and the demands of farm animals. School and factory schedules deprive the family of a significant block of time together in the middle of the day but correspondingly emphasize collective time (often around the television) in the evening. There is, furthermore, the prolongation of schoolwork into the evening. But the construction of the evening as a time for doing things, as opposed to quietly slipping into rest, demands interior lighting. This is reinforced by housing forms and practices that increasingly emphasize time spent indoors rather than in yards and under exterior, open-air roofed spaces. During my fieldwork in the 1980s, working-class Mexicans were just beginning this transition into lighted interior spaces and evening-oriented activities, and their use of electric lighting was still sparse to my North American eyes. But from a political ecology perspective, the lesson is clear: changes in the organization of time demand increasing use of electric lighting, produced mostly by burning fossil fuels while emitting greenhouse gases.

The political ecology of space is similar. While the largest user of fossil fuels, in the United States at least, is electric generation, the next largest source is internal-combustion engine vehicles for transportation (Barry Solomon, personal communication, 2001). The replacement of walking by motorized transportation had begun in Agua Prieta but had not progressed very far. Only about a quarter of working-class households I surveyed owned cars or trucks, and these households tended to use their vehicles more for hauling than for errands or commuting to work. But it was a quite small city, and people could walk or take collective vans (which operated as small businesses) to most destinations. Cities enlarge, however, as commerce moves from the small neighborhood store format to the large strip development store format, as industries locate in specialized areas, and as land prices dictate the separation of affordable housing from places of work and schooling. Then sheer distance and time required for walking combine to force people to use cars or large-scale collective transportation to commute.

Modern consumption does not arrive alone. It requires new sources of income and credit and travels along novel paths of trade and commerce. In northern Sonora, I identified what I call channels of consumption change that included U.S.-owned mine company stores providing ample credit for North American goods; migrant laborers in the United States bringing back money, appliances, and tools for personal and family use; and peddlers (often smugglers) bringing back U.S. consumer items for the Mexican market, a trade significant enough to have a distinctive name, *fayuca* (Heyman 1994b, 183–91). Through these mechanisms, some locations come to be modern in terms of shopping, available cash, credit, and needed inputs (gasoline, electricity), and others are seen as apparently backward and boring. The geographic pattern of consumption channels thus reshape regional space—in the Sonoran case, orienting people in their migratory moves and lifestyle decisions toward larger cities in general and the U.S. border in particular (Heyman 1991, 15).

As the term *channel* suggests (as in television channel), we must consider the mass media in the political ecology of consumption. Movies were the first industrially produced mass entertainment to penetrate northern Sonora, entering via mine company towns and border cities, and commercially recorded music followed soon afterward. Television came much later, but it is widespread; in 1986, 70 percent of working-class homes in Agua Prieta had televisions, a higher rate than for many other appliances.[5] Thinking about mass media raises the important question of power relations between consumers and capitalist marketers—to put it more plainly, of whether or not people's desires are manipulated by advertising and marketing. One school of thought emphasizes the powerful manipulation of images and symbols to promote consumption (Galbraith 1985 [1967], 163–81). The other view is that successful marketers and advertisers largely sell what the consuming public itself favors or are punished by the market and at most promote fine distinctions among products. Another version of the latter position is that people reinterpret the items and symbols they do consume (Miller 1997).

A political ecology of consumption might help overcome this dichotomy by drawing on Karl Marx's (1977 [1867], 163–77) concept of commodity fetishism. A fetish is an inanimate object to which people attribute lifelike powers; commodity fetishism refers to understanding people and relationships among them through the objects they exchange, including metaphorical objects such as television images. Such "object standing in for person/relationship" thought processes occur in a variety of cultural settings (Appadurai 1986), but capitalist relations particularly heighten this phenomenon because people receive the items and images as anonymous commodities purchased in impersonal markets from large corporations rather than producing such items themselves or obtaining them from local and regional markets. This means that even when consumers take an active stance, choosing goods from diversified marketers according to their own meanings and self-concepts, they may well fetishize social contexts, taking representative objects as the essence of groups and relationships.[6] It is rarely the case that commodities overtake all relationships; border Mexicans, for example, obtain many of their durable goods (appliances, furniture, and so on) from relatives and friends through gifts and sales, reinforcing rather than hiding the connection among persons, at least at the intimate level. Still, vital social phenomena come to be enacted as relationships among objects. In particular, households and communities dissolve into market segments of consumers, each designated by characteristic incomes and goods preferences, and each the target of particular marketing and advertising strategies.

The rise of commodified youth culture—which shapes a formative period in each person's life—is particularly important in this regard. Adolescence and young adulthood have long been marked by distinctive cultural practices in tension with adult-dominated society. But such phases end quickly, and young people are reintegrated into society, ready to succeed the roles of their parents. In border Mexico, as in many other places, the advent of migratory and local wage labor (starting in the early twentieth century) broke the need and duty of young people to defer to older generations; inheritance of resources like land and established community standing were no longer absolutely necessary for life. Instead, young people turned to new modes of relationship among people: factory labor markets, money from work in the United States, and even (for some youth) educationally based professional careers (Heyman 1990). These novel patterns favor commodity fetishism, emphasizing the person as a free agent, a money earner, a goods purchaser—that is, as a commodity her or himself—rather than son, daughter, brother, sister, and so on. Buying, possessing, and consuming personal goods with one's own money enacts this new sense of commodity-self. But ironically this commodity-self can be shared among youthful peers and is thus easily molded by mass-media entertainment and advertisers into a market segment marked by cheap, discretionary consumer goods like clothes, drugs, and music.

Of course, capitalist relations are never total, and young people rarely isolate themselves from the household relationships needed for everyday provisioning. This is especially the case for working-class Mexicans, who are so poor that children rarely can afford to live on their own and parents do and must claim part of their earnings for the family fund (unlike many U.S. youth, who tend to retain all their earnings for spending money). Instead, young people settle into a constant struggle with parents, as I will discuss, bringing some earnings home and retaining some for their own consumption. In Agua Prieta, for example, young women and men often bought with their factory wages knock-off designer blue jeans, using time-installment arrangements of four to eight weeks of payments since they have so little discretionary money. They could then own a stylish pair of denims just like the Americans and rich Mexicans they saw in glossy variety shows and soap operas. Emotions of desire and fulfillment poured into these purchases, constrained as these youths otherwise were—working at mind-numbingly repetitive assembly plant jobs, fighting with parents for money, saturated by the artificial paradise of television, and stimulated at work and in the neighborhood by peers who were seeing the same images and feeling the same emotions.

We thus return to the question of relative power between consumers and marketers. Under conditions of strong but incomplete commodity fetishism, marketers succeed precisely if they empower consumers to choose among the objects that they sell. Insofar as marketing is well informed and technically capable, it recognizes and heightens finely differentiated social groups and their specific motivating symbols and images (Fine and Leopold 1993). The selling of consumption involves popular will, then, but in such a way that it strengthens the message to buy commodities. These changes, for which I have used youth culture as an example, cover a variety of novel social relations with significant consequences, in which consumption is both a cause and a visible indicator.

Political ecology thus demonstrates consumption's interrelationships with other social, cultural, and geographic changes as well as changes in the biophysical environment.[7] As we consider the profundity of the changes in the sale of labor, the organization of household work, the relationships of child to parent and woman to man, the sense and expression of self, and so forth, simply urging people to be less consumerist is ineffective, if not condescending. Some of the goods just described are relatively discretionary (although usually imbued with compelling commodity symbolism), but a great deal of it—stoves, washing machines, electric lights, motorized transportation, and so on—are nondiscretionary since people have few alternatives about how to solve fundamental problems of organizing time, space, and the production of daily existence except to use the technologies available in the marketplace and the supplies organized by utilities. We can thus understand better the perspective of working-class Aguapretense, who wanted more consumption rather than less. Their desire was not a matter of unrestrained greed or dreams of luxury amid poverty but the dream of surviving and surpassing the endless challenges of balancing and sustaining a way of life built around flows of money and credit, commodities, water, and energy.[8] Taken together, however, these small flows are important ecologically, including scarce water in this desert region, fossil fuel energy sources used directly (gasoline, propane) and indirectly (electricity), firewood, and materials consumed through the whole life cycle from manufacture to solid waste. In this highly pressured context we can understand the public conflicts swirling around consumption in Agua Prieta.

The Immediate Politics of Consumption in Border Mexico

By using the word *immediate*, as in "the immediate politics of consumption," we draw a useful contrast with long-term changes already described. The word focuses us on aspects of consumption in which there was an actual or potential conflict, whether among organized groups or between individuals falling into consistent social categories (for example, parents and children, women and men). During the 1980s in Agua Prieta, the ecological effects of consumption were *not* on the immediate agenda, although there were glimmers of other kinds of environmental politics (such as toxic waste produced by maquiladoras).[9] Rather, protests over price increases were the clearest instance of consumption politics at that time. In early 1986, the Mexican governmental electric commission raised electric rates by 50 percent. This took place at a time when the government ran a significant deficit, faced intense international pressure to reduce subsidies and expenditures, and operated an inefficient electric grid with widespread theft by the poor and numerous hidden subsidies to the industries and farms of the rich. Middle-aged women (primarily) and men affiliated with a radical Roman Catholic parish in a working-class neighborhood organized a midday march to the local offices of the electricity commission, voicing their grievances and obtaining the commission's promise to review a few bills that seemed to have increased by especially high amounts. The electric rate protest grew out of the central role of electricity in household technology, the measurable challenge that bimonthly electric bills posed for households with limited income and savings, and the crucial role that middle-aged women played as the managers of household interests, especially in the consumption sphere (Heyman 1994b, 227).

This protest, although it was not associated with a political party or a broader movement, raises the question of the wider role of consumption in politics. The recent successful overturning of Mexico's authoritarian one-party regime began with student protests in Mexico City in 1968 but received significant impetus in the 1980s when Mexico's debt to foreign banks ballooned, resulting in extreme currency devaluations and budget cuts to maintain the repayment schedule. On the production side, this meant the closure or downsizing of many government agencies and state industries. On the consumption side, it was manifested in very high inflation and consequent loss of purchasing power and, for border dwellers, a sudden reduction in ability to shop on the U.S. side because of the sharply increased value of the dollar against the peso. One cannot single out the consumer crisis as the prime mover of political change in Mexico; long-standing resentment of imposed candidates, corruption, and other features of one-party rule played crucial roles as well. Nevertheless, unhappiness about price inflation was a significant subject of conversations in Agua Prieta and important motivation for people to switch allegiances from the governing party to the right-wing

National Action Party (PAN in Spanish), which in 2000 finally obtained the presidency and shattered Mexican one-party rule.

This case suggests that loss of purchasing power, especially through dramatic price increases (such as those in electric bills), powerfully mobilizes popular political movements and that such movements are perhaps most often associated with the right wing of the political spectrum, which largely blames activist policies and governments for the problem rather than demands them as a solution. This is, of course, a bold hypothesis that I am by no means prepared to justify, but it is worth thinking about in terms of the immediate political ecology of consumption. It suggests that the price increase route to resource conservation will produce significant popular resistance and that such consumption politics may feed right-wing movements that generally lack environmental agendas.

Protests and parties encompass our stereotypical view of politics, but there were other domains of significant conflict and mobilization around consumption in Agua Prieta. One domain appeared to the individuals concerned to be personal and idiosyncratic; but when studied in multiple households, it turned out to be quite extensive and important: conflicts over consumption between parents and children and between husbands and wives—that is, involving the politics of gender and generation. The main earners of wages in Agua Prieta formed two groups: men from their twenties up, who worked at a variety of jobs, such as truckers, construction laborers, broom factory workers, and warehousemen, and contributed (usually but not always) to the support of wives and children; and young adult children of both sexes, but especially women, who worked in maquiladoras and contributed to the support of parents and siblings. In contrast, the main users of wages (to buy groceries, pay bills, and so on) were middle-aged people; in some households, men controlled family spending but in most cases women (considered housewives) controlled collective expenditures (Heyman 1994b, 229).

This scenario created constant struggles inside families over personal versus collective spending—over how much of the husband's earnings were brought home to the wife, how much of the daughter's to her mother. It was generally acknowledged that wage earners were entitled to some share of the money (a rhetorical rule of thumb in Sonora was that working children living at home could keep half their earnings and turn over half to their parents); but the real exchange was negotiated, often with considerable conflict, family by family. Behind this was the tug of war between the cost of the shared items and inputs required to make households work (whose character we have discussed) and the individualizing aspects of consumption, notably the making of self-conscious style and peer group–oriented consumption among youth. This politics is reproduced inside each family as members face the inherently contradictory tendencies of contemporary consumption. In turn, the differential understandings,

practices, and power within households influence decision making and activities that use resources and affect the environment.

Another political phenomenon with interesting implications for ecology
was the struggle with the municipal government to get basic urban services,
including water, sewage, and electric lines and adequate filling of propane tanks.
This played into party politics in that local party operatives used these widespread desires to recruit and reward followers. We have already seen why these
energy and material inputs and outputs are crucial for modern consumers
houses. (Although different in character, one might add public schools to this
category.) Such goods are most efficient when delivered through large-scale, collective infrastructures—for example, water mains with feeder lines to individual
houses. For this reason, they can be termed *collective consumption*. Such collective activities significantly shape the urban form. The urban development pattern of Mexico—indeed, of much of the world—consists largely of people placing
houses and streets and later agitating to obtain basic infrastructure (such as
water and sewer mains) (Ward 1999). In spite of their significant cost to quite
pinched households, people strongly desire these utilities and make considerable sacrifices in terms of both connection charges and contributed in-kind
labor in digging trenches, laying pipe, and so on. The rationales are twofold: the
time and physical energy savings in not having to haul water from delivery trucks
or standpipes (and some form of sewage disposal, either septic tanks or drainage
mains, is required once people have piped water), and the ability to access a
more modern (better illuminated, cleaner) lifestyle with electricity, water, and
so on. Clearly, then, there is a profound trend toward locking large numbers of
households and wide swaths of towns and cities into collective infrastructures
that favor the high-volume flow of basic resources and energy.

Through this analysis, then, we begin to recognize that the environmental
effects of consumption often occur in the production and supply systems that
serve consumers rather than being done by consumers themselves. That is, they
are linked to the decisions of consumers, but the proximate source of environmental effects is the utility itself, usually a firm or a government agency. One
might compare this to the difference between the environmental effects of
throwing away a candy wrapper versus the greenhouse gases and particulates
emitted when the plastic is manufactured for that wrapper. The political implications are significant. They bring into view the often ignored politics of supply
organizations and collective or shared consumer technologies: how power is
generated, water supplied, household technologies designed. People in Agua Prieta had little concept of these questions, but then most advocates and analysts of
consumption ignore them also or blur them into a generalized consideration of
consumerism. Yet they constitute a vital agenda for political ecology to contribute to the politics of consumption.[10]

Fusing Knowledge and Action

Recognizing that contemporary consumption has deep causes, rescuing these causes from the oblivion of ordinary life and capitalist mystery, and perceiving the immense scale and distant environmental effects of consumption acts: such steps profoundly challenge our capacity for understanding and action. The challenge faces scholars, activists, and everyday consumers (such as the Aguapretense) alike. Yet taking these steps seems to be the only way forward. We have already seen flaws in two ways in which environmentalists commonly approach consumption-price incentives and moralized rhetoric. Exhortation from the outside seems unlikely to be effective in two regards: it focuses attention on environmentally marginal consumption acts, not crucial ones (in terms of energy and material flows); and it ignores the constructive and creative qualities of consumption, especially how consumer goods help people cope with the challenges of capitalist life. Rather, it seems that people (including the people of Agua Prieta, this writer, and the readers of this chapter) need to investigate the social and environmental chains extending outward from their own consumption acts toward larger contexts. Their learning process will require dialogue between study groups and experts, which will enable people to have a greater sense of ownership of understandings and new ideas about practices.[11]

The production, delivery, and consumption of water, for example, are crucial topics for the largely arid U.S.-Mexico border region and one for which the knowledge and decisions of householders are as important as those of authoritative experts. Sarah Hill (2003) describes a water health promotion project in Ciudad Juárez, Chihuahua, Mexico, and El Paso County, Texas, that contains elements of the learning process approach. Although the project encountered classic political ecological variation (caused by the local political history and urban land tenure geography of the study communities), Hill documents significant and enduring learning about water in even the most difficult situations. (On water as a consumer good generally, see Chappells et al. 2001.)

But knowledge is not enough. Consumers need greater capabilities to act. *Capabilities* combine material resources with opportunities to set goals and determine appropriate means of action (Sen 1999). Thinking of amplifying capabilities broadens the concept of development from supplying more and better stuff to include the process of increasing self-determination. It seems particularly useful in the consumption sphere, where the debate has been trapped between "more is better" and "more is worse" without consideration of what "more" does for people. We need to give people capabilities to solve their challenges of time and space and to build on their positive experience of and control over consumption.

Let us continue our water example, then. Access was sought by the Aguapretense to address increasing demands for healthiness and cleanliness within rigid time schedules, as described. Raising capabilities for women and children might well mean increasing access to and consumption of piped water. Given this context, knowledge of limited renewable water resources and depletion of fossil groundwater would be contradictory and perhaps ineffective if householders also do not have access to grants and loans to obtain water-efficient technologies for key domestic production processes (bathing, washing clothes and dishes, watering small gardens, and so on). But a program that paternalistically hands out water connections and technologies without popular goal setting and ownership of knowledge is likely to bog down in graft and false compliance. The concept of capabilities synthesizes both dimensions needed in practice and seems particularly well suited as a positive response to a political ecology critique of the status quo. (See Heyman 2003 on the relationship between critique and counterpart ideals.)

Ultimately, political ecology rests on understanding the importance of unequal power in our social-natural lives. Greed as an aspect of consumption assumes a certain level of power to command goods and resources, and guilt is the situational regret over doing this. By isolating the volition of the individual from its social context, these visions of consumption mystify the distribution of power in consumption and focus inward rather than toward an empathetic encounter with poorer and less empowered consumers' lives. They furthermore fail to capture the positive experience of consumption, its roles in satisfying our needs and enriching our practical and creative lives. At the same time, greed (if rhetorically exaggerated) captures some truth about the human relationship with biophysical flows and stocks, as consumption seizes the productivity of plants, animals, soils, aquifers, and so on for human use and returning most of the energy and mate- rials in relatively degraded form (Robertson 2001). In a sense, we produce our human selves by consuming and disposing of what surrounds us. Political ecology's critique, then, is not against consumption per se. Rather, it suggests that the arrangements by which we produce daily life matter profoundly.

NOTES

1. The literature on consumption and its environmental effects is voluminous. Fortunately, a few works identify and synthesize a great many sources. For consumption generally, consult Goodwin et al. (1997) and Miller (1995a, 1995b). Focusing specifically on the consumption-environment nexus, I recommend Cohen and Murphy (2001) and Stern et al. (1997), especially the chapter by Wilk. A valuable web site with both scholarly and lay articles on consumption is *http://www.jrconsumers.com*. Richard Wilk, an anthropologist at Indiana University, maintains the Global Consumer web page (http:// www.indiana.edu/~wanthro/consum.htm) and a page of graduate student reviews of books about consumption (http://www.indiana.edu/~wanthro/reviews.htm). The web page *http://dizzy.library.arizona.edu/ej/jpe/consumpt.htm* offers a short introduction to studying consumption in developing societies, also applicable to overdeveloped societies. Other notable works in anthropology include Antrosio (2002), Carrier (1995), Carrier and Heyman (1997), Chin (2001), Miller (1997, 2001), O'Dougherty (2002), Orlove (1997), Rutz and Orlove (1989), and Hansen (2000).

2. *Aguapretense* is the collective noun for the people of Agua Prieta, comparable to *New Yorkers* or *Californians.*

3. Another line of analysis draws attention to broad phases of capitalism, in particular the Fordist mass-production/mass-consumption nexus characteristic of the United States and the U.S.-dominated world system of the twentieth century. A succinct introduction is offered in Taylor's (1999) book on modernities.

4. James B. Greenberg initially worked on this method with me; the pioneering study is Lewis (1969). Another useful reference is Menzel (1995), a photographic compendium of homes and possessions around the world.

5. The introduction of television to Agua Prieta is an interesting case study in the political economy of consumption. Initially, televisions were brought back from shopping and migratory labor in the United States and were tuned to grainy American channels. In the late 1970s and early 1980s, the Mexican government installed transmitters in remote corners of the republic (notably along the northern frontier where the state feared losing political and cultural control), and households tuned into Spanish-language, mostly Mexican-origin programming from the multibillion-dollar, private but pro-government media conglomerate Televisa. A comparable anthropological study of television in Brazil is Kottak (1990).

6. Another effect of commodity fetishism involves the mystification of environmental and other forms of political action. The centralization of media production means that messages, even environmentalist ones, put recipients into a passive recipient role rather than a responsible one and come from outside rather than engage the local setting.

7. Status imitation is a widespread explanation of increased consumption: first the rich possess something, and then other classes imitate it. Such imitation has some explanatory force but needs to be viewed within a wider historical context of social change. In tributary relations of production, elites gain and express political domination through sponsorship of large parties and festivals, meaning that goods are collectively consumed. Under conditions of capital accumulation, elites cut back on costly redistribution in favor of personal and familial possession, some flaunted publicly (but not shared), some kept quite private (see, for example, Roseberry 1989, 1–2). In addition, cash incomes (perhaps from transnational migration, wage labor, and so on) become a novel means for subordinate classes to change their public status, escaping from a previously rigid class (or class-race) structure (Heyman 1994a, 139; Antrosio 2002, 112–13). On consumption and social inequality broadly, see Carrier and Heyman (1997).

8. In an article focusing on household economics (Heyman 1994b, especially 179–83), I suggested that we study the change from flow-conserving peasant households, which use cash, credit, and natural resources on annual and even longer cycles, to flow-through households, which gain income over short periods (weekly paychecks, for example) and pay monthly or bimonthly bills (such as utility charges) and consumer debts. Although both household economies use resource inputs and produce waste products, I suggest that the flow-conserving household economy probably has fewer extended environmental impacts than does the flow-through household.

9. More recently, a binational governmental environmental initiative—the Border Environmental Cooperation Commission (BECC, known as COCEF in Spanish)—has promoted a certain kind of collective environmental politics on the border, focusing on public works and remediation activities such as clean water, sewage treatment, and solid waste projects.

10. Taking these large-scale supply systems into consideration also gives us a better handle on the role of wealth inequality in the environmental effects of consumption. By demanding very different amounts of energy and goods from these systems, consumers with very different degrees of purchasing power share their environmental effects to considerably different degrees. It is estimated, for example, that each U.S. consumer uses eleven times the resources of each Indian consumer and that, in India, the national upper and middle classes account for most of that nation's output of greenhouse gases (Parikh et al. 1997).

11. My suggestion here owes much to an unpublished book manuscript by Marianne Schmink, Susan Paulson, and Elena Bastidas describing the project known as Managing Ecosystems and Resources with a Gender Emphasis (MERGE). A description of this project is available at *http://www.tcd.ufl.edu/merge/Case1Eng.html.*

REFERENCES

Antrosio, Jason. 2002. "Inverting Development Discourse in Colombia: Transforming Andean Hearths." *American Anthropologist* 104, no. 4: 1110–22.

Appadurai, Arjun, ed. 1986. *The Social Life of Things: Commodities in Cultural Perspective.* Cambridge: Cambridge University Press.

Carrier, James G. 1995. *Gifts and Commodities: Exchange and Western Capitalism since 1700.* London: Routledge.

———, ed. In press. *Confronting Environments: Local Environmental Understanding in a Globalizing World.* Walnut Creek, Calif.: Altamira.

Carrier, James G., and Josiah McC. Heyman. 1997. "Consumption and Political Economy." *Journal of the Royal Anthropological Institute.* 3, new series: 355–73.

Chappells, Heather, Jan Selby, and Elizabeth Shove. 2001. "Control and Flow: Rethinking the Sociology, Technology, and Politics of Water Consumption." In *Exploring Sustainable Consumption: Environmental Policy and the Social Sciences*, edited by Maurie J. Cohen and Joseph Murphy, 157–70. Amsterdam: Pergamon.

Chin, Elizabeth J. 2001. *Purchasing Power: Black Kids and American Consumer Culture.* Minneapolis: University of Minnesota Press.

Cohen, Maurie J., and Joseph Murphy, eds. 2001. *Exploring Sustainable Consumption: Environmental Policy and the Social Sciences.* Amsterdam: Pergamon.

Durning, Alan. 1992. *How Much Is Enough?* New York: Norton.

Fine, Ben, and Ellen Leopold. 1993. *The World of Consumption.* London: Routledge.

Galbraith, John Kenneth. 1985 [1967]. *The New Industrial State.* New York: New American Library.

Goodwin, Neva R., Frank Ackerman, and David Kiron. 1997. *The Consumer Society.* Washington, D.C.: Island Press.

Greenberg, James B. 1998. "The Tragedy of Commoditization: The Political Ecology of the Colorado River Delta's Destruction." *Research in Economic Anthropology* 19: 133–49.

Hansen, Karen T. 2000. *Salaula: The World of Secondhand Clothing and Zambia.* Chicago: University of Chicago Press.

Heyman, Josiah McC. 1990. "The Emergence of the Waged Life Course on the United States–Mexico Border." *American Ethnologist* 17, no. 2: 348–59.

———. 1991. *Life and Labor on the Border: Working People of Northeastern Sonora, Mexico, 1886–1986.* Tucson: University of Arizona Press.

———. 1994a. "Changes in House Construction Materials in Border Mexico: Four Research Propositions about Commoditization." *Human Organization* 53, no. 2: 132–42.

———. 1994b. "The Organizational Logic of Capitalist Consumption on the Mexico–United States Border." *Research in Economic Anthropology* 15: 175–238.

———. 1997. "Imports and Standards of Justice on the Mexico–United States Border." In *The Allure of the Foreign: Imported Goods in Post-Colonial Latin America*, edited by Benjamin S. Orlove, 151–83. Ann Arbor: University of Michigan Press.

———. 2001a. "United States Ports of Entry on the Mexican Border." *Journal of the Southwest* 43, no. 4: 681–700.

———. 2001b. "Working for Beans and Refrigerators: Learning about Environmental Policy from Mexican Northern-Border Consumers." In *Exploring Sustainable Consumption: Environmental Policy and the Social Sciences*, edited by Maurie J. Cohen and Joseph Murphy, 137–55. Amsterdam: Pergamon.

———. 2003. "The Inverse of Power." *Anthropological Theory* 3, no. 2: 139–56.

Hill, Sarah 2003. "The Political Ecology of Environmental Learning in Ciudad Juárez and El Paso County." In *Shared Space: Rethinking the U.S.-Mexico Border Environment*, edited by Lawrence A. Herzog. La Jolla, Calif.: University of California, San Diego, Center for U.S.-Mexican Studies.

Hornborg, Alf. 2001. *The Power of the Machine: Global Inequalities of Economy, Technology, and Environment.* Walnut Creek, Calif.: Altamira.

Kottak, Conrad P. 1990. *Prime-Time Society: An Anthropological Analysis of Television and Culture.* Belmont, Calif.: Wadsworth.

Lewis, Oscar. 1969. "Possessions of the Poor." *Scientific American* 221 (October): 114–24.

Marx, Karl. 1977 [1867]. *Capital: A Critique of Political Economy*, translated by Ben Fowkes, introduction by Ernest Mandel. Vol. 1. New York: Random House.

Menzel, Peter. 1995. *Material World: A Global Family Portrait.* San Francisco: Sierra Club Books.

Miller, Daniel, ed. 1995a. *Acknowledging Consumption: A Review of New Studies.* London: Routledge.

———. 1995b. "Consumption and Commodities." *Annual Review of Anthropology* 24: 141–61.

———. 1997. *Capitalism: An Ethnographic Approach.* Oxford: Berg.

———. 2001. *The Dialectics of Shopping.* Chicago: University of Chicago Press.

O'Dougherty, Maureen. 2002. *Consumption Intensified: The Politics of Middle-Class Daily Life in Brazil.* Durham, N.C. : Duke University Press.

Orlove, Benjamin S., ed. 1997. *The Allure of the Foreign: Imported Goods in Postcolonial Latin America.* Ann Arbor : University of Michigan Press.

Parikh, Jyoti K., Manoj K. Panda, and N. S. Murthy. 1997. "Consumption Patterns by Income Groups and Carbon-Dioxide Implications for India: 1990–2010." *International Journal of Global Energy Issues* 9, nos. 4–6: 237–55.

Rapp, Rayna. 1983. "Peasants into Proletarians from the Household Out: An Analysis from the Intersection of Anthropology and Social History." In *The Social Anthropology of Peasantry*, edited by Joan P. Mencher, 32–47. Bombay: Somaiya.

Robertson, A. F. 2001. *Greed: Gut Feelings, Growth, and History.* Cambridge, England: Polity.

Roseberry, William. 1989. *Anthropologies and Histories: Essays in Culture, History, and Political Economy.* New Brunswick, N.J.: Rutgers University Press.

Rutz, Henry J., and Benjamin S. Orlove, eds. 1989. *The Social Economy of Consumption.* Lanham, Md.: University Press of America.

Sen, Amartya. 1999. *Development As Freedom.* New York: Random House.

Sheridan, Thomas E. 1988. *Where the Dove Calls: The Political Ecology of a Peasant Corporate Community in Northwestern Mexico.* Tucson: University of Arizona Press.

Stern, Paul C., Thomas Dietz, Vernon W. Ruttan, Robert H. Socolow, and James L. Sweeney, eds. 1997. *Environmentally Significant Consumption: Research Directions.* Washington, D.C.: National Academy Press.

Taylor, Peter J. 1999. *Modernities: A Geohistorical Interpretation.* Minneapolis: University of Minnesota Press.

Thompson, E. P. 1967. "Time, Work-Discipline, and Industrial Capitalism." *Past and Present* 38: 56–97.

Wackernagal, Mathis, and William E. Rees. 1996. *Our Ecological Footprint: Reducing Human Impact on the Earth.* Gabriola Island, British Columbia: New Society.

Ward, Peter M. 1999. *Colonias and Public Policy in Texas and Mexico: Urbanization by Stealth.* Austin: University of Texas Press.

PART TWO

Social Hierarchies in Local-Global Relationships

8

Finding the Global in the Local

Environmental Struggles in Northern Madagascar

LISA L. GEZON

Political and economic control is a process, never complete and always shifting. Whether in the context of ideologies or the daily practices of power and enforcement, domination is constantly threatened by the varied and multiform resistance of those whose consent it relies upon as well as by changes in the political and economic frameworks in which power operates. Early theorists of globalization supposed that technological advances in the domains of transportation and communication would contribute to cultural homogenization and unilateral domination from centers of technological invention, dissemination, and control (see Friedman 2000, Jameson 1992). Anthropologists have pointed out, however, that despite the often overwhelming force of international finance institutions and capital investment schemes, predictions of global domination have not resulted in expected forms of political and economic control and culture change. Anna Tsing (2000b), for example, encourages scholars to free "critical imaginations from the specter of neoliberal conquest—singular, universal, global" and instead analyze capitalism as heterogeneous and shifting (144).[1]

Whatever one's take on globalization, conceiving the world as interconnected raises issues of scale and method. What connects people and places? How do we recognize articulations of power within and between places? How do landscapes themselves manifest global relationships? Finally, what kinds of research methods are necessary for answering those questions? This chapter explores possible ethnographic approaches in a world characterized by interconnections and sources of power external to the site of research. In two cases of shifting political affiliations in the Ankarana region of northern Madagascar, conflicts among multiple actors interacting in a single locale provide an informative arena for analyzing a conjuncture of interests, including those based locally, nationally, and internationally.

Scalar relationships between the local and the global do not exist in an a priori

way. The global domain and local places are historically situated cultural constructions. In recent decades, concepts of global and globalization have provided
a framework in which to discuss how places and people are connected. This study
demonstrates that connections between what we may refer to as local (geographic
spaces and resident people) and processes that we define as extralocal are often
performed within and are inseparable from specific locales. As Tsing (2000b)
points out, the "globe comes into being both as a culturally specific set of commitments and as a set of practices" (143). This view encourages a rethinking of
the dichotomy between local and global as separate domains because the global
is embedded within the local (Tsing 2000a). I focus in this chapter on analyzing
how scale, or relationships between what is local and what is not, comes about
in the context of specific actions and as the result of specific decisions.

International conservation movements and donor- or lender-initiated
neoliberal economic policies provide a point of departure for understanding the
globally connected local of the Ankarana Special Reserve in northern Madagascar. Observable actors in the local setting are (1) conservation personnel, represented by local nongovernmental organization (NGO) employees; (2) the indigenous
political-religious leader of the Antankarana people (called the Ampanjaka); (3)
Antankarana members of the Ampanjaka's patrilineage; and (4) Antankarana of
commoner descent living in and near the Antankarana ritual village center of
Ambatobe, which is located adjacent to the protected area. Not visibly present
but nevertheless an active part of local political interactions are national strategies, policies, and judicial processes and international donor and conservation
ideologies and practices.

Conflicts among these actors and groups expose tensions among identities,
cultural logics, and discourses of rights and responsibilities between people and
nonhuman environments. As Terre Satterfield (2002) points out in her analysis
of clashes between loggers and environmentalists in the U.S. Pacific northwest,
identities are marked by larger cultural forms and at the same time are "flexible
vehicles through which to challenge those forms" (8). The Ankarana cases suggest that identities are multiple, shift in meaning, and are situationally negotiated (Kottak 2003, 370).

Concerns about Method

The analysis in this chapter is based on research conducted over the past thirteen
years in the Ankarana region of Madagascar. Research methods have involved
satellite image analysis, surveys, structured formal interviews, ethnographic
mapping, and long-term participant observation, including sixteen months
spent living at the research site. Each method has contributed a valuable facet to
an investigation of the global within the local. Satellite image analysis has pro-

vided visible information about changing characteristics of human settlements, productive practices, and environment in time and space (also see Harwell 2000, Moran and Brondizio 1998, Nyerges and Green 2000). Face-to-face surveys and interviews have given me an opportunity to hear many people speak about specific topics of interest. A cornerstone of this research has been the long-term ethnographic practice of participant observation, which has contextualized survey and interview results.

The use of ethnography as a method again raises the critical issue of scale: how can such a localized research strategy be useful in studying regional dynamics or even global connectedness? In response to the analytical challenges of envisioning a globally connected world, Michael Burawoy (2000) has proposed the concept of global ethnography, recounting that global ethnographers have "had to rethink the meaning of fieldwork, releasing it from solitary confinement, from being bound to a single place and time" (4). George E. Marcus (1995) has argued in favor of carrying out ethnography in a mobile and multiply sited way so that comparison and juxtaposition become integral to a study. Nevertheless, he recognizes that the global is not "out there" to be discovered but "is an emergent dimension of arguing about the connection among sites" (99). In arguing for a "strategically situated (single-site) ethnography," Marcus suggests that "some ethnography may not move around literally but may nonetheless embed itself in a multi-sited context" (110). Indeed, ethnographic methods and an interest in case studies helped me to identify global connections in local sites through the examination of micro-interactions among actors who derive their authority from both local and extralocal sources.

Physical landscapes result in part from individual contests over social position and the rights those positions entail. Explanations of the biophysical environment are the purview of many disciplines, including biology, geology, forestry, agronomy, and, importantly, social sciences such as anthropology that explore human action in the contexts of meaning and social standing. Environmental understanding involves not only the measurement of soil fertility and the mapping of forest cover but also an awareness of what motivates people to cut down trees and make productive decisions that contribute to the leaching of soils. As such, ethnography remains a critical methodology in the hands of social scientists who are interpreting and explaining landscapes.

The cases analyzed in this chapter demonstrate the usefulness of understanding politics broadly to refer to both intentional and unintentional dynamics of power that occur in the context of everyday interactions, not just in the realm of formal decision making. Sherry B. Ortner (1989) argues that we consider as political "all relations in which the relative power, authority, agency, legitimacy, and so forth of actors is negotiated and defined" (194). Such a practice approach to power and politics informs an empirical study of how landscapes result from interactions among specific people in specific places, considering the processes through which decisions are made and contested and the nature of the articulations between local and nonlocal sites of influence.

The chapter begins by presenting an ethnographic setting and describing the recent historical context of conservation efforts internationally and within Madagascar. It continues with analysis of two case studies. In the first case, people living in a commoner village on the edge of the Ankarana protected area protested the prohibition against cutting wood for home construction. What made this case particularly interesting was that the Antankarana indigenous leader (the Ampanjaka), who was generally an advocate for the local people, supported the prohibition. The result was a tense standoff between the commoner village leaders, the conservation project staff, and the Ampanjaka. In the second case study, which examines a land privatization campaign as a component of western-led, neoliberal conservation strategies, the Ampanjaka again jeopardized his legitimacy when he appropriated land that was being farmed by members of both royal and commoner families.

This ethnographically rich presentation of case studies provides a framework for analyzing conflict in a way advocated by A. L. Epstein (1967) in his argument for a case method in studying law. He wrote: "Disputes are a universal feature of human social life. The central question thus becomes not do the Nuer have law, but, in any given society, in what ranges of social relationships do quarrels arise, what forms do they take, and by what means are they are they are handled" (206). Even in a study of global connections, the case study approach remains an important component for understanding the conjunctures of power and resistance in given sites.

Ethnographic Setting

Antankarana-identifying people locate their geographic home at the far northern reach of the Sakalava dynasty, which expanded along the west coast of Madagascar in the seventeenth and eighteenth centuries. As internal disputes threatened political cohesion, some branches of the Sakalava royal family moved north to establish their own political domains. In the far north, they called themselves Antankarana, or "people of the rocks," referring to the Ankarana limestone massif that is now a national protected area.

During the colonial era, the French officially recognized the Antankarana royal line and administered the local territories through the Antankarana leader, called the Ampanjaka, until the 1950s, when civil servants assumed these responsibilities. After independence in 1960, the royal network has continued to have political and religious authority in the lives of the local people. The Ampanjaka is influential in setting a ritual agenda, communicating with royal ancestors, extracting tribute in the form of rice and cattle, mediating certain conflicts, and serving as a liaison between local people and outside governing bodies.

Although the state does not officially incorporate the Ampanjaka or any other indigenous leaders into its governing structure, national leaders have often solicited the support of these local leaders because of their connection to the people.

The Antankarana people living around the Ankarana limestone massif mostly herd zebu cattle and grow rice. On the southern end of the massif, as in the village of Amalo (discussed later in the chapter), many people also grow a variety of cash crops, including sugarcane, tobacco, and cotton.[2] People throughout the region consult the Ampanjaka on religious matters, but he serves as a mediator only in land disputes within an area close to the Antankarana royal center, the village of Ambatoaranana, which is adjacent to the Ankarana Special Reserve. In other places where there are Antankarana-identifying people, local leaders take the lead in managing village-level political and economic affairs as either patrilineal leaders in family meetings or leaders in the state-sanctioned *Fokonolona* (village council).

Conservation

Post–World War II conceptions of conservation-oriented land management in Madagascar emerged from Truman-era western visions of economic modernization (Rostow 1960). As schemes for ensuring conservation of natural resources, protected areas fit into an overall strategy for developing industrialization and international trade. The logic of setting aside parcels for protection involves the assumption that local people will be able to meet their resource needs (for example, fuelwood, fruits, and game) in other ways. Conservation efforts have not been implemented in a uniform manner or without internal disagreements. Disputes among proponents of conservation have revolved around ways of bounding areas that need protection and the extent to which people living on the periphery of the protected areas are to be included in executing conservation strategies. Through the past several decades, conservation efforts and philosophies have swung from a colonial "fences" approach, emphasizing a national park model and boundary maintenance (Brandon et al. 1998, Kramer and van Schaik 1997), to an emphasis on the involvement of local people through integrated conservation and development projects (ICDPs) (Agrawal and Gibson 1999; Brechin et al. 2002, 2003; Furze et al. 1996; Western et al. 1994; Wilshusen et al. 2002; Wood 1995), and back again (Oates 1999, Redford and Richter 1999, Terborgh 1999, Terborgh et al. 2002).[3]

In 1984, Madagascar was one of the first African nations to develop, in collaboration with international conservation professionals, a national strategy for conservation and development. In the late 1980s, with funding and administrative support from the U.S. Agency for International Development (USAID), the World Bank, and other international donors and NGOs (such as World Wide Fund for

Nature), the Malagasy government instituted a number of ICDPs, which sought to address conservation through economic development. This included the Montagne d'Ambre ICDP in the far north, which includes the Ankarana Special Reserve. The ICDP model became a cornerstone of the first phase (1991–97) of Madagascar's fifteen-year, donor-led and -funded National Environmental Action Plan (NEAP) (Durbin and Ralambo 1994; Kull 1996; Gezon 1997a, 2000). The second phase of environmental funding in Madagascar then de-emphasized the ICDP and replaced it with a regional, or landscape, approach to conservation (Gezon 2000). Several factors led to the demise of ICDPs in Madagascar and else-where in the world, including their cost (USAID 1997); the need to target a popu-lation base broader than those people living immediately around protected areas; the biological need for habitats larger than those provided by official pro-tected areas (Hannah et al. 1998); and their overall ineffectiveness, which has often been related to the difficulties of incorporating local people into interna-tionally funded projects (Brandon and Wells 1992).

It is worth noting that the NEAP corresponded, was conditionally linked, and was ideologically compatible with structural adjustment programs that were designed to make Madagascar competitive in a global capitalist market econ-omy. Adrian Hewitt (1992) has argued that despite Madagascar's apparent will-ingness to participate in a national conservation plan, the government had little choice but to adopt conservation measures. Faced with increasing dependence on the international community for loans just to keep its population fed, the country had complex reasons for wanting to gain international favor. Christopher B. Barrett (1994) has taken a slightly different perspective, suggesting that the president at the time, Didier Ratsiraka, used the west's interest in the environment as a lever in his negotiations about general economic restructuring.

From a political ecology perspective, conservation in Madagascar since the 1980s must be understood in the context of its embeddedness within goals and projects of World Bank–style economic development and corresponding national and international ambitions for increasing the country's formal inte-gration into a global capitalist economy. The potential for this kind of economic growth is often used to justify environmental protection (Ferraro 2002) and has guided conservation practices in Madagascar, from the ICDP (see Gezon 1997a) to the land titling campaigns analyzed in the second case in this chapter.[4] The cases analyzed here reveal how the framework in which people make decisions has been significantly molded by discourses and practices at nonlocal levels—in particular, by the political and economic tides of late-twentieth-century struc-tural adjustment.

Around the world, people living on the edges of protected areas have felt the consequences of these types of conservation strategies, whose effects have been neither uniform nor predictable. The following analysis takes a case involving multiple parties, acting within a single geographic site, as a point of departure for understanding how existing cultural frameworks negotiate the hegemonic impact of outside forces and complicate the production of landscapes as envisioned by those from the outside who hold positions of power.

Case 1: Protected Area Boundaries and the Need for Construction Wood

A conflict emerged when people from the commoner village of Amalo broke ranks with the Ampanjaka over a question of access to the protected forest. The Ampanjaka, whose favor had been heavily courted by the leaders of the NGO charged with executing the ICDP project, had forbidden the villagers to cut trees for construction in the portion of the forest closest to their village. During the conservation project's initial phase (1989–91), before formal implementation of the NEAP, the project staff, especially the expatriate project director, strategized that the best way to get local people to cooperate was to enlist the good will of their political and religious leader, the Ampanjaka. He was thus named a *président d'honneur* (honorary president) of the conservation NGO early in that phase, and project staff called on him to participate in conceptualizing sustainable conservation. They sent him to a conference on conservation and development in Uganda, a gesture that greatly honored the Ampanjaka. In keeping with the logic of indirect rule, the project directors were hoping that if they had his favor, the people's cooperation would follow.

I became familiar with this situation in July 1991, when the interdisciplinary research team in which I participated visited several villages in a project to compare satellite images and aerial photos with what we saw on the ground and to gather general socioeconomic information on land-use patterns.[5] Since two previous visits in other villages had gone smoothly, our team was surprised to encounter resistance at our first village meeting in Amalo, situated on the southern end of the Ankarana limestone outcropping. The people of Amalo angrily insisted that we grant them permission to cut down trees to repair their houses. The villagers explained that the Ampanjaka had forbidden them to cut trees, threatening them with the condemnation of the royal ancestors. In response, they had selected a delegation of *rey amin'dreny* (elders) to visit the Ampanjaka to ask for permission to cut a limited number of trees just for local home construction. The Ampanjaka, to their surprise and dismay, announced that he supported the project's conservation initiatives and ordered them to stay entirely out of the protected forest.

After this refusal, the village elders openly warned the Ampanjaka and project representatives that they would soon be obliged to cut the trees anyway because their homes needed replacement or repair. In a cultural context in which indirection dominates in communication (Keenan and Ochs 1979), such a warning effectively threatened the legitimacy of the Ampanjaka and jeopardized his ability to interpret sacred ancestral prohibitions. We soon noticed that while the people had not yet openly defied the prohibition, they had indeed been cutting wood in the forest (as evidenced by recent ox-cart trails going into the forest and signs of cutting within it). There was no effective enforcement of the protected area boundary—I suspect because the park guard living in Amalo and hired by the project did not dare to report these infractions. Although there was no active enforcement of the protected area's boundaries, the people sought a legal solution to their lack of access so that they would not have to risk fines and imprisonment from the state and spiritual sanction from the ancestors via the Ampanjaka.

By the time I returned to the area in 1992–93, the conservation project leaders who were in place in 1991 (and who had originally garnered the Ampanjaka's support) had left; and his communication with the project had broken down. Preoccupied with recruiting new local and expatriate leaders and beginning new phases of funding, the project staff had become less active in both enforcing their policies and cultivating positive relations with the local people. Contrary to the advice of scholarship on effective protected-area management (West and Brechin 1991, Hough and Sherpa 1989), they had not actively engaged the Ampanjaka and the local people as participants in the project. As a result, the Ampanjaka began to feel less invested in the project and stopped enforcing the ban on cutting trees from the protected area. No one with whom I came into contact a year later—neither those close to the Ampanjaka nor people from Amalo—mentioned the conflict as a continued concern. In fact, the people of Amalo showed strong support for the Ampanjaka in the fall of 1992 during an Antankarana ceremony that was held in the protected area (Gezon 1997b).

In the early part of this conflict in Amalo, the interests of the local people (all commoners) opposed those of the Ampanjaka and the conservation project. Alliances then shifted when the project's connection with the Ampanjaka weakened. The conflict had erupted into an overt dispute that was not resolved through mediation or antagonistic confrontation. Rather, it subsided, perhaps temporarily, when both the project and the Ampanjaka backed off from asserting their authority. The local people were able successfully to assert their will to cut trees in the face of royal, state, and international prohibitions. This resonates with findings that grassroots movements often achieve success in the face of seemingly insurmountable odds, frequently by sheer persistence (Rocheleau et al. 1996). The potential strength of grassroots movements is indeed one reason explaining why processes of globalization cannot be taken as unilateral, inevitable, or predictable.

Case 2: The Ampanjaka and Agricultural Land

Two years later, in 1993, struggles over rights to land erupted in a conflict that only indirectly involved the conservation project yet reveals the deep and indirect scope of international regulatory forces that emerge through conservationist agendas via capitalist principles of free trade and private property. Specifically, it shows how tensions between local and state-level land tenure systems and patterns of use emerge in the context of internationally mandated and financed land privatization and titling schemes that have accompanied neoliberal-influenced ideologies of conservation.

Sponsored by a group of donors led by the World Bank, the NEAP mandated the Malagasy Service des Domaines to establish titles to the land around protected areas, based on the logic that if farmers had clear rights to land, they would have less need to cut more land from the forest. Although this case slightly predates official land titling campaigns, which were being fully implemented by 1995 (Leisz et al. 1995), it illustrates how competing claims to land may become far less negotiable once private titles exist. It also foreshadows the types of problems that a titling campaign would face in this region. The case illustrates the performative nature of scale making in the region, revealing how actors strategically draw on a variety of perspectives in shaping, contesting, and negotiating ownership and use.

The argument for encouraging private land ownership through campaigns to establish land titles is based on the logic that private landholders will be motivated to avoid land management schemes and practices that lead to the permanent degradation of their land or other material means of subsistence and will thus be more likely to avoid a "tragedy of the commons" (Hardin 1968) scenario. As one report on the Malagasy situation stated, "[a] lack of confidence [over rights] leads to a situation where the user believes he or she must use the resource today for fear that either it will not be there in the future, or that future access to it will be cut off" (Leisz et al. 1995, 60–61). In response, conservationist planners have emphasized individual rights, and international funding has contributed to state efforts to assign individual titles to the users of land around protected areas.

The "tragedy of the commons" argument has been challenged by evidence of numerous effective communal management schemes (McCay and Acheson 1987, Okoth-Ogendo 1987, Ostrom 1991, Peters 1994). The purported environmental advantage of private property has also been challenged by the argument that, in a capitalist economic system, private or legal corporate ownership leads to degradation through the tendency to extract as much profit as possible from given resources, externalize costs, and move on to new frontiers. This case presents another critique of moves toward privatization of land tenure. Land becomes concentrated in the hands of fewer people as land that was once held in common becomes titled to single individuals, often excluding others who held customary rights to it. In addition to lowering some people's quality of life, increased stratification can result in increased pressure on the land if landless people who once formed part of corporate landholding groups clear new productive land.

The Conflict

This case focuses on a dispute that surfaced just after the Antankarana flag-raising ceremony (see also Gezon 1995, Walsh 1998), which occurs approximately every five years and culminates in the ritual center of Ambatobe. As people were packing up the day after the ceremony, the Ampanjaka called a meeting of elder men from the royal family to announce that he was reclaiming some of the land surrounding the royal capital village—land that local people (both members of the royal family and commoners) had been farming for years. For the Ampanjaka, this was a simple assertion of his existing right as ultimate owner of all the land surrounding the royal village, which had been passed down to him from the royal ancestors. For the soon-to-be displaced land users, this was a violation of their customary ownership rights. A previous Ampanjaka had indeed granted rights to use the land to the ancestors of the current users; but in the minds of current users, the land had become their own.

The Ampanjaka decided to reclaim this land because he had a plan to convert its fields into cashew orchards and sugarcane plantations, whose profits would go toward amenities for the royal capital village, such as a large mosque and generators for electricity. He publicly justified taking the land with the argument that the people on the land in question were abusing their rights by selling and renting land instead of farming it themselves or returning it to him. He maintained that he had a title to all of the land he claimed, although this was never verified or directly questioned in the course of the proceedings to follow. Given the Ampanjaka's statements, people who had bought their land without getting permission from him were in danger of losing it. Anyone who was in the process of selling their land or of taking on paying tenant farmers could also lose it.

To most of the royal men, the Ampanjaka's plan sounded like a good, if perhaps overambitious, idea. For some, however, the prospect for development was tainted by the fact that part of the land being appropriated was their own. One high-ranking royal elder, Anjona, had recently completed a deal to sell his land for a large sum by Malagasy standards. The Ampanjaka ordered him to return payment to the new owner and give up the land. At the meeting, Anjona was visibly angered by the Ampanjaka's forcible revocation of his sale and appropriation of his land and at one point openly walked out. Nevertheless, the Ampanjaka did not seem annoyed by this dissension; Anjona was the only one who dared to show disapproval, and his expression of anger made him appear childish to the other royal men.

Overall, few royal families lost their land compared to the number of commoners from the nearby village of Amboly who lost theirs. The latter were less restrained than Anjona in showing their disapproval. By the time I left the region, at the end of November 1993, they had not yet reacted; but I learned from fellow researcher Andrew Walsh that they had threatened the life of the Ampanjaka's principal liaison with the village, Henri. They had also burned a pile of sugarcane cuttings that were going to be planted in one of the newly reclaimed fields. There seemed to be a general sense of discontent, with a real possibility of retributive action.

When I returned in 1995, I learned that only one man from Amboly had been held responsible for burning the cane cuttings and, more generally, for the discontent. People said that the state authorities in Ambilobe had handled his case and that he had received some punishment. (People were not too sure what the punishment was.) People had reinterpreted the dissent against the Ampanjaka as an unreasonable affront by one jealous and possibly crazy man; no longer did they refer to the burning as an indication of general discontent. People from the royal families in Ambatoaranana told me that everyone, even the royal elder Anjona, had come to recognize the Ampanjaka as the rightful owner of the land. Despite this later interpretation, accounts suggest that, at the time of the incident, dissatisfaction with the Ampanjaka's moves had been general throughout the community of Amboly, not particular to one man.

Pluralist Land Rights

The players in this case were the Ampanjaka, the royal family in Ambatoaranana, the commoners in the area, and the state as an implicit actor, conceived of as a potential mediator. Three land tenure and management systems came most obviously into play: traditional divine right, customary usage rights, and state-sanctioned legal rights. A fourth was not immediately apparent but was nevertheless important in shaping trends in land tenure and use: private property as a component of neoliberal reforms and encouraged in international conservation circles. First, the Ampanjaka's claims to authority were based on divine, ancestral, and historical right. According to this logic, all the land around the royal village belongs to the Ampanjaka and the royal ancestors. Anyone who farms it does so by their gracious permission. Local histories assert that a previous Ampanjaka, Tsialana I, claimed the land when he first moved to Ambatoaranana. Since then, people have come into the area and requested permission from the Ampanjaka to farm individual plots of land. By this reasoning, the Ampanjaka explained that, since the land is still his, he may decide how it is to be used and furthermore may reclaim it when he desires.

An overlapping system is that of local customary land tenure, which applies to commoners as well as to members of the royal family. In the local system of land ownership and management, individuals and corporate patrilineal groups have exclusive rights to use, buy, and sell land, with the understanding that royalty has no inherent right to this land. Under the system, individuals or groups obtain the land by either buying it, being the first to claim an unused portion of it, or asking permission from elders to claim ownership of it—not merely use rights.

When land is obtained in these ways, the users are assumed to have full and inalienable rights to it. Some farmers do not own the land they work on but are tenant farmers or renters, and they compensate the owners for the right to use the land. After the contract period, rights to the land return to the owner. Conflicts over use of land may be handled either by family or village councils. If they cannot be resolved by consensus at this level, state officials may be called in to mediate (Gezon 1995). In Ambatoaranana and the villages around it, people recognize that the Ampanjaka's ancestors claimed the land surrounding the villages as part of Antankarana territory; therefore, they are likely to take conflicts directly to the Ampanjaka for mediation. Yet there is no precedent in recent history for the Ampanjaka to behave like the owner of that land or reclaim access to land around the villages that he had previously granted to others.

The third land-use system is the state's. During the colonial period, the French systematized private ownership of land by granting titles to individuals. They gave large tracts of land to colonial companies for industry and extraction. They also provided local people with the opportunity to register their landholdings, although few local people did this. At independence in 1960, and until the present, the system of private ownership of smallholder agricultural lands has been maintained, despite the socialist revolution in the mid-1970s. While the socialist government nationalized large industry, it did not abolish the private property of small farmers. Many have recognized that having one's land registered with the state is the only way of ensuring state protection from encroachment. Nevertheless, most smallholdings were not officially registered with the state when the titling campaign began in 1995. The reason that titling was once again promoted in the 1990s can be tied to a fourth land-use system or ideology: conservation and neoliberal economic reform communities both identified private property as a mechanism for obtaining greater economic productivity as well as higher rates of conservation.

Confrontation of Tenure Systems: Local-Royal Contests

How and under what circumstances did specific actors, deriving their authority from different sources, come together to contest access rights? How did people creatively draw on multiple, often contradictory, systems of land management? The four land tenure systems intersected at a point in time, revealing contradictions that may have gone unnoticed without this conjunction. The Ampanjaka and the farmers cannot each hold inalienable rights to the land, for example, and this creates conflict that provides fertile ground for analysis. As Ortner notes (1999), in the "zones of friction (or worse) between 'cultures' . . . the clash of power and meaning and identity is the stuff of change and transformation" (8). In the cases analyzed here, conflicts and cultural clashes have resulted in negotiated and shifting patterns of resource access and use that can significantly affect the biophysical environment.

It was uncharacteristic for the royal elder Anjona to show such open defiance to the Ampanjaka. Even though Anjona is older than the Ampanjaka and a royal male, he remains a status subordinate. By burning the cuttings, the commoners from Amboly also reacted unusually harshly. At the same time, the Ampanjaka's decision to take peoples' land strongly clashed with local standards of fair land management. It was not clear that the Ampanjaka was the owner of the land in any practical sense since his predecessor had given the villagers the right to farm there without exacting any regular form of remuneration, such as a landlord would exact from tenants. In the people's opinion, then, the Ampanjaka did not have the right to take their land. His moves signaled an attempt to strengthen a regional base of indigenous authority in light of both state-sanctioned and locally exercised resource management practices and ideologies.

When the national cadastral project team arrived in the region in 1995 to issue titles, they did not go immediately to Ambatoaranana, the royal ritual center, around which the Ampanjaka makes the strongest claim to the land. Many felt that state officials remained wary of challenging his claims because state leaders had relied so heavily on the coastal kings for political support and for obtaining governability of the commoners and their resources. When the team did arrive in Ambatoaranana in the late 1990s, the Ampanjaka had organized a popular resistance to the titling campaign based on the argument that the state might then try to take some of the land that was not actively being farmed, thereby threatening the people's cultural patrimony. His actions had the effect of preserving intact his claim to all of the land, including agricultural land, based on customary rights. As of the summer 2003, for reasons unrelated to the land dispute, many people, both commoners and members of the extended royal family, had become disenchanted with the Ampanjaka; and some had even begun the process of obtaining titles for the land they farmed, despite his disapproval. The son of the anonymous commoner who had burned the cuttings was also reported to have returned to farming on the land that the Ampanjaka had taken away since the sugarcane and cashew plantations had never materialized.

In each of these cases, the Ampanjaka tried to extend his decision-making power over an increased number of people and material resources. His success in defining the terms of resource access corroborates Tsing's (2000b, 143) assertion that the global exists through contingent articulations among globalist, nationalist, regionalist, and local projects. Hegemony of any given project is only ever partial, although it often has significant consequences for people and physical landscapes.

Scale As Process: Agency and Identity in Claims Making

While the concept of globalization assumes the importance of global, or nonlocal, sources of authority in defining relationships of influence, the term *scale* recognizes that there are multiple levels of analysis but appropriately leaves open the character of the connections among people and places (if, indeed, there are any connections) and invites investigations into who influences whom. Many dictionary definitions of *scale* refer to relationships, in terms of distance or degree, between phenomena. Used in this sense, scale implies comparison and invokes a gradient. In the analysis of global connections, scale has two interrelated components: geographic scale and breadth of political legitimacy. In terms of the latter, the multiple forms of political power—those that derive from family or village leaders, from divine authority, from the state, and from international-globalist conservation agendas—do not interact as equal players. A concept of scale helps to place them analytically in a relationship based on the nature and extent (in terms of both geography and the number of people concerned) of their power in political discussions. The extent of influence ranges from very limited in the case of family leaders to very extensive in the case of international regulation of conservation. In terms of geography, scale also refers to the size and distance of the material implications of decisions made—with multinational corporations, for example, effecting ecological consequences far from the corporation's headquarters. Projects of scale making occur as people negotiate the extent of their political influence and the material impact of the decisions they make.

In a study of conflict, the subject of analysis is not merely contestations among individuals but the situated negotiation of connections, commitments, and subjectivities. Laura M. Ahearn (2001) argues that agency, or the ability of an individual to act, emerges within specific contexts and cannot be considered as ontologically prior to action itself. In these cases in Madagascar, culturally and socially situated individuals generate and enact agency as they negotiate overlapping norms for land use. Arturo Escobar (1998) points out that culture, or the processes of meaning making, and the politics of conflict are fully integrated: "Cultural politics is the process enacted when sets of social actors shaped by, and embodying, different cultural meanings and practices come into conflict with each other. . . . Culture is political because meanings are constitutive of processes that, implicitly or explicitly, seek to redefine social power" (64). Alf Hornborg (2001) points out the importance of remembering that the "asymmetrical distribution of resources and risks" that characterizes power relations does not reside in a static way within individuals but within situated interactions in which people negotiate their possibilities for effective action (1).

In conflicts, people negotiate cultural and social identities—in this case, according to their historical relationship to the land, their status as citizens versus royal subjects, and their competence to act as responsible adults. On learning that the Ampanjaka was taking his land, Anjona, the royal elder, acted like an adult Antankarana landowner who is both subject to and empowered by the norms of customary land tenure rights. Later, he acted like an elderly royal male, expressing a shifting evaluation of the conflict. He came to agree (at least publicly) that the Ampanjaka held ultimate rights to the land and that the Ampanjaka did this for the good of the Antankarana people. During the unraveling of the conflict, Anjona shifted his identity. While he had rights as a landowner in the system of customary law, he was not able, or perhaps willing, to articulate them effectively in challenging the more powerful claims of the Ampanjaka.

As for the anonymous commoner man who burned the sugarcane plants, the change in his agency apparently came not from shifts in the way he managed his own identity (for he was reported to be as angry in 1995 as in 1993) but from a change in the identity imposed from the outside. What changed was the extent to which he was perceived as being *able* to act in a socially meaningful way and, by extension, in a materially acceptable way. He was at first perceived to be a bold representative of public unrest in the face of a serious violation of customary land management practices. He positioned himself as a potential leader of a just rebellion against the king's appropriation of land. In the later scenario, he lost his public identity as a wronged landowner and became perceived as a contemptible and crazy (but ultimately harmless) man, whose unjustified actions would stand as a random act of vandalism. He arguably ceased to be an effective agent in that he was no longer able to make a difference through the exercise of power (Giddens 1984). People are also constrained in their ability to negotiate their identities and advocate for their interests.

Finally, the Ampanjaka negotiated his own agency. He acted in the first instance as an individual asserting rights to land: he held the meeting in which he announced his own personal vision. When challenged publicly, he did not provide a defense. Through his silence, he left the people to contemplate his legitimacy. In the eyes of many local people, especially the royal family, the Ampanjaka's agency and the rights associated with it merged with that of the royal ancestors. As a sort of living ancestor (Walsh 1998), he seemed to have inherited his land rights from those who had preceded him. The will of the ancestors proved to be a powerful resource that delegitimized Anjona and the commoner adherents to customary land tenure procedures while granting authority to the Ampanjaka.

This case suggests that agency is closely bound with a situational negotiation of identity—one that is negotiated both by and for oneself in a context of power relations. As Sara S. Berry (2001) has stated, "People act, . . . but the social effectivity of their actions depends not only on their own capacities but also on their access to sources of power that lie outside the individual and beyond his or her control" (xxv). While identities shift, none are free of constraint and opportunity. Scale making occurs through the movements of actors who are situated within, yet not determined by, their sociocultural milieu.

NOTES

1. I would like to thank the many people in Madagascar who have made this research possible. Funding for research in 2003 came from the National Geographic Society and a

Fulbright-Hays Faculty Research Abroad Fellowship. Earlier research was funded by a State University of West Georgia Faculty Enhancement Grant, the National Science Foundation, the National Aeronautics and Space Administration, the Wenner-Gren Foundation, Consortium for an International Earth Science Information Network (CIESIN), and the Population/Environment Dynamics Project of the University of Michigan. Thanks to Susan Paulson for carefully reading multiple drafts of this chapter.

2. All village names except for the royal center, Ambatoaranana, are fictional, as are the names of all individuals.

3. For an overview of the history of protected-area management discourse and practice as well as a strong argument in favor of including local people in project designs, see Brechin et al. 2002 and 2003 and Wilshusen et al. 2002.

4. Note that concern for sustainability has not been a consistent part of structural adjustment or other economic development approaches. Sachs et al. (1993) provides an important critique of the first world summit in Rio in 1990 and the Brundtland Report on sustainability that emerged from it. As has been evident in world economic and environmental summits, many northern nations, especially the United States, have been unwilling to take economic steps that embrace the need for long-term sustainability.

5. The project, "An Integrated Approach to Deforestation, Conservation, and Development in Madagascar," was funded by CIESIN. Conrad Kottak was the principal investigator, and John Colwell helped process satellite images. The field team consisted of myself, Glen Green, Kim Lindblade, and Phillip Block.

REFERENCES

Agrawal, Arun, and Clark C. Gibson. 1999. "Enchantment and Disenchantment: The Role of Community in Natural Resource Conservation." *World Development* 27, no. 4: 629–49.

Ahearn, Laura M. 2001. "Language and Agency." *Annual Reviews in Anthropology* 30, no. 1: 109–37.

Barrett, Christopher B. 1994. "Understanding Uneven Agricultural Liberalization in Madagascar." *Journal of Modern African Studies* 32, no. 3: 449–76.

Berry, Sara S. 2001. *Chiefs Know Their Boundaries: Essays on Property, Power, and the Past in Asante, 1896–1996*. Portsmouth, N.H.: Heinemann.

Brandon, Katrina, Kent H. Redford, and Steven E. Sanderson, eds. 1998. *Parks in Peril: People, Politics, and Protected Areas*. Washington, D.C.: Nature Conservancy/ Island Press.

Brandon, Katrina, and Michael P. Wells. 1992. "Planning for People and Parks: Design Dilemmas." *World Development* 20, no. 4: 557–70.

Brechin, Steven R., Peter R. Wilshusen, Crystal L. Fortwangler, and Patrick C. West, eds. 2002. "Beyond the Square Wheel: Toward a More Comprehensive Understanding of Biodiversity Conservation As Social and Political Process." *Society and Natural Resources* 15, no. 1: 41–65.

———, eds. 2003. *Contested Nature: Promoting International Biodiversity with Social Justice in the Twenty-first Century*. Albany: State University of New York Press.

Burawoy, Michael. 2000. *Global Ethnography: Forces, Connections, and Imaginations in a Postmodern World*. Berkeley: University of California Press.

Durbin, Joanna, and J. Ralambo. 1994. "Role of Local People in Successful Maintenance of Protected Areas in Madagascar." *Environmental Conservation* 21, no. 2: 115–20.

Epstein, A. L. 1967. *The Craft of Social Anthropology*. Oxford: Pergamon.

Escobar, Arturo. 1998. "Whose Knowledge, Whose Nature? Biodiversity, Conservation, and the Political Ecology of Social Movements." *Journal of Political Ecology* 5: 53–82.

Ferraro, Paul. 2002. "The Local Costs of Establishing Protected Areas in Low-Income Nations: Ranomafana National Park, Madagascar." *Ecological Economics* 43, nos. 2–3: 261–75.

Friedman, Thomas L. 2000. *The Lexus and the Olive Tree: Understanding Globalization*. New York: Anchor.

Furze, Brian, Terry De Lacy, and Jim Birckhead, eds. 1996. *Culture, Conservation and Biodiversity: The Social Dimension of Linking Local Level Development and Conservation through Protected Areas*. Chichester, England: Wiley.

Gezon, Lisa L. 1995. "The Political Ecology of Conflict and Control in Ankarana, Madagascar." Ph.D. diss., University of Michigan, Anthropology Department.

———. 1997a. "Institutional Structure and the Effectiveness of Integrated Conservation and Development Projects: Case Study from Madagascar." *Human Organization* 56, no. 4: 462–70.

———. 1997b. "Political Ecology and Conflict in Ankarana, Madagascar." *Ethnology* 36, no. 2: 85–100.

———. 2000. "The Changing Face of NGOs: Structure and Communitas in Conservation and Development in Madagascar." *Urban Anthropology* 29, no. 2: 181–215.

Giddens, Anthony. 1984. *The Constitution of Society*. Los Angeles: University of California Press.

Hannah, Lee, Berthe Rakotosamimanana, Jorg Ganzhorn, Russell Mittermeier, Silvio Olivieri, Lata Iyer, Serge Rajaobelina, John Hough, Fanja Andriamialisoa, Ian Bowles, and Georges Tilkin. 1998. "Participatory Planning, Scientific Priorities, and Landscape Conservation in Madagascar." *Environmental Conservation* 25, no. 1: 30–36.

Hardin, Garrett. 1968. "The Tragedy of the Commons." *Science* 162, no. 3859: 1243–48.

Harwell, Emily E. 2000. "Remote Sensibilities: Discourses of Technology and the Making of Indonesia's Natural Disaster." *Development and Change* 31, no. 1: 307–40.

Hewitt, Adrian. 1992. "Madagascar." In *Structural Adjustment and the African Farmer*, edited by Alex Duncan and John Howell, 86–112. London: Overseas Development Institute.

Hornborg, Alf. 2001. *The Power of the Machine: Global Inequalities of Economy, Technology, and Environment*. Walnut Creek, Calif.: Altamira.

Hough, John, and M. N. Sherpa. 1989. "Bottom Up vs. Basic Needs: Integrating Conservation and Development in the Annapurna and Michiru Mountain Conservation Areas of Nepal and Malawi." *Ambio* 18, no. 8: 434–41.

Jameson, Frederic. 1992. *Postmodernism, or, the Cultural Logic of Late Capitalism*. Durham, N.C.: Duke University Press.

Keenan, Edward L., and Elinor Ochs. 1979. "Becoming a Competent Speaker of Malagasy." In *Languages and Their Speakers*, edited by Timothy Shopen, 113–58. Cambridge, Mass.: Winthrop.

Kottak, Conrad. 2003. *Anthropology: The Exploration of Human Diversity*. 10th ed. New York: McGraw-Hill.

Kramer, Randall, and Carel van Schaik. 1997. "Preservation Paradigms and Tropical Rain Forests." In *Last Stand: Protected Areas and the Defense of Tropical Biodiversity*, edited by Randall Kramer, Carel van Schaik, and Julie Johnson, 3–14. New York: Oxford University Press.

Kull, Christian A. 1996. "The Evolution of Conservation Efforts in Madagascar." *International Environmental Affairs* 8, no. 1: 50–86.

Leisz, Stephen, Andrea Robles, and James Gage, with Haingo Rasolofonirinamanana, Hantanirina PulchJrie, Rivo Randriamanantsoa Ratsimbarison, Raymond Lemaraina, Jean Aime Rakotoarisoa, Karen Schoonmaker Freudenberger, and Peter Bloch. 1995. *Land and Natural Resource Tenure Security in Madagascar.* Madison: University of Wisconsin, Land Tenure Center.

Marcus, George E. 1995. "Ethnography in/of the World System: The Emergence of Multi-Sited Ethnography." *Annual Review in Anthropology* 24, no. 1: 95–117.

McCay, Bonnie J., and James M. Acheson, eds. 1987. *The Question of the Commons: The Culture and Ecology of Communal Resources.* Tucson: University of Arizona Press.

Moran, Emilio F., and Eduardo Brondizio. 1998. "Land-Use Change after Deforestation in Amazonia." In *People and Pixels: Linking Remote Sensing and Social Science*, edited by Diana Livermann, Emilio F. Moran, Ronald R. Rindfuss, and Paul C. Stern, 94–120. Washington, D.C.: National Academy Press.

Nyerges, Endre A., and Glen Martin Green. 2000. "The Ethnography of Landscape: GIS and Remote Sensing in the Study of Forest Change in West African Guinea Savanna." *American Anthropologist* 102, no. 2: 271–89.

Oates, John F. 1999. *Myth and Reality in the Rain Forest: How Conservation Strategies Are Failing in West Africa.* Berkeley: University of California Press.

Okoth-Ogendo, H.W.O. 1987. "Tenure of Trees or Tenure of Lands." In *Land, Trees, and Tenure*, edited by John Raintree. Madison: University of Wisconsin Press.

Ortner, Sherry B. 1989. *High Religion: A Cultural and Political History of Sherpa Buddhism.* Princeton, N.J.: Princeton University Press.

———. 1999. *The Fate of "Culture": Geertz and Beyond.* Berkeley: University of California Press.

Ostrom, Elinor. 1991. *Governing the Commons: The Evolution of Institutions for Collective Action.* Cambridge: Cambridge University Press.

Peters, Pauline E. 1994. *Dividing the Commons: Politics, Policy, and Culture in Botswana.* Charlottesville: University Press of Virginia.

Redford, Kent H., and Brian D. Richter. 1999. "Conservation of Biodiversity in a World of Use." *Conservation Biology* 13, no. 6: 1246–56.

Rocheleau, Dianne, Barbara Thomas-Slayter, and Esther Wangari, eds. 1996. *Feminist Political Ecology.* London: Routledge.

Rostow, Walter W. 1960. *The Stages of Economic Growth: A Non-Communist Manifesto.* Cambridge: Cambridge University Press.

Sachs, Wolfgang, ed. 1993. *Global Ecology: A New Arena of Political Conflict.* London: Zed.

Satterfield, Terre. 2002. *Anatomy of a Conflict: Identity, Knowledge, and Emotion in Old-Growth Forests.* Vancouver: University of British Columbia Press.

Terborgh, John. 1999. *Requiem for Nature.* Washington, D.C.: Shearwater.

Terborgh, John, Carel van Schaik, Lisa Davenport, and Madhu Rao. 2002. *Making Parks Work: Strategies for Preserving Tropical Nature.* Washington, D.C.: Island Press.

Tsing, Anna. 2000a. "The Global Situation." *Cultural Anthropology* 15, no. 3: 327–60.

———. 2000b. "Inside the Economy of Appearances." *Public Culture* 12, no. 1: 115–44.

U.S. Agency for International Development (USAID). 1997. "Strategic Objective Agreement: Annex 1, Amplified Description." Internal document. Madagascar.

Walsh, Andrew. 1998. "Constructing 'Antankarana': History, Ritual and Identity in Northern Madagascar." Ph.D. diss., University of Toronto.

West, Patrick C., and Steven R. Brechin, eds. 1991. *Resident Peoples and National Parks: Social Dilemmas and Strategies in International Conservation.* Tucson: University of Arizona Press.

Western, David, Michael R. Wright, and Shirley C. Strum, eds. 1994. *Natural Connections: Perspectives in Community-Based Conservation.* Washington, D.C.: Island Press.

Wilshusen, Peter R., Steven R. Brechin, Crystal L. Fortwangler, and Patrick C. West. 2002. "Reinventing a Square Wheel: Critique of a Resurgent 'Protection Paradigm' in International Biodiversity Conservation." *Society and Natural Resources* 15, no. 1: 17–40.

Wood, David. 1995. "Conserved to Death: Are Tropical Forests Being Over-Protected from People?" *Land Use Policy* 12, no. 2: 115–35.

9

Symbolic Action and Soil Fertility

Political Ecology and the Transformation of Space and Place in Tonga

CHARLES J. STEVENS

Anthropologists studying human-environment relations confront two related challenges: first, how to tease out the multitude of ecological, social, cultural, political, and historical influences through and in which knowledgeable actors live; second, how to convey to one's peers and students the illustrative qualities of ethnographic events that help us to understand the interplay of these diverse influences. Clifford Geertz (1973), of course, is widely recognized for just such an eloquent portrayal of ethnographic events in his thick description of the Balinese cockfight. William Roseberry's (1989) commentary on Geertz's work has provided a political-economic contextualization of the publicly displayed meaning of the cockfight, adding a rich and necessary aspect to the process of doing ethnography in a globalized world. Roseberry noted that the political-economic contexts of Indonesian colonial domination were necessary elements for comprehending the significance of cockfighting among Balinese villagers. Such contextualizations strike me as fundamental to understanding and explaining the political in political ecology, particularly in rethinking situations formerly constructed in the colonial imagination as discretely bounded cultures and landscapes.

When I was in the south Pacific Kingdom of Tonga carrying out dissertation research, my conception of political ecology as the merging of political economics and cultural ecology was expressed in my project goals and methods as a blend of the "rather pedestrian neo-functionalism" of my mentor, Robert McC. Netting (1993, ix), and the historical approach of Eric Wolf (1982). My research goals included understanding the ongoing transformation of Tongan agriculture from a 2,500-year-old agroforestry system to an increasingly capital-intensive system oriented toward both market and subsistence activities in the context of rapid population growth. In keeping with Wolf, I could no longer conceive of

Tongan agriculture or society as an isolated and bound system, so I worked to locate Tongan farming families in a global system in which family economies were linked through relatives to the economies of Los Angeles, Salt Lake City, Sydney, and Auckland. I spent sixteen months in Tonga, mapping agricultural fields and town lots, collecting detailed household budgets, estimating agricultural yields per unit of land and unit of labor, and learning the history of land and agricultural management from as many farmers as would tolerate my questions. In short, I was "counting all the potatoes." Since I was interested in the issue of sustainability (and in keeping with my scientific roots), I settled on soil fertility as a measurable indicator of the comparative sustainability of farmers' management strategies and collected soil samples from different agricultural fields for this purpose. For all of my so-called objective documentation of the contemporary Tongan political ecology, I received some of my deepest insights about contemporary Tongan life from events and issues that fell outside the realm of quantitative methodology.

In Tonga, allegiances, cultivars, and families are distributed on a historically and culturally constructed ecoscape devoted to the stable production of farinaceous crops.[1] Informed by archaeological, historical, and ethnographic evidence, I see the transformation of Tongan productive inequalities and Tongan agroforestry as deeply interconnected.[2] These transformations occur simultaneously in a world in which the unintended consequences of decisions made in the Tongan past now manifest themselves both ecologically and politically.[3]

In addition to gathering objective measures of household economics and soil fertility, I attempted to contextualize contemporary Tongan political economy and ecology by interpreting a specific event: a feast celebrating the birthday of a chief, today called a *nopeli* (noble). Here, I witnessed a demonstration of political symbolic action that had significant historical, political, and cultural relevance to the authentication of a modern and transformed Tongan commoner identity. Once depicted in the ethnographic and historical literature as profoundly subservient to chiefs and royalty, commoners are now asserting democratic rights and have in other ways transformed relationships with people in positions of genealogical superiority. The transformation of relations between commoners and chiefs in Tonga began when commoners were granted inalienable rights to agricultural lands in the late nineteenth century. In this constitutional act, the authority of chiefs over the resources and labor of commoner smallholders diminished, a diminution that was constantly exacerbated by Tonga's integration into wider political-economic spheres. The events at the feast seemed to assert commoner economic independence as well as commoner expectations that chiefly appropriation of their resources be met with administrative competence not delivered by the reigning noble.

The Feast

Traditionally in Tonga, both production and the hierarchical relations of production were celebrated by presentations of produce to chiefly and royal lineages during the annual 'inasi festival, the main event in a series of feasts held at the ta'u lahi harvest season that ran from March to September (Helu 1994, 41).Commoners presented ceremonial yams to the upper classes, pantomiming the bounty of their harvest by feigning struggle under the weight of a single yam and praising various gods, including 'Alo 'Alo, a god of weather, vegetation, and soil (Ferdon 1987, 87; Martin 1981 [1817], 303). 'Inasi means "sharing out or apportioning" (Martin 1981 [1817], cited in Ferdon 1987), and 'inasi was timed by the planting and the maturation of the prized Kahokaho yam variety, events that coincided with the spring and fall equinoxes (Ferdon 1987, 84). Ceremonies smaller than the spring and fall feasts were also held (82); and they, too, involved the redistribution of food and koloa (goods) according to the differential status among participants. The redistribution of agricultural yields at the 'inasi festival and other feasts legitimized and reproduced an intricate social system of extended and complex family and hierarchical relations. Power and status were manifested in redistribution.

The constitutional changes brought about in the nineteenth century by the unification of the kingdom by Taufa'ahau Tupou I, first king of Tonga, as well as the influence of British political organization and the Methodist church, changed the organization of the feasting rituals. The contemporary manifestation of the 'inasi festival is a series of feasting and religious celebrations beginning in the first week of December and ending with uike lotu (prayer week) in the first week of January. Commoner households purchase, produce, and present all of the food at the feasts; and during prayer week, families own certain feasting times. A second series of feasting events in May is associated with the annual church convention in the capital Nuku'alofa, where, again, the commoners supply all of the food for convention participants. Additionally, there are feasts for marriages, smaller faka'afe (feasts) given for girls' first and twenty-first birthdays, and occasional impromptu feasts to mark visits by expatriate family members or guests. There is also substantial exchange of resources between related households at funerals. It is not common for households, drawing on an extensive set of reciprocal obligations among kin, to be obliged to host four or five feasts per year. With each feast involving the presentation of perhaps 2,000 dollars (1,300 U.S. dollars) in food, these ceremonialized obligations are significant impositions on household resources.

Feasting obligations require long-range planning by farmers, and an unexpected feast demanded by a chief or noble may upset otherwise carefully managed smallholder resources. Such was the case in the second week of January of my second year in Tonga, when demands for four pola (large trays to carry food for a feast) were delivered to leaders of the village where I was staying. The feast was called to celebrate both the noble's birthday and his return after a long absence. After the Christmas feasting season and with farming households anticipating the feasts in May, this sudden demand for resources caught many families off guard.

When I asked high-ranking villagers about where the demand for the feast had originated, I received only rhetorical responses meant to stifle further questioning. I concluded that the demand had originated from the noble himself and that his request had passed through the *matapule* (talking chiefs) to the village leaders. My invitation to the feast came as one of the serendipitous events that occur in the field; I was, at the time, also involved in a traditional wedding ceremony. I rushed out of the house vaguely irritated at having my involvement in the wedding interrupted and found myself in a feasting venue that was to include a dramatic display of commoner displeasure.

The feast demand occurred when commoner parliament members were spearheading a movement for democratization of a monarchial government characterized by unequal representation in parliament (Hau'ofa 1994b, Hills 1993). The democratization movement subsequently lost its momentum (James 1995, 2001, 260) but has resurged recently after parliamentary action outlawed media criticisms of the monarchy (Australian Broadcasting Corporation 2003). At the time of my stay in the kingdom, the democratization movement was flourishing, empowered not only by the inequalities evident in the parliamentary system but also by a belief among farmers that a member of the royal family had attempted to corner a lucrative market in agricultural export. Coincidentally, in another village close to where I worked, commoners had recently refused to use their own resources to provide their noble with a demanded feast. Instead, the commoners negotiated with their noble: they agreed to provide the labor for the feast but refused to use their own stocks without compensation. I was told that such insubordination was unprecedented, but in the end the noble agreed to compensate the farmers for the resources they had invested in the pola.

The Tongan term *pola* refers literally to materials made by plaiting or weaving coconut leaves or fibers as well as to those activities done with pola. Hence, pola can refer to both the tables on which food for feasts is placed and to the feast itself. A table-of-food pola is expensive; and since many families have multiple feasting demands during the course of a year, they must carefully plan their allocation of resources for feasts and family obligations as well as resources required for subsistence. To contribute a pola, a family might garner from its own stocks six piglets, the quarter sections of one large pig, one roasted goat, two large baked fish, eighty kilograms of yams, about fifty kilograms of sweet potatoes, and three twenty-kilogram giant taro. Preparation could take the better part of two days, including collection of firewood and purchasing of goods the family could neither produce themselves nor store in sufficient quantities. Pola often include food not usually affordable to smallholders, such as lobster, octopus, and large pelagic fish.

Women preparing their portion of the pola may spend a morning collecting shellfish in the tidal flats and catching crabs in the mangroves. Much of the food and most of the decorations, however, have to be purchased. Chicken legs from Alabama; aluminum foil, wheat flour, and canned meat from Australia; decorative papers, balloons, and Chinese noodles for *sopo sui* (chop suey) from Taiwan; soft drinks from the Coca-Cola and Pepsi plants in Honolulu; curry powder, cornstarch, and sugar from Fiji; pudding mix, canned fruit and vegetables, and ice cream from New Zealand are purchased from Morris Hedstrom, Burns Philip, and Adiloa's *falekoloa* (store) in Nuku'alofa. Onions for the *'ota ika* (marinated fish), bell peppers, carrots, and tomatoes for the sweet and sour chicken, and an extra basket of large sweet potatoes are purchased at Talamahu market. An additional basket of *'ufi* (yams), if needed to complete a pola, cost sixty dollars (Tonga) at the time of the feast, amounting to half a week's income for salaried workers. Pola themselves now reflect the local and global interconnectedness of Tongan smallholders.

The feast for the noble's birthday involved forty such pola from the eight villages in this noble's *Tofia* (estate): in pure scale of presented food products, it was not the biggest feast I witnessed, but it was the grandest and most involved. In addition to the pola, there were three hours of traditional dances, in which each village's troupe presented *ma'ulu'ulu*, *ta'olunga*, *soke*, and other Tongan dances. The organizers touted the celebration as a distinctly Tongan affair; and in this context, the dances were "symbolic anchors of community" (Gupta and Ferguson 2002, 69). Distinguishing the feast from less ambitious presentations were amplified music, an emcee, the presence of members of the royal family and ministers of the realm, high-ranking church members, and an assortment of dignitaries, some of whom presented what seemed, even to the Tongan commoners who attended, interminable oratories. The scene progressed for so long that food rotted in the tropical sun, and family members waiting in the parking area honked horns voicing their displeasure at the extended course of events. Young men who were told to stop dancing because their time was over (an announcement that conveyed an un-Tongan concept of time) continued their dance through to its conclusion, cheered by the crowd. An obviously intoxicated noble from a neighboring estate delivered an endless speech; and when he finally uttered the Tongan equivalent of "in conclusion," the crowd erupted in applause, horns honked, and audible sighs could be heard emanating from those sitting very close to the noble's own dais. I had never witnessed such public display of impertinence or such clear disrespect.

At last, the noble for whom the feast was being held came around to make his speech and to accept a gift of *tapa* cloth and fine mats from the villagers. He had been sitting with King Taufa'ahau Tupou IV's daughter at the head of the horseshoe that formed the feasting area. His last gesture was to cut a birthday cake. As soon as he had done so, the crowd spontaneously began singing, in English, "Happy Birthday to You."

"Stop singing this *pālangi* [European] thing," the emcee admonished. "This is a Tongan event!" But they didn't stop. The song was sung to its conclusion, followed by long and enthusiastic period of laughing and clapping. The feast ended in prayer.

Something important had happened. I asked a number of people of various social rankings if what I had seen was a demonstration of the commoners' displeasure with the nopeli. Those of higher rank in the village shrugged off the event as tu'a childishness. Those of the tu'a class were heard days later still singing "Happy Birthday" and laughing out loud as they walked through the village.

"Was the singing of 'Happy Birthday' a commoner way of sending a message to the noble?" I asked a teacher colleague of mine at the local high school.

"You're a very smart guy," was the reply.

"How could I miss it?" I answered.

The symbolic action that I had witnessed conjured up thoughts about forms of resistance, about the negotiation of tradition, and of continuously and historically constructed identity. In the particular estate where I did my fieldwork, the tu'a had sided in the nineteenth-century civil war with the heathen and anti-Christian faction against their chief's alignment with the recently converted Christian and soon-to-become-first-monarch of a united Tonga, Taufa'ahau Tupou I. In fact, the commoners had essentially revolted against their chief, who returned to enact his revenge against the renegades at the fort of Hule, where the last of the Hihifo heathens were defeated. These historical events are played out in contemporary political arrangements in which chiefs use the first person when discussing the actions of their chiefly ancestors: the past is embodied in the contemporary office holder. In meetings where nobles present instructions for commoners' obligations, direct reference to the rebellion chides the commoners into obedience. Commoners, on the other hand, both pride themselves on their rebel image and are embarrassed that their rebellion was anti-Christian. Hule, the fortification where the last of the heathen commoners were defeated, is still obvious on the landscape and is approached with some reverence by local visitors. When I heard the tu'a singing "Happy Birthday," I thought the past was not so far behind.

But there were more immediate concerns about this noble and his public presentation. Some people in the village, a community that demonstrated pride in being traditional, had voiced displeasure about their noble's behavior. Not only was his demand for resources in the feast presented at an unreasonable time, just after the feasting season, when commoner stocks were depleted; but there were also rumors that the chief and his wife (who was not from the main island, Tongatapu) were less demonstrative of chiefly status than many of the older villagers cared to accept. Rumors of the noble's behavior had entered a gossip network that makes the Internet look slow and puritanical by comparison. Gossip that the noble's children spoke no Tongan and attended English-speaking private schools passed quickly through the villages. A noble whose family was observed only irregularly at church but who was rumored to attend the liquor-serving Nuku'alofa Club added insult to perceived injury. Some commoners regarded the chief's demand for a celebration to honor an uneventful birthday and an unremarkable trip as unjustified posturing. In the context of a democratization movement and the increased economic independence of commoners, a chief behaving in an un-Tongan manner deserved at least symbolic retribution.

Historical Context

The drama enacted in this feast discloses the emergent transformations of social structure in a highly negotiated and contested network of reciprocal relationships that are deep and wide, temporal and spatial, material and semiotic. The same global interconnections and historical contexts inform not only the transformation of Tongan smallholder and commoner agency and intentionality but also the alteration of Tongan agro-ecology. In a Tongan world characterized by a recent history of labor outmigration by a people whose very soul lies in movement and network building across an oceanic seascape (Hau'ofa 1994a), the prospect of locating ecological transformations in simple proximate causes seems unpromising.

James Gifford (1929) and Marshall Sahlins (1958) present classic descriptions of timeless genealogical relations between *Tu'i* (royalty), *ho'eiki* (chiefs), and tu'a in Tongan and, more generally, Polynesian social structure. In these accounts, the royal lineage is deified, chiefs occupy an elevated and administrative position, and commoners work the land and are subservient to chiefs. Past depictions of the relations among the classes (see Mariner's account written by Martin in 1817) depict chiefs as having rather despotic domination over commoners. Sione Latukefu (1974) describes a social organization that is characterized more by interdependency among the classes than by chiefly despotism. In contemporary Tongan social organization, however, the relations among classes are not characterized by an absence of commoner political power as some official histories indicate (Bott 1981, 1982; also see Gifford 1929, Kaeppler 1971, Wood 1978 [1932]).

In the past, social relations among commoner families and between commoners and chiefs were mediated by a host of status differentials and rankings of occupational groups. This resulted in a complex social organization that governed the production and distribution of agricultural goods and *koloa* (valuables) prominently displayed during the 'inasi festival. Interdependencies among social ranks, occupational groups, and farming families were a vital dimension of a highly productive agroforestry system long maintained on attenuated island environments. The Tongan agroforestry system managed by commoners and administered by chiefs provided society's subsistence, and it was characterized by genetically diverse cultivars and complex production cycles that guarded against overexploitation of the resource base.

Taufa'ahau Tupou I initiated changes in agriculture in the late 1800s by mandating that commoners sell copra (dried coconut) to make contributions to the church (Campbell 1992, Latukefu 1974). This had the initial affect of integrating Tonga into an external political economic community. Moreover, the political organization adopted by the new kingdom of Tonga was greatly influenced by British missionaries, who, although unsure of their proper role in the formation of the Tongan state, were enthusiastic in their efforts to institute Methodist guidelines into Tongan constitutional statehood. The formation of judicial and governmental standards required for Tonga's recognition as an independent nation followed intervention, but not colonization, by Great Britain. Constrained by the costs of imperialism, Great Britain grudgingly imposed its control only after Germany displayed imperial ambitions in the South Pacific.

A process of increased economic and ideological independence of commoners was initiated in the 1830s with the drafting of the Code of Vava'u, the legal and political forerunner of the Tongan constitution drafted in 1875. The structure of the constitutional monarchy effectively decreased both the numbers and the power of paramount chiefs. Moreover, the constitution granted commoners inalienable use rights to land heritable through the patrilineage, thus creating the preconditions for commoner economic independence from the chiefs. The alienation of chiefs from control over the means of production continued with the introduction of Christianity, which granted even commoners a direct relationship with God. As well, government financing of universal education that included teaching English as a second language provided commoners with valuable tools for engaging with the world without chiefly mediation.

Avoidance of direct colonization spared Tonga's land from permanent appropriation by foreign interests, but it did not spare Tonga from the imposition of British notions of political organization. A centralized monarchy under Taufa'ahau Tupou I and the consolidation of power in Tonga legally delimited the number of chiefly titles and removed much of the power from many chiefs who had administered production among their *kainga* (extended kin). The power of chiefs to accumulate surplus production from commoners and control the distribution of land was substantially diminished in the civil wars of the nineteenth century and replaced by the power of the monarchy and the church.

The nineteenth century also brought the introduction of a number of crop plants, some of which were easily integrated into Tongan agroforestry, and the sum of which contributed to the declining health of what had been a largely sustainable system. Unknown traders introduced cassava to Tonga in 1830, greatly enhancing the productive capacities of Tongan farmers and allowing them to extend the agricultural cycle several years before returning the land to regenerative fallow. Cassava, now the staple of Tongan households, and the cocoyam, drought-tolerant and more productive than *Calocassia taro*, relegated yams to ceremonial significance and eliminated households' need for storage techniques and facilities. The traditional agroforestry system easily incorporated cassava and cocoyams, and village households maintained traditional land-management techniques and forms of communal distribution of labor and resources well into the mid-twentieth century. The wide sharing of perishable resources, such as seasonal fruit and large catches of fish in pola (here *pola* refers to communal fishing activities involving coconut-fiber nets), are examples of the long tradition of productive agroforestry and nonmarket distribution networks.

During World War II, allied troops—first New Zealanders and then Americans—came to Tonga and precipitated changes in Tongans' relationships with each other and their land. Many Tongans had the opportunity to provide labor and food items to the American troops, exposing commoners to a level of material wealth never before experienced. After the war, a small number of Tongans were allowed to migrate to the United States, initiating an export of labor that lasted into the 1980s. The involvement of Tongans in the global economy of the modern era also took commoners to New Zealand and Australia, further providing smallholders with economic alternatives beyond market and subsistence agriculture.

Agricultural production of a small number of cultivars for the market was advocated by both Tongan and New Zealand government representatives after World War II in production schemes meant to mark Tonga's formal integration into the global market. While these schemes contributed to the economic independence of commoner households, they presented a qualitatively different form of agriculture than did the premarket system. The introduction of market monocropping of watermelon and bananas in the 1960s and squash in the 1980s had a far more dramatic effect on human-land relations in Tonga than did the introduction of cassava and cocoyams. Bananas, watermelon, and squash all require significant departures from traditional land-management practices, including the use of tractor tillage, pesticides, and fertilizers. The ecological consequences of introducing industrialized agriculture would not be recognized until the early 1970s.

After perhaps thirty years of banana and watermelon production and significant population in-migration to the main island of Tongatapu, Tongan farmers began to notice a decline in soil fertility and decreasing crop yields. The presence of non-agriculturally productive civil servants and entrepreneurs in the economic center of the kingdom in Nuku'alofa prompted the production of surplus for the urban market beyond production required by families. Export production of bananas and squash intensified the overexploitation of soil reserves by decreasing fallow cycles and diminishing plant diversity. The transformation of a complex agriculture system with a wide diversity of subsistence crops into a simplified system of monocropping small numbers of market cultivars occurred over a full century. The modern Tongan agroforestry system was at its peak of change during my field research in 1991–93, and production was characterized by a host of both industrial and indigenous land-management activities.

The combination of labor outmigration with privatized agricultural production brought newfound wealth and new forms of status in education and employment that were not previously granted to commoners. Status distinctions in the past had been marked by chiefs' economic and social superiority. As Wendy Cowling (1990) has noted, and as my research among Tongan-Americans confirms, outmigration has enhanced commoner status as it has diminished chiefly status.[4] These changes were presaged by the increased privatization of landholdings in Tonga granted through the constitution that marked the formation of the Tongan nation-state and fostered independent economic strategizing by smallholders previously dependent on subsistence agriculture and the largess of landowning chiefs.

Structural descriptions of Tongan social organization in anthropology tend to overlook both the interdependency among the classes and the political agency of commoners.[5] Today, while formal recognition is afforded to chiefs at feasts and *fonos* (community meetings), the increasing economic independence of smallholders has diminished commoner loyalties in many parts of Tonga. In the village where I stayed, lack of traditional respect took the form of vicious rumors about higher-ranking village families and what commoners thought of as the un-Tongan behavior of some nobles. Along with increased demands for the democratization of the Tongan parliamentary government, an increasingly vocal oppositional press, and political-ideological influences from Tongans in New Zealand, Australia, and the United States, loyalty to higher-ranked peoples was diminishing, particularly among younger Tongans. Suspicion that the noble had not presented a proper role model for *anga fakaTonga* (the Tongan way) fueled disgruntlement among village commoners over the chief's unexpected demands for resources. The commoners were now largely independent of the noble's control but remained invested in the cultural significance of commoner-chiefly relations. The public and symbolic display of displeasure performed at the feast allowed commoners to simultaneously exhibit their contemporary economic independence and their deep cultural heritage.

While Tongan commoner households are still substantially dependent on agricultural production for subsistence (Stevens 1997), they are incorporated into a globalized political economy through the operation of a migration, remittances, aid, and bureaucracy (MIRAB) economy (Bertram and Watters 1985). While many scholarly works locate Tongan commoners in a global network (Benguigui 1989; Connell and Lea 2002; Connell 1986, 1988, 1991; Helu 1985), few works other than Cathy A. Small's (1999) or Mike Evans's (2001) focus on the transformations of commoner material and social life brought by these new political-economic relations. Tongan commoner households now manage a variety of economic alternatives (wage labor, civil service, subsistence and market agriculture, remittances) used to meet social obligations as well as enhance standards of living along westernized concepts. These new relations of production have had a number of contemporary consequences, including alterations in household production and consumption practices (Stevens 1997), disruption of local demographic patterns brought by labor migration, rapid degradation of the agricultural resource base (Evans 1999, James 1993, Stevens 1999), demands for democratization of the constitutional monarchy (Hau'ofa 1994b, Hills 1991; also see James 1995), and greater economic investment in technology and telecommunications (van Fossen 1999).

Creative reworking of household production and consumption patterns are expected outcomes of changing political-economic contexts (Greenberg and Park 1994). In Tonga, however, predictions that an economic middle class separate from genealogical status would develop (Benguigui 1989, Helu n.d., Needs 1988) have not been played out because households with higher genealogical rankings have also tended to gain preferred access to higher-paying civil service jobs and greater economic well-being (Stevens 1997, 291). Nevertheless, production and consumption patterns have changed in all but the most impoverished households in the village in which I stayed in Tonga, and only those impoverished households remained completely dependent on subsistence agriculture. Some of these changes are due to the demographic imbalances brought by labor migration, resulting in a loss of people in the working and reproductive age groups between thirty and forty-five years old.

The effect of population change on the landscape varies from island chain to island chain. In Ha'apai, the villages are generally composed of the elderly and children. Those of working age have migrated to Nuku'alofa (Evans 2001), and much agricultural land lies fallow and unproductive. In Tongatapu, an influx of migrants, population pressure, and subsequent conversion of land to market production have contributed to soil degradation and loss of botanical diversity, as I will discuss. There, farmers are converting to industrialized forms of agriculture to produce squash and sugar beets for international export. On 'Eua, farmers are growing traditional crops for sale to agriculturally nonproductive households in Nuku'alofa. But the effects of labor outmigration on Tongatapu are more insidious with regard to landscape alteration. Many young men without access to their own agricultural allotments gain the use of allotments owned by relatives overseas. In many instances these allotments are extensively ploughed and used for market crop production since nonowners, concerned only with immediate returns on their labor, are not particularly interested in the possible long-term consequences of their short-term uses of the land.[6]

The major market crop in 1987–93 was either squash for the Japanese market, which afforded households a rapid return on labor and capital expenses, or cassava, which served as a source of ad hoc household cash. This allowed the addition of imported lamb "flaps" (sheep ribs) or tinned meats to the traditional *haka* (stew of cassava in coconut milk) that typifies the daily fare. These processes influenced the landscape because farmers were required to alter their traditional system of swidden agriculture by using tractor tillage, adjusting fallow periods, and applying fertilizers. The farmers with whom I studied practiced twelve different fallow cycling systems, many of which dramatically shortened a traditional system of three productive years followed by five fallow years, organized in a counterclockwise rotation of one-acre plots in a three-hectare allotment. I frequently found systems of semiproductive fallow fields growing pineapples or remnants of taro used to supplement market or household subsistence needs. Some farmers had abandoned fallow cycles entirely and engaged in large-scale market production, in part necessitated by their dependency on the chemical fertilizers needed to replenish soil fertility (Clarke 1994, Clarke and Thaman 1993, Thaman 1990).

While tractor tillage greatly eases agricultural labor requirements, tractors damage or kill deciduous tree saplings, damage coconut tree roots, and encourage the spread of Guinea grass. These effects diminish soil fertility and decrease the soil's capacity to hold water (Halavatau 1991, Stevens 1996, Trangmar 1992). While the relationship between tillage techniques, chemical fertilizers, and soil structural and chemical fertility are complex, decreasing fallow periods, infiltration of Guinea grass, and increasing use of tractors and chemical fertilizers seem to contribute to the net result of decreased soil structural fertility, decreased botanical diversity (James 1993, Stevens 1996), increased soil acidification, and increased rates of nutritional leaching from soils. Siua Halavatau (1991, 1992) and his colleagues (Halavatau et al. 1992) provide data on the consequences of changed agricultural production on the soils in Tongatapu. Halavatau's greatest concern is with the loss of organic matter in the soil and the decrease of water-stable aggregates in the soil: "The major threat to the Tongan agricultural systems [*sic*] is the breaking of the nutrient cycling system by cutting of forests and loss of nutrients as a result of logging, increased frequencies of shortened fallow period, or permanent cultivation" (Halavatau et al. 1992, 108).

The New Zealand Soil Bureau's analyses of soils in Tonga show there are two variations of one soil type, an *udic mollisol*, in the estate where I worked (Cowie et al. 1991, Gibbs 1976). *Fahefa* soils are found in the southern portion of the estate, and *Fatai* soils comprise the larger soil type in the northern three-quarters of the estate. Fatai and Fahefa soils are not distinguished by differences in chemical profiles; rather, Fahefa soils are well drained and Fatai soils less well drained. J. P. Widdowson (1992, 18) has argued that variations in soil chemical or physical properties on different agricultural plots in this area of Tongatapu must be due to differences in land-management techniques since the inherent soil type is the

same throughout. The consequences of agricultural transformation from a traditional system of farinaceous agriculture to industrial market crop production
can be seen in changes in soil fertility and, specifically, as chemical fertility is
replaced by fertilizers, in soil structure and the soil's capacity to hold water.

Realizing the complex historical, social, and political processes that have
induced farmers to change production activities, I sought to test the consequences of certain land-management activities on soil structure. I collected soil
samples from fifty-nine different sites that had production histories ranging
from long-term fallow to continuous monocropped production for the market.
The sampling procedure was to collect soil samples from plots that could be
placed along a continuum of production from long-term fallow to five years of
continuous production. Samples were collected from long-term fallows of up to
forty-five years, short-term fallows of both mixed brush and grass types, and a
range of productive histories from the first year of production to the fifth year of
production in a number of different management regimes. I categorized these
different land-management regimes into four basic types:

1. Monocropped production of squash for export, characterized by extensive
   plowing and use of fertilizers and chemicals
2. Very intensive subsistence and market production characterized by occasional plowing and application of external inputs; usually involving multiple years of mixed production and shortened fallow periods
3. Subsistence production characterized by farinaceous crops with limited
   plowing and fallow-production ratios equal to or greater than 1 to 0 (for
   example, five years' fallow to five years' production)
4. Land area fallow and out of production for more than three years

L. M. Potter (1986) attempted this approach to testing the consequences of
land management on soil fertility, but he was not able to reach any firm conclusions regarding declines in soil fertility or the repercussions of declining soil fertility for continued agricultural production in Tonga. The soil's physical condition
and ability to hold water are reflected in the soil fertility parameter called water-
stable aggregates. Extensive plowing and insufficient addition of raw organic matter to the soil diminish soil's water-holding abilities. Green manuring, grazing on
fallow, carrying manure to fields, or regular and lengthy fallow regimes restore
organic matter to the soil. Soil organic matter facilitates the availability of soil nutrients to plants, enhances the soil's water-holding ability, and reduces soil erosion.
Moreover, evidence suggests that grass fallows return less organic matter to the soil
than fallows with a high diversity of deciduous plants (Van Wambeke 1992, 76).

The soil chemical and structural fertility measures I used in the study
included pH; total nitrogen; water-stable aggregates; organic carbon; exchangeable calcium, magnesium, potassium, and sodium; Olsen phosphorous; cation
exchange capacity; percentage of base saturation; and carbon-nitrogen ratio.

TABLE 9.1

New Zealand Soil Bureau: Ranges of Soil Fertility Indices

Level	pH	Organic Carbon	Total Nitrogen	Carbon-Nitrogen Ratio	Olsen Phosphous	Cation Exchange Capacity
Very high	7.6+	>20	>1.0	>24	>50	>25
High	7.5–6.6	10–20	0.6–1.0	16–24	30–50	25–40
Medium	6.5–5.3	4–10	0.3–0.6	12–16	20–30	12–25
Low	5.2–4.5	2–4	0.1–0.3	10–12	10–20	6–12
Very low	< 4.5	< 2	< 0.1	< 10	<10	< 6

The New Zealand Soil Bureau has established ranges for some of these measures for Tongan soils. The figures provide a basis for the interpretation of the findings of soil fertility in my study (see table 9.1).[7]

Soil organic matter is important for stable agricultural systems, and its presence is expressed in soil analyses as total organic carbon and/or total nitrogen. The primary sources of these compounds are living organisms that decompose organic matter and return nutrients to the soil in a form available to plants. The amount of the organic matter itself is based on how much biomass remains in the system, which in turn depends on the availability of nutrients, the amount of rainfall and solar radiation, and the age of the vegetation. Traditional agricultural management with long-term success protects and enhances soil organic matter for the health of the system.[8] Adding chemical fertilizers replaces the nutrients necessary for plant growth but does not replace the organic matter on which soil biology, structure, and water-holding abilities are based. Since the sample size was small (fifty-nine), a nonparametric method of quantitative analysis was used to determine if difference in soil fertility measures were statistically significant. According to these calculations, the differences in soil fertility between the four land-management types were statistically significant at the 0.05 level for five of the eleven parameters: total nitrogen, water-stable aggregates, organic carbon, Olsen phosphorous, and pH. Decreases in total nitrogen, water-stable aggregates, organic carbon, and pH can all be attributed to frequent plowing and overexploitation of soil resources. These indices of soil fertility reflect changes in the structure of the soil but not its chemical fertility. The differences in the other six measures reflect soil chemical fertility, and these were not expected to be revealing because of fertilizer application on plowed fields. The significant differences in the five measures, four of which are relevant to preservation of soil organic matter and the soil's ability to hold water, illuminate the possible consequences of a transformed agriculture.

TABLE 9.2

Soil Fertility Measurements

Measure	Monocropped Production	Subsistence and Market Production	Subsistence Production	Land Fallow
% of base saturation	96.08	96.92	96.33	96.82
Cation exchange capacity	39.80	44.20	39.40	46.90
Carbon-nitrogen ratio	19.23	19.09	20.00	17.94
Exchangeable calcium	32.20	33.20	30.00	36.80
Exchangeable potassium	1.30	1.88	1.80	2.01
Exchangeable magnesium	4.50	6.00	5.70	5.90
Exchangeable sodium	1.07	1.16	1.17	1.16
Olsen phosphorus	29.00	24.30	17.70	11.10
Organic carbon	5.00	4.70	5.10	5.70
pH	6.08	6.38	6.40	6.36
Total nitrogen	0.26	0.25	0.28	0.31
Water-stable aggregates	48.90	46.00	55.70	62.00

The findings of the soils analysis of the Nukunuku farmlands are summarized in table 9.2, showing the median scores in each of the soil fertility measurements for the four management regimes described in the text.

Conclusion

Place and space, together with the structured relations of production that characterize Tongan social organization, have been significantly transformed in a process of globalization, as have the structured relations of production that characterize Tongan social organization. The data suggest that the alteration of Tongan means of production, ownership and control over land, and the integration of foreign cultivars and ideologies are all related to changes in soil fertility. The immediate precipitating factor in the degradation of soil fertility and botanical diversity can be located with equal facility in population change, changes in market-based demands, or tractor tillage. Indeed, no simple precipitating factor seems singularly persuasive. The historical political ecology approach of this study reveals that these processes of agricultural change, while accelerated since the 1960s, began in 1865 and have involved a host of interceding and interrelated variables.

Tongan commoner households strategically intensify their economic activities in and out of agriculture to adjust to changing political-economic contexts. Their ability to act on economic alternatives originated with the granting of inalienable rights to land. There has been increased individuation of productive ownership since the constitution of 1865; and more recent migrations of relatives to the United States, New Zealand, and Australia has allowed for a freer flow of pālangi ideas. The past decade in Tonga has been characterized by demands for government democratization and commoners' expression of new views about the rank and status of their nobles. Indeed, the process of labor migration has altered the relative statuses of Tongan actors so that genealogical rank no longer automatically grants respect and economic prestige.

Evidence of emergent transformations in the balance of power in productive and social relations in Tonga can be illuminated by ethnographic events that are not merely anecdotal but deeply disclosing and significant. The birthday feast, for example, demonstrated transformations in the political and economic relations among actors on the Tongan stage. Understanding transformations in the environment requires greater understanding of the social relations of the actors who are responsible for those environmental transformations. The maintenance of ritual structures has political relevance; these structures index relations of production and mark emergent changes in socially structured, productive relations of power. The ritual event is significant in both its historical antecedence and as a contemporary context for negotiation of the social transformations of a globalized Tongan polity. Part and parcel of the context in which this symbolic action occurred are changing agricultural management practices, changing commoner access to wealth, and transformations of the environment. The birthday celebration reflects a changing political-ecology economy, as do changing botanical features and lowered soil fertility. Contemporary political ecology is well served by both quantitative and qualitative data and by the various methodologies required to obtain these forms of information to explain and contextualize the complexities of human-environment relations.

NOTES

1. *Farinaceous* refers to starchy root and tree crops that characterize Pacific and some of Central and South American agroforestry. These crops include true yams from the

genus *Dioscorea*, sweet potatoes (*Ipomoea batatas*), taro (*Colocasia esculenta*), and breadfruit (*Artocarpus altilis*).

2. Patrick Kirch, David Steadman, and Michael Spriggs have conducted archaeological research in the Pacific. Historical references include Martin (1981 [1817]), Campbell (1992), Wood (1978 [1932]), and Latukefu (1974). Documentation of Pacific agro-forestry has been done by Clark (1994), Clark and Thaman (1993), Thaman (1994), and Stevens (1996, 1999). Political-economic analyses have been most notably provided by Connell and Lea (2002). The ethnographic literature on Tonga and the South Pacific is extensive.

3. Research on agroforestry in Tonga was funded by the Wenner-Gren Foundation for Anthropological Research (grant number 5391). Some portions of this chapter were included in a paper presented at the annual meeting of the American Ethnological Society in 2001. I want to thank Susan Paulson, Lisa L. Gezon, Lynn Stevens, and Mark Peterson for reviewing early drafts of the chapter.

4. The Wenner-Gren Foundation for Anthropological Research funded research on demographic change in Tonga (grant number 6503).

5. See Evans (2001) for a persuasive and nuanced discussion of the contemporary social organization of Tongan village commoners.

6. The most important market crop in Tonga has been squash produced for the Japanese market. With its three-month growing season, squash gives smallholders a rapid return on their investment of labor and external inputs. Sugar beets were introduced in 1991 and have not yet gained wide popularity. Tonga produces high-quality vanilla. Vanilla production is labor-intensive but requires little external inputs and does not seem to have a negative effect on soil fertility.

7. *pH:* testing the relative acidity or alkalinity of the soils. A pH between 6.5 (slightly acid) to 5.3 (moderately acid) is considered optimal.

   Total nitrogen: a major nutrient in soils that indicates, with organic carbon, the amount of organic matter in the soil. Ideal levels of total nitrogen for the tropical soils in Tonga lie between 0.6 and 1.0; 0.3 to 0.6 is in the medium range for this parameter.

   Water-stable aggregates: a measure of the structural fertility of the soil. It decreases with increased extensive tillage and indicates the soil's susceptibility to leaching of nutrients.

   Organic carbon: a measure of the amount of organic matter in the soil. High levels indicate high nutrient levels and the soil's capacity to avoid leaching of nutrients. Nutrients are released from the reserve of organic carbon.

   Exchangeable calcium, magnesium, potassium, and sodium: measures of these micronutrients in the soil demonstrate their availability to plants and show their relative availability in soluble form as anions or cations. High ratings would be 10–20 for calcium, 3–7 for magnesium, 0.8–1.2 for potassium, and 0.7–2.0 for sodium.

   Olsen phosphorous: measures the amount of available phosphorous in the soil for rea-sons similar to the exchange capacities just described. A range of 30–50 is high.

   Cation exchange capacity: nutrients in soil must be in a form readily absorbed by plant roots; that is, calcium, magnesium, potassium, and sodium must be in simple sol-uble forms, not locked up in complex chemical structures where they cannot be absorbed. A high cation exchange capacity along with high organic matter indi-cates a high level of available nutrients in the soil. Optimal ranges are 25–40. The measure tells about the relative replaceability of cation (positively charged ions) on the surface of clay or humus particles, those easily available to plants, and measures the state of soil leaching.

Percentage of base saturation: expressed as a percentage of cation exchange capacity. It measures the extent to which the surface of soil particles is occupied by exchangeable basic cations. A range of 60–80 percent is high; a moderate range is 40–60 percent.

Carbon-nitrogen ratio: an indicator of the state of decomposition of organic matter in the soil. A carbon-nitrogen ratio greater than 15 indicates high amounts of raw or poorly decomposed organic matter in the soil.

8. See Netting's (1968) classic *Hill Farmers of Nigeria* for an ethnographic account and Altieri (1995) and Gleissman (1998) for agro-ecological accounts of the significance of soil organic matter in regenerative and stable agriculture.

REFERENCES

Altieri, Miguel. 1995. *Agroecology: The Science of Sustainable Agriculture.* Boulder, Colo.: Westview.

Australian Broadcasting Corporation. 2003. "Tonga: Large Crowd Turns Out in Support of Democracy." June 10, 2003. Transcript.

Benguigui, Georges. 1989. "The Middle Class in Tonga." *Journal of the Polynesian Society* 98, no. 4: 451–63.

Bertram, I. G., and R. F. Watters. 1985. "The MIRAB Economy in South Pacific Microstates." *Pacific View Point* 26, no. 3: 497–519.

Bott, Elizabeth. 1981. "Power and Rank in the Kingdom of Tonga." *Journal of the Polynesian Society* 90, no. 1: 7–81.

———. 1982. "Tongan Society at the Time of Captain Cook's Visits: Discussions with Her Majesty Queen Salote Tupou (with the Assistance of Tavi)." Memoir no. 44. In *The Polynesian Society.* Wellington, New Zealand: Polynesian Society.

Campbell, Ian C. 1992. *Island Kingdom: Tonga Ancient and Modern.* Christchurch, New Zealand: Canterbury University Press.

Clarke, William C. 1994. "Traditional Land Use and Agriculture in the Pacific Islands." In *Land Use and Agriculture: Science of Pacific Island Peoples,* edited by John Morrison, Paul Geraghty, and Linda Crowl, 2: 11–38. Suva, Fiji; Institute of Pacific Studies.

Clarke, William C., and Randall R. Thaman, eds. 1993. *Agroforestry in the Pacific Islands: Systems for Sustainability.* New York: United Nations University Press.

Connell, John. 1986. "Population, Migration, and Problems of Atoll Development in the South Pacific." *Pacific Studies* 9, no. 2: 41–58.

———. 1988. "Sovereignty and Survival: Island Microstates in the Third World." *Research Monograph,* no. 3. Sydney: University of Sydney, Department of Geography.

———. 1991. "Island Microstates: The Mirage of Development." *Contemporary Pacific* 3, no. 2: 251–87.

Connell, John, and John P. Lea. 2002. *Urbanization in the Pacific.* Sydney: Routledge.

Cowie, J. D., P. L. Searle, J. P. Widdowson, and G. E. Orbell. 1991. *Soils of Tongatapu, Kingdom of Tonga.* Lower Hutt, New Zealand: Department of Scientific and Industrial Research.

Cowling, Wendy. 1990. "Motivations for Contemporary Tongan Migration." In *Tongan Culture and History,* edited by Phyllis Herda, Jennifer Terrell, and Neil Gunson, 187–205. Canberra: Australian National University, Department of Pacific and Southeast Asian History.

Evans, Mike. 1999. "Is Tonga's MIRAB Economy Sustainable? A View from the Village and a View without It." *Pacific Studies* 22, nos. 3–4: 137–66.

———. 2001. *The Persistence of the Gif: Tongan Tradition in Transnational Context.* Ottawa: Wilfred Laurier University Press.

Ferdon, Edwin. 1987. *Early Tonga: As the Explorers Saw It, 1616–1810.* Tucson: University of Arizona Press.

Geertz, Clifford. 1973. *The Interpretation of Culture.* New York: Basic Books.

Gibbs, H. S. 1976. *Soils of Tongatapu, Tonga.* Wellington: New Zealand Soil Bureau.

Gifford, James. 1929. "Tongan Society." *Bishop Museum Bulletin*, no. 61. Honolulu: Bernice P. Bishop Museum.

Gleissman, Stephen R. 1998. *Agroecology: Ecological Processes in Sustainable Agriculture.* Chelsea, Mich.: Ann Arbor Press.

Greenberg, James B., and Thomas K. Park. 1994. "Political Ecology." *Journal of Political Ecology* 1, no. 1: 1–12.

Gupta, Akhil, and James Ferguson. 2002. "Beyond 'Culture': Space and the Politics of Difference." In *The Anthropology of Globalization*, edited by Jonathan Xavier Inda and Renato Rosaldo, 65–80. London: Blackwell.

Halavatau, Siua M. 1991. "Effects of Cultivation on Water Stable Aggregates and Organic Matter Content of Tongan Soils." Nuku'alofa, Tonga: Ministry of Agriculture, Forestry, and Fisheries. Unpublished manuscript.

———. 1992. "Effects of Tillage and Fallow on the Productivity of Tongan Soils." Nuku'alofa, Tonga: Ministry of Agriculture, Forestry, and Fisheries. Unpublished manuscript.

Halavatau, Siua, T. V. Menu, and F. S. Pole. 1992. "Perception of Soil Fertility/Management Problems Facing Tonga." In *Proceedings of the Soil Fertility and Land Evaluation Workshop, Kingdom of Tonga, 3–7 February 1992*, edited by B. B. Trangmar, 103–12. Lower Hutt, New Zealand: Department of Scientific and Industrial Research.

Hau'ofa, Epeli. 1994a. "Our Sea of Islands." *Contemporary Pacific* 6, no. 1: 147–62.

———. 1994b. "Thy Kingdom Come: The Democratization of Aristocratic Tonga." *Contemporary Pacific* 6, no. 2: 415–28.

Helu, 'I. Futa. 1985. "Tonga in the 1990s." Paper presented at a meeting of the New Zealand Institute for International Affairs, May.

———. 1994. "The Ethnoscience of the Cultivation of the Frail Kahokaho." In *Land Use and Agriculture: Science of Pacific Island Peoples*, edited by John Morrison, Paul Geraghty, and Linda Crowl, 2:39–50. Suva, Fiji: Institute of *Pacific Studies*.

———. N.d. "A Short General Profile of the Socio-Economic and Political Situation." Unpublished manuscript.

Hills, Rodney C. 1993. "Predicaments in Polynesia: Culture and Constitutions in Western Samoa and Tonga." *Pacific Studies* 16, no. 4: 115–29.

James, Kerry E. 1991. "Migration and Remittances: A Tongan Village Perspective." *Pacific Viewpoint* 32, no. 1: 1–23.

———. 1993. "Cutting the Ground from under Them? Commercialization, Cultivation and Conservation in Tonga." *Contemporary Pacific* 5, no. 2: 215–43.

———. 1995. "The Kingdom of Tonga: Political Review." *Contemporary Pacific* 7, no. 1: 164–67.

———. 2001. "Tonga: Political Review." *Contemporary Pacific* 13, no. 1: 258–60.

Kaeppler, Adrienne. 1971. "Rank in Tonga." *Ethnology* 10, no. 2: 174–93.

Latukefu, Sione. 1974. *Church and State in Tonga: The Wesleyan Methodist Missionaries and Political Development, 1822–1875.* Canberra: Australian National University Press.

Martin, John. 1981 [1817]. *Tonga Islands: William Mariner's Account.* Nuku'alofa, Tonga: Vava'u.

Needs, Andrew P. 1988. *New Zealand Aid and the Development of Class in Tonga.* Palmerston North, New Zealand: Massey University.

Netting, Robert McC. 1968. *Hill Farmers of Nigeria.* Seattle: University of Washington Press.

———. 1993. *Smallholders, Householders: Farm Families and the Ecology of Intensive, Sustainable Agriculture.* Stanford, Calif.: Stanford University Press.

Potter, L. M. 1986. *Tongan Soils: Site Characteristics and Management Practices.* Smallholder project. Armidale, Australia: University of New England.

Roseberry, William. 1989. *Anthropologies and Histories: Essays in Culture, History, and Political Economy.* New Brunswick, N.J.: Rutgers

Sahlins, Marshall. 1958. *Social Stratification in Polynesia.* Seattle: University of Washington Press.

Small, Cathy A. 1999. *Voyages: From Tongan Villages to American Suburbs.* Ithaca, N.Y.: Cornell University Press.

Stevens, Charles J. 1996. "The Political Ecology of a Tongan Village." Ph.D. diss., University of Arizona.

———. 1997. "Gender, Labor, Production, and Consumption: Smallholder Agriculturalists in the Kingdom of Tonga." *Research in Economic Anthropology* 18: 281–329.

———. 1999. "Taking Over What Belongs to God: The Historical Ecology of Tonga Since European Contact." *Pacific Studies* 22, nos. 3–4: 189–220.

Thaman, Randall R. 1990. "Agrodeforestation and the Neglect of Trees: Threat to the Well-Being of Pacific Societies." South Pacific Regional Environmental Programme. Occasional paper, no. 5. Noumea, New Caledonia: South Pacific Commission.

———. 1994. "Pacific Island Agroforestry: An Endangered Science." In *Land Use and Agriculture: Science of Pacific Island Peoples,* edited by John Morrison, Paul Geraghty, and Linda Crowl, 2:191–222. Suva, Fiji: Institute of Pacific Studies.

Trangmar, B. B. ed. 1992. *Proceedings of the Soil Fertility and Land Evaluation Workshop, Kingdom of Tonga, 3–7 February 1992.* Lower Hutt, New Zealand: Department of Scientific and Industrial Research.

Van Fossen, Anthony. 1999. "Globalization, Stateless Capitalism, and the International Political Economy of Tonga's Satellite Venture." *Pacific Studies* 22, no. 2: 1–26.

Van Wambeke, Armand. 1992. *Soils of the Tropics: Properties and Appraisals.* New York: McGraw-Hill.

Widdowson, J. P. 1992. "Soil Resources of Tonga and Their Potential." *Proceedings of the Soil Fertility and Land Evaluation Workshop, Kingdom of Tonga, 3–7 February 1992,* edited by B. B. Trangmar, 17–24. Lower Hutt, New Zealand: Department of Scientific and Industrial Research.

Wolf, Eric. 1982. *Europe and the People without History.* Berkeley: University of California Press.

Wood, A. H. 1978 [1932]. *History and Geography of Tonga.* Nuku'alofa, Tonga: Kalia.

10

Gendered Practices and Landscapes in the Andes

The Shape of Asymmetrical Exchanges

SUSAN PAULSON

The Andean region is characterized by extraordinary geographic and ecological diversity and a great complexity of cultural practices and patterns. Across the Andes, rural families manage dissimilar and often distant geographic and ecological spaces; numerous species and varieties of plants and animals; multiple economic systems and relations; and a wide gamut of knowledge, techniques, and organizational strategies. Relations among these elements have been orchestrated through politics of resource allocation and management in which social differentiation and interdependence—expressed in gender, generational, ethnic, and spatial terms—are key factors. Andean forms of social organization (notably, ethnic-based polities called *ayllus*) have been widely interpreted as sophisticated technologies for environmental management (Alberti and Mayer 1974, Izko 1992, Healy 2001, Masuda et al. 1985, Molina Rivero 1987; Murra 1956). Anthropologists have also analyzed gender meaning and practice and the symbolic gendering of Andean space (Arnold and Yapita 1996, Harris 1980, Isbell 1997, Rösing 1997, Sikkink 1997). In this chapter, I draw on both traditions to explore the processes through which gendered environmental practices shape and give meaning to landscapes and the processes through which changes in biophysical environments influence gender identities and relations.[1]

This chapter describes practices and relations of farming, herding, and cooking in one region of the central Andes that produce and reproduce people and places in culture-specific ways. It also explores how these practices and landscapes have been changing in relation to regional and global processes of agricultural modernization. The case study begins with the startling erosion and degradation of mid-watershed slopes registered in the 1980s and 1990s in Bolivia and the reduced productivity and social value described by many of the women who manage these slopes for grazing livestock, collecting fuelwood, and other purposes. Although both problems have been documented in many parts of the developing world, this study explores new conceptual and methodological approaches to understanding links between them. First, it uses participatory research methods that facilitate the examination of social and ecological dimensions of local productive practices. Second, it establishes a multiscale frame of reference to consider relations among rural farms and farmers, near and distant landscapes, urban produce and labor markets, and national-international interests and processes. Finally, an analytic focus on gender and socioeconomic differences, together with the asymmetrical exchanges that shape and express those differences, helps to identify power dynamics in these diverse sites and processes. Gender is understood here as a social and cultural system that organizes and gives meaning to our bodies, practices, relationships, and the world around us with symbolic reference to sex and sexuality. Like systems of production and kinship with which they interact, gender systems function in all human societies, and their manifestations vary widely across time and space.

In the tradition of Piers Blaikie's (1985) early assessment of land degradation, this study does not interpret increasing erosion and reduced productivity as local problems to be addressed through technical solutions. Instead, it scales up to consider wider relations of power and difference that facilitate the flow of energy away from mountain communities—specifically, away from spaces and resources used mainly by women. Drawing on Alf Hornborg's (2001, 1) definition of power as "a social relation built on an asymmetrical distribution of resources and risks," the analysis developed here locates power and politics in the material and meaningful relations of difference surrounding the distribution and exchange of resources as well as in the national and international policies and ideologies that influence the productive processes and markets through which such exchanges take place.

This study is part of an ongoing effort to better understand relationships between two disturbing phenomena manifest in many parts of Latin America: environmental degradation and social inequality (Painter and Durham 1995, Paulson 1998). Both phenomena have been consistently identified as causes or results of impoverishment, deforestation, loss of soil fertility, migration, poor health and nutrition, breakdown of families and communities, and other problems. Yet they are often treated separately in research and action that focus on either ecological or social issues. This chapter uses political ecology concepts and analyses to consider how environmental degradation and social inequality interact to produce these symptoms. (See also studies collected by Guha and Martínez-Alier 1997, Peet and Watts 1996, and Rocheleau et al. 1996.)

A Study of Gendered Practices and Landscapes

Highland Carrasco is an arid mountainous region in Cochabamba, Bolivia, with an average altitude of 2,800 meters and annual rainfall of 60 centimeters. The

Figure 10-1. Perched tree in the Carrasco region of Bolivia.
Photo by Brian Schultz

area has suffered increasingly severe erosion over the past two decades, creating deep gullies, contributing to flash floods, and reducing the viability of present farming strategies (Calvert and Alandia 1993, Paulson and Schultz 1995). The relatively low biodiversity of this high, dry region, together with its long history of human presence and people's visible impact on the landscape, make it ineligible for the wilderness-style conservation models currently applied in parts of the Bolivian lowlands (see fig. 10.1).

Instead, a number of nongovernmental organizations (NGOs) working in the region developed programs to study and address ecological degradation by collaborating with local farmers. I reviewed field records of several organizations to gather information on crops and animals raised in the communities, diseases and other problems that affected them, biodiversity and biomass in grazing areas, and measures of soil depth and analyses of soil constitution.[2] One organization collaborated with farmers to document soil erosion by planting metered stakes deeply in the ground at different locations and marking the soil levels at regular intervals. Another fenced off sectors of hillside to measure regeneration of biomass and plant diversity in relation to areas used for pasture and collection. All of these organizations supported local responses to environmental problems via land-management techniques designed to reduce erosion (such as contour plowing and soil retention walls); the use of improved stoves, bio-energy converters, and other technologies to reduce fuelwood consumption; and the planting of trees. Parallel to these conservation efforts, the projects addressed "social problems" that had been identified, including poverty and migration, through development interventions designed to increase residents' income, such as the agricultural improvement project described later in this chapter.

The ongoing struggles of conservation and development efforts to mitigate the ecological and social problems identified in the region suggest that we need new ways to look at how ecosystems and social systems interact. Analytic frames that encompass multiple aspects of systems stretching across dissimilar and non-contiguous places, such as those developed by political ecologist Karl Zimmerer (1999, 2000), are useful in Carrasco Province, which extends over an arid highland region, a tropical lowland region, and the steep lush cascades in between (see fig. 10.2). Many residents of highland Carrasco, especially men, travel regularly to the tropical lowland region where they tend farms or work as laborers, often in the production and processing of coca and cocaine. Although ancient foot trails link highland and lowland Carrasco, the shortest vehicle road between them takes travelers a hundred miles east to Cochabamba City, then another hundred miles northwest to Chimoré. Other residents, mostly young men, travel to eastern Bolivia or Argentina to seek work in commercial agriculture or construction. Trucks and buses that make the day-long journey from highland Carrasco to Cochabamba City or Santa Cruz carry out migrant workers (mostly men) and marketers (mostly women) with their produce and then transport back to the rural mountain communities manufactured goods and agricultural inputs, along with (new) ideas and values. What goes on in these distant places, and the movements and exchanges among them, influences the people and landscapes of highland Carrasco.

Methodologies for Studying Gendered Practices and Landscapes

Tools for studying resource management with attention to gender were developed and disseminated in the 1990s, provoking much new research as well as ongoing methodological and conceptual revisions (Balarezu 1994, CARE Perú 1994, Feldstein and Poats 1989, GENESYS 1994). In 1994 and 1995, I worked with a number of Bolivian researchers, including Teresa Blanco, Javier Fuentes, Rosario León, and Rosario Valenzuela, to apply some of these tools in highland Carrasco.[3] Our efforts to implement the new methodologies generated a considerable amount of information and also led to numerous confusions and debates, well worth considering for the extent to which they illuminated political dimensions of environmental practice *and* research.

After spending time observing and participating in farm labor, we organized focus groups to catalog men's and women's activities on daily hour sheets and annual calendars. While early research on gender and labor had established lists of men's-versus-women's activities, adding temporal dimensions to these exercises complicated such schemata. It turns out that at vital moments in the agricultural

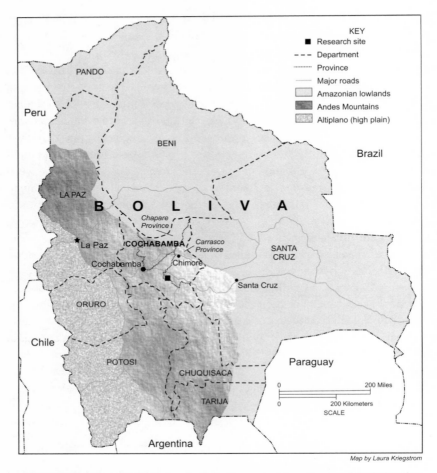

FIGURE 10-2. Map of Bolivia showing how the central department of Cochabamba
extends across high mountains and low rainforest.

cycle, such as planting and harvesting seasons, women spend a great deal of time
and energy on what is often considered the male domain of commercial crops. At
different times of the year, when animals are sheared, treated for parasites, or
butchered, men spend significant time and energy with animals, which are often
considered a female domain. Calendars show that while men's migrational patterns complemented the agricultural cycle to some degree, outside demand for
seasonal labor (notably during commercial rice and sugarcane harvests in
Bolivia's eastern lowlands) competed with on-farm demands in ways that sometimes overburdened those left at home—mainly women, children, and older
people. Uneven access to financial resources shaped women's experience during
these periods of male migration: some women characterized these times as long

hours of heavy labor, while for others the hours were spent supervising and cooking for hired male laborers.

The next steps of our research—participatory mapping and transect walks—were designed to develop spatial and ecological dimensions of the activity calendars by allowing us to observe, and ask about, where diverse activities took place, what resources they involved, and how various actors accessed and controlled those places and resources. We asked groups of men and women to draw maps illustrating the plants, animals, water, and other resources that they use during the year. While each group portrayed a unique set of resources and spaces, including distant locations, the maps drawn by women shared certain perspectives vis-à-vis men's maps. While men prioritized cultivars, for example, women drew and named more wild plants. In a series of day-long transect walks, a local man or woman led one or more researchers on a narrated hike that started from a high point of interest (such as the intake of an irrigation system or a high pasture) and continued to a point below the community (perhaps a choice fishing spot or a neighboring hamlet).

Narratives generated during these walks touched on men's ability to cultivate food plants and women's contribution to the fertility of animals and soil through livestock management. A widower described his difficulties in securing the manure necessary for maintaining agricultural soils; he depended on bags of manure from a married daughter. The way in which these roles relate to gendered landscapes was expressed by an elderly Carrasco man: "I'm at my field all day. Here, nowhere else. This is my place, where I feel good. The house, that's for women. I even eat my lunch here, and take my siesta right here, under the tree." A woman in the same community sighed that her teenage son had complained about pasturing the sheep; he felt that only women and children, not men, should be in the hills with the herds.

During mapping and transect exercises, we asked questions about relationships between individuals and their resources. While the terms of tenure and ownership reflected in our questions elicited valuable discussion, their limitations were made evident by responses such as that of a woman who remarked, "What do you mean, do I own or use these sheep? My duty is to make sure that the herd is healthy and reproduces." Our applications also revealed that research tools were limited by the static assumption that gender identities exist as two discrete categories: men and women. When Carrasco residents were asked to describe women's resources and responsibilities, several asked, "What woman? A young woman [sipas]? Or a mature woman with family [warmi]?" Others differentiated the rights and responsibilities of widows from those of married women, suggesting that the essentialist category *woman* does not coincide with the multiple gender identities and resource-management roles at play in the community. Thus, we became aware of how women's sexual status, and the politics involved therein, is fundamental to the organization of resource management. While our field research was guided by tools based on the admittedly problematic assumption of two static gender categories, the analysis strives to take into account some of the variables, such as socioeconomic status and age, that intersect with gender and to recognize that historical changes give rise to contradictions between the symbolic organization of gender systems and everyday practice.

Organization of Labor and Space

When asked whether certain tasks were carried out by men or women, many community members insisted that "everyone is involved with everything." Our research team came to understand the gendered organization of labor as a series of nested complementarities in which certain tasks or responsibilities are considered feminine or masculine, while subactivities below each rubric involve differentiated collaboration between men and women. Indeed, everyone was involved but not in an undifferentiated way.

In the communities studied, agriculture is generally considered to be a male domain and is, in practice, the principal focus of most men's labor when they are not migrating. Women, for their part, are more closely associated, both practically and symbolically, with the care of livestock (medium-sized herds of sheep and goats, a few cows) and collecting fuelwood, forage, fruits, and herbs. At the same time, each of these sectors encompasses multiple levels of participation.

Within the agricultural sector, for example, men in the region take greater responsibility for main crops (primarily wheat, potatoes, and some corn), which are cultivated in the larger, flatter fields, whereas women have greater responsibility for and participation in secondary crops (broad beans, peas, quinoa, amaranth, squash, and others), which are planted in scattered hillside patches and garden plots or intercropped with corn or around wheat. A larger portion of the main crop is destined for sale, whereas secondary crops, which women administer according to culinary and ritual customs, are mostly consumed or traded. Both spatial and social organization of crops can vary significantly across regions; in higher altitudes, for example, *quinoa* or *tarwi* are often cultivated in larger fields by men. In spite of variations in specific practices, anthropologists working throughout the Andes have noted gendered practice and meaning in cropping patterns (Rösing 1997, Weismantel 1988).

Within the main crops, there are internal differences. For commercial production, led by men, most families use improved seed that provides higher yields and depends heavily on modern training, technology, and inputs that men often obtain from agricultural extension programs. Women tend to play larger roles in the cultivation of local varieties of wheat and potatoes, which are variously resistant to droughts, floods, frost, and plagues. Even within each crop and each field, gendered actors apply different knowledge, skills, and strategies. Family members work side by side in some activities and take different roles in others. With wheat, for example, men tend to prepare the earth and sow the seed, while women and children do much of the weeding. With potatoes, men plow the field with oxen, while women plant the potatoes in the soil.

In sum, different activities, spaces, and knowledges are nominally feminine or masculine, while in practice men and women collaborate at specific points within these domains. This practical organization is meaningful as well. Women's selection, storage, and planting of seed potatoes, for example, are symbolically charged through their identification with Pachamama, the female force behind soil fertility, who is said to "nourish the potatoes at her breast."

Geographies of Interdependence

The next analytic step is to move beyond lists of men's and women's activities to explore relations between different activities and spaces—relations that are practical and meaningful in economic, ritual, cosmological, erotic, and ecological terms. Attention to these relationships helps us to see how ecological dynamics among diverse flora, fauna, and spaces are mediated by gendered social relations.

In the Andes, the interdependence of agriculture and livestock is widely recognized as a basic land-management strategy, and universities and institutions locate farm research and extension in the integral field of *ciencias agropecuarias* (agro-husbandry sciences). Yet in contrast to agriculture and livestock raising, remarkably little research or technical support has focused on the management of hillsides and other noncultivated areas. Besides agricultural parcels and pasture lands, the Carrasco landscape is characterized by networks of paths and canals lined with grasses, shrubs, and trees; corridors of trees and bushes; fallow fields and irregular, rocky, or inclined slopes covered with greenery; and forested ravines in steeper parts of the watershed. Men and women residents explained that these areas serve as physical barriers against wind and water erosion; shade for humans, animals, and crops; biological barriers against crop-specific pests and diseases; and nesting places for birds and animals. They also produce forage, fuelwood, green fertilizer, fruits, roots, and medicinal and culinary herbs. Land-management research and extension projects have often neglected these uses because they do not have market value (and thus are not labeled *productive*) and because women and children (not men) invest large amounts of time and energy in them. Over time, the tendency of scientific and policy initiatives to prioritize commercial products and men's productive activities has contributed to uneven development of mountain landscapes.

Gender organization and meaning influence local topographies in countless other ways. In many families, when a man plants a parcel of wheat on a slope, his wife or daughters plant around it a living fence of tarwi, amaranth, or other robust native plants that protect against erosion and repel pests. Adolescent girls often plant and tend beans between the rows of corn, referring to them as "my beans." Men and women affect the landscape through different purposes and practices of germplasm management. In this region it has been mostly men who obtain improved seed through agricultural extension institutions, while in situ selection and intercommunity exchange are carried out by men and women who manage different species and varieties of seed and select for different character-istics within varieties (Watson and Almanza 1994). Women describe seed selec-tion as a strategy to assure family nourishment within changing ecological and socioeconomic contexts. Women and men also affect semi-domesticated and wild grasses, shrubs, and trees by fostering, discouraging, or otherwise affecting their growth through collection, pasturing, and other practices.

If we look at the landscape in nutritional terms, we see large fields of main crops (significant providers of carbohydrates, calories, and energy) and many smaller swatches of diverse crops that contribute specific proteins, vitamins, and minerals. These species and proportions are reflected in the daily soups cooked and eaten in the communities and in the seasonal foods that mark the annual calendar: bread from a certain wheat baked for All Saints Day, fresh corn soup at Christmas, cabbage and lamb at Carnival (Paulson 2003). Culinary prac-tices and preferences not only reflect but also influence the spatial organization of the landscape as gender-specific knowledge and technique in relation to seed selection, food production, menu planning, and meal preparation play a signifi-cant role in environmental change or sustainability (Weismantel 1988).

In sum, gender influences the organization of diverse sectors, spaces, species, knowledge, and responsibilities: it saturates the landscape. At the same time, it is increasingly apparent that neither social relations nor ecological conditions nec-essarily tend toward equilibrium and that neither exists in isolation from forces outside community territory (Zimmerer 2000, Zoomers 1998). So in addition to exploring the multiple relations among roles, practices, and resources within these mountain farming communities, we also need to explore their dynamic evolution in larger spatial and historical contexts.

A National and Global Push toward Agricultural Modernization

A central question for political ecology is how the social and ecological character-istics of local communities are connected to, and influenced by, forces and events that extend beyond them. Relations between Andean men and women and their resources have changed throughout history in response to many kinds of factors, proximate and distant. Irene Silverblatt (1987) argues that during the fifteenth century, specific political and religious hierarchies that developed with the expansion of the Inca Empire contributed to a significant growth of male control over human and environmental resources. In the following century, the European conquest provoked dramatic shifts in gender order and resource use. In response to Europe's insatiable desire for silver, Spanish viceroy Francisco de Toledo (who governed from 1569 to 1581), mounted a massive program of rotating obligatory mining labor (*mita*) that was designed to draft one-seventh of all adult males in indigenous communities and managed to secure some 12,600 draftees (*mitayos*) annually (Larson 1988, 60). Each year, countless women took over the responsibilities of absent men in their home communities, while thousands of women left their animals and children in the care of others and accompanied men to mining cities to earn what was necessary to feed and clothe them both (Zulawski 1990).

By the time of independence (1825), much of highland Bolivia was organized into a feudal-like mode of production in which elite families (called *hacendados*) owned large tracts of land, while indigenous farmers (*colonos*) paid tribute in exchange for access to small bits of land and water. Although arrangements varied by region and through time, the greatest part of the tribute was usually extended via male labor on hacienda fields and through shares of harvest from colono crops. In these contexts, colono women often sought and managed a variety of peripheral resources, which they used to provide food and clothing for their families (Larson 1988).

Bolivia's 1953 agrarian reform led to the redistribution of much of the land-based resources formerly controlled by hacendado families in Cochabamba. In the following decades, the Bolivian government (motivated by political goals that included a drive for national food self-sufficiency), in collaboration with international funding agencies (motivated by political goals that included a push for economic growth that would facilitate debt payment), promoted a series of modernization policies and programs directed toward intensifying small farm production and increasing the quantity of Bolivian produce sold in national markets. These programs generally promoted land privatization, expansion of area cultivated with commercial crops, and increased yields per unit of land (Urioste 1987, 11); and all extended services directly to male farmers. For decades, little or no effort was invested in studying, supporting, or improving systems for managing grazing lands, wooded ravines, fallow cycles, and other practices that interact and overlap with individual management of commercial agricultural plots. And most agricultural and land-management projects did not take women and their activities and resources into account until the 1990s. Thus, for the past few generations, the decisions and actions of farmers and institutions in Carrasco have been situated in a field of national and international actions and programs that have promoted modernizing political visions and have reconfigured gender relations by allocating modern knowledge and power directly to men. Resulting changes have contributed to new opportunities and new roles, as well as new kinds of exploitation, for farmers in rural Cochabamba (Lagos 1994).

An Agricultural Modernization Project in Carrasco

Specific processes of agricultural modernization have been widely analyzed, criticized, and debated in terms of ecological impacts, on the one hand, and gender impacts, on the other (Carney and Watts 1990; Finan 1997, 82; Kabeer 1994; León de Leal and Deere 1980; Mackenzie 1998; Murray 1994). The following example explores connections between some social and environmental impacts of agricultural modernization.

Through the 1980s, and until its program was changed significantly in the mid–1990s, an internationally funded NGO implemented a relatively typical agricultural modernization project whose major activities included technical training and institutional support to farmer syndicates and wheat producer associations (whose members were virtually all male) for the production of improved wheat that could be certified as high-quality seed; provision on credit of wheat seed and chemical inputs (to those men who had sufficient land and were willing and able to take the risk); and sale on credit of tractors and threshing machines (to a few men who had land titles to use for collateral). The stated general goal of the program was to improve the quality of life of local farm families.

Technically, the project was a tremendous success and squarely fulfilled its operational goals of increasing the area of land cultivated in improved wheat, yield per hectare, net output of certified wheat seed, and cash income of participants. But how did these achievements affect the quality of life of local families? If quality of life is measured by net income, the condition of some families certainly improved. If we define quality of life to include ecological and cultural well-being, however, or a degree of sovereignty over one's labor and resources, answers to the question lie beyond the NGO project indicators.

In light of our previous characterization of labor organization, it is clear that this project, like many others carried out in the region, was directed to selected sectors, spaces, and social groups. Agricultural production was strengthened, but not silviculture or livestock management; commercial production was improved, but not production for family consumption or exchange; monoculture of improved varieties was expanded, but not the cultivation of diverse local species and varieties. Individual production on private plots was supported, while cooperative management of communal spaces was ignored. Men's activities and efforts were strengthened, but not women's. In sum, commercial production was expanded in ways that would compromise certain aspects of the social and environmental context.

In terms of the spatial organization of the landscape, this project (and, more importantly, the regional historical process of which it is but a minor part) motivated and facilitated expansion of the agricultural frontier, impelling farmers to open larger fields on increasingly steep slopes, which displaced and degraded the communal spaces that women and poorer families had been using for multiple purposes. Consequent overgrazing and intensified fuelwood collection in reduced green areas has contributed to deforestation and erosion, leading some observers to conclude that women and land-poor peasants are the main perpetrators of ecological destruction (see discussion in Zimmerer 1993b).

As green areas are degraded and eroded with the expansion of commercial agriculture, women have to take their herds longer distances to find forage, which takes a toll on the health and vitality of both women and livestock. Increasingly, families are forced to sell livestock or arrange for it to be pastured in other communities. Reduced access to manure limits women's capacity to reproduce the fertility of the soil, while reduced access to milk and meat hamper their efforts to sustain family labor through nourishing food. For many families, reallocation of land, labor, and water to commercial fields has coincided with reduced quantity and variety of complementary crops, contributing to increased dependence on purchased foodstuffs and consequent changes in menus and recipes. Even within main crops, diversity has been reduced in the region. Women explained that they used to plant multiple varieties of wheat to guarantee a minimal family diet in the face of climate risks; fulfill specific nutritional, cooking, and storage characteristics; and serve as key ingredients in traditional meals prepared throughout the ritual cycle. Since improved wheat that suffers wind-induced cross-pollination cannot be certified, farmers were advised to curtail their traditional cultivation of diverse varieties. Finally, although the tractors and threshing machines provided by the program easily reduced aspects of men's labor in commercial wheat fields, women's and children's tasks (notably weeding) were increased by the greater area and density of improved wheat and stringent certification standards.

As women lose access to key resources, and as the resources that they do control become degraded, their work becomes less efficient and productive; and many respond to this loss by increasing the time and energy invested in their work. Even so, some of the women interviewed expressed concern that they were failing to provide good food for their families and livestock and failing to assure the health and fertility of soils, animals, and people. These changes in biophysical conditions and social practices affect gender meanings and values. One man complained, "The cost of buying fertilizers and food for the family is constantly increasing, and we men have to earn more and more money to buy these things that everyone used to make at home." Women testified: "My husband hits me because I don't cook well, like they used to." "My mother-in-law criticizes me because I don't make my herd multiply like she did." "My child got sick because I was off herding on a distant mountainside."

Seeking Equality or Equilibrium?

The institutional trajectory took an interesting turn in the early 1990s, when representatives of the major funding agency, OXFAM Netherlands, evaluated the

project using indicators disaggregated by sex to discover that virtually all participants and direct beneficiaries were men and that men accrued disproportionate social value from training and support provided by the project. The gender
evaluation was carried out by social scientists and not linked to an environmental impact study.

Consequent demand for a gender focus evoked an initial response typical of
the times: incorporate women into productive activities. The NGO helped form
an association of women wheat producers, began to distribute improved seed
and chemical input packets to women, and provided technical training to female
members. This resolutely liberal response exemplifies a widespread reformist
approach aimed at ensuring the integration of women into development. Kay
Warren and Susan Bourque (1991) describe the theory behind this kind of effort:
"To the extent that feminists and development critics defined access [to technology and resources] as the crucial issue, the logical solution was to equalize it"
(28).

In the Carrasco case, women in wealthier families, in which both husband
and wife gained access to improved seed packages, did enjoy benefits of their
integration into development. They valued the opportunity to participate in a
formal organization and converse with extension workers. The sale of certified
seed provided income that allowed them to buy more foodstuffs and farm inputs
and to hire other women to assist them. Thus, certain better-off women were lib-
erated from increasingly burdensome "female chores" and could pursue other
activities allowing them to obtain greater status and income. In the words of one
woman participant, "with the proceeds from the wheat, I've begun selling *chicha*
(corn beer); now I have cash all the time and can do what I want to."

While improved conditions enjoyed by the new women producers looked
good on gender evaluations, they were tied to increasingly inequitable distribution of natural, financial, and technical resources within the community. The
access of certain families to a double quota of seed, credit, and technical support
allowed those families to consolidate private control over greater extensions of
cultivated land. This affected poorer families, who had earned a livelihood by
pasturing other people's livestock, gathering and selling fuelwood, and doing
other activities that depend on watershed resources outside of private agricultural plots. Thus, the expansion and intensification of private agricultural plots
at the expense of communally managed areas and resources affects land-poor
families in a disproportionate way, often pushing them to further degrade the
surrounding resources. A single mother of five explained, "It's not worthwhile to
work on the hillsides anymore. There is no fuelwood left, not even grass for the
little animals. Now mostly I wash clothes; there are three or four women who pay
me by the dozen to wash. And I had to send my daughter, the second one, to
Cochabamba City to work as a maid."

Voices such as hers suggest that the difficult situation of rural women is inextricably tied to the degradation of the hillsides that they manage. Starting in the mid–1990s, the NGO in question began to respond to these local voices and visions with programs for improving small livestock management, conserving soils and pastures, and harvesting runoff waters. The NGO also advanced a campaign to raise gender consciousness within the institution (Zambrana and Wade 1997).

Scaling Up: Wider Webs of Interdependency and Power

The asymmetrical exchanges that develop in relations among diverse humans, natural resources, and geographic spaces have long been of central concern in Marxist theory and have been explored on a global scale by dependency and world system theorists (Frank 1967, Wallerstein 1984). Hornborg (2001, 35–48) endeavors to generate a more comprehensive theoretical framework by bringing these social science notions of value and exchange together with thermodynamic analyses of energy to analyze the kinds of social-environmental issues and situations discussed in this book. Without pretending to breach gaps of understanding between current notions of economic value and biophysical energy, I find that the move to consider both types of phenomena within one frame of analysis allows me to explore new models for understanding the dynamics of diverse and interconnected exchange relations.

In Carrasco watersheds, energy from organic matter, forage, moisture, and soil on slopes, combined with women's collecting and herd-management efforts, subsidizes the productivity of agricultural plots located on flatter stretches. With the expansion of commercial agriculture and increasing seasonal migration, less time and energy are being invested in practices that work to maintain the vitality, biomass, and biodiversity of the slopes. An increasing asymmetry between efforts invested in production versus those invested in the regeneration of conditions of production has been documented in other communities in the Cochabamba Department (see Cortes 2001). Karl Zimmerer (1993a), for example, "demonstrates that soil erosion in the Bolivian Andes worsened during recent decades (1953–91) due to changes in production as peasants shifted labor from conservation techniques to nonfarm employment" (1659).[4]

In regional markets, agricultural products obtain market values too low to maintain the social and ecological resources necessary to continue producing them, let alone fuel the development and socialization of new generations of farmers (Lagos 1994, Urioste 1987). When men migrate to sell their labor, their work is similarly valued with wages too low to reproduce new workers. Those left at home scramble to make up the deficit, often overexploiting their ecological resources and their own labor in the process.

In Bolivia, this constant drain of human, economic, and ecological energy has contributed to degradation and abandonment of farming regions and an exodus from highland communities, resulting in the rampant growth of tropical colonies and new urban satellites, many of whose inhabitants are refugees from failed farms (Dandler 1987, Ledo 2002). While remarkably low prices of domestic food crops in Bolivian markets drain small farms and farmers, they also help allow employers to maintain shockingly low wages. Displaced farmers join the masses who exchange their labor for these low wages, contributing to competitive production and export in areas of agrobusiness, commercial forestry, and mining, as well as coca and cocaine, to the benefit of international investors, businesses and consumers. In the 1990s, conditions of wage labor were so unfavorable in Bolivia that dozens of men from the Carrasco highlands traveled to Argentina to find work. Today, after the traumatic crash of the Argentine economy, many are returning home empty-handed, some on foot.[5]

In this chain of asymmetrical exchanges, we can identify a net flow of energy and economic value away from women, sheep, and mountainsides toward urban centers and, ultimately, international poles of wealth. Numerous analysts have brought attention to the fact that rural hinterlands and indigenous women suffer the most immediate symptoms of degradation in processes of global development (Kabeer 1994, Braidotti et al. 1994). Among others, Maria Mies and Vandana Shiva (1993, 50) argue that both nature and women have been colonized and exploited for the short-term profit motives of affluent societies and classes and that the discursive marginalization of their energy as an externality has enabled dominant groups to continue expanding economic production.

Yet if women and nature are the losers of global economic development, our case certainly does not suggest that men and culture are winners. Men farmers in Carrasco, even ones with successful participation in the kind of modernization project profiled here, are also exploited by the low market value of their produce and labor in a system of multiple inequalities. Moreover, the very success of their development initiatives makes them vulnerable to increased dependency on volatile markets, reduced nutritional security, environmental degradation, weakening of community solidarity, and new kinds of family tensions.

Political and economic decisions that favor the development of certain natural resources and certain social groups can dangerously overexploit and undermine other aspects of the shared environment—often unwittingly, sometimes consciously. Although some critics speak of rural women and hinterlands as being marginalized or excluded from modernization processes, this case suggests that they are very much involved in asymmetrical relations of development. Rural women are vital actors in complex networks of inequitable exchanges built on gender, space, and socioeconomic differences. Neither the construction of these differences nor the exchanges that develop among differentiated groups are free from influence of international political and economic interests. And these social relations of exchange are deeply embedded in and expressed through the material resources and places in which people move and which they continually shape and re-create.

Implications for Research, Development, and Conservation

This chapter explores multiple levels of action and analysis in a study of changing relationships between labor practices and environments in the Bolivian Andes. In the context of recent historical processes promoting the expansion and intensification of commercial agriculture, environmental spaces and resources controlled and managed by men from wealthier families are taking on greater prominence, while those managed primarily by women and poorer families are reduced and degraded in greater proportion. Although social roles and ecological systems vary through space and time, the general processes manifested in this case resonate widely. In all known human groups, practices, knowledge, and resources take on gender meanings and are organized by gender in ways that influence the biophysical environment. In the process, differentiated actors become associated with different resources and dimensions of the landscape in ways that influence their identities, their social value, and their power. Throughout the world, these associations and meanings are changing in response to widely varied modernizing processes.

Another broad implication of this study is that local gender-social systems and landscapes are influenced in both material and meaningful ways by forces and processes that extend far beyond community territory. Some of the concepts, values, and mechanisms of agricultural modernization illustrated in this case were developed in North Atlantic countries and disseminated via global markets, international development policies and programs, and other means. Many have been widely questioned in the past two decades; and government agencies and NGOs, including the NGO described here, have begun to experiment with more integral, participatory, and ecologically balanced approaches (Healy 2001). This chapter throws critical light on key assumptions and forces that continue to influence processes of modernization and define their putative goals: development and quality of life. Since the United Nations Statistical Commission adopted the first system of national accounts in 1953, calculations of economic production, consumption, income, investment, and savings have been used to measure and compare the health and development of nations, while similar indicators have been applied to measure the quality of life of development-project beneficiaries. Ideas of sustainable development, introduced into global discourse via the 1987 Brundtland Report, have promoted greater equity for future generations by calling for progress toward economic development that could be sustained without depleting natural resources or harming the environment. In the 1990s, the United Nations and others expanded the scope of development by including indicators of life expectancy, adult literacy, and school enrollment, together with gross domestic product, in its human development index (UNDP 2001). Yet power, a factor that emerges so prominently in this case study, is still remarkably absent from dominant measures of development and quality of life. How can we redefine human and sustainable development to encompass questions of power over one's body and one's labor; power to control one's resources and territory; and the relative balance of power necessary to engage in equitable and just exchanges of labor, produce, resources, and money?

One lesson learned from this study is that approaches to development and conservation questions that recognize relations among social, ecological, and political dimensions of the environment come up with analyses and responses different from those of sector-specific approaches. This requires moving beyond analytic frameworks and program strategies that treat phenomena such as hillside degradation, women's marginalization, and men's market exploitation as separate problems. Programs throughout Latin America have responded to perceived gender asymmetries with attempts to empower women by incorporating them into productive economic projects that do little to address (and sometimes exacerbate) the environmental degradation and resource loss that is often a critical factor in women's disempowerment.[6] In response to deforestation and erosion, projects have attempted to protect hillsides through retention walls, terraces, fenced-off areas for regeneration, and other approaches that do not address the social and gender situations that led to the overuse and abuse of those hillsides in the first place and sometimes increase demands on women's labor or reduce their access to resources. Benjamin S. Orlove and Stephen Brush (1996) argue that anthropological approaches have had important effects and have great potential for moving conservation projects away from narrowly defined efforts to preserve single species toward more integral programs involving local people and their knowledges, biological resources, and policy concerns. The political ecology methods and analyses demonstrated here might help to realize that potential.

Another lesson from this study is that responding to social-environmental problems in the immediate place of degradation is often not sufficient; we must look beyond proximate causes to discover links with multiple ecological zones, markets, and social and political processes. This requires the use of broader spatial-temporal lenses as well as collaboration among ideas, tools, and people from multiple disciplines. In the case discussed here, that means considering demographic studies of migration practices; economic analyses of agricultural commodification, produce and labor markets; and agro-economic and legislative studies of land reform in Bolivia. It also means looking at the generation and exchange of social capital in the form of knowledge and information (Bebbington 1998). Further work will require investigating the impact on these social and ecological processes of significant changes in governance resulting from the implementation of Bolivia's Law of Popular Participation, passed in 1994 with a mandate to enlarge the powers and autonomy of municipal governments and legitimize the participation of community members and groups in local government (Medeiros 2001).

Finally, this case underscores the need to examine asymmetrical relationships between regimes of knowledge and value in a world where the resources for inventing natures and cultures are unevenly distributed (Escobar 1999). Even in isolated Carrasco, highly political western ideas and methods circulate in the powerful guise of objective reality and technical necessity. Dominant ideas of agricultural modernization and indicators of development progress have isolated commercial production and prioritized it over the rest of life. In the region studied, men have for decades been labeled *producers* and received public esteem and technical and financial support in their work with cash crops. At the same time, women have been associated with *reproduction*, a category conspicuously absent from agricultural improvement and resource-management projects and spuriously associated with the modern housewife. These ideas, values, and indicators influence farmers' decisions to invest in commercial agricultural fields to maximize and sustain cash crops and to neglect steep hillsides, rocky uneven areas, and pasturelands. So in addition to analyzing social, ecological, and political dimensions of productive practice and exchange, we need to examine the forms of knowledge and value that motivate and inform them.

NOTES

1. Research and analysis contributing to this chapter were supported by the United Nations Food and Agriculture Organization, Forests, Trees, and People Project; OXFAM Netherlands; and Catholic Relief Services. I would like to thank the many Bolivian farmers and researchers who engaged in conversations contributing to my understanding of this case. Sincere thanks also go to the colleagues who invited me to present papers on this study, and provided fruitful feedback, at the Latin American Studies Program, Cornell University (2001); the Center for Tropical Research and Development, University of Florida (2001); and the Environment and Development Advanced Research Circle, University of Wisconsin (2002), where Karl S. Zimmerer was especially helpful. Some aspects of this study were addressed in a chapter on multiple tenure arrangements (Paulson 2001) and an article about agroforestry practices (Paulson 2000).

2. The organizations were Centro de Servicios a la Producción de Trigo, Centro Internacional de la Papa, Instituto Boliviano de Tecnología Agropecuaria, and Programa de Asistencia Agrobioenergética al Campesino.

3. During the decade that I lived and worked in the Department of Cochabamba, my understanding of this part of Carrasco also developed through collaborative research with Centro de Servicios a la Producción de Trigo, as member of an environmental impact assessment team with the Cochabamba Regional Development Project, and through an evaluation of gender and participation in an integrated agro-ecology project called Programa de Asistencia Agrobioenergética al Campesino (Paulson and Schultz 1995).

4. Similar processes have been documented in other Andean regions and in Peru were insightfully analyzed by Collins (1988).

5. Personal communication from Stuart Rockefeller, whose ethnographic research spans communities in Potosí, Bolivia, as well as the Buenos Aires barrios where community members live as migrant laborers.

6. According to Kabeer (1994), "The WID [Women in Development] neglect of the inter-connections between production and reproduction in women's lives is echoed, for instance, in USAID [U.S. Agency for International Development] policy, which in 1979 officially defined WID projects as those which increased women's participation, oppor-tunity and income-earning capacities. Explicitly excluded from the WID definitions are those projects in which women are recipients of goods (such as contraception or health projects) or of food and services for themselves or their children" (30).

REFERENCES

Alberti, Giorgio, and Enrique Mayer, eds. 1974. *Reciprocidad e intercambio en Los Andes Peru-anos.* Lima: Instituto de Estudios Peruanos.

Arnold, Denise, and Juan de Dios Yapita. 1996. "Los caminos de género en Qaqachaka: Saberes femeninos y discursos textuales alternativos en Los Andes." In *Ser mujer indí-gena, Chola o Birlocha en la Bolivia postcolonial de los años 90*, edited by Silvia Rivera Cusicanqui, 303–92. La Paz, Bolivia: Ministerio de Desarrollo Humano.

Balarezu, Susana. 1994. "Guía metodológica para incorporar la dimensión de género en proyectos forestales participativos." Quito, Ecuador: United Nations Food and Agricul-ture Organization, Forest, Trees, and People Project.

Bebbington, Anthony. 1998. "Sustaining the Andes: Social Capital and Policies for Rural Regeneration in Bolivia." *Mountain Research and Development* 18, no. 2: 173–81.

Blaikie, Piers. 1985. *Political Economy of Soil Erosion in Developing Countries.* London: Longman.

Braidotti, Rosi, Ewa Charkiewicz, Sabine Hausler, and Saskia Wieringa. 1994. *Women, the Environment, and Sustainable Development: Towards a Theoretical Synthesis.* Lon-don: Zed.

Calvert, Donald, and Segundo Alandia. 1993. "Evaluación ambiental para el proyecto de Desarrollo Regional de Cochabamba (CORDEP)." La Paz, Bolivia: USAID Proyecto.

CARE Perú. 1994. *Género y Desarrollo, Guía del facilitador.* Lima, Peru: CARE Perú.

Carney, Judith, and Michael Watts. 1990. "Manufacturing Dissent: Work, Gender, and the Politics of Meaning in a Peasant Society." *Africa* 60: 207–41.

Collins, Jane L. 1988. *Unseasonal Migrations: The Effects of Rural Labor Scarcity in Peru.* Princeton, N.J.: Princeton University Press.

Cortes, Genevieve. 2001. "Rooted Migrants, Land, and Rural Development in the Valle Alto of Cochabamba, Bolivia." In *Land and Sustainable Livelihood in Latin America*, edited by Annelies Zoomers, 59–70. Amsterdam: Royal Tropical Institute.

Dandler, Jorge. 1987. "Diversificación, procesos de trabajo y movilidad espacial en los valles y serranías de Cochabamba." In *La participación indígena en los mercados surandinos*, edited by Olivia Harris, Brooke Larson, and Enrique Tandeter, 639–82. La Paz, Bolivia: Centro de Estudios de la Realidad Económica y Social.

Escobar, Arturo. 1999. "After Nature: Steps to an Antiessentialist Political Ecology." *Current Anthropology* 40, no. 1: 1–30.

Feldstein, Hilary, and Susan Poats. 1989. *Working Together: Gender Analysis in Agriculture.* Vols. 1 and 2. West Hartford, Conn.: Kumarian.

Finan, Timothy. 1997. "Changing Roles of Agriculture in Global Development Policy: Is Anthropology (Out)Standing in Its Field?" *Culture and Agriculture* 19, no. 3: 79–84.

Frank, Andre Gunder. 1967. *Capitalism and Underdevelopment in Latin America: Historical Studies of Chile and Brazil.* New York: Monthly Review Press.

Gender in Economic and Social Systems Project (GENESYS). 1994. "Gender in Economic and Social Systems: Gender Analysis Toolkit." Washington, D.C.: U.S. Agency for International Development.

Guha, Ramachandra, and Juan Martínez-Alier. 1997. *Varieties of Environmentalism: Essays North and South.* London: Earthscan.

Harris, Olivia. 1980. "The Power of Signs: Gender, Culture, and the Wild in the Bolivian Andes." In *Nature, Culture, and Gender,* edited by Carol P. MacCormack and Marilyn Strathern, 70–94. London: Cambridge University Press.

Healy, Kevin. 2001. *Llamas, Weavings, and Organic Chocolate: Multicultural Grassroots Development in the Andes and Amazon of Bolivia.* Notre Dame, Ind.: University of Notre Dame Press.

Hornborg, Alf. 2001. *The Power of the Machine: Global Inequalities of Economy, Technology, and Environment.* Walnut Creek, Calif.: Altamira.

Isbell, Billie Jean. 1997. "De inmaduro a duro: Lo simbólico femenino y los esquemas Andinos de género." *In Más allá del silencio: Las fronteras de género en los Andes,* edited by Denise Arnold, 253–301. La Paz, Bolivia: Centre for Indigenous American Studies and Exchange/Instituto de Lengua y Cultura Aymara.

Izko, Xavier. 1992. *La doble frontera: Ecología, política y ritual en el Altiplano Central.* La Paz, Bolivia: Editorial Hisbol, Centro de Estudios de la Realidad Económica y Social.

Kabeer, Naila. 1994. *Reversed Realities: Gender Hierarchies in Development Thought.* London: Verso.

Lagos, Maria Laura. 1994. *Autonomy and Power: The Dynamics of Class and Culture in Rural Bolivia.* Philadelphia: University of Pennsylvania Press.

Larson, Brooke. 1988. *Colonialism and Agrarian Transformation in Bolivia: Cochabamba, 1550–1900.* Princeton, N.J.: Princeton University Press.

Ledo, Carmen. 2002. "Poverty and Urbanization in the Cities of the National Economic Corridor of Bolivia." Ph.D. diss., Department of Architecture and Urban Planning, Delft University, the Netherlands.

León de Leal, Magdalena, and Carmen Diana Deere. 1980. *Mujer y capitalismo agrario: Estudio de cuatro regiones Columbianas.* Bogotá, Colombia: Asociación Colombiana para el Estudio de la Población.

Mackenzie, A. Fiona D. 1998. *Land, Ecology, and Resistance in Kenya, 1880–1952.* Oxford: Heinemann.

Masuda, Shozo, Izumi Shimade, and Craig Morris, eds. 1985. *Andean Ecology and Civilization.* Tokyo: University of Tokyo Press.

Medeiros, Carmen. 2001. "Civilizing the Popular? The Law of Popular Participation and the Design of a New Civil Society in 1990s Bolivia." *Critique of Anthropology* 21, no. 4: 401–25.

Mies, Maria, and Vandana Shiva. 1993. *Ecofeminism.* London: Zed.

Molina Rivero, Ramiro. 1987. "La tradicionalidad como medio de articulación al mercado: Una comunidad pastoril en oruro." In *La participación indígena en los mercados surandinos,* edited by Olivia Harris, Brooke Larson, and Enrique Tandeter, 603–38. La Paz, Bolivia: Centro de Estudios de la Realidad Económica y Social.

Murra, John. 1956. "The Economic Organization of the Inca State." Ph.D. Diss., Department of Anthropology, University of Chicago.

Murray, Douglas L. 1994. *Cultivating Crisis: The Human Cost of Pesticides in Latin America.* Austin: University of Texas Press.

Orlove, Benjamin S., and Stephen Brush. 1996. "Anthropology and the Conservation of Bio-diversity." *Annual Review of Anthropology* 25: 329–52.

Painter, Michael, and William Durham. 1995. *The Social Causes of Environmental Destruction in Latin America.* Ann Arbor: University of Michigan Press.

Paulson, Susan. 1998. *Desigualdad social y degradación ambiental en America Latina.* Quito, Ecuador: Abya Yala.

———. 2000. "La diferencia e interdependcia social en el manejo agroforestal." *Agroforestería en Las Américas* 7, no. 25: 8–14.

———. 2001. "No Land Stands Alone: Social and Environmental Interdependency in a Bolivian Watershed." In *Land and Sustainable Livelihood,* edited by Annelies Zoomers. Amsterdam: Royal Tropical Institute.

———. 2003. "New Recipes to Live Better with Pachamama." In *Imaging the Andes: Shifting Margins of a Marginalized World,* edited by Ton Salman and Annelies Zoomers, 251–71. Amsterdam: Aksant.

Paulson, Susan, and Brian Schultz. 1995. *Evaluación de proyecto: Difusión de la agropecuaria alternativa, Provincia Carrasco.* La Paz, Bolivia: Catholic Relief Services.

Peet, Richard, and Michael Watts. 1996. *Liberation Ecologies: Environment, Development, Social Movements.* London: Routledge.

Rocheleau, Dianne, Barbara Thomas-Slayter, and Esther Wangari. 1996. *Feminist Political Ecology: Global Issues and Local Experiences.* London: Routledge.

Rösing, Ina. 1997. "Los diez géneros de Amarete, Bolivia." In *Más allá del silencio: Las fronteras de género en los Andes,* edited by Denise Arnold, 77–93. La Paz, Bolivia: Centre for Indigenous American Studies and Exchange/Instituto de Lengua y Cultura Aymara.

Sikkink, Lynn. 1997. "El poder mediador del cambio de aguas: Género y el cuerpo político condeno." In *Más allá del silencio: Las fronteras de género en los Andes,* edited by Denise Arnold, 94–122. La Paz, Bolivia: Centre for Indigenous American Studies and Exchange/Instituto de Lengua y Cultura Aymara.

Silverblatt, Irene. 1987. *Moon, Sun, and Witches: Gender Ideologies and Class in Inca and Colonial Perú.* Princeton, N.J.: Princeton University Press.

United Nations Development Program (UNDP). 2001. *Human Development Report 2001: Making New Technologies Work for Human Development.* New York: United Nations Press.

Urioste, Miguel. 1987. *Segunda reforma agraria: Campesinos, tierra y educacion popular.* La Paz, Bolivia: Centro de Estudios para el Desarrollo Laboral y Agrario.

Wallerstein, Immanuel. 1984. *The Politics of the World-Economy.* New York: Cambridge University Press.

Warren, Kay, and Susan Bourque. 1991. "Women, Technology, and International Development Ideologies: Analyzing Feminist Voices." In *Gender at the Crossroads of Knowledge: Feminist Anthropology in the Postmodern Era,* edited by Micaela di Leonardo, 278–311. Berkeley: University of California Press.

Watson, Greta, and Juan Almanza. 1994. *Manejo in situ de cultivares de papa: Caracterización, producción difusión y el rol de género en Cochabamba.* Cochabamba, Bolivia: Centro Internacional de la Papa/Programa de Investigación de la Papa.

Weismantel, Mary J. 1988. *Food, Gender, and Poverty in the Ecuadorian Andes.* Philadelphia: University of Pennsylvania Press.

Zambrana, Jaime, and Samantha Wade. 1997. "Análisis participativo de género como medio de cambio social." In *Teorías y prácticas de dénero: Una conversación dialéctica,* edited by Susan Paulson and Mónica Crespo, 37–50. Cochabamba, Bolivia: Embajada Real de los Paises Bajos.

Zimmerer, Karl S. 1993a. "Soil Erosion and Labor Shortages in the Andes with Special Reference to Bolivia, 1953–91: Implications for 'Conservations-with-Development.'" *World Development* 21, no. 10: 1659–75.

———. 1993b. "Soil Erosion and Social (Dis)courses in Cochabamba Bolivia: Perceiving the Nature of Environmental Degradation." *Economic Geography* 69, no. 3: 312–27.

———. 1999. "Overlapping Patchworks of Mountain Agriculture in Peru and Bolivia: Toward a Regional-Global Landscape Model." *Human Ecology* 27, no. 1: 135–65.

———. 2000. "The Reworking of Conservation Geographies: Nonequilibrium Landscapes and Nature-Society Hybrids." *Annals of the Association of American Geographers* 90, no. 2: 356–69.

Zoomers, Annelies. 1998. "Estrategias campesinas: Algunas consideraciones teóricas y conceptuales." In *Estrategias campesinas en el surandino de Bolivia: Intervenciones y Desarrollo rural en el norte de Chuquisaca y Potosí*, edited by Annelies Zoomers, 13–34. Amsterdam and Bolivia: Royal Tropical Institute/Centro de Estudios para el Desarrollo Laboral y Agrario.

Zulawski, Ann. 1990. "Social Differentiation, Gender, and Ethnicity: Urban Indian Women in Colonial Bolivia, 1640–1725." *Latin American Research Review* 25, no. 2: 93–113.

11

Undermining Modernity

Protecting Landscapes and Meanings among the Mi'kmaq of Nova Scotia

ALF HORNBORG

This chapter focuses on the involvement of Mi'kmaq Indians in preventing a mountain on Cape Breton Island, Nova Scotia, from being turned into a granite quarry.[1] The struggle illustrates how the cultural, existential, and political dimensions of environmental engagement are enmeshed. I identify a fundamental polarity between local and nonlocal interests, incentives, and perspectives, in which the nonlocal tends to be represented by abstract discourse far removed from the experiential realities of local meanings and life worlds. As local meanings are threatened by development projects, social movements mobilized to protect them tend paradoxically to be drawn into the abstract, discursive practices of their opponents, generating ambiguities and rifts in the movements themselves. By evoking the mountain's sanctity and threats of violent resistance, however, the Mi'kmaq activists managed to transform the terms of environmental negotiation while projecting an image of ethnic revival and unity that publicly transcended internal divisions. Rather than interpret this strategy simply in terms of political opportunism, anthropologists might understand the evocation of spirituality as an attempt to represent in public discourse those local meanings that are systematically excluded from the abstract mind frame of modernity.

In recent years, throughout the world, environmental and indigenous movements have been developing a kind of conceptual symbiosis. In the media and several popular books (such as Suzuki and Knudtson 1992), environmentalists have used the image of the ecological native to sharpen their critique of industrialism. Conversely, indigenous activists increasingly have employed environmental arguments in their struggles for the rights of native minorities. In this chapter, I reflect on the convergence of environmental and indigenous activisms in relation to issues of modern identity construction, social differentiation, and local-global connections. My empirical point of departure is a movement to stop a proposed granite quarry on Cape Breton Island, Nova Scotia, in the early 1990s;

and my theoretical aim is to situate this movement in a larger field of discourse on development and environment. Investigation of this case can be seen as part of a larger project analyzing the ways in which technology is based on unequal exchange in the world system, which increasingly generates a global polarization of wealth and impoverishment. In a recent book resulting from this project (Hornborg 2001), I argue that we are caught in a collective illusion about the nature of modern technology, preventing us from recognizing that our machines are ultimately a social mode of redistributing resources and risks.

While this chapter focuses on conditions and dynamics of political activism in Nova Scotia, the quarry conflict simultaneously illustrates issues of environmental justice and the distribution of risk among social groups. The controversy highlights how technology and spirituality represent two alternative sources of ontological security. The modern, secular culture of risk reduction (Beck 1992 [1986]) in the economic centers of the world system aims to generate ontological security through, for instance, improved roads, while the disempowered in the periphery resort to spirituality. The quarry controversy illuminates how the modern project of development pursues its utopian vision of security through local, technological risk reduction, while generating and exporting other kinds of risk such as deterioration of both the natural environment and sources of identity.

Like people elsewhere in North America, the indigenous people of Nova Scotia have spent recent decades reevaluating their cultural identity. Fourth World consciousness is gaining momentum as the self-confidence of western civilization is challenged by the environmental movement and other forms of internal critique. The growth of a "red consciousness" has also been inadvertently encouraged by Canadian Indian policy (Lithman 1978). This was dramatically highlighted in the summer of 1990 at Quebec's Kahnesatake reserve, where militant Mohawk warriors mobilized to prevent a Mohawk burial ground from being converted into a golf course, an incident that prompted demonstrations of sympathy among indigenous nations throughout Canada, including the Nova Scotia Mi'kmaq.

I begin here with a historical contextualization of Mi'kmaq land and resource use. After presenting the case of the quarry conflict, I discuss the negotiation of identity that occurs in the midst of competing claims about environmental control and management. Specifically, I problematize the discourse of indigenous spirituality and environmental sensitivity, analyzing how it has become increasingly legitimate in such confrontations to call upon images of sacredness. Several themes weave through the sections that follow, including the relationship between the local and the global, the circumstances of socially differentiated movements, and the changing role of anthropologists in studying and speaking on these issues.

My analysis of local-global articulations rests on a concept of modernity as a process that abstracts, encompasses, and disempowers the local. I argue that the *global* is not a place, nor is the *modern* a time in history or a generalized state of technological development. Rather, any reference to the global or modernity must identify systems of power where access to resources and risks is unequally distributed. As for social movements, I point out the processes by which local-interest groups appropriate the very discourse that subsumes them, thereby legitimizing claims to local sacred sites by referring to abstract concepts of indigenous rights and spirituality. Yet I reject a simplistic analysis that native claims to spirituality are purely instrumental and politically goal-oriented and argue for the need to recognize the spiritual underpinnings of social movements as experientially real.

My study of a grassroots environmental movement required methods that went beyond, but included, participant observation in a given locale. I combined casual on-site interviews with a reading of historical documentation on subsistence and land use, newspaper reports on the case, unpublished reports by advocacy groups and industry, and correspondence found in organizations' files. I attended public meetings to observe the sites of contestation of identities and rights. This multipronged approach allowed me to understand the complexity of local interests and also to link local happenings and perspectives with the nonlocal. At the most general level, my investigation was informed by the conviction that there are fundamental connections between the objective and the subjective dimensions of environmental crisis: that the physical threats to ecosystems and the existential threats to identities and meanings are expressions of the same, underlying logic of modernity.

The Mi'kmaq: A Brief Environmental History

Five hundred years ago, Cape Breton (called *Unama'kik* by the Mi'kmaq) was one of the seven districts of the Mi'kmaq nation (Mi'kma'kik), which embraced the modern Canadian provinces of Nova Scotia and Prince Edward Island and adjoining parts of New Brunswick, Quebec, and Newfoundland. The Mi'kmaq are an Algonquian-speaking people who have inhabited the area for at least 3,000 years. Before the arrival of Europeans, they were primarily fishermen, hunters, and gatherers, spending the warmer half of the year fishing along coasts and rivers and moving inland to hunt moose, beaver, and other game in the winter. Despite reports of taboos and other signs of respect for the game animals and their supernatural masters (Denys 1908 [1672]), this delicate relationship between people and their subsistence resources seems to have been undermined by the fur trade. Spurred by this trade, natives have been important agents in the depletion of game stocks in much of eastern Canada.

The European colonization of coasts and rivers in the seventeenth and eighteenth centuries pushed much of the Mi'kmaq population permanently inland to hunt. Many retreated to the district of Unama'kik, now known as Cape Breton Island, which long remained a wilderness with few European settlers. As game

was depleted and the fur trade moved west, the Mi'kmaq resorted to craft production for the European settlements. Now that neither hunting nor fishing was
a viable mode of subsistence, history turned the Mi'kmaq into a nation of bas-
ketmakers. Baskets, produced mainly for tourists, are still emblems of their ethnic identity.

During World War II, the Department of Indian Affairs attempted to concentrate the native population of Nova Scotia into two large reserves, Eskasoni on
Cape Breton and Shubenacadie on the mainland. In 1958, it divided the Nova
Scotia Mi'kmaq into twelve bands, five of them on Cape Breton. The Mi'kmaq
population of Cape Breton now numbers about 5,000 people. Except for formal
contact (for example, with storekeepers, teachers, doctors, and police), their five
reserves are socially isolated from the rest of the population of the island. They
are ethnically marginalized pockets of *Gemeinschaft* in an economically marginalized part of Canada.

Actors and Arguments in the Public Process

In 1989, a local corporation called Kelly Rock announced its plans to open a so-
called superquarry—one of the three largest in the world—on Kelly's Mountain,
located on a peninsula between St. Ann's Bay and the Great Bras d'Or inlet to the
Bras d'Or Lakes, on Cape Breton Island. Kelly Rock planned to ship 5.4 million
tons of crushed granite gravel annually (for use as concrete aggregate, asphalt
topping, and so on) to the eastern United States. The quarry would start as a strip
mine 2,300 feet across and 200 feet deep, and the granite would be transported
to a shipping wharf by means of a 600-foot shaft. This so-called "glory hole"
method would minimize the visibility of the operations. Almost invisibly, the
company maintained, the mountain could yield 2,500 tons of rock every working
hour for the next twenty to forty years and provide an estimated total of 103 jobs.
Once a month, about half a million tons would be blasted loose. The seven shore-
line crushers would be at work twenty-four hours a day. The crushed gravel
would then be washed in sizable settling ponds. The shipping wharf would be
equipped to receive 60,000-ton ships about twice weekly and to stockpile perhaps a half million ton of gravel (equivalent to almost five football fields piled
thirty feet high). Space would also be required for a number of thirty-ton trucks,
conveyor belts, and administrative buildings. Kelly Rock estimated that the project would require about forty acres but negotiated an agreement in principle to
obtain almost 4,000 acres of Crown land on the mountain from the provincial
government.

Opposition to the quarry was immediately evident, primarily from some
local residents organized as the Save Kelly's Mountain Society (SKMS) and from
Mi'kmaq traditionalists affiliated with the Grand Council of the Mi'kmaq. The
SKMS was organized within weeks of Kelly Rock's announcement, which was

made on September 5, 1989, at a public meeting for the residents of the St. Ann's Bay area. Also in September 1989, Mi'kmaq traditionalists organized a demonstration in Englishtown, the community closest to the proposed quarry site. The protesters told the press that they represented the grand chief of the Mi'kmaq Grand Council (*Cape Breton Post*, September 26, 1989). They arranged a ceremony with drumming and chanting and requested a major historical and archaeological study of the mountain, emphasizing that it is the sacred abode of the Mi'kmaq god Kluskap and the point of his prophesied return.

In response to the debate on the status of the mountain, staff from the Nova Scotia Museum laid out the facts in October 1989:

> Traditionally, Cape Breton is the site of three "doors" into the World Beneath The Earth, the place where the Mi'kmaq spirit-helper and culture-hero Kluskap went when he left the Earth World behind. . . . The third door, which is considered quite an important site due to the presence of the rock called "Kluskap's Table," and the rock called "The Mother-in-law" or "The Grandmother," is a cave in a cliff washed by the sea, on Kelly's Mountain at Cape Dauphin. Traditionally, it is called Kluskap's Cave, Kluskap's Door, or Kluskap's Wigwam. Although known to the Mi'kmaq for generations, this cave was first recorded in anthropological literature only in 1923. (Whitehead 1989)

The museum staff continued by quoting one of Elsie Clews Parsons's (1925) informants almost seven decades earlier: "At Cape Dolphin (Dauphin), Big Bras d'Or, there is a door through the cliff, Gluskap's door. Outside, there is a stone like a table. Indians going hunting will leave on it tobacco and eels, to give them good luck. They do this today" (87). Finally, the museum report concluded: "Offerings are said to have been made at this cave for generations, up into the twentieth century, and it is a tradition still being carried out today. Traces of gifts made to Kluskap have been noted in the presence of deposits of fish bones on the rock in front of the cave entrance 'Kluskap's Table'. On a recent visit to the site, Museum staff noted offerings of tobacco and sweet fern inside the cave itself, and in holes in the rock of the Table" (Whitehead 1989).

A year later, in October 1990—only weeks after dramatic confrontations between soldiers and natives at Oka, Quebec—a more militant demonstration made the headlines. At an information meeting called by the Victoria County Committee for Development and attended by the Kelly Rock president, members of three separate Mi'kmaq bands turned up, all wearing army camouflage dress. "At all costs," they said, "we will blockade the road to the quarry. We are preparing for war" (*Harrowsmith*, January–February 1991). This group of militant Mi'kmaq activists, some of whom had assisted the Mohawk warriors at Oka, became known as the Mi'kmaq Warrior Society. The Warrior Society later also operated under the name Sacred Mountain Society (SMS). The SMS presents itself as "the only First Nations environmental organization in Atlantic Canada," declaring that "funds will be utilized to support environmental struggles affecting all peoples within the Mi'kmaq territory" (*Nova Scotia Environmental Network News*, April–May 1993).

Opponents to the quarry have pointed to at least seventeen different ways in which it might harm the environment, including the nearby Bird Islands seabird sanctuary, the Bras d'Or Lakes spawning grounds, local lobster stocks, and the bald eagles on the mountain itself. Critics argue that the project was proposed in Nova Scotia only because U.S. environmental laws would never allow it to be built in New England. According to the national magazine *Earthkeeper*, "the province is reported to have the most relaxed environmental legislation and lowest prosecution rates for environmental crimes in the country, and word is spreading" (3:91). The issue thus immediately emerged as a problem of environmental justice as well.

Whereas SKMS immediately began listing a number of separate concerns about the impact of the proposed quarry, the Mi'kmaq organizations initially focused on the threats to Kluskap's Cave. As discussions continued, however, the SKMS and the SMS increasingly pooled their arguments. The chairman of the SKMS realized that "the challenge by the Cape Breton Micmacs may pose an even tougher hurdle for the company to cross" than purely environmental arguments might be (*Inverness Oran*, February 1991). He emphasized that "more study is needed to look at Mi'kmaq concerns" (*Micmac News*, April 19, 1991). In an article in *Earthkeeper* (January–February 1991), he makes the Mi'kmaq argument his own: "This mountain is Sacred. It contains a Sacred Cave. Even the absurdities of the proposal pale in comparison with this reality: what is threatened for the People of the Dawn is not Kelly's Mountain, but Glooscap's Mountain." Conversely, the SMS's information package lists many of the arguments advanced by SKMS. It even concludes with the observation that "the super quarry is contrary to the concept of sustainable development." According to a survey conducted by members of the Victoria County Committee for Development early in 1990, however, only 34 out of 404 residents in the Englishtown area were opposed to the quarry. Many local people saw the 103 jobs that Kelly Rock hoped to create as a dying community's chance to survive.

When Kelly Rock submitted its own environmental impact assessment to the provincial Department of the Environment in November 1989, the SKMS successfully challenged its validity and requested a federal environmental review. The decision to conduct such a review took some time, but in early March 1991 the federal and provincial governments agreed to establish a joint federal-provincial environmental assessment review (EAR) panel to review the quarry project. Later that month, the names of the five members of the panel were announced; and final guidelines for the preparation of terms of reference for their report were completed on May 8, 1991.

The Union of Nova Scotia Indians (UNSI), based in Sydney, Cape Breton, actively participated in the review process from the start. In an April 1991 submission, the union suggested a number of changes to the EAR guidelines, many of which were incorporated into the final version. In early May, the UNSI also requested that an aboriginal person be added to the panel. The UNSI president wrote: "The mountain is of cultural and spiritual significance to the Mi'kmaq of Nova Scotia as the site to which Glooscap will return and the location of his cave. We are concerned about the impact that the quarry would have on this interest, as well as its impact on fish and wildlife."

The provincial and federal environment ministers immediately agreed, and in December 1991 they appointed a captain of the Mi'kmaq Grand Council as the sixth member of the panel. Moreover, a few weeks previously, the EAR panel had announced the hiring of a Mi'kmaq linguist as a "technical specialist [to] provide the Panel with expertise in Micmac communication and interpretation [and to] advise on issues related to Micmac culture."

In late January 1992, Kelly Rock submitted its draft terms of reference for the EAR, but they were immediately returned because they did not satisfy the final guidelines. In October 1992, the revised terms of reference were finally approved by the provincial minister of the environment. The proponent had "turned itself inside out" to demonstrate that it would consider all possible impacts of the quarry (*Inverness Oran* 1991).

A few months later, however, Kelly Rock announced that, for economic reasons, it would not be proceeding with the EAR at this time. It now seems highly unlikely that the granite quarry on Kelly's Mountain will ever materialize. It is difficult to assess the importance of environmentalist protests in determining Kelly Rock's decision; but it is probably safe to assume that if the SKMS and the Mi'kmaq traditionalists had not raised their voices in September 1989, construction would have begun as planned in May 1990. Opponents of the quarry may have achieved their immediate aim as portrayed in the media, but there is definitely more to it than this. By reading between the lines, we can provide valuable insights into the cultural fabric and the structural tensions of modern civilization itself.

Environmental Discourse As Negotiation of Identity and Credibility

To the Mi'kmaq traditionalists, the struggle against the quarry was not only a matter of keeping the mountain undisturbed but also an opportunity to redefine their identity as native people in ways to which most Cape Bretoners were unaccustomed. Journalists readily cooperated with the traditionalists in projecting the new image of Mi'kmaq culture, but the message was received with skepticism in many quarters. The president of Kelly Rock responded that radical natives were simply using the occasion to further their land-claims issue (*Inverness Oran*, February 1991). He was not alone in brushing aside the Mi'kmaq protests as part of a larger strategy. In a sense, of course, any behavior is strategic inasmuch as it aims to communicate something. But the little group of drummers who so effectively helped to turn public processes against the quarry had much more profound objectives in mind than land claims.

Two questions come to mind if we focus on this meta-communicative dimension of Mi'kmaq environmentalism: what are the different levels of their message? And why is it so potent today? A discourse constantly remolds its own framework of rules. By testing various messages on one another, the participants negotiate a shifting field of credibility. But the limits of credible discourse have a tenuous relationship to real motives and objectives. These two levels must be investigated separately. For instance, we can safely assume that the primary motive of Kelly Rock was not to generate local opportunities for employment, yet this is the message that was continually presented in the media (*Toronto Star*, June 20, 1991). The president of Kelly Rock is thus an unlikely person to question the motives professed by the Mi'kmaq traditionalists. The issue is not whether all the motives of the participants have been exposed or truthfully presented but whether those offered are accepted by the public (media, authorities, and so on) as legitimate. Suffice it to say that the struggle to stop the quarry on Kelly's Mountain suggests a shift in the range of credible public discourse when compared to the environmental debate on Cape Breton a mere decade previously. The framework is no longer restricted to "jobs-versus-the-environment" or "jobs- versus-health." Nor is it even constrained by the rational-scientific environmental assessment approach. The pivotal contribution of indigenous activists to environmental discourse is to redefine its framework so that it is now increasingly legitimate to evoke concepts of sanctity.

Initially, there were attempts to define the spiritual approach as incomprehensible. According to an article in the *Micmac News* (March 15, 1991) covering a March 1991 meeting between Kelly Rock and Mi'kmaq representatives (UNSI and the Micmac Association of Cultural Studies), the "Micmac leaders view the proposed rock development as a cruel and disrespectful way to treat Mother Nature and the Great Spirit." The president of Kelly Rock is quoted as responding, "We don't fully understand each other's concerns at this time and we wish to see what steps can be taken to alleviate your concerns." On another occasion, a representative of the federal EAR office in Hull, Quebec, said that "the Panel is going to need help in understanding what is said here" (*Micmac News*, April 19, 1991).

Problems of communication seem unavoidable when elements of traditionalist discourse enter the rational, analytical discourse of bureaucracy. A predictable problem, for instance, is how an assessment instructed to conceptually break down Kelly's Mountain into "valued ecosystem components" will be able to deal with holistic perspectives such as those embodied in the Mi'kmaq view that the mountain is sacred. Referring to Gordon Beanlands and Peter Duinker

(1983), the EAR final guidelines for preparation of the terms of reference propose that the study should "identify an initial set of valued ecosystem components (VEC's) to provide a focus for subsequent activities." This approach immediately defines the proper relationship to the mountain as one of analysis, fragmentation, and objectification rather than holism and participation. Turning a mountain into gravel is facilitated by first breaking it down conceptually.

The approach of the Mi'kmaq traditionalists exposed inadequacies in the categories of the public framework for dealing with multifaceted issues such as those concerning Kelly's Mountain. The SMS turned to the Nova Scotia Human Rights Commission (NSHRC), arguing that, "like any other spiritual beliefs we have certain sites that are more important than life itself." In its information package, the SMS explains that "the degree of offense would be equal to that felt by Christians if a super quarry were placed at the Holy Sepulcher, or by Hebrews if the wailing wall were removed for a motel, or by Muslims if a casino were placed in Mecca." The NSHRC replied that it did "not see the complaint as coming within the confines of the Nova Scotia Human Rights Act" and referred it to the Department of Culture. The Nova Scotia Museum, in turn, responded that "since the cave is not an archaeological site, it does not fit within the usual interpretation of the Special Places Protection Act." (All quotations in this paragraph are from correspondence in the SMS files.)

Although many Cape Bretoners may have found the image of the ecological and spiritual native difficult to reconcile with ingrained local stereotypes, at a more abstract level most were probably well prepared to receive the new message. The Mi'kmaq traditionalists reenacted a message that rings familiar to the non-native majority of North America. In many people it evoked a strain of collective guilt handed down through the generations and reinforced by genre books and films such as *The Last of the Mohicans* and *Dances with Wolves*. Considering the extent to which our image of the ecological native is a projection of non-native writers, from James Fenimore Cooper on (see Francis 1992), the dominant culture may be seen as inviting native people to protest against it in specific ways. In an almost Jungian way, natives are offered a niche in the dominant cosmology as speakers of spiritual truths of which everybody is, at heart, aware. Mainstream North Americans want them to say the things they cannot say themselves.

If presenting themselves as protectors of Mother Earth is an emblem of Native Americans' opposition ideology (Larsen 1983), the choice of this emblem is not entirely their own. This social constructivist perspective does not detract from the authenticity or significance of their critique. On the contrary, it recognizes that the First Nations, in articulating a new framework for environmental debate, are being assigned an important historical mission. Their leading actors, I would add, are acutely aware of these processes; but rather than feeling deconstructed, they recognize a real opportunity to fill their sense of ethnic identity with new and profound meaning. A constructivist account of Mi'kmaq spiritual resurgence need not be de-authenticating. Anthony Giddens (1990) visualizes a "radicalised modernity" that, rather than succumb to the postmodern dissolution of the self, encourages "active processes of reflexive self-identity" (150). Thus, in a sense, the "traditionalist" who reflects on the Mi'kmaq revival is radically modern: "the nativeness is growing. And it's fortunate. If I were to fight for this mountain fifteen years ago, I'd be locked up in one of the mental hospitals. My people would have signed me in. . . . Some of our elders . . . I would have never believed fifteen years ago would be walking around with eagle feathers, going to powwows, dancing."

The Authentic and the Corrupt

By positioning themselves as uncompromisingly opposed to the quarry, the Mi'kmaq traditionalists evoke a dualistic archetype of Indian-white relations. Native people are presented as the oppressed guardians of authentic, spiritual values, whereas the dominant, non-native culture is identified with corrupt power and a materialistic greed for money. But when I discussed this polarity with several Mi'kmaq, I soon realized that it was applicable to more than the ethnic, Indian-white dichotomy. Precisely the same opposition recurs in the way in which many natives present the difference between the two forms of Mi'kmaq government: the traditional Grand Council, on one hand, and the system of band chiefs and councils organized and funded by the Department of Indian Affairs, on the other. Derogatory remarks about the chief and council invariably focused on various forms of corruption, such as favoritism and mismanagement of funds. In the context of reserve life, where funding is a scarce resource to compete for, being entrusted with the allocation of funds seems sufficient to warrant suspicion (see Larsen 1983, 79–81).

It is obvious that the same moral polarity that at one level serves to define Indian-white relations can be applied at another level to divide native communities. The concept of native people who have adopted a white mentality is a commonly evoked archetype. The two parallel systems of Mi'kmaq government employ distinctly separate modes of self-presentation, in terms of both speech and dress. The Grand Council affiliates often appear in traditional dress and adopt a befitting, serene idiom, whereas chief and council tend to dress and speak like mainstream bureaucrats. It is evident that competence in bureaucratic discourse is an asset in careers funded by the Department of Indian Affairs. In effect, bureaucratic modes of behavior and interaction are rewarded with funding.

In various other contexts as well, adversaries were characterized as people who have betrayed fundamental values and sold themselves to money and power. Conspicuously often, they were also charged with mismanagement of the funds they had secured. From the perspective of some traditionalists, the adversaries were also impostors. Their most essential critique focused on lack of authenticity. At one level, this was simply a matter of observing that a successful fundraiser was not really Mi'kmaq and that he should not be diverting funds that ought to be enjoyed by those who were. At another level, adversaries were characterized as "wannabes" whose self-construction as traditionalists was not accepted as credible or legitimate.

In view of all the internal divisions reflecting the ambiguity and contextuality of the Indian-white dichotomy, much of the significance of an issue such as Kelly's Mountain is that it united, at a higher level, virtually all those who define themselves as Mi'kmaq. Even though there has been overt disagreement on the methods to be used in the struggle, opposition to the quarry became an expression of ethnic identity. The issue presented an opportunity to publicly define Mi'kmaq culture as opposed to mainstream values, an act of definition that may have been as helpful to many Mi'kmaq as it was instructive to non-natives. Whether a band chief, a Grand Council Catholic, or a Mi'kmaq warrior, at this level the message was the same.

Objectifying Modernity: Conceptual Encompassment As Power

Although modernity's genesis can be traced to European history, it would be misleading to refer to it as an aspect of European culture, contrasting, for instance, with native Amerindian culture. The polarity of local-versus-global identity is now equally evident all over the world. This polarity is generated by the systems of national and international integration (state, market, and movement; see Hannerz 1989) that require centralization, mobility, and specialized, supralocal interest groups. Finally, although there are great differences among people in terms of how far they have been drawn into modernity, the polarity is not primarily a mode of classifying individuals but a tension that most people would recognize as running down the middle of their existence. It could be approximated by a series of linked conceptual dualities, thus:

Embedded	Disembedded
Local	Global
Irreplaceable	Interchangeable
Experience near	Experience far
Sensory	Reflexive
Subjectivity	Objectification
Holism	Fragmentation

These two polar modes of relating to the world interact with each other in terms of social processes that have significance for the negotiation of environmental issues such as those surrounding Kelly's Mountain. I have already indicated that modernity is a strategy of conceptual encompassment of local life worlds. When the cognitive approach of modern science and technology is applied to society, as in economics and administration, it is always used as a means of manipulation and control. By objectifying local life worlds into abstractions such as "labor," "consumers," or "voters," the language of the administrators constitutes a relationship of power. Because such language provides access to supralocal power structures, proficiency in abstract modes of discourse is a kind of social capital accumulated through what we know as education. In spite of its emancipatory goals, the modern educational system remains fundamentally an institution for equipping a select minority of the world's population with the conceptual means to dominate the remainder. Modernist perspectives tend to objectify, encompass, and transcend the concrete realities of place.

At a public seminar on indigenous perspectives of sustainable development, I recorded an interchange between a Canadian marine biologist (B), a local Mi'kmaq youth (M), and a United Nations observer from an indigenous minority in Russia (R) that highlights the role of education in the asymmetrical articulation of local and global identities:

B: From my experiences in all the countries that I've worked in, including Canada, one of the biggest problems that the aboriginal groups have is a lack of education. . . .

M: The thing I want to say is, the education part. . . . It's kind of a disagreement, when he says that, you know . . . that he's smarter than I am, you see? That's not the case. Are you smarter than I am? How much education do you have? . . . I might not be a biologist . . . but . . . it's really bullshit. It's the people inside, if they want to save the Mother Earth. It's the people inside, if they care, really. . . . It's the spirituality part. We have to treat each other with respect, show respect to people and to Mother Earth. . . . I'm just a human being. . . . I speak from my heart, and that's the way it should be. Education, the biologists, and everything else goes out the window, and that's all I have to say, and thank you for listening to me.

R: Education is not bullshit. Education is a way . . . to go and achieve the goal which you need. . . . The United Nations . . . is not a god. . . . It's a very big building with very small rooms, and in each of the rooms there are very small people, and if you learn about those people, and if you learn the way to get in there, then you can use it. Because we live in a very strange world. The great warrior nowadays is not a brave with bow or tomahawk; it's a very sneaky lawyer with a fax machine.

To become a great warrior today generally means to adopt a modernist, global frame of mind. Ambitious local actors will appropriate abstract modes of discourse to gain access to external funding and other forms of recognition. Conversely, global actors from the outside will attempt to evoke local frameworks and reference points for purposes of political or commercial infiltration. Through such dialectical instrumentalities (local actors adopting global modes and vice versa), local and global language continuously mingle and shade into one another. But the relationship between local and global actors is not symmetrical in terms of power. It is one thing to promote a local cause by adopting a language that outside powers will recognize and another to promote an abstract cause (such as share of voters or the market) by adopting a language that local people will listen to. A local cause can at times be served by an abstract nonlocal language, but an abstract nonlocal cause masqueraded in local language deserves to be more closely examined. The essential difference is whether the actors themselves are ultimately guided by local incentives, deriving from the specifics of place-based life worlds, or by abstract motives (such as capital accumulation) that have no regard for place.

Here, of course, is a central problem of modernity: the adoption of a decontextualized discourse is itself a distancing from place; and if this means entering into one of modernity's specialized sectors for identity construction, even one as benevolent as environmental activism, there will be a corresponding shift of motives. If the individuals have to choose whether to define themselves in terms of local or abstract reference points, the movement from local to global will tend to be irreversible; and there will be a constant co-optation of local voices into placeless, guild-like frameworks. Without the constant, experience-near resonance of place, these voices risk forgetting the contexts in which they were raised, devoting themselves to the perfection of their own objectified intonation, echoing in the empty labyrinths of disembedded abstraction.

This brings us to the subsumptive nature of modernity's global language. The confrontation between the local Mi'kmaq youth and the educated few who would be spokespeople for indigenous minorities evokes the perennial paradox of power. Can local voices ever ring unadulterated in global institutions? To confront modernity through public discourse is, paradoxically, to be absorbed by it. This is the predicament of movements. Self-reflection and self-objectification tend to mold activists according to public images such as those of the "environmentalist" or the "indigenous" representative. There is a subtle transformation in motives as critique is progressively institutionalized and the focus is shifted from the source of indignation to the skills of self-presentation. Yet there are obviously also ways in which local voices can unite, often in unexpected ways, to challenge—or even subvert—a dominant paradigm.

Spirituality As Revolt against Modernity

While subsuming the mainstream of critique that it generates, modernity simultaneously pushes countercultural movements toward extremist positions, including the threat of violence. When dominant word games fail them, the chronically disempowered may seek more potent forms of expression. In a television interview, a young Mi'kmaq warrior described the effects of his camouflage uniform:

"I walk into Woolco, and I have everybody's eyes watching me as I walk all through the store. People won't turn their back on me now, when I walk into a store."

To start discussing the historical and contemporary "facts" of the spiritual significance of Kelly's Mountain to the Mi'kmaq would be to miss the point of the activists' message. Theirs is a message about contemporary social relationships, not history or religion. Evoking A. O. Hirschman's (1970) terminology *exit* and *voice*, the new native voices pose an alternative to the self-destructive patterns that for so long have crippled the indigenous minorities of North America. Their growing impact on the mainstream environmental debate fulfils an old prophecy of native revival. Their invocation of spirituality draws on potent archetypes to become a revolt against the language of modernity, yet their mode of self-definition is radically modern.

When a person begins to talk about his or her own culture, it is a sign that another life world is being objectified and decontextualized. It would seem that a vital way to resist the power of modernity would be to refuse to let one's life world thus be encompassed. From a purely theoretical perspective, such a strategy would have to be based on some kind of boundary drawing between the local and the global. To pursue this line of reasoning, we must once again consider the extent to which discourse emerges within specific political and economic settings. Concepts such as development and employment opportunities are part and parcel of the way in which the capitalist world economy is organized. The decontextualizing cosmology of the economists, which aspires to engulf all local systems of meaning, is a means to open local communities and ecosystems to outside exploitation. In other words, the impact of the disembedded language of modernity upon the material world facilitates ecological destruction. Against this background, we can appreciate why both the Mi'kmaq traditionalists and proponents of a biocentric deep ecology have chosen to revolt against mainstream language. They are trying to redesign the definition space (see Ardener 1989) of environmentalist discourse.

The concept of sanctity is radically opposed to modernity and commodification because it posits irreplaceable and incommensurable values (Kopytoff 1986). But is not sanctity itself an abstract and disembedded concept? At this point, I would like to make a distinction between *abstract* and *disembedded*. A living relationship to place can provide abstract thought with the sensory resonance and experience-near reference points that distinguish a spiritual from a completely secular frame of mind. The destructive tendencies in modernity are generated not by abstract thought in itself but by disembedding and secularizing abstraction. Robin Grove-White (1993) calls environmentalism "a new moral discourse for technological society," suggesting that "some of the deeper shades of recent 'green religiosity'" can be read as a dissatisfaction with objectivistic, atomizing, and trivializing representations and express a "need to address authentic human concern about deeper mysteries of existence." These, he adds, are "far from insignificant matters" (24–25).

Modern, objectivist rationality claims a monopoly on legitimate knowledge construction, suggesting a confusion of map and territory. But to the extent that there is such a thing as an absolute truth, there will always be more than one set of words to represent it. Spiritual and deep ecology approaches to environmental issues suggest a renewed concern with the performative dimension of our narratives. It could be argued that they represent the logical next step beyond the paralysis of postmodernism. If there is a sense in which humans are indeed the authors of their world, the postmodern discovery that this is the case should ultimately inspire responsibility rather than nihilism. If we have to recover a metaphorical idiom capable of sustainably relating us to the rest of the world, the reflexive experience of modernity now leaves us no other choice than to learn how to handle the awareness that this is what we should be doing.

To clarify what I think the Mi'kmaq environmentalists meant by the concept of spirituality, I believe it signifies a propensity to see beyond the surface. In the way that it is used among many Mi'kmaq, spirituality has to do with relating. It refers to the emotive states that are evoked in human subjects in the process of relating to each other and the natural world. The fact that the concept is frequently used to describe a proposed difference between Mi'kmaq and white indicates that the former perceive the latter as somehow less apt to relate—that is, less sensitive to the emotive dimension of being in the world. This observation is a cultural datum worth examining in its own right. If there is such a thing as cultural variation in personhood (Shweder and Bourne 1984), it is not invalid to propose that such sensitivity may be one of the parameters to investigate.

Beyond Nostalgia and Cynicism: Indigenous Environmentalism and the Politics of Ecological Irony

Most Mi'kmaq environmentalists that I spoke with explicitly referred to the spiritual aspect of their struggle to safeguard Kluskap's sacred mountain. I am convinced that the concept of spirituality signified an experiential reality for most of them; it was not just an instrumental accessory in their self-construction. But contemporary anthropology would undoubtedly have difficulty buying the image of themselves that the Mi'kmaq traditionalists were projecting through the media. This is not only because modern natives are generally not accepted by anthropologists as representative of their premodern ancestors but also because the whole idea of a premodern condition is increasingly dismissed as a modern construction. It is ironic that the image of the spiritual, ecological native, though widely disseminated by previous generations of anthropologists, is now being systematically dismissed as romanticism by anthropology precisely when (or because?) it is gaining a popular foothold.

Perhaps an adequate representative of such earlier generations, Richard B. Lee (1988) has observed that there is now "a considerable industry in anthropology . . . to show the primitive as a Hobbesian being—with a life that is 'nasty, brutish and short.'" In the current climate of opinion, he notes, "no one is going to go broke" by appealing to cynicism (253). Roy F. Ellen (1993) captures the currently fashionable opinion in his assertion that the "myth of primitive environmental wisdom" does not make sense "except in relation to the recognition that such an illusion serves an important ideological purpose in modern or postmodern society" (126).

But cynicism, too, has its ideological purposes. Dwelling on examples of unwise natural resource management among indigenous peoples today is not a very good argument for dismissing indigenous environmentalism because it also rests on essentialist premises. The opposite argument is not that indigenous peoples are somehow inherently (genetically?) prone to deal wisely with their environment but that the social condition and mind frame of premodern existence contains elements that may be more conducive to wise management than the modern mind frame does (Anderson 1996, Bateson 1972, Rappaport 1979). If we define a premodern condition in terms of an experiential immersion or embeddedness in a local, socio-ecological context, we would have to concede that the degree to which people have been drawn into modernity varies significantly among regions, occupations, and individuals. Even if, for the moment, anthropologists have lost sight of any way of curbing the ongoing commodification of the planet, we have no reason to terminate the long-standing anthropological project of investigating the role of the capitalist world market in dissolving such premodern conditions. To focus on the processes through which local experience is fragmented and absorbed by modernity could be a step toward the protection and resurrection of place.

On the last weekend of July in every year since time immemorial, several thousand Mi'kmaq from all the reserves in the Atlantic provinces gather on a little island in the Bras d'Or Lake on Cape Breton that is said to have been a ritual center long before a French mission was established there in the seventeenth century. For several days, the participants immerse themselves in their own specificity, visiting relatives among the tightly packed cabins, drinking tea, gossiping, and sharing the atmosphere of a place dense with lifelong memories. It is a place and time for celebrating several kinds of irreplaceable reference points for identity in terms of social relations, objects, and space. It is precisely this specificity, or noninterchangeability, that is the common denominator of kinship, ritual paraphernalia, and sacred places and that generates such a profound sense of familiarity with the laughing faces, the statue of St. Ann, and the well-trodden paths.

As an outside observer of such intensely meaningful events, I have felt convinced that a primary objective of anthropology should be to understand the very relation between the local and the disembedded. This includes not only local strategies of resistance (and accommodation) to modernity but also, crucially, those very supralocal processes and discursive practices through which local life worlds are being encompassed, marginalized, and disempowered.

Culture, Modernity, and Power: The Relevance of Anthropology

The confrontation between the newborn Mi'kmaq Warrior Society and the mining company was a struggle at many levels: between the local and the global, between spirituality and capitalism, between identities anchored in uniquely meaningful places and identities anchored in boardrooms. It thus highlighted the elusive but pervasive polarity between the modern and the nonmodern, not as periods in history or sectors of world society but as modes of life into which we are all variously drawn. Kluskap's sacred mountain came to represent strong emotional and spiritual attachment to the concrete specifics of a unique place; and it was obvious that a primary threat to it—and to Mi'kmaq identity—was the very language that was imposed on it from the outside, aspiring to define it as an abstract assemblage of natural resources or quantifiable ecosystem components. Anthropology is in a unique position to critically scrutinize the political dimensions of such discursive practices.

The Mi'kmaq were finally successful in reshaping the discursive space of these negotiations to make it permissible to refer to the mountain as sacred. The underlying message was that neither the mountain nor Mi'kmaq identity is negotiable. Ironically, however, in the process, what had been an argument grounded in the wordless phenomenology of local life worlds seemed to have become fetishized into formal, legal discourse, turning the mountain into a monument and the self-professed traditionalists into thoroughly modern activists. Perhaps it is an inevitable paradox that whatever is to be rescued from modernity is drawn into the orbit of modern reflexivity precisely because it is recognized as worth rescuing. The paradox is currently obvious in the struggle to salvage traditional or indigenous knowledge systems, which are thus reified by the very structures that continue to marginalize them. The degree of reflexivity that is generated in such processes certainly poses an immediate threat to traditional sources and systems of meaning, but the various ways in which Mi'kmaq traditionalists are able to revive such meanings suggest a resilience beyond the reach of reflexivity. Reflexivity and abstraction are employed contextually as political instruments for safeguarding those crucial spaces where meanings can continue to be generated as reflexivity recedes and surrenders to experience.

NOTES

1. This chapter draws on material and analysis found in chapter 12 of my book *The Power of the Machine: Global Inequalities of Economy, Technology, and Environment* (2001). I am grateful to Rowman and Littlefield, Publishers, for permission to use that material as a basis for the present chapter.

REFERENCES

Anderson, Eugene N. 1996. *Ecologies of the Heart: Emotion, Belief, and the Environment.* Oxford: Oxford University Press.

Ardener, Edwin. 1989. *The Voice of Prophecy and Other Essays.* Oxford: Blackwell.

Bateson, Gregory. 1972. *Steps to an Ecology of Mind.* New York: Ballantine.

Beanlands, Gordon, and Peter Duinker. 1983. *An Ecological Framework for Environmental Impact Assessment in Canada.* Halifax, Nova Scotia: Dalhousie University.

Beck, Ulrich. 1992 [1986]. *Risk Society: Towards a New Modernity.* London: Sage.

Denys, Nicholas. 1908 [1672]. *Concerning the Ways of the Indians: Their Customs, Dress, Methods of Hunting and Fishing, and Their Amusements.* Halifax: Nova Scotia Museum.

Ellen, Roy F. 1993. "Rhetoric, Practice and Incentive in the Face of the Changing Times: A Case Study in Nuaulu Attitudes to Conservation and Deforestation." In *Environmentalism: The View from Anthropology*, edited by Kay Milton, 126–43. London: Routledge.

Francis, Daniel. 1992. *The Imaginary Indian: The Image of the Indian in Canadian Culture.* Vancouver, British Columbia: Arsenal Pulp.

Giddens, Anthony. 1990. *The Consequences of Modernity.* Cambridge: Polity.

Grove-White, Robin 1993. "Environmentalism: A New Moral Discourse for Technological Society?" In *Environmentalism: The View from Anthropology*, edited by Kay Milton, 18–30. London: Routledge.

Hannerz, Ulf. 1989. *Scenarios for Peripheral Cultures: Symposium on Culture, Globalization, and the World-System.* New York: State University of New York at Binghamton.

Hirschman, A. O. 1970. *Exit, Voice, and Loyalty.* Cambridge: Harvard University Press.

Hornborg, Alf. 2001. *The Power of the Machine: Global Inequalities of Economy, Technology, and Environment.* Walnut Creek, Calif.: Altamira.

Kopytoff, Igor. 1986. "The Cultural Biography of Things: Commoditization as Process." In *The Social Life of Things: Commodities in Cultural Perspective*, edited by Arjun Appadurai, 64–91. Cambridge: Cambridge University Press.

Larsen, Tord. 1983. "Negotiating Identity: The Micmac of Nova Scotia." In *The Politics of Indianness: Case Studies of Native Ethnopolitics in Canada*, edited by Adrian Tanner, 37–136. St. John's, Newfoundland: Memorial University of Newfoundland.

Lee, Richard B. 1988. "Reflections on Primitive Communism." In *Hunters and Gatherers.* Vol. 1, *History, Evolution, and Social Change*, edited by Tim Ingold, David Riches, and James Woodburn, 252–68. New York: Berg.

Lithman, Yngve. 1978. *The Community Apart: A Case Study of a Canadian Indian Reserve Community.* Stockholm Studies in Social Anthropology, no. 6. Stockholm: University of Stockholm, Department of Social Anthropology.

Parsons, Elsie Clews. 1925. "Micmac Folklore." *Journal of American Folklore* 38: 87.

Rappaport, Roy A. 1979. *Ecology, Meaning, and Religion.* Richmond, Calif.: North Atlantic Books.

Shweder, Richard A., and Edmund J. Bourne. 1984. "Does the Concept of the Person Vary

Cross-Culturally?" In *Culture Theory: Essays on Mind, Self, and Emotion*, edited by Richard A. Shweder and Robert A. LeVine, 158–99. Cambridge: Cambridge University Press.

Suzuki, David, and Peter Knudtson. 1992. *Wisdom of the Elders: Sacred Native Stories of Nature*. New York: Bantam.

Whitehead, Ruth Holmes. 1989. *Kluskap's Cave: Documentation of Micmac Oral Tradition*. Halifax: Nova Scotia Museum.

PART THREE

Forest Visions

12

Shade

Throwing Light on Politics and Ecology
in Contemporary Pakistan

MICHAEL R. DOVE

A fool sees not the same tree that a wise man sees.

–William Blake, *The Marriage of Heaven and Hell* (1979 [1793], 89)

Until a generation ago, influenced by a much older nature-culture dichotomy in western thought, studies of environment and society were generally kept strictly apart, pursued by the natural and social sciences, respectively.[1] The rise of human ecological approaches in the 1960s and 1970s represented a radical critique of and break from this dichotomy in that they explicitly integrated human beings into ecological studies. Nevertheless, political dimensions were characteristically missing from these early human ecological studies: the relevance of power, inequality, and the state to resource use and degradation was not explored. Human ecologists had critically asked of previous ecological studies, "Where are the people?" But they themselves came to be criticized for having no answer to questions such as "Where is the state?" (see chapter 2). Scholars (many working in a neo-Marxist tradition) who were then paying attention to the exercise of power in national and global systems were generally not interested in the environment and natural resources. These complementary lacunae contributed to the subsequent rise of political ecology, which, in pioneering works by Piers Blaikie (1985) and Blaikie and Harold Brookfield (1987), among others, brought wider political factors into analyses of local relations between society and environment. In time, however, other scholars, led by Andrew P. Vayda, have argued that this paradigmatic shift has meant that, whereas politics were once ignored, now they are overly privileged—that an "ecology without politics" has merely been replaced by a "politics without ecology" (Vayda and Walters 1999, 168).

How do we contribute to this debate without simply fueling what might be

called, following Jacques Derrida (1978, 280-281), a cycle of reciprocal destruction? I suggest that the answer lies not in debating the balance between politics
and ecology but in rethinking what we mean by ecology and politics in the first
place. In this chapter, I illustrate one path we might follow by drawing on a multiple-
year study of rural resource use that I carried out in the late 1980s in the rainfed
districts of Pakistan's Punjab and Northwest Frontier provinces.[2] In the course of
the study, I discovered a widespread, coherent, indigenous constellation of beliefs
and practices regarding tree shade and its management within the context of on-
farm tree-crop interactions.[3] These beliefs diverged greatly from western scientific
concepts of shade and, of most importance, directly contradicted the accepted
wisdom of Pakistan's government foresters that farmers were not interested in
trees and knew nothing about them.[4]

According to my study, farmers in the region interpret the on-farm interaction between annual crops and trees in terms of *sayah* (tree shade). Tree shade is
conceived of as an emission and is thought to have density, temperature, taste,
and size. Farmers believe that the character of shade and its impact upon their
crops varies by tree species and also by season and land type (see table 12.1). This
complex system of beliefs attests to farmers' commitment to the management of
tree-crop interactions and contradicts government foresters' beliefs that farmers are hostile to the presence of trees on farms. The farmers' belief system collapses a dichotomy between tree and crop, forest and farm, and indeed nature
and culture that serves the interests of the forest department. My analysis of this
system suggests that the most quotidian resource practices may have profound
political implications; that environmental knowledge is often (if not always) partisan knowledge (Haenn 1999); and that cultural meaning cannot be divorced
from political-economic dynamics. My interest in everyday knowledge and practice, as well as in problematizing customary ways of dividing up the world, draws
on work done on the theory of practice (Bourdieu 1977 [1972], Ortner 1984).

The suggestion that environmental knowledge and practice do not belong
to an ontologically distinct realm from politics and power has important methodological implications. Although my official mandate in Pakistan was to study
farmers, I was obliged to give equal attention to foresters. As the chief social scientist on a social forestry project, I spent as much time objectifying the project
as I did its ostensible subjects. This dual focus required me to adopt multiple
roles and perspectives. Such a task was inherently problematic but not without
potential, as Jennifer Pierce (1995) articulates when writing about her dual roles
of participant and observer in a U.S. law firm, a stance that she calls the *outlaw
position*: "The outlaw position is a multiple and discontinuous identity whose
movement between positions proves to be a critical advantage in uncovering the
'regimes of power' in the workplace. Further, I suggest that it is through the
responses I elicit in my movement between positions that I unveil the complex
operations of . . . power in the field" (96).

TABLE 12-1

Characteristics of Tree Shade

Dimension of Tree Shade	Range of Variation	Cause of Variation
Length and Width	Small to large	Lopping Species variation Cardinal orientation
Height	Short to tall	Species variation
Duration	Brief to long	Orientation in field
Density	Light to dark	Species variation Seasonal variation Diurnal variation
Temperature	Cold to hot	Species variation
Taste	Bitter to sweet	Species variation
(Root length)	Short to long Shallow to deep	Species variation Species variation
(Litter quality)	Few to many nutrients	Species variation

Note: Parentheses indicate that a dimension has secondary importance.

Pierce's principal insight is that the inherent tension between the roles of participant and observer has pedagogical value. I also found this to be true. Many of the insights in my study were initially stimulated by foresters' reaction to my efforts to widen the scope of my research to encompass not just the behavior of the farmers but the foresters themselves. In effect, these insights were stimulated by my own movement between the roles of project participant and project observer. This sort of movement is often demanded when we study the local-level environmental relations and extralocal politics that constitute much of the avowed subject matter of political ecology.

I begin my analysis by presenting some background information on the development project in which I worked and the methodology of my study of Pakistani farmers. I then discuss the limitations of this methodology in understanding the agendas and behavior of Pakistani foresters, who became for me a subject of study themselves. In the context of divergent farmer and forester agendas, I discuss farmers' beliefs regarding tree shade, its impact on crops, and their practices for managing that impact and conclude with an analysis of the political dimensions of shade beliefs and the implications of this analysis for the future study of environmental knowledge in particular and political ecology in general.

Setting and Methods

Historically, most of Pakistan was covered by tropical thorn forest, which merges into dry, subtropical, evergreen forests in the hilly regions in the northern and western part of the country (Champion et al. 1965, 111). Today, however, the vegetation in most of Pakistan's arid lowlands ranges from a "scrub preclimax" at best (40) to rocky wastes at the worst (Khan 1994). The forest cover of the country has so dwindled that Pakistan today has one of the smallest forest covers (3.2 percent) of any country in the world (World Bank 2001, 139).[5] The loss of the country's forest cover has meant an increasing scarcity of biomass fuels for the rural population. Households that once burned mostly fuelwood must now burn complex and intensively managed combinations of wood, small branches and twigs, wild grasses and reeds, agricultural and stable waste, and livestock dung. Surveys show that almost two-thirds of all dung produced is now burned as fuel instead of being returned to the land as fertilizer (Campbell 1992).

The Forestry Planning and Development (FP&D) Project (1985–93), jointly funded by the government of Pakistan and the U.S. Agency for International Development (USAID), was the first national-level social forestry project in Pakistan and was designed to address the ill-effects of deforestation.[6] Its ultimate goal was to expand tree planting and thus the production of fuelwood, fodder, and timber on farmlands, especially those of the *barani* (rainfed) tracts of the Punjab and Northwest Frontier provinces (see fig. 12.1), thereby improving rural welfare and sustaining the long-term economic and ecological viability of small farms. Its more immediate goal was to assist the Pakistan Forest Service to develop the institutional capacity to work with farmers and thus help to change the basic function of the forest service from protecting the state forests from the rural population to serving this same population. To this end, the project included a program to train foresters in agroforestry, a program of research on agroforestry systems, and a field program to demonstrate the viability of agroforestry systems that provided farmers with extension advice and free seedlings for planting on their own lands. Responsibility for overall supervision of the project lay with a special cell established in the federal office of the inspector-general of forests, to which several expatriate technical advisors hired by USAID were attached (including myself), while responsibility for field operations lay with project offices established in each of the provinces involved.

I was attached to the FP&D project for nearly four years (1985–89) as chief social scientist in charge of contacting, studying, and advising the federal government about the project's farmer clientele. With the assistance of a team that I assembled of nine Pakistani social scientists, I carried out a multiple-year study of farmers throughout the project region to discover what their fuel, fodder, and timber needs were; how well they were meeting those needs with their current farm forestry practices; and what extension services from the forest service

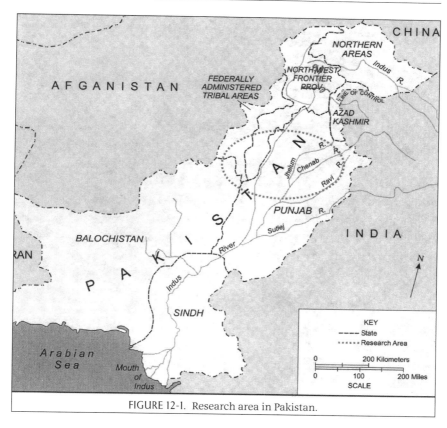

FIGURE 12-1. Research area in Pakistan.

would help them to do better.[7] Many of our forester counterparts openly questioned whether or not small farmers had any interest in farm forestry, so we made the extent of small farmer interest in on-farm cultivation of trees a central part of the study.

Given the nationwide scope of the project and the need to attend to macro- as well as microlevel factors (see chapter 2), I devised a multistage approach to the farmer study, progressing from a broad but shallow focus to a narrow and intensive one (see fig. 12.2). The first stage, a type of rapid rural appraisal, consisted of group interviews concerning overall patterns of rural resource use with officials and local luminaries in each of twenty-five *tehsil* (subdistricts) of the eleven project districts (Kohat, Dera Ismail Khan, and Karak in Northwest Frontier Province; Attock, Chakwal, Rawalpindi, Sargodha, Sialkot, Gujrat, and Jhelum in Punjab Province; and Nasirabad in Baluchistan Province). The second stage consisted of group interviews (one with village officials, one with ordinary villagers) concerning village resource patterns in 118 villages.[8] The third stage consisted of individual interviews on household resource-use patterns in 1,132 households in 63 villages.[9] The fourth stage consisted of more in-depth inter-

Number of Villages	Stages of Research	Number of Households
13	7. Daily records	13
13	6. Shade study	100
40	5. Village in-depth interview	n.a.
40	4. Household in-depth interview	589
63	3. Household survey	1,132
118	2. Village survey	n.a.
n.a.	1. Rapid rural appraisal	n.a.

FIGURE 12-2. Multistage survey methodology.

views on farm ecology and economics in 40 of these same villages and 589 of these same households. Some of the thornier questions that arose in these interviews were subsequently pursued in group discussions with key informants and village leaders in each of these same forty villages, which represented the fifth stage of the study. Several topics that arose in the course of the study that appeared to merit further sustained study (including the indigenous conception of tree shade) were investigated in a further round of intensive interviewing with one hundred households in a sample of thirteen villages—the sixth stage of the study. Finally, to quantify some aspects of daily farm resource use, key informants in each of these thirteen villages were hired to keep daily records of farm forestry—related activities for a period of eighteen months, which represented the seventh and final stage of the study. The methodological principles of this multistage approach were as follows: (1) each successive stage focused on a subset of the sample of the prior stage (so the smallest sample was studied in all seven stages, whereas the largest or widest sample was studied in just the first stage); (2) each successive stage of the study produced the criteria used to select the narrower sample (of villages and households) for the next stage; and (3) the findings of each stage were used to direct the questioning in each subsequent stage.

This multistage and multilevel methodology enabled the research team to transcend the narrow scope of traditional village studies while preserving some of their ethnographic strengths. It crossed the boundaries of locale, class, ethnicity, and—most important, perhaps—scale, allowing us to talk about a variety of different levels of resource use, ranging from subhousehold to national. But it became evident while this research was still underway that there was yet another boundary that we needed to cross—that between the rural population and the state, between the common farmers who were supposed to be our subjects and the state foresters who were supposed to be our counterparts. The most critical challenge of this research turned out to be the need to adapt our methodology to rethink the basic concepts of research subject and object.

Methodology Redux: The Forest Department

Many of the initial field visits in the farmer study were carried out in the company of our official counterparts from the forest departments of Northwest Frontier, Punjab, and Baluchistan. These provincial foresters invariably steered us toward the so-called progressive villages in each subdistrict, which in practice meant villages with irrigation, villages on paved roads, villages close to forestry offices, and so on (see Chambers 1983, 1–27). The foresters also steered us toward "progressive" farmers, meaning the ones with extensive holdings and often with political office or influence as well.[10] When we met with these elite farmers, they usually asked whether the project would offer them the tractors, low-interest loans, and other sorts of expensive subsidized resources that they were used to receiving from their government patrons. When we announced that all the project offered was a modest number of free seedlings of fuel-, fodder-, and timber-providing species, they were openly contemptuous.[11] Their reaction to this offer contrasted with the reaction of common farmers, who were typically delighted at the prospect of getting anything at all for free from the government.

These field experiences with the project foresters led me to add an additional topic to our study: the forest service itself and its relations with both elite and nonelite farmers. Therefore, while directing the farmer study, I also carried out an ethnography of the forest service. (See chapter 2 on the emphasis in political ecology on studying institutions.) I gathered data by participating in several dozen forest service meetings, workshops, and field trips; analyzing forest department documents; and taking part in informal discussions with forest officers.[12]

It quickly became clear from this institutional ethnography that forester-farmer dynamics could only be understood within the context of a complex historical process, which involved not just the loss of natural resources (the focus of both the forest service and foreign donors) but a change in their location and control. This change was best articulated by the senior Pakistani forester in the project, who suggested that a historic shift in tree cover was occurring, with or without state assistance, from the domain of the state to the domain of private farmers. This shift, which is also attested to by historical-ecological evidence (Dove 1995), was not simply a shift in tenure but a literal displacement of tree cover from state to private lands. The socioeconomic niche favorable to tree growth was waning on public lands but waxing on private lands. Evidence of this shift was provided by the data gathered in the farmer study: 49 percent of the farmers interviewed reported prior tree planting on their lands. And the percentage of farmers reporting tree planting would have been much higher if fruit trees (the cultivation of which has a much longer history in Pakistan) had been included in the analysis (Cernea 1989, 4–5).

This historic displacement was threatening to the forest service, whose political capital was traditionally based on how much forest area it controlled and how much revenue it contributed to government coffers. As these declined, so, too, did the forest service's share of the state budget. Taken together, these developments led to a debate regarding the need to reorient the forest service toward a public service role with a constituency that would prominently include small farmers.

The Pakistan Forest Service traditionally has had distinct relations with two different rural clienteles. From one clientele, the peasantry, the forest service extracted fees for approved use of forest resources (grazing cattle and gathering fuelwood) and fines and bribes for unapproved uses.[13] For the other clientele, the principal landlords in each district, the service provided subsidized tree plant- ings on their lands, within a broader pattern of reciprocal economic and politi- cal ties between the government and the rural elite (Fortmann 1988, 57). Many foresters initially assumed (incorrectly) that the FP&D project was designed to ben- efit this same elite clientele. Their assumption that scarce government resources should be directed toward rural elites needs to be interpreted in light of the fact that the foresters are part of this elite themselves. The higher-level officers in the forest service all do their formal degree training at the Pakistan Forest Institute in Peshawar, a prestigious institution modeled after the Indian forestry school in Dehra Dun. Once posted in Pakistan's rural areas, forest officers command con- trol of not only valuable natural resources (namely, forests and grazing lands) but also important infrastructural resources, including offices and homes, staff and salaries, means of transportation and communication, and access to the other branches of government. These resources combine to make forest officers some of the most powerful political figures on the rural landscape, especially in Pak- istan's poorer and more remote rural districts. This stature contributes to their identification with the rural elite as opposed to rural poor.

The foresters' traditional belief that rural elites were the appropriate focus for material and technical expertise, whereas the rural poor were the appropri- ate focus for surveillance, was supported by a set of beliefs that denied small farmers' interest in and knowledge of on-farm tree cultivation (Dove 1992). Most project foresters maintained that small farmers did not have trees on their farms, did not want them, and would not agree to plant them. In the exceptional cases where this was not true, they insisted that small farmers would only plant large blocks of exotic species for market sale and not for on-farm needs for fuel,

TABLE 12-2						
Obstacles to Tree Cultivation (by percentage)						
Lack of Water	Hard to Protect	Crop Impact	Lack of Seedlings	Pests and Disease	Soil Problems	None
39	38	29	11	9	8	7

Note: These are the percentages of farm households that report each obstacle, and households could report more than one obstacle

timber, and fodder. The foresters glossed the small farmers as being not "tree-minded." When presented with incontrovertible evidence of tree cultivation by small farmers, one project forester retorted that this represented only a casual commitment but was "not from the heart." Central to these beliefs was the idea that small farmers and trees did not mix and that, more generally, agriculture and silviculture did not mix. Their belief in this fundamental incompatibility supported the status quo in forester-farmer relations and mitigated against the department's evolution toward a public service organization.

The foresters' beliefs regarding farmers' lack of tree-mindedness were decisively contradicted by the findings of my study (Dove 1992). Among the farmers surveyed, 87 percent reported having existing trees on their farms, of which about one-half were planted and most of which were scattered about the farmland or located within the house or farmhouse courtyard (as opposed to being grouped in linear or block plantings).[14] Further, two-thirds of the farmers surveyed expressed interest in working with the project to establish small plantings (meaning fewer than 1,000 trees) of multipurpose native species to meet their households' fuel and timber needs.[15] These findings clearly reflected an existing, successful integration of tree cultivation into the farming landscape.

This integration is also reflected in the findings of the farmer study regarding the perceived obstacles to on-farm tree cultivation. The major reported obstacles to on-farm tree cultivation were not farmers' lack of interest or experience but the normal challenges of the farming-forestry interface. Thus, whereas the foresters were proposing to devote large amounts of project resources to farmer "motivation," the farmers themselves were concerned with how best to manage the perennial farm-forestry problems of water scarcity, free-ranging cattle, and competition with annual crops (see table 12.2). Central to their efforts to manage these problems was their conception of tree shade.

Farmers' Shade Beliefs

The retreat of Pakistan's state forests does not mean that trees have vanished from the countryside. Trees abound in all graveyards and religious shrines, where they provide shade for the pious and eternal blessings for the planter.[16] Trees are found in the enclosed courtyards of every rural home, providing shade, fodder, and fruit. The greatest numbers of trees are found on the farmlands themselves: in clusters around water holes and tanks, where Moghul rulers decreed the planting of banyan (*Ficus bengalensis*); around wells and Persian wheels, where they shade the circling oxen; and in hedgerows along field boundaries, where they provide protection from wind and livestock incursions and yield fuel and fodder. The number, species, location, and growth of on-farm trees are carefully managed to balance their perceived benefits against their perceived costs, referring largely to deleterious effects on agricultural land and crops. This balance is most often articulated within farmers' discourse about sayah (tree shade).

Farmers in the rainfed tracts of Pakistan conceive of tree shade not as the absence of something (such as light) but as the presence of something that the tree itself emits. This emission has four major characteristics: density, temperature, taste, and size (see table 12.1). Each is believed to vary with the tree species; and of most importance to the farmer, the impact of shade on food crops is thought to vary accordingly. The varying character of tree shade is well expressed in a proverb of the Pushto-speaking tribes of the region: "Look at the tree before sitting under its shadow" (Ahmed 1975, 56).

First, regarding size, Pakistani farmers are acutely conscious of the length and width of the area that is shadowed by a tree; and one of their motives for pruning is to reduce the height and width of a tree's crown and thereby the extent of its shade. They favorably compare the natural shape of a tree such as the Indian olive (*Olea ferruginea Royle*), slender and casting less shade, with one such as the Persian lilac (*Melia azedarach L.*), broader and casting more shade.[17] In addition to length and width, some farmers assign another dimension to shade: height or vertical movement. Speaking of a tall tree such as the Persian lilac, they say that its shade cools as it "descends" from the tree's top to earth. A final dimension, time, is also important. Farmers are very conscious of the duration of a tree's daily shadow on the land, which varies principally according to the location of the tree vis-à-vis the land in question. Thus, farmers say that one reason it is better to plant a tree at the edge of a field instead of the center is so its shade will cover the field for only half the day (morning if it is on the eastern edge, afternoon if on the western) instead of covering some part of the field all day long.

After size, the second most important dimension of shade is its density—the depth and uniformity of its darkness—which appears to be a measure of the amount of sunlight that passes through the tree's foliage. Farmers say, for example, that sissoo (*Dalbergia sissoo Roxb.*) and white mulberry trees (*Morus alba Linn.*) have especially dense shade because their leaves are very thick and opaque. As a result, the amount of sunlight filtering through them is limited, and their shade is dark. There are also seasonal and diurnal dimensions to shade thickness. Farmers say that shade is thicker during the summer than during the winter, and

they say that it is thicker at midday than during the morning or afternoon. Whatever its cause, farmers say that thick shade is generally bad for crops.

The third dimension of tree shade is temperature, which farmers say is
immediately perceptible to anyone standing under the tree. Thus, it "feels cold"
under a sissoo tree or a siris tree (*Albizia lebbek (L.) Benth.*), while it "feels hot"
under a tamarisk (*Tamarix aphylla (L.) Karst.*).[18] Farmers attribute variation in
shade temperature, in part, to variation in shade density. Thus, they say that
thin-leaved trees such as the Indian jujube (*Zizyphus mauritania Lam.*) have hot
shade, while thick-leaved trees such as the sissoo and white mulberry have cold
shade.[19] More generally, the temperature of a tree's shade is associated with the
temperature of the tree itself, which the farmers apprehend indirectly. Thus,
farmers say that the Indian olive is cold because it casts little shade (since shade
is a crop-threatening and hence "hot" impact) and because its leaf litter enriches
the soil (which is seen as a fertility-enhancing and hence "cool" impact). In contrast, mesquite (*Prosopis juliflora (Swartz) DC*) and babul (*Acacia nilotica (L.)
Willd. ex Del.*) are said to be hot trees because they thrive not only in hot regions
but in hot seasons as well, losing their leaves only during the cold season. Of
most importance, any tree in whose shade crops fare especially poorly is said, by
inference, to have hot shade. The temperature of a particular tree's shade does
not vary with the season, although its value to the farmers may. Thus, farmers
say that they stake their livestock under the hot shade of the Indian jujube in the
winter but under the cool shade of sissoo in the summer. The same principles
are applied to tree products as well as tree shade. Thus, farmers feed their livestock the leaves of the hot Indian jujube to counteract the cold of winter and the
leaves of the cold sissoo to counteract the heat of illness. The farmers themselves
eat the leaves of the hot tamarisk to counteract the cold of sexual impotence (see
also Watt 1889–96, 6:3, 410).

The fourth dimension of tree shade is taste, which encompasses bitterness
and sweetness. The taste of shade cannot be perceived directly. Farmers infer it
from other characteristics of the tree or from its effects on proximate crops.
Thus, farmers say they know that the shade of the Persian lilac is bitter because
its sap, fruit, and even the crops growing under it all taste bitter. In contrast, the
sweet taste of the Indian jujube's sap indicates that its shade is sweet. The taste
of a tree's leaves may also indicate whether its shade is bitter or sweet. Taste
extends even to the wood: farmers say that the bitterness of the wood of the
neem tree (*Azadirachta indica A. Juss.*) gives it its well-known resistance to ter-
mites (CSIR 1986, 64; NAS 1980, 1:114).[20] Because of these insecticidal properties,
other observers have reported that the shade of the neem tree is considered to
be healthy for people (Ahmed and Grainge 1986, 205).[21] According to George
Watt (1889–96), "a popular belief exists that a leper can be cured if he can live
exposed under a *neem* tree for 12 years" (1:218).[22]

Shade Impact and Management

Farmers say that the impact of shade on crops is often but not always negative. They attribute these negative impacts to reduction in the amount of sunlight that reaches the crops and especially to exacerbation of undesirable soil conditions. Thus, farmers say that when the soil is overly wet after rainfall or irrigating, shade keeps it from drying out. Similarly, when the soil is overly cold and dry, shade keeps it from being warmed and energized. Farmers associate both conditions with lack of soil strength and fertility. Further, these effects are believed to vary according to the type of land and the season of the year (see fig. 12.3). Farmers say that shade's augmentation of soil moisture has an extremely negative impact on irrigated land because it aggravates extant problems with waterlogging. Its de-energizing of the soil has a similar negative impact on rainfed land because it aggravates extant problems with soil fertility. Likewise, the cooling impact of shade on the soil is most harmful during the winter, whereas it is sometimes even beneficial in the summer. To a limited extent, farmers also say, the impact of tree shade varies according to the type of crop planted under it. For example, particularly "hot" crops such as the chili pepper (*Capsicum spp.*) are said to grow better than other crops do under shade.

At one level of farmer discourse, shade refers to all of the effects of a tree on crops; but at another level, the effects of a tree's shade and the effects of its roots are distinguished. Farmers believe that the impact of tree roots is always negative, unlike the impact of its shade. Whereas shade makes the topsoil wet, roots make the subsurface soil dry. This is thought to be a function of the tree's need to consume energy (that is, nutrient matter), which is hot and thereby requires an offsetting amount of coolness from water.[23] When the tree takes this water from the subsurface soil, the soil's energy will be negatively affected. (This is said to be more true in the case of shallow-rooted trees such as the Persian lilac or the white mulberry than in the case of more deeply rooted trees.) Farmers say that if the soil can be sufficiently irrigated, however, this effect can be neutralized or even transformed into a positive impact. Consequently, they believe that the impact of roots is worse in rainfed lands than in irrigated ones. Indeed, a significant minority of farmers with irrigated lands deny that tree roots have any deleterious effect on crops. Since the major limiting factor in agriculture on irrigated lands is not lack of water but its overabundance, farmers tend to see the wetting impact of tree shade as worse than the drying impact of tree roots. For farmers with rainfed lands, on the other hand, the chief agricultural constraint is lack of water; so they tend to view the impact of tree roots as worse than that of tree shade (see fig. 12.3).

A minority of farmers identify a third aspect of tree impact on crops: leaf and flower litter. That effect is thought to vary according to the availability of irrigation water to prevent the crops from being "burned" by the "hot," nutrient-laden litter. Some farmers carry this argument so far as to attribute all ill-effects of trees to their litter, holding shade (or roots) to be irrelevant by comparison.[24] Trees said to have the worst litter are the Persian lilac and the babul. The Indian olive, in contrast, is said to have good litter.[25]

Pakistani farmers have a management system for tree shade that is based on a variety of regional intellectual traditions, including Ayurveda, which draws on classical Sanskrit sources (Bhishagratna 1963, Sharma and Dash 1976); and Unani Tibb (Greco-Arabian medicine), which draws on the classical works of Hippocrates and Galen, especially the medieval works of Avicenna (Shah 1966, Gruner 1930). Farmers' shade beliefs appear to represent an example of what Claude Lévi-Strauss (1966) called *bricolage* or James C. Scott (1998) has more recently called *metis:* namely, a practically oriented, context-specific recombination of elements. Although the shade beliefs draw on formal knowledge systems such as Ayurveda, they do not themselves constitute a formal, self-conscious system of knowledge. If you asked Pakistani farmers about their system of belief regarding

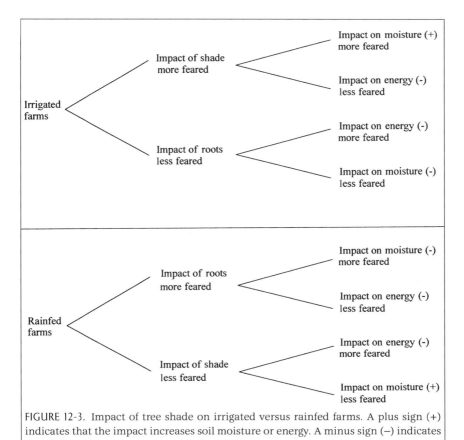

FIGURE 12-3. Impact of tree shade on irrigated versus rainfed farms. A plus sign (+) indicates that the impact increases soil moisture or energy. A minus sign (−) indicates that the impact decreases soil moisture or energy.

tree shade, you might well be told that there is no such system (Fairhead and Leach 1996, 285).

The central management principle in these beliefs involves the combination and segregation of opposing qualities—hot and cold, wet and dry, bitter and sweet—to attain desired agricultural outcomes (see Kurin's [1983] analysis of Pakistani food crops). In the case of tree shade, the desired outcomes are to mitigate (or at least not exacerbate) the constraining properties of the land and the season in which a farmer is working: too much wetness in irrigated land, too much dryness in rainfed land, and too much cold in winter. Farmers' responses to shade depend on the context. In most cases, a particular tree and its shade is neither absolutely good nor absolutely bad but good or bad on a particular type of land in a particular season. In this and other respects, the management system is whole-heartedly empirical: Pakistani farmers use sight, taste, touch, and causal inference from trees' effects on crops to inform their concepts of tree shade.

Farmers possess a variety of techniques for applying these management principles. The first consists of selecting and planting those tree species believed to have more beneficial and less destructive shade, a selection that varies somewhat according to the local ecology and desired land use (Jones and Price 1985, 327). A second technique consists of selecting appropriate spacings and locations. For linear plantings, this entails spacing trees widely to prevent shade from adjoining trees from overlapping and to thus avoid day-long coverage over crops underneath; planting trees along east-west as opposed to north-south axes (Stigter 1984, 207) to minimize the length of the shadow cast; and planting trees on the east side of the field to ensure that the field receives the warmth of the afternoon sun. A third management technique consists of actively removing all undesirable tree species in all inappropriate locations on and around the fields.

With grown trees, farmers employ two other important management strategies. The first is watering proximate crops by hand, especially in rainfed lands, to offset trees' water uptake. The second and perhaps most important strategy is pruning, especially during the winter, just before the planting of the winter crops (Michie 1986, 238).[26] Farmers maintain that pruning not only increases the amount of sunlight reaching the crops but also adds to the energy and hence fertility of the soil as it reduces the amount of energy that the tree draws out of the soil. Some farmers also believe that pruning weakens tree roots and thereby further reduces their drain on soil energy.[27]

Conclusion

Tree shade may not appear to have much to do with politics.[28] Such apparent political irrelevance has served as the starting point for a number of political ecological studies that employ a variation of Ludwig Wittgenstein's (1974) metaphor of the magic drawer. This refers to the act of conceptually putting something into a drawer and closing it, then turning around, reopening the drawer, and removing the same object with an exclamation of surprise. (See chapter 2 on the search for hidden functions in ecological anthropology in the 1960s.) I could work that magic here by disingenuously presenting shade as a strictly local and agricultural subject, only then to reveal its extralocal and political dimensions. For example, I could have focused on the classical origins of the Unani Tibb elements in shade beliefs and drawn into the analysis Alexander the Great's passage through the region. Then I could have argued that what appears to be an indigenous system of knowledge is really a product of ancient geopolitical struggles. Or I could have traced these struggles into contemporary times by emphasizing the link between the FP&D project and the wider program of 1980s U.S. technical assistance to Pakistan and the U.S.-led opposition to the Soviet-backed regime in Afghanistan—the latest act at the time of this study in the so-called "great game" that extralocal powers have played in this region for centuries.[29] But there are two related problems with this type of analysis. The stylized "discovery" of unsuspected political dimensions is based on an artificial dichotomization of political and everyday life, which in turn is based on a limited and dated conception of politics and the exercise of power. In political ecology, ecological anthropology, and allied fields, these older approaches to power have increasingly been supplanted by poststructural approaches (as noted in chapter 2). Raymond L. Bryant (2000), for example, urges us to turn away from framing environmental debates in terms of material struggle toward a focus on struggles over the social construction of environmental knowledge (see Brosius 1999).[30]

The Pakistani case represents just such a struggle. The shade beliefs that have been analyzed here are premised on tree-crop interactions and the articulation of domains—tree and crop, forest and farm, forest department and farmer, indeed nature and culture—that the forest department has felt politically bound to maintain as oppositions. The farmers' shade discourse is all about negotiating this boundary—the shade beliefs represent a practical guide to the mediation of tree-crop interactions—while the foresters' farmer discourse focuses on constructing and reifying this boundary (epitomized in their characterization of the farmers as "anti-tree"). The shade beliefs represent an ability to make discriminations that the forest department denies; they open a conceptual space that the forest department refuses to admit exists. Whereas the manifest goals of the farmers' discourse are agronomic and those of the foresters' discourse are silvicultural, both clearly also have political implications: the farmers' discourse challenges state authority; the foresters' discourse reasserts it. These political implications are inherent in the two discourses. As Scott (1998) writes, "situated, local knowledge"—like that of both the Pakistani foresters and the farmers—is inherently "partisan knowledge" (318). It is partisan because it is socially constructed (as chapter 2 notes). The social constructedness of knowledge is what enables power to be expressed at the epistemological level.

Nevertheless, the link between farmer and forester discourses is more complex than a simple opposition. By making it possible for farmers to manage tree-crop interactions, farmers' beliefs implicitly open the possibility of forest department collaboration with farmers. This possibility challenges the forest department so long as it ignores or denies such an opening. Denial, in the form of foresters' statement that farmers are "anti-tree," is thus in some sense evoked by the farmers' shade beliefs. In other words, the farmer and forester discourses are linked. Not only does each help to explain the other, but the forester discourse probably owes its development to the farmer discourse. Without elaborate farmer beliefs and practices addressing on-farm tree management, an elaborate forester discourse that dismisses such beliefs and practices would be unnecessary. As Nora Haenn (1999) suggests in her study of opposing but linked environmental discourses in Mexico, we need to start examining the interdependence of such constructs and ask if their pairing serves some purpose (Sivaramakrishnan 1995).

My research in Pakistan has a variety of implications for practice. Most obviously, this system of tree shade management has relevance for development analysts in Pakistan and elsewhere in South Asia. Whereas scientific research on agroforestry dates back at most two generations, this indigenous system is centuries or even millennia old. The system foregrounds the challenge of tree-crop interactions and the need to study relevant dimensions of trees: the shape and height of their canopies; the extent of ground area they shade; and the light, temperature, and humidity differentials of their shade (Jones and Price 1985, 327)—matters of central interest to farmers in the region but still of little interest to government foresters.[31] It also directs us to look at how this pattern of interest and disinterest articulates with wider political-ecological relations.

My research shows that the study of indigenous environmental knowledge and practice cannot be separated from the study of politics, although efforts to separate them can be revealing. At the time of my research, little if any of the rural social scientific research being done in Pakistan was relevant to the policies and practices of the forest service; and filling this gap was one of my explicit goals in the FP&D project. But social science research on the knowledge and practices of small farmers was so threatening to the forest service's status quo that it was stiffly resisted, at least initially. This was made clear at the Pakistan Forest Institute, the country's preeminent institution for professional training of forest officers, where my efforts to develop courses on rural development sociology were initially countered by a request to instead develop more traditional social science materials on rural social structure. This request can be read as an explicit call for the continued separation of social science and policy and the continued distancing of farmer resource practices and knowledge from forestry programs, policy, and politics. The Pakistan Forest Institute's initial reaction to applied social science—indeed, the response of the country's forest service as a whole—shows how the separation in development between agrarian ecology and politics is itself socially constructed.

NOTES

1. The research on which this analysis is based was supported by the Forestry Planning and Development Project, jointly funded by the government of Pakistan and the U.S. Agency for International Development, under the direction of the inspector-general of forests and under contract to the Winrock International Institute for Agricultural Development. The author was assisted in data gathering by Riaz Ahmad, Sarfraz Ahmad, Nisar Ahmed, Abul Hassan, Zafar Iqbal Marwat, Umar Farooq Marwat, Zafar Masood, Shamsul Qamar, Jamil A. Qureshi, Nazir Shahzad, and Gul Muhammad Umrani. He is indebted to Carol Carpenter, Lisa L. Gezon, and Susan Paulson for insightful readings of previous drafts. He alone, however, is responsible for the final analysis presented here.

2. One irrigated district of Baluchistan was also included in the project.

3. I will refer to this system of knowledge as *indigenous*, although the term is problematic (Agrawal 1995, Ellen et al. 2000).

4. For an exegesis and problematizing of western concepts of shade, see, for example, Casati (2003) and Smith (1973).

5. Note, however, that these measures of deforestation focus on the contraction of contiguous forests managed by the state and largely ignore the expansion of tree cover on private farmlands, which is one of the points of this analysis.

6. The project was one of many responses to the so-called fuelwood crisis that came to the fore in international development circles in the 1970s, the validity of which has since been disputed by retrospective studies (Arnold et al. 2003).

7. I was assisted by a Pakistani sociologist throughout the project, and we hired eight additional field assistants, all with some social science background and all native speakers of the local languages in the provinces to which they were assigned. The field assistants worked in pairs to minimize non-sampling error. I also visited each field team every one or two weeks to participate in interviews and review completed interview schedules. All the researchers were male: in part, because of the radicalizing impact on Islam of the Soviet Union's invasion of Afghanistan, it was not possible to hire female field assistants or interview female members of farm families, which was an admitted weakness of the study.

8. The villages were selected for variation in terms of the presence or absence of the FP&D project; distance to roads, urban areas, forest department offices, state forests, refugee camps, and traditional migratory routes of herders; the presence or absence of irrigation; the presence or absence of *shamilat* (communal forests); population size; the predominance of landlords versus small farmers; government characterization as a progressive versus a backward village; and geographical location.

9. The households in each village were randomly selected. If the village was included in the FP&D project, up to one-half of these random selections were made from lists of project participants. In addition, two village officials were selected for interview in each village.

10. When we expressed to one district forest officer our desire to meet with farmers, he replied that he could have "all of the farmers" in the district in his office in twenty minutes. He got on the telephone, and a half-dozen landlords of large estates shortly thereafter drove up to his office to be interviewed (Dove 1994). It was politically difficult for the

foresters to introduce important guests to poor farmers instead of their landlord clients, just as it was difficult for the foresters to deliver project resources to the former as opposed to the latter.

11. These negative responses prompted foresters' efforts to adapt the project resources to their clients' needs, initially by raising the ceiling on the number of seedlings that could be given to any one household, subsequently by using project funds to build nurseries for elite farmers in which they could raise seedlings to sell to poor farmers.

12. A formal study of forester beliefs was vetoed by senior forest service officials.

13. The oppositional character of forester-farmer relations is reflected in Cernea's (1985, 271) report that, at the time of his study in Azad Kashmir, one out of every five households was involved in ongoing litigation with the forest service.

14. Among the farmers interviewed, 74 percent and 60 percent, respectively, reported scattered versus courtyard plantings, whereas just 10 percent and 3 percent, respectively, reported linear versus block plantings.

15. Among the farmers surveyed, 35 percent requested fewer than one hundred seedlings, and another 51 percent requested fewer than 1,000 seedlings. The tree species requested by the households interviewed were as follows: babul (*Acacia nilotica*), 48 percent; sissoo (*Dalbergia sissoo*), 46 percent; eucalyptus (*Eucalyptus spp.*), 44 percent; poplar (*Populus spp.*), 17 percent; leucaena (*Leucaena leucocephala*), 8 percent; phulai (*Acacia modesta*), 8 percent; and others, 18 percent. Note that these are the percentages of farm households that requested each species. Each household could request more than one species.

    Households desired planted trees for the following reasons: fuelwood, 91 percent; timber, 72 percent; sale, 46 percent; fodder, 13 percent; other, 7 percent; and uncertain, 6 percent. Once again, these are the percentages of farm households that reported each use. Each household could mention more than one use.

16. Proscriptions against tree felling in such places are strictly followed (see Gold and Gujar 1989), which has led Pakistani foresters to study their vegetation as the closest remaining approximation of the country's historic vegetation (Chaghtai et al. 1983, 1984; Khan 1994).

17. Stewart (1869) says of the olive, "Its foliage looks more dense than it really is, and it gives a rather chequered shade" (140). Of the lilac, Khan (1965) observes that it has a "spreading crown" (28).

18. Stewart (1869) says of the tamarisk, "it furnishes a very insufficient guard from the sun" (92).

19. This perceived difference in the temperature of shade is likely to be due not just to less sunlight beneath the tree but also to more humidity (Shankarnarayan et al. 1987, 81).

20. The leaf, bark, and fruit of the neem tree all have insecticidal properties (CSIR 1986, 361; NAS 1980, 2:40).

21. The belief that tree shade affects human health is ancient. Pliny (1938) writes: "Onesicritus says that in parts of India where there are no shadows there are men five cubits and two spans high [approximately eight feet tall], and people live a hundred and thirty years, and do not grow old but die middle-aged" (2:525). Recent work on the impact of diminished ultraviolet light on human stature actually supports Onesicritus, at least with respect to stature (O'Dea 1994).

22. The shade of some trees is also believed to affect spiritual health or fortune. The shade of the siris tree (*Albizzia lebbek* [L.] Benth.), for example, is widely believed to be

unlucky because its leaves have a droopy or wilted appearance (see also Stewart 1869, 55; Watt 1889–96, 1:158). According to Kane (1974, 2:400), a verse from the classical Yam-smrti prohibits Vedic study under the shade of certain trees, including salmali or silk cotton (*Salmalia malabarica* or *Bombax heptaphyll*); slesmataka (*Cordia latifolia*); and madhuka (*Bassia latifiolia*) (see Gruner [1930, 185] on "trees of bad temperament"). Discussing the peepal tree (*Ficus religiosa Linn.*), one or two large specimens of which customarily stand over village tanks or water holes and provide some of the widest, thickest, and most appreciated midday shade, farmers say that they fear to sit or even pass under its shade at night because of the spirits believed to inhabit it (Mansberger 1987, 161).

23. Pakistani farmers conceptualize the effect of chemical fertilizers on their crops in a similar manner: fertilizers require the coolness of irrigation or rain to work effectively; otherwise, they will burn the crops (Kurin 1983, 289–91).

24. Since litter can shade soil just as much as foliage can, some of these ill-effects may still be due to shade. Stigter (1984) calls litter a "natural shading mulch" (211).

25. The litter and soil impacts of the babul tree have been found to be relatively poor, at least in comparison with *Prosopis cineraria* (L.) Druce (Singh and Lal 1969; Shankarnarayan et al. 1987, 81).

26. Pruning, according to Foley and Barnard (1984), is "an aspect of tree management that conventional forestry has largely ignored" (38).

27. An unrelated benefit of pruning is the contribution that the pruned branches make to household fuel and fodder supplies, especially in the winter, when fuel supplies are under greatest pressure because of high consumption and fodder supplies are under greatest pressure because of a lack of sources (Supple et al. 1985).

28. Recent studies, such as Schroeder's (1993, 1999) on the management of shade by Gambian landlords to assert their political control and economic advantage over female tenants, show how central a role shade can play in the micropolitics of agroforestry.

29. The Soviet Union's 1979 invasion of Afghanistan precipitated an enormous increase in developmental aid from the United States to Pakistan, including funding for the social forestry project in which this research was conducted.

30. For an example of the sort of struggle Bryant is advocating and one that also involves tree shade, see Dove and Carpenter (2005) on the famous "poison tree" (*Arbor toxicaria* or *Antiaris toxicaria*) of the seventeenth-century East Indies.

31. The immense scope for studies of tree-crop interactions is suggested in Ong and Huxley (1996).

REFERENCES

Agrawal, Arun. 1995. "Dismantling the Divide between Indigenous and Scientific Knowledge." *Development and Change* 26: 413–39.

Ahmed, Akbar S. 1975. *Mataloona Pukhto Proverbs.* Karachi, Pakistan: Oxford University Press.

Ahmed, S., and Grainge, M. 1986. "Potential of the Neem Tree (*Azadirachta* indica) for Pest Control and Rural Development." *Economic Botany* 40, no. 2: 201–9.

Arnold, Michael, Gunnar Köhlin, Reidar Persson, and Gillian Shepherd. 2003. "Fuelwood Revisited: What Has Changed in the Last Decade?" CIFOR occasional paper, no. 39. Bogor, Indonesia: Center for International Forestry Research.

Bhishagranata, K. K., ed. and trans. 1963. *The Sushruta Samhita.* 3 vols. Varanasi, India: Chowkhamba Sanskrit Series Office.

Blaikie, Piers. 1985. *The Political Economy of Soil Erosion in Developing Countries*. New York: Longman.

Blaikie, Piers, and Harold Brookfield. 1987. *Land Degradation and Society*. London: Methuen.

Blake, William. 1979 [1793]. *The Marriage of Heaven and Hell*. In *Blake's Poetry and Designs*, edited by Mary Lynn Johnson and John E. Grant, 85–102. New York: Norton.

Bourdieu, Pierre. 1977 [1972]. *Outline of a Theory of Practice*, translated by Richard Nice. Cambridge: Cambridge University Press.

Brosius, J. Peter. 1999. "Green Dots, Pink Hearts: Displacing Politics from the Malaysian Rain Forest." *American Anthropologist* 101, no. 1: 36–57.

Bryant, Raymond L. 2000. "Politicized Moral Geographies: Debating Conservation and Ancestral Domain in the Philippines." *Political Geography* 19: 673–705.

Campbell, Tim. 1992. "Socio-Economic Aspects of Household Fuel Use in Pakistan." In *The Sociology of Natural Resources in Pakistan and Adjoining Countries: Case Studies in Applied Social Science*, edited by Michael R. Dove and Carol Carpenter, 304–29. Lahore, Pakistan: Vanguard Press for the Mashal Foundation.

Casati, Roberto. 2003. *The Shadow Club: The Greatest Mystery in the Universe, Shadows, and the Thinkers Who Unlocked Their Secrets*, translated by Abigail Asher. New York: Knopf.

Cernea, Michael M. 1985. "Alternative Units of Social Organization Sustaining Afforestation Strategies." In *Putting People First: Sociological Variables in Rural Development*, edited by Michael M. Cernea, 267–93. New York: Oxford University Press and the World Bank.

———. 1989. "User Groups As Producers in Participatory Afforestation Strategies." World Bank discussion paper, no. 70.

Chaghtai, S. M., N. A. Rana, and H. R. Khattak. 1983. "Phytosociology of the Muslim Graveyards of Kohat Division, NWFP, Pakistan." *Pakistan Journal of Botany* 15, no. 2: 99–108.

Chaghtai, S. M., A. Sadiq, and S. Z. Shah. 1984. "Vegetation around the Shrine of Ghalib Gul Baba in Khwarra-Nilab Valley, NWFP, Pakistan." *Pakistan Journal of Forestry* 34, no. 3: 145–50.

Chambers, Robert. 1983. *Rural Development: Putting the Last First*. London: Longman.

Champion, Harry G., S. K. Seth, and G. M. Khattak. 1965. *Forest Types of Pakistan*. Peshawar: Pakistan Forest Institute.

Council of Scientific and Industrial Research (CSIR). 1986. *The Useful Plants of India*. New Delhi: CSIR.

Derrida, Jacques. 1978. *Writing and Difference*, translated by Alan Bass. Chicago: University of Chicago Press.

Dove, Michael R. 1992. "Foresters' Beliefs about Farmers: A Priority for Social Science Research in Social Forestry." *Agroforestry Systems* 17, no. 1: 13–41.

———. 1994. "The Existential Status of the Pakistani Farmer: A Study of Institutional Factors in Development." *Ethnology* 33, no. 4: 331–51.

———. 1995. "The Shift of Tree Cover from Forests to Farms in Pakistan: A Long and Broad View." In *Tree Management in Farmer Strategies*, edited by J. E. Michael Arnold and Peter Dewees. Oxford: Oxford University Press.

Dove, Michael R., and Carol Carpenter. 2005. "The 'Poison Tree,' and the Changing Vision of the Indo-Malay Realm: 17th Century–20th Century." In *Environmental Change in Native and Colonial Histories of Borneo*, edited by Reid Wadley, 65–89. Leiden, the Netherlands: Koninklijk Instituut voor Taal-, Land-, en Volkenkunde.

Ellen, Roy F., Alan Bicker, and Peter Parkes, eds. 2000. *Indigenous Environmental Knowledge and Its Transformations*. Amsterdam: Harwood.

Fairhead, J., and M. Leach. 1996. *Misreading the African Landscape: Society and Ecology in a Forest-Savanna Mosaic*. Cambridge: Cambridge University Press.

Foley, Gerald, and Geoffrey Barnard. 1984. *Farm and Community Forestry*. London: International Institute for Environment and Development.

Fortmann, Louise. 1988. "Great Planting Disasters: Pitfalls in Technical Assistance in Forestry." *Agriculture and Human Values* 5: 49–60.

Gold, A. G., and B. R. Gujar. 1989. "Of Gods, Trees, and Boundaries: Divine Conservation in Rajasthan." *Asian Folklore Studies* 48: 211–29.

Gruner, O. Cameron. 1930. *A Treatise on the Canon of Medicine of Avicenna*. London: Luzac.

Haenn, Nora. 1999. "The Power of Environmental Knowledge: Ethnoecology and Environmental Conflicts in Mexican Conservation." *Human Ecology* 27, no. 3: 477–91.

Jones, J. R., and Norman Price. 1985. "Agroforestry: An Application of the Farming Systems Approach to Forestry." *Human Organization* 44, no. 4: 322–31.

Kane, Pandurang Vaman. 1974. *History of Dharmasastra (Ancient and Mediaeval Religious and Civil Law)*. 2d ed. Poona, India: Bhandakar Oriental Research Institute.

Khan, Abdul Hamid 1965. *Fodder Shrubs and Trees in Pakistan*. Lyallpur: West Pakistan Agricultural University.

Khan, A. U. 1994. "History of Decline and Present Status of Natural Tropical Thorn Forest in Punjab." *Biological Conservation* 67, no. 3: 205–10.

Kurin, Richard. 1983. "Indigenous Agronomics and Agricultural Development in the Indus Basin." *Human Organization* 42, no. 4: 283–94.

Lévi-Strauss, Claude. 1966. *The Savage Mind*. Chicago: University of Chicago Press.

Mansberger, J. R. 1987. "In Search of the Tree Spirit: Evolution of the Sacred Tree (*Ficus religiosa*)." Master's thesis, Department of Geography, University of Hawaii.

Michie, Barry H. 1986. "Indigenous Technology and Farming Systems Research: Agroforestry in the Indian Desert." In *Social Sciences and Farming Systems Research*, edited by Jeffrey R. Jones and Ben J. Wallace, 221–44. Boulder, Colo.: Westview.

National Academy of Sciences (NAS). 1980. *Firewood Crops: Shrub and Tree Species for Energy Production*. 2 vols. Washington, D.C.: National Academy of Sciences.

O'Dea, J. D. 1994. "Possible Contribution of Low Ultraviolet Light under the Rainforest Canopy to the Small Stature of Pygmies and Negritos." *Homo* 44, no. 3: 284–87.

Ong, Chin K., and P. A. Huxley, eds. 1996. *Tree-crop Interactions: A Physiological Approach*. CAB International.

Ortner, Sherry. 1984. "Anthropological Theory Since the Sixties." *Comparative Studies in Society and History* 26, no. 1: 126–66.

Pierce, Jennifer. 1995. "Reflections on Fieldwork in a Complex Organization: Lawyers, Ethnographic Authority, and Lethal Weapons." In *Studying Elites Using Qualitative Methods*, edited by Rosanna Herz and Jonathan B. Imber, 94–110. Thousand Oaks, Calif.: Sage.

Pliny. 1938. *Natural History*, translated by H. Rackham. 10 vols. Cambridge: Harvard University Press.

Schroeder, Richard A. 1993. "Shady Practice: Gender and the Political Ecology of Resource Stabilization in Gambian Garden/Orchards." *Economic Geography* 69, no. 4: 349–65.

———. 1999. *Shady Practices: Agroforestry and Gender Politics in the Gambia*. Berkeley: University of California Press.

Scott, James C. 1998. *Seeing Like a State*. New Haven, Conn.: Yale University Press.

Shah, Mazhar H. 1966. *The General Principles of Avicenna's Canon of Medicine*. Karachi, Pakistan: Naveed Clinic.

Shankarnarayan, K. A., L. N. Harsh, and S. Kathju. 1987. "Agroforestry in the Arid Zones of India." *Agroforestry Systems* 5, no. 1: 69–88.

Sharma, R. K., and V. Bhogwan Dash, eds. and trans. 1976. Caraka Samhita. Varanasi, India: Chowkhamba Sanskrit Series Office.

Singh, K. S., and P. Lal. 1969. "Effect of Khejari (*Prosopis spicigera Linn*) and Babool (*Acacia arabica*) on Soil Fertility and Profile Characteristics." *Annals of Arid Zone* 8, no. 1: 33–36.

Sivaramakrishnan, K. 1995. "Colonialism and Forestry in India: Imagining the Past in Present Politics." *Comparative Studies in Society and History* 37: 3–40.

Smith, K. R. 1973. "The Age of Enlightenment Ends." *Journal of Irreproducible Results* 20: 27–29.

Stewart, J. L. 1869. *Punjab Plants, Comprising Botanical and Vernacular Names, and Uses of Most of the Trees, Shrubs, and Herbs of Economical Value, Growing within the Province.* Lahore, British India: Government Press.

Stigter, C. J. 1984. "Traditional Use of Shade: A Method of Micro-Climate Manipulation." *Archives for Meteorology, Geophysics, and Bioclimatology* 34, series B: 203–10.

Supple, K. R., A. Razzaq, Ikram Saeed, and A. D. Sheikh. 1985. *Barani Farming Systems of the Punjab: Constraints and Opportunities for Increasing Productivity.* Islamabad, Pakistan: National Agricultural Research Centre.

Vayda, Andrew P., and Bradley B. Walters. 1999. "Against Political Ecology." *Human Ecology* 27, no. 1: 167–79.

Watt, George. 1889–96. *A Dictionary of the Economic Products of India.* 6 vols. Calcutta: Superintendent of Government Printing.

Wittgenstein, Ludwig. 1974. *On Certainty.* Rev. ed., edited by G.E.M. Anscombe and G. H. von Wright, translated by Denis Paul and Gertrude E. M. Anscombe. Oxford: Blackwell.

World Bank. 2001. *World Development Indicators.* Washington, D.C.: World Bank.

13

A Global Political Ecology
of Bioprospecting

HANNE SVARSTAD

Political ecology merges concern for aspects in the natural environment (ecology) with a focus on relationships between people-environment and people-people (political). The burgeoning literature in political ecology deals with environment and development issues, emphasising the perception of problems among various stakeholders and others (Blaikie and Brookfield 1987, Bryant and Bailey 1997, Peet and Watts 1996, Stott and Sullivan 2000; also see chapter 2). Political ecology attempts to understand various types of influences across scales, sometimes also involving multiple spaces.

Usually political ecology students start their projects by examining a situation at the local level and then spread gradually into an increasingly wider context—beginning, for instance, with the land user, following the seminal work of Blaikie and Brookfield (1987). In this chapter, however, I argue that it is sometimes useful to begin with the global features of a phenomenon. I present four steps that elaborate a global political ecology approach and show how I have studied the phenomenon of bioprospecting within each step. Bioprospecting implies that researchers and company agents travel to various parts of the world to collect samples of biological material and related indigenous knowledge in order to develop commercial products such as modern medicines. Step 1 employs a political economy approach to situate the activity. Step 2 moves from the global economic practice of, in this case, bioprospecting to the global production of discourses about it. Local-level case studies come in as step 3, and here I present bioprospecting by an American company, Shaman Pharmaceuticals, in an area in Tanzania. Finally, in step 4, I compare the discourses identified in step 2 with other human-environment discourses.

If a student tries to cover all the suggested steps thoroughly in the same analysis, she or he may have to spend much more time than is available for a delimited study. Covering all four elements may therefore require the student to undertake several subprojects over time or to cooperate with other researchers. There are at least two reasons why it may be worthwhile to organize multiyear, multisited, and multidisciplinary research projects to deal with issues on both local and global scales. On the one hand, the ways in which an issue is treated in global discourses often provides an important context for interpreting specific cases on the local level. On the other hand, case-specific experiences on the local level may shed light on how an issue is handled globally. In other words, the approach focuses on a global phenomenon so as to allow for movement in a hermeneutic circle between global and local scales.

Step 1: Studying the Political Economy of Global Practice

The political aspect of political ecology often draws from a broader tradition of political economy in which social relations of production are emphasized with a focus on access and control over resources. To understand aspects of bioprospecting in local-practice cases as well as global discourses about the phenomenon, it is useful to establish a picture of the global activity, including historical context and the current involvement of various actors. Although such work may be restricted to a small desktop study, it may also be expanded into a major focus and involve field visits and interviews with key actors.

Bioprospecting is an economic activity that has increased in significance and received considerable attention since the early 1990s. The search for new uses of biological materials may be as old as humanity itself, and it constitutes a fundamental feature of human development. During the past few centuries, colonial powers have expended much effort on searching for useful biodiversity all over the world. Thus, present bioprospecting activities in tropical countries such as Tanzania can be seen as a new phase in a long history. The Swahili word for Europeans is *wazungu*—literally, "those who travel around." White men in Africa have always traveled around searching for various things: the source of the Nile, gold, ivory, and, from the very beginning, usable plants.

The great European voyages of discovery during the seventeenth and eighteenth centuries were dedicated not simply to exploration but also to accumulation. Botanical and zoological gardens became centers of calculation in which knowledge was concentrated to obtain mastery of the resources (Foucault 1970, Parry 2000). Kenyan social scientist Calestous Juma (1989) argues that the introduction of genetic material and related technology into the economic system has been a crucial source of economic growth, when combined with institutional reorganization. In the nineteenth century, the power of colonial Britain was to a large degree based on the transportation of plants around the globe. For instance, tea was brought from China for cultivation in India and then to a number of other British colonies; rubber was transferred from Brazil to Southeast Asia. Cinchona, the plant yielding quinine, a treatment for malaria, was brought from the Andes to India and other parts of the world, thus facilitating military, political, and economic expansion. Botanical gardens of colonial powers, such as Kew Gardens in England, were key agents for these movements. The exchange of genetic resources helped Great Britain expand its colonies, and the introduction of genetic resources was a major factor in the development of the United States into a leading agricultural nation (Juma 1989).

Biochemicals have made an important contribution to the development of modern medicine. An estimated 42 percent of the twenty-five best-selling drugs worldwide are biologicals, natural products, or medicines derived from natural products (Newman and Laird 1999). Recently, much bioprospecting has taken place in tropical countries found to be very rich in biodiversity: rainforests may contain more than half of all species in the world (Wilson 1988).

Literature on bioprospecting from the early 1990s points to the pharmaceutical industry's resurgence of interest in biodiversity as a potential source of novel chemical compounds (Aylward 1993, McChesney 1996, Reid 1993–94, ten Kate 1995). This move came after decades of emphasis on synthetic chemistry and so-called rational drug design, although some plant-based drugs were also discovered and brought to the market during the period. Technological development has been highlighted as a core reason for the renewed interest in drug discovery from biological sources (Reid 1997). The development of automated screening techniques has increased the speed with which chemicals can be tested by a factor of one hundred, thereby making it a cost-effective alternative (Reid 1993–94). Furthermore, biotechnology makes possible the transfer of genetic material between species, thus enhancing the range of product development and increasing the demand for novel genetic and biochemical resources (Reid et al. 1993, 115; Krattiger and Lesser 1995, 211). A return to searching nature for medicinal material can also be associated with a lack of major successes in rational drug design research (Principe 1996, 191).

In addition to these mainly technological factors, changes in property rights concerning genetic resources may also underlie the resurgence of bioprospecting. Until recently, genetic resources have generally been handled as open-access resources, implying that anybody could freely collect and use them without permit or payment. Two factors have changed this situation. First, new possibilities in the field for patents and other intellectual property rights have created private ownership and commodification of genetic resources that have been subject to scientific alteration (Kloppenburg 1988). Second, and to a large extent as a reaction of developing countries to the first change, the Convention on Biological Diversity (CBD) provides an international legal instrument for source countries to claim national sovereignty over those genetic resources that have not been subject to alteration by conventional science. The principle of national sovereignty is stated in the convention's article 3. Article 15 specifies that access to genetic resources is subject to mutually agreed terms and the providing country's prior informed consent (United Nations 1992). Like most economic activities, the future of bioprospecting is unpredictable. It depends on factors such as further technological developments and political decisions surrounding access to genetic resources (Reid 1997, ten Kate 1995).

If we look at the various actors in bioprospecting, we can make a major distinction between bioprospectors, on the one hand, and traditional healers and local people who are primary providers of local knowledge and plant samples, on the other. Furthermore, bioprospectors can be divided into two major groups: producers and intermediaries. Pharmaceutical producers develop and produce medicines. They are predominantly multinational companies with headquarters in the United States, Europe, or Japan; and today all the largest pharmaceutical companies are involved in collecting and screening biological material.

Intermediaries in bioprospecting are actors who collect samples of biological material, such as plant species, for screening or conduct parts of the research to develop medicines. In cases of bioprospecting in developing countries, intermediaries may be foreign or local. Shaman Pharmaceuticals is a prominent example of a global bioprospecting intermediary active throughout the 1990s. The company started its operations in San Francisco in 1990 and has based its plant collection on local and traditional knowledge from many countries around the world. In 2002, Shaman closed down; and a new company, PS Pharmaceuticals, bought most of its intellectual property (Svarstad 2003).

In sum, bioprospecting is an activity directed by corporate product development, which links different actors and spaces into global chains. It is a recent part of a long history of investigating nature for human use. Much bioprospecting for medicinal plants resembles the simple dependency theory model of André Gunder Frank (1967): raw material gathering in the south (satellites, periphery) and industrial development in the north (metropolis, core). But there are also patterns in bioprospecting that imply north-north and south-south relations.

Step 2: Studying Discourse Production among Global Actors

The second step of my political ecology approach shifts the focus from global economic practice to discursive practices on a global level. In this analysis, I use a definition of *discourse* commonly employed by social scientists, referring to ways of understanding the world or some part of it. It is a socially constructed meaning system (Jørgensen and Phillips 1999), "a shared way of apprehending the world. Embedded in language, it enables those who subscribe to it to interpret bits of information and put them together into coherent stories or accounts. Each discourse rests on assumptions, judgements, and contentions that provide the basic terms for analysis, debates, arguments, and disagreements" (Dryzek 1997, 8).

I use the term *discourse* to refer to a conception of a realm of understanding that may be shared by a small or a large group of people on the local, national, international, or global level. Actors involved in the discourse participate (in varying degrees) in its production, reproduction, and transformation through written and oral statements. These statements possess certain regularities, not only with regard to content (or message) but also by their use of some shared expressive means—for instance, certain meta-narratives and rhetorical devices such as metaphors.[1] A discourse analysis implies the examination of statements to identify and depict discourses.

Some discourse analysts tend to de-emphasize agency. Michel Foucault (1980), who has offered seminal contributions to social science discourse analysis, deals with individual human beings not as acting subjects and producers of behavior and thought but as products of historical frameworks and discourses (also see Kendall and Wickham 1999). This view has been criticized by several authors (for example, Fish 1993, Fox 1998), and I agree with those who consider it valuable to go beyond describing social constructs such as discourses to get a picture of the actors involved in constructions, reconstructions, and practices.

The concept of discourse implies recognition of a certain structure or stability of specific social constructs. In line with a focus on actors, however, discourses must also be seen as targets for larger or smaller transformations. Meaning cannot be settled once and for all. A discourse may be reproduced in a relatively stable manner over a period of time, or it may be subject to considerable transformation and decline.

Different discourse analysts have applied a range of concepts concerning the relations between discourses. With reference to Antonio Gramsci's (1997 [1948–51]) hegemony theory, some discourse analysts use the term *hegemonic discourse* (Hajer 1995, Jørgensen and Phillips 1999, Laclau and Mouffe 1985). A discourse may be labeled hegemonic if it dominates thinking and is translated into institutional arrangements (Hajer 1995, 60–61). I find it useful to apply the notion of leading discourses to refer to discourses that are strong but do not dominate perceptions on a topic or the generation of policies and practices.

My data collection regarding global discourses on bioprospecting encompasses participatory observation in meetings and conferences as well as the examination of written sources. Study of contributions to various e-mail discussion forums have been particularly useful. My research resulted in the identification and analysis of two leading global discourses on bioprospecting from the early 1990s until today (Svarstad 2000, 2003). In some contexts (such as a conference), each discourse is as strong as the other; in other contexts, one has hegemonic standing.

The Bioprospecting Win-Win Discourse

According to the first discourse, bioprospecting provides opportunities for a super win-win situation. Benefits may be generated for conservation, development in source countries, local providers of genetic resources and knowledge, new medicines for patients, and profit for industry.

A professor at Cornell and founder of the field of chemical ecology, Thomas Eisner (1989, 1991) was an early contributor to this discourse. He termed the activity *chemical prospecting* and proposed that it should be substantially intensified. In response to concerns about species extinction and the concomitant loss of chemical compounds of great potential value for useful products such as medicines, Eisner argued for the establishment of screening laboratories in the developing world that could support conservation programs.

The CDB has been important for the elaboration of the win-win discourse. The CBD was negotiated from the late 1980s until the 1992 Earth Summit in Rio de Janeiro and came into force in December 1993. Its three objectives are conservation of biodiversity, sustainable use of components, and fair and equitable sharing of benefits from the use of genetic resources (United Nations 1992, art. 1). Several commentators believe that bioprospecting can contribute to all three objectives, supporting economically poor but biodiversity-rich countries in the south while providing the world with new medicines and companies with revenues (see Baker et al. 1995, Mugabe et al. 1997, Reid et al. 1993, ten Kate 1995). Such viewpoints have been adopted by various conservation organizations as well as those directly involved in promoting and undertaking bioprospecting activities. In 1993, the World Resources Institute published a seminal work on bioprospecting, maintaining that, "Done well, biodiversity prospecting can contribute greatly to environmentally sound development and return benefits to the custodians of genetic resources—the national public at large, the staff of conservation units, the farmers, the forest dwellers, and the indigenous people who maintain or tolerate the resources involved" (Reid et al. 1993, 2).

Positive links between human health, on one side, and conservation and bioprospecting, on the other, are given particular weight in the anthologies edited by Michael J. Balick et al. (1996) and Francesca Grifo and Joshua Rosenthal (1997). Nevertheless, even authors with a positive attitude toward bioprospecting often stress that the existence of an appropriate institutional environment in the source countries is a critical prerequisite for the realization of benefits.

The win-win discourse merges discourses produced among four main groups of actors. The first is constituted by scientists in various fields of natural product studies and ethno-sciences (for example, ethnobiology, -botany, and -pharmacognocy). The second group comprises natural scientists who belong to the specialization known as conservation biology. The third group consists of conservationists in organizations such as the World Wide Fund for Nature (WWF), the World Resource Institute, and the World Conservation Union (IUCN). Finally, the fourth group of actors comes from the pharmaceutical industry. Scientists obviously have an interest in increased attention to and funding of their fields of specialization. Similarly, conservationists are concerned about promoting conservation and securing funding for this goal. The pharmaceutical industry, for its part, has an interest in gaining access to biodiversity for medicine development while achieving social credibility for their activities. By presenting their objectives and activities in terms of the win-win discourse, members of all four groups may increase their legitimacy.

The Biopiracy Discourse

The biopiracy discourse vehemently resists the commercial collection, development, and patenting of modern medicines based on the biodiversity and traditional knowledge of the south. Advocates of this discourse emphasize the issues of rights and equity for indigenous peoples, local peasants, and healers. They do not believe that bioprospecting will provide satisfactory benefits for these groups.

Solidarity activists for the rural poor and indigenous people of the developing world are the main actors in the construction and reconstruction of the biopiracy discourse. In the forefront are the North America–based Rural Advancement Foundation International (RAFI); the Europe-based Genetic Resources Action International (GRAIN); and the Third World Network, operating mainly in Asia.[2]

The biopiracy discourse developed as a response to the increased attention given to bioprospecting in the 1990s. RAFI coined the term *biopiracy* as a response to Walter V. Reid et al.'s (1993) positive presentation of bioprospecting (Mooney 2000). In a booklet, RAFI (1994) referred to northern (particularly U.S.) concerns about loss of royalties on pirated pharmaceuticals and agricultural chemicals. The organization compared this loss to what it calculates as a larger loss for the south: a reverse piracy from the north, which uses seeds and medicines from the biodiverse south (RAFI 1994). It characterized biopiracy as a global pandemic, arguing that "there are few places on earth where rural people are not facing biopirates who aim to extract their knowledge and resources" (RAFI 1995, 1).

Metaphors of the discourse have been used with considerable sarcastic humour. Media events related to the arrangements of the Conferences of the Parties to the CDB, the RAFI/ETC Group, and alliances in the Coalition against Biopiracy present Captain Hook Awards in categories such as "greediest," "most offensive," and "most dangerous." They also present Cog Awards (cogs are ships designed to repel pirate attacks) (ETC Group 2002, RAFI 2000, 2004).

GRAIN (1993, 3) has characterized the current exploration of biodiversity for commercially valuable resources as a continuation of the activities of the colonial powers when they searched for plant products many centuries ago. Similarly, one Inter Press Service press release has defined biopiracy as "the stealing of plants for commercial purposes" (Portillo 1999).

The Philippines-based Southeast Asia Regional Institute for Community Education (SEARICE) is a nongovernmental organization (NGO) actively campaigning against biopiracy in cooperation with RAFI/ETC Group and GRAIN and has established a Southeast Asian anti-biopiracy program (RAFI 2000). According to

SEARICE (1997), bioprospecting is a factor involved in destroying the rainforests as well as local and indigenous cultures.

In the biopiracy discourse, patenting is often seen as a major mechanism of exploitation. For instance, Martin Khor (1996) of the Third World Network has defined biopiracy as "the granting of patents on biological materials, such as genes, plants, animals and humans" (73). Likewise, Janet Bell (1997) writes that the CBD goal of "equitable sharing of benefits" is "a difficult goal if the bio-prospector can slash intellectual property rights over whatever he/she finds" (2). Vandana Shiva (1997, 81) characterizes the introduction of intellectual property rights concerning life forms as a means of legalizing biopiracy and maintains that patents "protect this piracy of the wealth of non-Western peoples as a right of Western powers" (5).

Narrative Analysis

When analyzing the two discourses, I realized that the use of narratives in both cases plays an important role. I here use the term narrative to conceptualize accounts of a specific event that are produced and reproduced within a discourse. On the topic of bioprospecting, specific cases of the activity are subject to the production of one type of narrative in the bioprospecting win-win discourse and another in the biopiracy discourse. The narratives in each discourse have very similar structures regarding the cast of actors. Thus, there is a meta-narrative of each discourse.

WIN-WIN NARRATIVES. In the win-win discourse, narratives about specific arrangements show how bioprospecting can lead to various benefits. An impor-tant narrative is constituted by positive accounts of the cooperation between the Costa Rican institute INBio and the pharmaceutical company Merck, starting with an agreement in September 1991. INBio received 1,135,000 in U.S. dollars for collection and preparation of samples for Merck. Furthermore, 10 percent of the up-front benefits and 50 percent of any royalties were assigned to the Costa Rican authorities responsible for managing the country's national parks (Mateo 2000, Reid et al. 1993). In late 1991, I observed this win-win narrative presented directly to the CBD negotiators.

Shaman Pharmaceuticals and a related organization, the Healing Forest Conservancy, have produced several win-win narratives based on their experi-ences with bioprospecting and benefit sharing. While INBio has stressed conser-vation as a major aim for benefits, Shaman's description of the recipients of benefits emphasizes the "indigenous, tribal or native" people (Moran 1997, 246). With cooperators, Shaman has presented win-win narratives from its bio-prospecting in countries such as Ecuador (King 1994), Belize (Chinnock et al. 1997), and Nigeria (Carlson et al. 1997).

The cast of actors in win-win narratives involves two groups of heroes. The first consists of the bioprospectors themselves, who share benefits with recipients in source countries. The second includes local healers and other people who contribute medicinal plants and traditional knowledge and inadvertently promote conservation. Bioprospecting is seen as one solution to circumstances in which local economic activities indirectly cause biodiversity loss. All such narratives concentrate on presenting bioprospecting as a positive activity. There are no villains or victims, only heroic winners.

BIOPIRACY NARRATIVES. The biopiracy meta-narrative is what Emery Roe (1991, 1995) calls a counter-narrative to the bioprospecting win-win meta-narrative. The various biopiracy narratives focus on different stages in the bioprospecting process, but all constitute examples in which bioprospecting and patenting inevitably end up as exploitation. Well-known win-win narratives of specific cases are usually met by constructions of specific counter-narratives. For instance, the supposed success story of the 1991 INBio-Merck agreement was countered by a narrative in which the benefits to Costa Rica were low and no benefits were offered to indigenous people (Kloppenburg and Rodriguez 1992, Mooney 2000).

Counter-narratives have also been produced against Shaman's win-win narratives (see, for example, RAFI and Cultural Survival Canada 1997, Reyes 1996), arguing that the company in specific cases provided questionable compensation for indigenous knowledge. Attention has also been drawn to particular patents as well as business connections between Shaman and larger pharmaceutical corporations.

The win-win narratives are generally found in anthologies and journals of an academic, scholarly bent. Biopiracy narratives occasionally find such outlets but are more often disseminated in NGO newsletters and on electronic listservs.[3] Thus, the biopiracy narratives tend to have broader and more effective dissemination.

The biopiracy narratives see bioprospectors as villains—as biopirates. The casts of actors in these narratives also include victims. These encompass the developing world and its poor people in general but, more specifically, indigenous people, traditional healers, peasants, and other local possessors of traditional knowledge of medicinal properties of plants. No groups stand out as heroes in the biopiracy narratives.

It is important to recognize the contexts in which discourses are produced. Bioprospecting win-win narratives are often made by bioprospectors themselves, who thus have inside knowledge of the cases, although the bioprospectors are not independent observers. On the other hand, the discursive practices of the biopiracy discourse are totally separate from the social practice of bioprospecting, and the narratives produced are often based on rather weak empirical knowledge.

Step 3: Conducting Local Field Work in the Context
of Global Discourses

Step 3 implies that social scientists conduct independent and sound, in-depth studies on cases of the phenomenon in local spaces. Perceptions of local participants are studied in relation to and at a critical distance from the global discourses.

I present here in brief the main findings from my case study of Shaman Pharmaceuticals' bioprospecting activities in one area of Tanzania (Svarstad 2003). In 1995, the company arranged a collection expedition and thereafter provided benefits to the communities it had visited. Company collectors described the case as a win-win narrative, emphasizing mutualism and reciprocity in the relationship they created with local cooperators and providers of traditional knowledge. All participants were presented positively (like heroes), and the story contained no villains or victims. Shaman's collectors hoped that the experiences would stimulate new ideas about how private-sector research can support traditional medicine and the self-determination of traditional and indigenous peoples.

During the collection, traditional healers and other local people were asked to describe how they used medicinal plants for certain diseases. Then the plants were collected for screening in Shaman's laboratory. Shaman collected fifty-five species of plants used to treat non-insulin–dependent diabetes mellitus, respiratory syncitial virus, and hepatitis. After the expedition, the company provided short-term reciprocity for local projects in funds amounting to 6,500 U.S. dollars. In the first of the two involved districts, those funds were spent on construction materials for building a center for the district association of traditional healers. In the second district, the funds were divided among five visited villages and spent on items for village clinics and schools. Each local participant also received a salary of approximately five U.S. dollars a day. As long-term reciprocity, the company planned to allocate benefits to all collaborators from part of the company's income from selling the products. As medium-term reciprocity, the company contributed money to an institute that had been its main research cooperator in Tanzania.[4]

I followed in the footsteps (rather, the Jeep tracks) of the collection mission and interviewed traditional healers and other local people who had met the bioprospectors. I also observed that the money provided for the center in the first district was enough to half-complete a house.

In long qualitative interviews, I found that most of the healers who had experiences with bioprospecting were ambivalent about the activity, although I also found some very positive and very negative opinions.

The ambivalent healers wanted more bioprospecting, but they were not quite satisfied with the experience. I found four factors to explain their reaction. First, possible economic gains had some importance; but contrary to the impressions offered by both global discourses, that factor played a minor role among

local actors when compared with other issues. Second, healers wanted bioprospecting so they could gain access to additional knowledge from the modern
scientific system. Some healers identified themselves as modern and scientific,
while others emphasized more traditional aspects, such as the role of spirits and
dreams in expansions of their pharmacopoeias. Nonetheless, the traditionalists
were as eager to gain access to additional knowledge as the modernists were; and
most were disappointed about the extent to which they had so far been able to
gain knowledge from the bioprospectors.

Third, bioprospecting in the region enhances the acceptance of traditional
healing practices and healers' social status. The degree of tolerance that national
and local governments display toward traditional healing can vary; and in this
particular local area, traditional practitioners are sometimes viewed rather negatively. One of my informants, for instance, said, "The child who fails in other jobs
is the one who is chosen by his father to become a traditional healer. Therefore,
traditional healers are not among the smartest people." Bioprospecting, however,
implies that scientists from the modern health system come all the way from Dar
es Salaam and even prosperous countries in the north to this remote locality to
learn about medicinal plants from the traditional healers.

Finally, traditional healers have devised strategies of securing benefits from
bioprospecting. After its experience with Shaman, the local branch of their organization decided not to give bioprospectors plant names and recognizable plants
again. They agreed instead to provide unrecognizable substances so that the healers
could become more powerful in their relationship with researchers and companies.

Shaman presents the case as a model for cooperation and local participation, with a particular emphasis on the participation of women through the
involvement of traditional birth attendants. The collectors arranged meetings
with local participants to obtain prior informed consent as well as carry out reciprocity discussions. But in my interviews with women who had cooperated with
Shaman, I found that company collectors had not involved these women in the
meetings or even told them that the collection expedition had been followed by
donations to the community. Moreover, contrary to the image presented by
Shaman, traditional birth attendants in this area were not a group with much
knowledge about medicinal plants.

Should the case be interpreted in line with the win-win narrative? I did not
find that conclusion reasonable. Then what about seeing the case as biopiracy
and thereby as an example arguing against such external interventions? That
interpretation seemed to be paternalistic and inappropriate in light of the fact
that most traditional healers wanted more bioprospecting.

In accordance with ordinary bioprospecting practice, the company would in
this case have sole rights for patents. As I have mentioned, patenting is often
treated as a major cause of exploitation in the biopiracy discourse. But surprisingly, when looking into implications of patenting for relevant actors in this and

similar cases, I have not found evidence supporting such a conclusion. On the contrary, the patenting mechanism also protects the interests of local actors against the piracy of other corporate interests. A precondition is that local actors obtain an acceptable agreement for sharing benefits with the bioprospector.

Instead of aligning itself with either of the two global discourses and their meta-narratives, this case illuminates the fact that adequate benefit sharing must rely on more than the ethics of the involved bioprospector. At the national level, a suitable institutional framework for bioprospecting is a prerequisite if healers are to benefit.

When doing in-depth research of bioprospecting cases, it is possible to go back to the discourses and meta-narratives themselves and point to ways in which their reduction of the complexity of the world may be harmful to actors. This is indeed important with discourses that often are labeled *mainstream*. It may be even more important, however (although it is still too rare), for radical social scientists to critically examine so-called radical discourses to identify misunderstandings that may have harmful consequences on actors meant to be subjects of solidarity.

Step 4: Contextualizing Discourses

As shown, in my fieldwork in Tanzania, I found that neither the win-win narrative nor the biopiracy narrative provided an adequate framework to describe the bioprospecting activities of Shaman Pharmaceuticals. To a large extent, this conclusion can be explained by the knowledge gained through study of the case itself. But to understand how narratives of the two discourses are produced and reproduced, it is necessary to contextualize them within other human-environment discourses. Looking at the situation from a horizontal perspective, I found clusters of discourses about issues that are interpreted in similar ways. A vertical perspective reveals hierarchies of discourses that address views about larger and larger issues. In other words, there are scales among the discourses.

Horizontally, the win-win discourse belongs to a cluster of win-win discourses related to the management of biodiversity and other categories of natural resources. All discourses in this cluster focus on conservation and sustainable use of natural resources as well as provision of some benefits from that use to local people and governments. Similarly, the biopiracy discourse belongs to a cluster of partly overlapping discourses related to biodiversity. I call them *populist discourses* because they emphasize solidarity with local people (often poor peasants) while claiming that external interventions degrade local livelihoods and exploit people.

In a study involving four social scientists, we compared discourse formations of the four different global issues of climate change, deforestation, desertification, and bioprospecting (Adger et al. 2001). By analysing the three additional issues in the manner I had done for bioprospecting, we identified a cluster of leading discourses that resemble the biodiversity win-win discourses. These win-win discourses are based on development optimism and faith in the opportunities for conservation and local benefits in poor countries through exchanges with private and public parties from industrialized countries.

The identified win-win discourses can be related to the political and economic discourse of neoliberalism. None, however, can be associated with free-market scenarios. Instead, they are based on a belief in the creation of various win-win situations through partnership among global economic actors and local people regulated and controlled by national institutions.

We also identified leading populist discourses concerning desertification, deforestation, and global change. In populist discourses, foreign economic relations are perceived as negative interventions rather than possibilities for trade and income. Local and traditional knowledge is generally seen as sustainable practice, and local people are seen as being better off when left alone. Roots of these perceptions can be traced back to self-reliance advocacy of the dependency school of the 1970s and 1980s. Since the 1990s, a trend toward poststructuralist writing has emerged in this discourse, one in which development and foreign intervention are more or less categorically rejected (see, for example, Broch-Due and Schroeder 2000, Peet and Watts 1996, Yapa 1996).

Despite considerable differences in their approaches, the win-win and populist discourses also have some striking similarities. Both clusters share a concern for environmental questions. Both also see the importance of human use of natural resources. Thus, both clusters focus on the importance of combining conservation and use, although the differences become apparent in the question of whether or not foreign industrial use and conservation interventions are acceptable. Nevertheless, all these discourses emphasize combining conservation with use. In contrast, preservation discourses focus entirely on the maintenance of nature without a concern for human use of natural resources. In the four issues, preservation discourses constitute historical predecessors to present conservation and use approaches. For any conservationist to be taken seriously in most contexts today, conservation efforts must be combined with a concern for use aspects and thereby benefits to people on a local and/or national level.

Contrasting the hegemony of the conservation and use discourses, viewpoints can also be found in each of the four areas that question the existence or gravity of the environmental issue. They challenge claims concerning serious losses of biodiversity, deforestation, desertification, and the existence or importance of climate change. W. Neil Adger et al. (2001) point to extensive and fairly influential denial claims concerning climate change and desertification.

As mentioned in my discussion of step 3, I found in my in-depth studies of cases of bioprospecting that it is unreasonable to conclude that patenting is a key element of exploitation, despite the biopiracy discourse's strong claims.

Rather, condemnation of patenting is an important element of the biopiracy discourse that must be understood in the context of other populist environmental discourses. Patenting constitutes what we may call a *discursive symbol* in biopiracy and other populist discourses concerning biodiversity and has reached the biopiracy discourse from other discourses in the same cluster rather than stemming directly from experiences on the ground.[5] Categorical rejection of patenting provides a simple answer to a cluster of complex questions about decisions for granting specific patents and policy questions related to patent legislation and various international agreements. Policy questions on patenting have to do with source countries as well as recipient countries of biodiversity. By making patenting a general symbol of exploitation, solidarity-oriented people get a simple key to interpretation and action. The popularity of these discourses is based on a high degree of trust in the analysis of a small number of main discourse producers and a striking lack of tradition for critical examinations of core elements of common beliefs. Conclusion leaps between discourses, like the way in which patenting has leaped into the biopiracy discourse, is the type of feature that may be revealed by comparing the identified discourses to related ones. But to identify aspects that have leaped into a discourse without being grounded in sound knowledge of cases, it is necessary to investigate cases.

Conclusion

Using examples from studies of bioprospecting, this chapter has applied a global political ecology approach to the study of both global and local aspects of a global phenomenon. Steps 1 and 2 study the global political economy of the practice, on the one hand, and discourse production, on the other. Step 3 focuses on case studies of the phenomenon in local spaces, giving researchers a closer look at the practice and actors considered in step 1. Furthermore, step 3 relates back to step 2 by comparing local experiences to claims and features of global discourses and meta-narratives. This comparative perspective can illuminate the case studies and shed critical light on global discourse production. Finally, in step 4, discourses on the chosen topic are contextualized in relation to other human-environment discourses. Thus, on a higher discourse scale, it is possible to point to ways in which discourses are related to each other and how different phenomena are subject to similar simplifications.

NOTES

1. Later in the chapter I concentrate on narrative production in accordance with meta-narratives and delimit the scope by not looking into the role of other expressive means.

2. In 2001, RAFI changed its name to ETC Group (pronounced "et cetera"), an acronym for Action Group on Erosion, Technology, and Concentration. GRAIN's office is located in

Barcelona, Spain. In 1998 GRAIN started an e-mail list serve called BIOIPR, operated from Los Banos in the Philippines.

3. Among these list serves are those provided by GRAIN, ETC Group, a list concerning indigenous knowledge, and others.

4. This amounted to about 14,000 U.S. dollars, along with payment from Shaman for services bought from the institute.

5. I got the chance to experience one example of the creation of a biopiracy narrative when my research team conducted a study of a Norwegian case of bioprospecting. An NGO magazine, followed by some of the largest media in Norway, presented the research results but totally changed the conclusions about the role of the involved patents to fit the construction of a biopiracy narrative (Svarstad 2002).

REFERENCES

Adger, W., Neil Benjaminsen, A. Tor, Katrina Brown, and Hanne Svarstad. 2001. "Advancing a Political Ecology of Global Environmental Discourses." *Development and Change* 32, no. 4: 681–715.

Aylward, Bruce A. 1993. "The Economic Value of Pharmaceutical Prospecting and Its Role in Biodiversity Conservation." Discussion paper, no. 93–05. London: International Institute for Environment and Development, London Environmental Economics Centre.

Baker, J. T., R. P. Borris, B. Carte, G. A. Cordell, D. D. Soejarto, G. M. Cragg, M. P. Gupta, M. M. Iwu, D. R. Madulid, and V. E. Tyler. 1995. "Natural Product Drug Discovery and Development: New Perspectives on International Collaboration." *Journal of Natural Products—Lloydia* 58, no. 9: 1325–57.

Balick, Michael J., Elaine Elisabetsky, and Sarah A. Laird, eds. 1996. *Medicinal Resources of the Tropical Forest: Biodiversity and Its Importance to Human Health.* New York: Columbia University Press.

Bell, Janet. 1997. "Biopiracy's Latest Disguises." *Seedling* 14, no. 2: 2–10.

Blaikie, Piers, and Harold Brookfield. 1987. *Land Degradation and Society.* London: Methuen.

Broch-Due, Vigdis, and Richard A. Schroeder, eds. 2000. *Producing Nature and Poverty in Africa.* Stockholm: Nordiska Afrikainstitutet.

Bryant, R. L., and S. Bailey. 1997. *Third World Political Ecology.* London: Routledge.

Carlson, T. J., M. M. Iwu, S. R. King, C. Obialor, and A. Ozioko. 1997. "Medicinal Plant Research in Nigeria: An Approach for Compliance with the Convention on Biological Diversity." *Diversity* 13, no. 1: 29–33.

Chinnock, Julie Anne, Michael J. Balick, and Silviano Camberos Sanchez. 1997. "Traditional Healers and Modern Science: Bridging the Gap: Belize, a Case Study." In *Building Bridges with Traditional Knowledge*, edited by A. Wigston, D. Paul, and C. Peters. New York: New York Botanical Garden Press.

Dryzek, John S. 1997. *The Politics of the Earth: Environmental Discourses.* Oxford: Oxford University Press.

Eisner, Thomas. 1989. "Prospecting for Nature's Chemical Riches." *Issues in Science and Technology* 6, no. 2: 31–34.

———. 1991. "Chemical Prospecting: A Proposal for Action." In *Ecology, Economics, and Ethics: The Broken Circle*, edited by F. H. Bormann and S. R. Kellert. New Haven, Conn.: Yale University Press.

ETC Group. 2002. "Biopiracy +10." *ETC Communiqué* 75 (March–April): 1–10.

———. 2004. "Captain Hook Award Ceremony 2004." *New Item*, February 12.

Fish, Vincent. 1993. "Poststructuralism in Family Therapy: Interrogating the Narrative/Conversational Mode." *Journal of Marital and Family Therapy* 19, no. 3: 221–32.

Foucault, Michel. 1970. *The Order of Things: An Archaeology of the Human Sciences.* New York: Random House.

———. 1980. "Truth and Power." In *Michel Foucault: Power/Knowledge: Selected Interviews and Other Writings, 1972–1977*, edited by C. Gordon. Brighton, England: Harvester.

Fox, Nich J. 1998. "Foucault, Foucauldians, and Sociology." *British Journal of Sociology* 49, no. 3: 415–33.

Frank, André Gunder. 1967. *Capitalism and Underdevelopment in Latin America.* New York: Monthly Review Press.

Genetic Resources Action International (GRAIN). 1993. "Bargaining over the Benefits of Biodiversity." *Seedling* 10, no. 3: 2–10.

Gramsci, Antonio. 1997 [1948–51]. *Selections from Prison Notebooks*, edited and translated by Quintin Hoare and Geoffrey Nowell Smith. London: Lawrence and Wishart.

Grifo, Francesca, and Joshua Rosenthal, eds. 1997. *Biodiversity and Human Health.* Washington, D.C.: Island Press.

Hajer, Maarten A. 1995. *The Politics of Environmental Discourse: Ecological Modernization and the Policy Process.* Oxford: Clarendon.

Jørgensen, Marianne Winter, and Louise Phillips. 1999. *Diskursanalyse som teori og metode.* Frederiksberg, Denmark: Roskilde Universitetsforlag/Samfundslitteratur.

Juma, Calestous. 1989. *The Gene Hunters: Biotechnology and the Scramble for Seeds.* London: Zed.

Kendall, Gavin, and Gary Wickham. 1999. *Using Foucault's Methods.* London: Sage.

Khor, Martin. 1996. "The Worldwide Fight against Biopiracy." *Race Class* 37, no. 3: 73–77.

King, Steven R. 1994. "Establishing Reciprocity: Biodiversity, Conservation, and New Models for Cooperation between Forest-Dwelling Peoples and the Pharmaceutical Industry." In *Intellectual Property Rights for Indigenous Peoples: A Sourcebook*, edited by T. Greaves, 69–82. Oklahoma City: Society for Applied Anthropology.

Kloppenburg, Jack R., Jr. 1988. *First the Seed: The Political Economy of Plant Biotechnology, 1492–2000.* Cambridge: Cambridge University Press.

Kloppenburg, Jack R., Jr., and Silvia Rodriguez. 1992. "Conservationists or Corsairs?" *Seedling* 9, nos. 2 and 3: 12–17.

Krattiger, A. F., and W. H. Lesser. 1995. "The 'Facilitator': Proposing a New Mechanism to Strengthen the Equitable and Sustainable Use of Biodiversity." *Environmental Conservation* 22, no. 3: 211–15.

Laclau, Ernesto, and Chantal Mouffe. 1985. *Hegemony and Socialist Strategy: Towards a Radical Democratic Politics.* London: Verso.

Mateo, Nicolás. 2000. "Bioprospecting and Conservation in Costa Rica." In *Responding to Bioprospecting: From Biodiversity in the South to Medicines in the North*, edited by Hanne Svarstad and Shivcharn S. Dhillion, 45–55. Oslo: Spartacus.

McChesney, J. D. 1996. "Biological Diversity, Chemical Diversity, and the Search for New Pharmaceuticals." In *Medicinal Resources of the Tropical Forest: Biodiversity and Its Importance to Human Health*, edited by Michael J. Balick, Elaine Elisabetsky, and Sarah A. Laird, 11–18. New York: Columbia University Press.

Mooney, Pat. 2000. "Why We Call It Biopiracy." In *Responding to Bioprospecting: From Biodiversity in the South to Medicines in the North*, edited by Hanne Svarstad and Shivcharn S. Dhillion, 37–44. Oslo: Spartacus.

Moran, Katy. 1997. "Returning Benefits from Ethnobotanical Drug Discovery to Native Communities." In *Biodiversity and Human Health*, edited by Francesca Grifo and Joshua Rosenthal, 243–63. Washington, D.C.: Island Press.

Mugabe, John, Charles Victor Barber, Gudrun Henne, Lyle Glowka, and Antonio La Viña. 1997. "Managing Access to Genetic Resources." In *Access to Genetic Resources: Strategies for Sharing Benefits*, edited by John Mugabe, Charles Victor Barber, Gudrun Henne, Lyle Glowka, and Antonio La Viña, 5–32. Nairobi: ACTS Press.

Newman, David J., and Sarah A. Laird. 1999. "The Influence of Natural Products on 1997 Pharmaceutical Sales Figures, Appendix A." In *The Commercial Use of Biodiversity: Access to Genetic Resources and Benefit-Sharing*, edited by Kerry ten Kate and Sarah A. Laird, 333–36. London: Earthscan.

Parry, Bronwyn. 2000. "The Fate of the Collections: Social Justice and the Annexation of Plant Genetic Resources." In *People, Plants, and Justice: The Politics of Nature Conservation*, edited by C. Zerner, 374–402. New York: Columbia University Press.

Peet, Richard, and Michael Watts, eds. 1996. *Liberation Ecologies: Environment, Development, Social Movements*. London: Routledge.

Portillo, Zoraida. 1999. *Biopiracy: A New Threat for the Amazon*. Inter Press Service, Rome. Distributed January 6, 1999, by GRAIN's list serve BIOIPR.

Principe, P. P. 1996. "Monetizing the Pharmacological Benefits of Plants." In *Medicinal Resources of the Tropical Forest: Biodiversity and Its Importance to Human Health*, edited by Michael J. Balick, Elaine Elisabetsky, and Sarah A. Laird, 191–218. New York: Columbia University Press.

Reid, Walter V. 1993–94. "The Economic Realities of Biodiversity." *Issues in Science and Technology* 10, no. 2: 48–55.

———. 1997. "Technological Change and Regulation of Access to Genetic Resources." In *Access to Genetic Resources: Strategies for Sharing Benefits*, edited by John Mugabe, Charles Victor Barber, Gudrun Henne, Lyle Glowka, and Antonio La Viña. Nairobi: ACTS Press.

Reid, Walter V., Sarah A. Laird, Carrie A. Meyer, Rodrigo Gámez, Ana Sittenfeld, Daniel H. Janzen, Michael A. Gollin, and Calestous Juma, eds. 1993. *Biodiversity Prospecting: Using Genetic Resources for Sustainable Development*. Baltimore: World Resources Institute.

Reyes, Viki. 1996. "The Value of Sangre de Drago." *Seedling* 13, no. 1: 16–21.

Roe, Emery M. 1991. "Development Narratives, or Making the Best of Blueprint Development." *World Development* 19, no. 4: 287–300.

———. 1995. "Except-Africa: Postscript to a Special Section on Development Narratives." *World Development* 23, no. 6: 1065–69.

Rural Advancement Foundation International (RAFI). 1994. *Conserving Indigenous Knowledge: Integrating Two Systems of Innovation: An Independent Study by the Rural Advancement Foundation International Commissioned by the United Nations Development Program*. New York: RAFI.

———. 1995. "Biopiracy Update: A Global Pandemic." *RAFI Communiqué* (September–October): 1–10.

———. 2000. "The Captain Hook Awards for Outstanding Achievements in Biopiracy." *RAFI News*, May 17.

Rural Advancement Foundation International (RAFI) and Cultural Survival Canada. 1997. "Sangre de Drago." *BioPirates*, log no. 4. June.

Shiva, Vandana. 1997. *Biopiracy: The Plunder of Nature and Knowledge*. Boston: South End.

Southeast Asia Regional Institute for Community Education (SEARICE). 1997. *A Proposal for a Program on Biopiracy in Southeast Asia: Involving the Grassroots in Regulating Access to Biological and Genetic Resources and Indigenous Knowledge*. Quezon City, The Phillipines: SEARICE.

Stott, P., and S. Sullivan, eds. 2000. *Political Ecology: Science, Myth, and Power.* London: Arnold.

Svarstad, Hanne. 2000. "Reciprocity, Biopiracy, Heroes, Villains, and Victims." In *Responding to Bioprospecting: From Biodiversity in the South to Medicines in the North*, edited by Hanne Svarstad and Shivcharn S. Dhillion, 19–35. Oslo: Spartacus.

———. 2002. "Analysing Conservation-Environment Discourses: The Story of a Biopiracy Narrative." *Forum for Development Studies* 29, no. 1: 63–92.

———. 2003. "Bioprospecting: Global Discourses and Local Perceptions: Shaman Pharmaceuticals in Tanzania." Ph.D. diss., University of Oslo.

ten Kate, Kerry. 1995. *Biopiracy or Green Petroleum? Expectations and Best Practice in Bioprospecting.* London: Overseas Development Administration.

United Nations. 1992. *Convention on Biological Diversity.* Nairobi: United Nations Environmental Program.

Wilson, Edward O. 1988. "The Current State of Biological Diversity." In *Biodiversity*, edited by Edward O. Wilson and Frances M. Peter, 3–18. Washington, D.C.: National Academy Press.

Yapa, Lakshman. 1996. "What Causes Poverty? A Postmodern View." *Annals of the Association of American Geographers* 86, no. 4: 707–28.

14

The Emergence of Collective Ethnic Identities and Alternative Political Ecologies in the Colombian Pacific Rainforest

ARTURO ESCOBAR AND SUSAN PAULSON

The emergence of collective ethnic identities in the Colombian Pacific and similar regions reflects the irruption of the biological as a global concern and the cultural or ethnic as a political issue. This situation is evidenced in the new Colombian constitution's expressed desire to construct a pluri-ethnic and multicultural society. To what extent does the emergence of these unprecedented identities constitute a new context for biodiversity discussions? Is it possible to articulate an alternative view of biodiversity conservation grounded in the aims and needs of the movements? In this chapter, we explore three basic conceptual questions: what is biodiversity and how did the concept emerge? What meanings and applications of biodiversity are being advanced by certain social movements in Colombia? And how do these alternative approaches to biodiversity reconfigure the discursive and political terrain?[1]

Although the term *biodiversity* has concrete biophysical referents, it is a discursive invention of recent origin. The language and meaning developed around the concept of biodiversity weave together a complex network of actors—from international organizations and northern nongovernmental organizations (NGOs) to scientists, bioprospectors, and local communities and social movements—all with diverging biocultural perspectives and political stakes. Through the cultural politics they enact, social movements advance an approach to biodiversity conservation and appropriation that differs from dominant expressions. This approach is couched in terms of cultural difference, territorial defense, and some measure of social and political autonomy. In subscribing to a view of biodiversity that is linked to cultural and territorial defense, these social movements articulate an alternative political ecology framework that works to reconfigure the discursive and political terrain so that particular issues (such as territorial control, alternative development, intellectual property rights, genetic resources, local knowledge, and conservation itself) take on new dimensions; they can no longer be reduced to the managerial and economizing prescriptions offered by dominant views. In the alternative political ecology of social movements, formerly marginal sites, such as local communities and social groups, come to be seen as emergent centers of innovation and alternative worlds.

The aim of the chapter is to contribute to imagining such alternative worlds. It highlights the constructions of nature and culture harbored in the political strategies that social movements develop in their encounters with environmental destruction and their struggles for biodiversity conservation. To this end, it brings together information and understanding obtained through diverse research methods carried out across multiple spaces and scales and encompassing what we usually distinguish as political, economic, and ecological phenomenon. The investigation includes a textual analysis of global discourses on biodiversity and development, a summary of Colombia's 1991 constitution reform and Ley 70 that together granted black communities of the Pacific region collective rights to the territories they have traditionally occupied, and a critical assessment of national and international development institutions and conservation organizations working in Colombia. To this we add an ecological characterization of the region in question, including rivers, mangroves, foothills, and forest, and ethnographic information on local practices that contribute to shaping riverine lifeways and territories.

The centerpiece of the study is multiyear ethnographic research on and with the Proceso de Comunidades Negras, a network of black social movement organizations in the Pacific, and its processes of knowledge production that have generated concepts that reconfigure links among culture, identity, territory, and region. This study looks at the movement's analysis of traditional production systems of river communities with their multiple subsistence and economic activities, kin-based social relations, strong oral traditions, religious practices, and particular forms of knowledge and use of forest ecosystems. It also analyzes the movement's transnationalizing processes and the dynamics through which its activists produce knowledge and practice in their encounters with the state, NGOs, and scientific and development experts.

These multiple paths of research draw on concepts that help us understand politics, economy, and ecology and their relation to each other. The chapter begins with a look at the concept of biodiversity as developed in global discourses and networks. After introducing the social movement of black communities in the Pacific rainforest, attention turns to an alternative conceptualization of biodiversity as "territory plus culture" that is emerging in the context of the movement, together with innovative definitions of "region-territory" as a cultural-natural space of ethnic groups and life corridors associated with the riverine production systems.

Biodiversity Discourses and Networks

Does biodiversity exist? Is there a discrete reality of biodiversity different from the infinity of living beings, including plants, animals, microorganisms, and homo sapiens and their interactions, attractions and repulsions, co-creations and destructions? From a biological standpoint, one could say that biodiversity is the sum effect of all natural complexity and that it could be specified in functional and structural terms. Yet current scientific energy is geared not toward theorizing biodiversity per se but toward assessing the significance of biodiversity loss to ecosystem functioning and ascertaining the relation between biodiversity and the services that ecosystems provide.[2] Broadly disseminated definitions of biodiversity do not create a new object of study outside of biology and ecology, yet the term "biodiversity" is often used to refer to situations that go well beyond the natural science domain. As critical studies of science have shown, the act of naming a new reality is never innocent. What views of the world does this naming shelter and propagate? Why has this new way of naming been invented at the end of a century that has seen untold levels of ecological destruction?

Poststructuralist approaches suggest that it is useful to examine biodiversity not as a true object to be progressively revealed by science but as a historically produced discourse. Michel Foucault (1980) shook social science and medicine by suggesting that sex does not exist as a universally given entity but is an artificial construct elaborated through the employment of sexuality as a historical discourse. Is biodiversity similarly a construct around which a complex discourse of nature is being built? If biodiversity works in the same way as sexuality does, the biodiversity discourse will anchor an entire apparatus for the dispersion of new truths throughout vast social domains.

The emergence of the biodiversity discourse is a response to the problematization of survival motivated by the destruction of nature; as Edward O. Wilson (1993) has argued, "biological diversity is the key to the maintenance of the world as we know it" (19). The idea of biodiversity irrupted in the world theater of science and development in the late 1980s. Key textual markers of this emergence were the publication of *Global Biodiversity Strategy* (WRI/IUCN/UNEP 1992) and the Convention on Biological Diversity (CBD), signed at the Earth Summit in Rio de Janeiro in 1992. Subsequent texts and elaborations, from a plethora of United Nations and NGO meeting reports to Global Environment Facility (GEF) project descriptions, continue to be framed by this discourse.

The ferment of activity that characterizes the biodiversity field today is novel but not without historical precedents. One antecedent is found in the history of botanizing during the ages of empire and exploration, when "overseas collectors made up the most extensive scientific network in the world" (Mackay 1996, 39). During this time, plant collecting linked questions of culture, knowledge, empire, and economy. Historians of science and empire (Miller and Reill 1996) use lessons from this kind of past experience to illuminate today's biodiversity debates.

As a scientific discourse, biodiversity is a prime instance of the co-production of technoscience and society that works through networks. Scholars in the field of science and technology studies analyze technoscientific networks as chains of sites characterized by a set of heterogeneous parameters, practices, and actors in which each actor's identity affects and is affected by the network. Intervention in the network is done by means of objects (from plants and genes to various technologies); actors (prospectors, taxonomists, planners, experts); strategies (resource management, intellectual property rights); models (of ecosystems, species population dynamics); and theories (of development, restoration). These interventions affect and motivate translations, travels, mediations, appropriations, and subversions throughout the network. The work of activists of the Colombian Pacific region constitutes one site on this global network (and also a network of its own) that encompasses local communities, concepts, and ecosystems.

The biodiversity network originated in the late 1980s and early 1990s out of conservation biology, where the idea of biodiversity (Takacs 1996) first flourished. It soon articulated a master narrative of biological crisis ("if you want to save the planet, this is what you must do, and here are the knowledge and resources to do it") launched globally at what has been called the first rite of passage to the transnation state, the 1992 Rio Summit (Ribeiro 1997). The biodiversity narrative created obligatory parameters for the construction of particular discourses. The process translates the complexity of the world into simple narratives of threats and possible solutions. This simplified construction could be effectively summarized by paraphrasing Daniel Janzen's motto about biodiversity: "you've got to know it to use it, and you've got to use it to save it" (Janzen and Hallwachs 1993). In a few years, an entire network was established that amounted to what Stephen Brush (1998) has aptly called a tremendous invasion into the public domain. Yet in contrast to other instances of technoscience, the biodiversity network has not resulted in a stable construction. As we shall see, counter-simplifications and alternative discourses produced by subaltern actors also circulate actively in the network, with important effects.

The biodiversity discourse has generated an increasingly vast institutional apparatus that systematically organizes the production of forms of knowledge and types of power, linking one to the other through concrete strategies and programs. International institutions, northern NGOs, botanical gardens, universities and research institutes in the developed and developing worlds, pharmaceutical companies, and the great variety of experts located in each of these sites occupy dominant nodes in the network. As they circulate through the network, truths are transformed and reinscribed into other knowledge-power constellations. They are alternatively resisted, subverted, or re-created to serve other ends—for instance, by social movements that become themselves the sites of important counter-discourses.

At the risk of oversimplifying, we find it useful to identify four major posi-

tions produced by the biodiversity network to this date, characterized as globalocentric, developing-world sovereignty, biodemocracy, and cultural autonomy. We
stress that each position is itself heterogeneous and diverse and that the entire
biodiversity field is extremely dynamic and rapidly changing. The globalocentric
perspective, the dominant view in the network, emphasizes efficient resource
management administered by experts, as manifest in the Convention of Biological Diversity (CBD). This view derives from dominant institutions, such as the
World Bank and big northern environmental NGOs, and is supported by industrialized countries. It is based on a particular representation of the threats to biodiversity and strives to identify symptoms and implement expedient responses
rather than address underlying causes. This perspective proposes appropriate
mechanisms for biodiversity management, including in situ and ex situ conservation and national biodiversity planning. It focuses on intellectual property
rights as the chief mechanism for the compensation and economic use of biodiversity. It also promotes the problematic practice of bioprospecting, which often
has serious affects, including the loss by small farmers and indigenous peoples of
rights to their own plants and knowledge.

   The dominant globalocentric perspective is challenged by some developing-
world governments, which, without questioning it in a fundamental way, seek to
renegotiate the terms of biodiversity treaties and strategies. Although there is
great variation in the positions adopted by these governments, they tend to
emphasize issues of sovereignty, particularly in international fora such as the CBD.
Some countries strongly oppose policies favored by industrialized nations, such as
certain aspects of intellectual property rights; others call on rich countries, particularly the United States, to negotiate on key issues such as technology transfer and
biosafety protocols.

   Progressive NGOs are a greater challenge to the dominant resource management orientation. They see the globalocentric perspective as a form of bioimperialism and counter it by promoting biodemocracy. By reinterpreting threats to
biodiversity to focus on habitat destruction by megadevelopment projects, monocultures of the mind, agriculture promoted by capital and reductionist science,
and the consumption habits of the north, biodemocracy advocates shift attention
away from symptoms of environmental degradation appearing in the south and
point to the north as the root of the diversity crisis. These advocates promote a
radical redefinition of production away from the logic of uniformity and toward
the logic of diversity. Progressives oppose private intellectual property rights and
advocate collective rights that recognize the intrinsic value and the shared character of knowledge and resources. This view contests the most cherished constructs
of modernity, such as positivist science, the law of the market, and individual
property and ownership. The NGOs advancing this position constitute subnet-
works at national and transnational levels that are still poorly understood.

   Finally, a second challenge to the globalocentric perspective has been crafted by social movements that explicitly construct a political strategy for the defense of territory, culture, and identity. While having many points in common with the progressive NGO perspective, this view is distinct conceptually and politically and occupies a different role in the biodiversity network. Activists in these movements use widespread concern for biodiversity as a conduit for efforts to protect their entire life project, not just their genetic resources. In many cases, concern about biodiversity has followed from broader struggles for territorial control. In Latin America, a number of valuable experiences have taken place in this regard, chiefly in conjunction with the demarcation of collective territories in countries such as Bolivia, Brazil, Colombia, Ecuador, and Peru. The experience of one such movement is outlined in this chapter, highlighting the broader perspective on biodiversity that it has developed.

Power and Practice in Diverse Models of Nature

A fundamental asymmetry of power is embodied in the discourses on biodiversity that represent modern science and economics versus those arising from local knowledge and practice. Although some attention is now given to local knowledge in biodiversity debates (particularly around the discussion and implementation of article 8.j of the CBD), this attention is insufficient and often misguided because local knowledge is refunctionalized to serve the interest of western-style conservation rather than understood in its own terms. Beyond the political economy argument of capital's predation of local ecologies and knowledge (Shiva 1997), there are basic cultural and epistemological considerations at play, particularly insofar as local and modern forms of knowledge entail different ways of apprehending the world and appropriating the natural (Leff 1997).

Anthropologists, geographers, and others are demonstrating with increasing eloquence that many rural communities in the developing world construct nature in strikingly different ways from prevalent modern forms. Ethnographic studies unveil a coherent set of practices of thinking about, relating to, and using the biological, such as Michael R. Dove's study of Pakistani farmers' (chapter 12) conceptualization and management of tree shade and Anne Ferguson and Bill Derman's study of conflicting approaches to water use in Zimbabwe (chapter 4). The project of documenting cultural models of nature was formulated some time ago (Strathern 1980) and has achieved a remarkable level of sophistication in recent years (Descola and Pálsson 1996, Gudeman and Rivera 1990). Although there is no unified view of what constitutes a cultural model of nature or how these models operate cognitively and socially, it is widely recognized that many local models do not rely on a nature-society dichotomy. Unlike modern western constructions, with their strict separation between biophysical, human, and supernatural worlds, local models in many non-western contexts are often predicated on links of continuity among these spheres and embedded in social relations that cannot be reduced to modern capitalist terms.

Recent anthropological approaches are treating local knowledge as "a practical, situated activity, constituted by a past, but changing, history of practices" (Hobart 1993, 17). This approach assumes that knowledge can work more through a body of practices than by relying on a system of shared, context-free knowledge. This practice-oriented view of local knowledge has its origin in a variety of theoretical positions, voiced by thinkers ranging from Martin Heidegger to Pierre Bourdieu. A related trend emphasizes the embodied aspects of local knowledge, explored by Susan Paulson (chapter 10) in the context of places, practices, bodies and physical movements of differentiated social actors. For Tim Ingold (1995, 1996), our knowledge of the world can be described as a process of enskillment in the context of our practical engagement with the environment. Humans, in this view, are embedded in nature and engaged in situated, practical acts. For Paul Richards (1993), local agricultural knowledge must be seen as a set of time- and context-specific improvisational capacities rather than as a coherent indigenous knowledge system, as previous literature has suggested. These welcome trends give rise to new questions regarding the nature and modes of operation of local knowledge (Escobar 1999a) that might strengthen our framework for discussions of biodiversity conservation and related issues, such as intellectual property rights.[3]

These questions are being actively explored in two separate but increasingly interrelated domains: political ecology theory, particularly that which explores alternative ecological rationalities (Leff 1995a), and social movements in biodiversity-rich regions. Whereas the former aims to develop a new paradigm of production that incorporates, for any given ecosystem and social group, cultural, ecological, political and technoeconomic factors in the assessment of strategies that may be ecologically and culturally sustainable, the latter attempt to construct an alternative view of development and social practice through self-conscious and locally grounded political strategies. As this chapter will demonstrate in its examination of how a particular social movement (a network of black communities in the Pacific rainforest region of Colombia) addresses questions of biodiversity and sustainability from the perspective of culture and politics, both projects have much to contribute to each other.

Social Movements and New Politics of Ecology, Ethnicity, and Territory

Since the end of the 1980s, the Pacific rainforest region of Colombia has been undergoing an unprecedented historical process: the emergence of collective ethnic identities and their strategic positioning in culture-territory relations. This change is set in a national context that includes the neoliberal opening of the national economy to world markets after 1990 and integration into the Pacific Basin economies as well as substantial reform of the national constitution in 1991 that, among other things, granted black communities of the Pacific region collective rights to the territories they have traditionally occupied. Internationally, tropical rainforest areas such as the Pacific region are increasingly recognized as housing the majority of the biological diversity of the planet. The emergence of collective ethnic identities in the Colombian Pacific and similar regions reflects a double historical movement with worldwide implications: the irruption of the biological in global concerns for conservation and the unprecedented political role of the cultural and the ethnic in efforts to construct more pluri-ethnic and multicultural societies.

The Pacific Coast region of Colombia covers a vast area (about 70,000 kilometers) stretching from Panama to Ecuador and from the westernmost chain of the Andes to the ocean. It is a unique rainforest region, one of the world's most biodiverse in scientific terms. About 60 percent of the region's 900,000 inhabitants (800,000 Afro-Colombians; about 50,000 Embera, Waunana, and other indigenous people; and mestizo colonists) live in the few larger cities and towns; the rest inhabit the margins of more than 240 rivers, most of which flow from the Andes toward the ocean. These black and indigenous peoples have maintained distinct material and cultural practices in relation to the rest of the nation, such as multiple subsistence and economic activities involving agriculture, fishing, hunting, gathering, and small-scale gold mining and timber collecting for the market. They are characterized by extended families and matrilocal social relations, strong oral traditions and religious practices, and particular forms of knowledge and use of the diverse forest ecosystems. The continued existence of significantly different cultural practices is notable in a heretofore invisible region that is finally attracting national and international attention. (For a general introduction to the region's black cultures and current situation, see Escobar and Pedrosa 1996.)

Social movements theorists have recently turned their attention to the notion of cultural politics, understood as the process through which sets of social actors shaped by and embodying different cultural meanings and practices come into conflict with each other. In this conceptualization, meanings and practices that are usually excluded from conventional definitions of politics are understood as political, including practices theorized as marginal, oppositional, residual, emergent, alternative, dissident, and the like, all of them conceived in relation to a given dominant cultural order. Culture is political because meanings are constitutive of processes that, implicitly or explicitly, seek to redefine social power. When movements employ alternative conceptions of nature, woman, development, economy, democracy, or citizenship that unsettle dominant cultural meanings, they enact a cultural politics; and in the case studied here, those cultural politics are inextricably intertwined with ecology (Alvarez et al. 1998).

In the Colombian Pacific region, the interplay of these dynamics since 1990 has contributed to the emergence of important black and indigenous movements that have progressively come to tackle ecological questions.[4] Since 1993, the Proceso de Comunidades Negras (PCN; the name translates as Process of Black Communities, a network of more than 140 local organizations), has assumed a leading role in the struggle to exercise the constitutional rights granted to black communities and the defense of their territories. The PCN emphasizes the social control of the territory as a precondition for the survival, re-creation, and strengthening of culture. In the river communities, activists' efforts have been geared toward advancing a participatory pedagogical process on the meaning of the new constitution; debating the fundamental concepts of territory, development, traditional production practices, and use of natural resources; and strengthening the organizational capacity of the communities. This sustained effort lay the basis, in 1991–93, for the elaboration of a proposal for the law of cultural and territorial rights called for by the 1991 constitution (Ley 70, approved in 1993) and a call to firm up a series of political-organizational principles.

The collective discussion of the proposal for Ley 70 was a decisive space for the development of the movement. This process was advanced at two levels: one centered on the daily life and practices of the black riverine communities, the other on an ideological and political reflection advanced by activists. The first level worked with the rubric of what was referred to as "the logic of the river"; it relied on the broad participation of local people in the articulation of their own rights, aspirations, and dreams. The second level maintained the rivers and their settlements as referents and sought to transcend the rural domain to raise the question of black people as an ethnic group beyond what could be granted by the law. This level saw a rearticulation of the notions of territory, development, and the social relations of black communities with the rest of the country.

The movement has been growing in conceptual and political sophistication. The Third National Conference of Black Communities convened in September 1993 in the predominantly black town of Puerto Tejada, south of Cali. It proposed the movement's goal to be the consolidation of a social movement of black communities for the reconstruction and affirmation of cultural identity, leading to an autonomous organizing strategy for the achievement of cultural, social, economic, political, and territorial rights and for the defense of natural resources and the environment. One of the central features of the conference was the adoption of a set of political-organizational principles concerning the key issues of identity, territory, autonomy, and development:

1. Reaffirmation of identity (the right to be black), which identifies culture and identity as organizing axes of both daily life and political practice to all.
2. Right to the territory (as the space for being), which conceives of the territory as a necessary condition for the re-creation and development of a black

cultural vision and a habitat where black people develop their being in and with nature.

3. Autonomy (the right to the exercise of being and identity), particularly in the political realm, and with the aspiration of a certain degree of social and economic autonomy.
4. Right to construct an autonomous perspective of the future, particularly an autonomous vision of development based on black culture.
5. Solidarity with the struggles for rights of black people throughout the world.

The activists made a strategic move in defense of certain cultural practices of the river communities that are seen as embodying resistance to capitalism and modernity and being elements for alternative ecological rationalities. Although often couched in culturalist language, this defense is not essentializing: it responds to current challenges faced by the communities and the possibilities presented by a cautious opening toward forms of modernity such as biodiversity conservation and alternative development. Identity is thus seen in both ways: as anchored in traditional practices and forms of knowledge and as an always-changing project of cultural and political construction. In this way, the movement builds on the submerged networks of cultural practices and meanings of the river communities and their active construction of lifeworlds (Melucci 1989) and also takes these networks as the basis for a political conception of identity that has more to do with the encounter with modernity (state, capital, science, biodiversity) than with timeless and bounded identities.

Gender is also becoming salient in the agenda of ethnocultural organizations and related identity construction. Although it is still given insufficient attention, the fact that many of the top leaders and activists of the movement are women committed to an ethnocultural approach is acting as a catalyst for the articulation of gender issues. In 1992, the first meeting of black women of the Pacific Coast attracted more than five hundred participants; a network of black women's organizations now exists and is gaining visibility in various domains of activity, particularly since 1995 (Rojas 1996), and discourses of gender and biodiversity are also slowly emerging (Camacho 1996). Although most women's organizing efforts are still couched in conventional "women in development" terms (Lozano 1996), the number of activists committed to a simultaneous gender and ethnic mobilization is increasing (Asher 1998); and the need to embrace gender as an integral aspect of the movement, as opposed to promoting the creation of separate women's organizations, was recognized in 1994.

An Alternative Political Ecology Framework

Through their encounter with instances of environmental conflict and initiative, movement activists are crafting an entire political ecology that provides important elements for a redefinition of biodiversity appropriation and conservation. In this section, we analyze the alternative views, concepts, and proposals for biodiversity conservation advanced in these social movements.

Between the time of the new constitution and Ley 70, when biodiversity was barely spoken about in the region, and the late 1990s, significant terrain was covered. One important factor has been the intensive and active engagement of river communities and PCN activists with the internationally funded Pacific Biodiversity Conservation Project. (Proyecto Biopacífico was implemented between 1993 and 1998, with 9 million dollars allocated to the initial three-year period [see GEF/PNUD 1993].) Also important is the increasing transnationalization of the movement as activists travel to places in North and South America and Europe to participate in meetings such as COP–3 in Buenos Aires (1996), the People's Global Action against Free Trade in Geneva (1997 and 1998), and the United Nations Working Group on Indigenous Populations (1998). Although no one could say that biodiversity has become the overriding concern of the movement, it is clear that the movement's construction of a political strategy for the region is increasingly enmeshed with the biodiversity network and that the PCN, Proyecto Biopacífico, and other actors have created a local-regional site that constitutes a network of its own. The relations among culture, territory, and natural resources constitute a central axis of strategy building both within movement organizations and in their dealings with the state. At the same time, disagreements on views of natural resources have created tensions among community organizations and between some community sectors and ethnocultural organizations.

These tensions are related to the overall intensification of development, capitalism, and modernity in the region (Escobar and Pedrosa 1996). First, the growing migration to the Pacific of peasants, proletarians, and entrepreneurs displaced from the interior of the country is having a visible ecological and social impact arising chiefly from the different cultural logic that these actors bring with them. Second, the government continues to insist on implementing conventional development plans for the region intended to create infrastructure for the large-scale arrival of capital. Third, government policies for the protection of natural resources have consisted of conventional measures, including the expansion of natural parks and the implementation of social forestry programs with little or no community participation. Only the small but symbolically important Proyecto Biopacífico has attempted, even if in ambiguous ways, to incorporate the demands of the organized black communities. Finally, the drug cartels have also entered the region in the form of big mining, agro-industrial, and tourist projects, with momentous consequences that are still difficult to assess.

The vulnerability and insufficient organizational level of the black communities has been revealed in a variety of cases of environmental conflict between local communities and state, timber, mining, and agro-industrial interests. These conflicts have made evident not only the weakness of the state agencies in charge of the protection of natural resources but also frequent collusion between state functionaries and the private business interests exploiting the resources they are supposed to protect. Finally, government measures to control environmental abuses are often late and inefficient. On the positive side, movement organizations have extracted partial but important victories in some environmental conflicts, and black organizations have been able to use some of these instances of conflict to build inter-ethnic alliances with indigenous movements. Insofar as the study of environmental conflict and its distributional effects is a central feature of political ecology (Martínez-Alier 1995), the Pacific region of Colombia has important lessons for the field.

In their interaction with community, state, NGO, and academic sectors, PCN activists have progressively articulated a political ecology framework that incorporates concepts of territory, biodiversity, life corridors, local economies, alternative development, and territorial governability.[5] The demarcation of collective territories has led activists to develop a conception of territory that highlights articulations between patterns of settlement, use of spaces, and resource-use practices and meanings. This conception is validated by recent anthropological studies that document the cultural models of nature that exist among black river communities. Riverine populations evidence longitudinal and discontinuous settlement patterns along the rivers in which multiple economic activities (fishing, agriculture, small-scale mining and forest use, hunting and gathering, subsistence and market activities) are combined and articulated according to the location of the settlement in the upper, medium, or lower segment of the river. This longitudinal dimension articulates with a horizontal axis regulated by the knowledge and use of multiple resources, ranging from those that have been domesticated or are found close to the river margin (including medicinal herbs and food crops) to the undomesticated species found in the various layers of forest away from the river. A vertical axis (from the infraworld to the supraworld, populated by benevolent or dangerous spirits) also contributes to articulating the patterns of meaning and use of resources. These various axes depend on social relations between communities, which in some parts of the Pacific entail inter-ethnic relations between black and indigenous communities as well as inter-river social and ecological relations (Del Valle and Restrepo 1996).

One important contribution of the Proyecto Biopacífico has been to initiate research and conceptualization of the traditional production systems of the river communities. For Proyecto Biopacífico staff and PCN activists alike, it is clear that these systems are geared more toward local consumption than to the market and accumulation. As such, they have operated as forms of resistance, even if they have also contributed to the region's marginalization. Also commonly appreciated is the fact that, until a few decades ago, traditional practices were largely sustainable to the extent that they enabled the reproduction of the cultural and biophysical ecologies. Among those practices highlighted are the sustained use of forest and soil resources through low-intensity exploitation, shifting use of productive space over broad and different ecological areas, manifold and diverse agricultural and extractive activities, family- and kindred-based labor practices, and horticulture. Conceived in terms of adaptive productive systems, this research has provided useful tools for community and social movement planning and reflection. It is also revealed that in many of the rivers these systems are under increasingly heavy stress, chiefly by growing extractivist pressures, and in some cases have become untenable. Under these conditions, novel economic and technological strategies are seen as necessary; these strategies should be capable of generating resources for conservation (Sánchez and Leal 1995).

Activists have introduced other important conceptual innovations, some of which have come about in the process of negotiation with the staff of the biodiversity conservation project. The first is the definition of biodiversity as "territory plus culture." Closely related is a view of the entire Pacific rainforest region as a region-territory of ethnic groups—that is, an ecological and cultural unit laboriously constructed through the practices of the communities. The region-territory is also thought about in terms of life corridors, veritable modes of articulation between sociocultural forms of use and the natural environment. There are, for instance, life corridors linked to the mangrove ecosystems; to the foothills; and to the middle part of the rivers, extending toward the inside of the forest; and those constructed by particular activities, such as traditional gold mining or women's shell collecting in the mangrove areas. Each corridor is marked by particular patterns of mobility, social relations (gender, kindred, ethnicity), use of the environment, and links to other corridors. Each involves a particular use and management strategy of the territory. In some parts of the region, life corridors rely on inter-ethnic and inter-river relations.

These concepts have been arrived at and filled out as much through direct engagement with river communities in the mapping of particular territories as through engagement with national and transnational actors and events. The ensuing political ecology is thus based on a complex view of ecocultural dynamics. Government strategies tend to lack this complexity when they divide the territory according to other principles (such as the topographical outline of the river basin) that overlook the networks that articulate various rivers together. Precisely because they are blind to sociocultural dynamics, conventional approaches tend to fragment the culturally constructed spatiality that helps to constitute particular landscapes.

The region-territory is a category of inter-ethnic relations that points toward the construction of alternative models of life and society; it is a conceptual unit and also a political project and a mode of ethnic management. It entails an attempt to explain and manage biological diversity from inside the ecocultural logic of the Pacific. The demarcation of collective territories fits into this framework. Government dispositions violate the framework by dividing up the

Pacific region among collective territories, natural parks, areas of use, and areas of sacrifice where megaprojects are to be constructed. This is why it would be quite difficult to articulate a conservation strategy based on the principles proposed by the PCN with the ecodestructive strategies of national development that prevail in the country.

Because conceptualizations of territory do not necessarily correspond with the long-standing practices of the communities, where rights to land are allocated on different bases (according to kin, tradition of occupation, and so on), some observers see the emphasis on collective territories as a mistake of the movement based on a misperception of their strength. At the same time, we emphasize that the region-territory is also a result of collective (inter- and intracommunity) ecocultural practices. The territory is seen as the space of effective appropriation of the ecosystem—that is, as those spaces used to satisfy community needs and for social and cultural development. For a given river community, this appropriation has longitudinal and horizontal dimensions, sometimes encompassing several river basins. Thus defined, the territory not only traverses several landscape units but also embodies a community's life project. The region- territory, in contrast, is conceived as a political construction for the defense of the territories and their sustainability. In this way, the region-territory is a strategy of sustainability, and sustainability is a strategy for the construction and defense of the region-territory. What these strategies seek to sustain includes cultural processes of signification, biological processes of ecosystem functioning, and technoeconomic processes of resource use. In other words, sustainability is not conceived here only in terms of biological species or singular activities or only on economic grounds. It must respond to the integral and multidimensional character of the practices of effective appropriation of ecosystems. The region-territory thus can be said to articulate the life project of the communities with the political project of the social movement. In sum, the political strategy of the region-territory is essential to strengthening specific territories in their cultural, economic, and ecological dimensions.

Current pressures on activists and communities to prepare river-based development and conservation plans entail many contradictions in terms of existing local practices. Activists are painfully aware of these contradictions as they embark on the planning process and try to buy time for strategies that respond more closely to local realities and aspirations. This explains why for many people of the Pacific the loss of territory would amount to a return to slavery or, worse perhaps, to becoming "common citizens." The struggle for territory and against slavery involves strengthening and transformation of traditional production systems and local markets and economies, pressing on with the collective titling process, and working toward organizational strengthening and the development of forms of territorial governability. Despite the fact that the primary interests of the country's conservation establishment (whether state agencies or NGOs) are genetic resources and habitat protection, not the ecocultural demands of the movement,

PCN activists find in biodiversity discussions and programs an important space for struggle that partly converges with the strategies of these actors. Regarding the possibility of slowing down the most predatory activities by capital and the state, biodiversity discussions are of utmost importance to black and indigenous movements.

The Proyecto Biopacífico and the PCN have struggled to advance the shared goal of constructing the region in ways that markedly contrast with dominant views. They have developed a more complex view of the Pacific and the socio-economic cultural and political forces that shape it and have amply demonstrated the lower impact of traditional systems on biodiversity. While debunking the perception that the forest is being destroyed by poor blacks and Indians, they have carried out some concrete projects that have strengthened local organizations. As an example of persistent and intense negotiation of a development-conservation strategy between the state and a social movement, the experience has left novel lessons for both sides. For Proyecto Biopacífico planners, for instance, it was important to learn to go along with the organizational dynamic of community and social movement, so different from that of a project cycle. Scientifically oriented project staff in charge of developing a map of the region's bio-diversity found this particularly hard to accept. The tension between natural science and social science approaches to biodiversity is as real in the Colombian case as it is elsewhere, including the CBD, even if it cannot be reduced to a simple question of disciplinary training. Once the initial distrust was overcome, it was vital for PCN activists to accept, however provisionally, Proyecto Biopacífico staff members as allies among the many antagonists facing them.

Finally, we can refer this movement and conceptualization back to academic positions. We can, for instance, link it to Félix Guattari's (1995) conception of territory as "the ensemble of projects and representations where a whole series of behaviors and investments can pragmatically emerge, in time and in social, cultural, aesthetic and cognitive space"—that is, as an existential space of self-reference where "dissident subjectivities" can emerge (23, 24). Similarly, the definition of biodiversity proposed by the movement provides elements for reorienting biodiversity discourses according to local principles of autonomy, knowledge, identity, and economy (Shiva 1993). Finally, the activists' efforts to theorize local practices of resource use contribute to a growing awareness that nature is not an objective entity existing outside human history but is deeply produced in conjunction with the collective practice of humans who are integrally connected to it (Descola and Pálsson 1996).

Conclusion

The dismantling of Proyecto Biopacífico in 1998 (also the writing date of texts contributing to this chapter) coincided with the region's accelerated immersion into the armed conflict that engulfs much of the country and from which it had remained relatively immune until the mid–1990s. Involving left-wing guerrillas, right-wing paramilitaries, and the army, and complicated by the increasing presence of drug mafias, the conflict has caused massive displacement, even from already titled collective territories. Although it is impossible to summarize here this sad turn of events, it is relevant to point out the following:

1. This deathly process is fueled by economic interests intent on appropriating and exploiting the region's resources in the most conventional ways.
2. Local-based social movements are opposed to all forms of armed presence since from their perspective the interests of the communities do not coincide with any of the armed actors.
3. Many activists and local leaders have had to leave the region, and there has been massive displacement from many areas, even already titled collective territories.
4. All these events have negated almost a decade of gains by black and indigenous movements and communities. Confronted with this situation, activists are focusing on redressing displacement by emphasizing a general defense of the territory without abandoning completely their environmental and cultural concerns. (See Escobar [2003] for an extended discussion of current displacement and PCN's ways of dealing with it.)

More constructively, and going beyond the Pacific case, we want to end by discussing briefly the potential for fruitful dialogue between political ecologies arising from academic and social movements. Visions generated in social movements of the Pacific resonate with current scholarly proposals to rethink production as the articulation of ecological, cultural, and technoeconomic productivities (Leff 1992, 1995a, 1995b). As Enrique Leff (1995b) insists,

> Sustainable development finds its roots in the conditions of cultural and ecological diversity. These singular and non-reducible processes depend on the functional structures of ecosystems that sustain the production of biotic resources and environmental services; on the energetic efficiency of technological processes; on the symbolic processes and ideological formations underlying the cultural valorization of natural resources; and on the political processes that determine the appropriation of nature. (61)

In other words, the construction of alternative production paradigms, political orders, and sustainability are interdependent aspects of the same process; and this process is advanced in part through the cultural politics of social movements and communities in the defense of their modes of nature and culture. The project of social movements thus constitutes a concrete expression of the search for alternative production and environmental orders envisioned by political ecologists. The dialogue with intellectual-activists such as those from PCN can be advanced through collaborative research about how diverse groups characterize and implement their engagement with the natural world. We academics still have relatively little experience with this type of collaborative research and are unsure about the theoretical, methodological, and political repositionings they might entail for us. The case presented here provides glimpses of the immense scope of possibility opened up by such collaboration.

There is much more to understand about various positions on biodiversity and about the networks that sustain and are sustained by them (King 2001). Work should entail ethnographies of networks that are just emerging at this time, including those in the field of bioprospecting, analyzed by Hanne Svarstad in chapter 13. More ethnographic research is needed on how various organizations articulate their visions and issues (for example, on genetic resources, patenting of life forms, indigenous knowledge) in terms of science, gender, nature, culture, and politics. These organizational networks are prime examples of the emergent set of transnational practices and identities that link virtual and place-based modes of activism and enact a cybercultural politics that is increasingly and paradoxically important for the defense of physical places (Ribeiro 1998, Escobar 1999c).

Much work remains to be done on diverse cultural models of nature. Ethnographically, the focus should be on documenting for diverse groups the ensembles of meanings and uses that characterize their engagement with the natural world. From a multiplicity of cultural models so described, we can posit a number of questions. Is it possible to launch a defense of local models of nature in the scope of biodiversity appropriation and conservation debates? In what ways would current concepts of biodiversity and local knowledge have to be transformed to make this reorientation possible? Finally, which social actors could best advance such a project? And how?

In sum, we have argued in this chapter for a view of biodiversity as a construction that constitutes a powerful interface between nature and culture and originates a vast network of sites and actors through which concepts, policies, and ultimately cultures and ecologies are contested and negotiated. This construction has a growing presence in the strategies of both governments and social movements in many parts of the world. The social movement of black communities of the Colombian Pacific region, for instance, enacts a cultural politics that is significantly mediated by ecological concerns, including biodiversity. Despite the negative forces opposing it, and in the climate of certain favorable ecological and cultural conjunctures, this movement might represent a real defense of the social and biophysical landscapes of the region. That defense has been advanced through a slow and laborious construction of Afro-Colombian identities that articulate with alternative constructions of development, territory, and biodiversity conservation. The social movement of black communities can thus be described as one of cultural and ecological attachment to a territory, even as an attempt at creating new existential territories. Despite its precariousness, this articulation of a link among culture, nature, and development constitutes an alternative political ecology framework for biodiversity discussions. The movement can be seen as an attempt to show that social life, work, nature, and culture can be organized in ways that differ from what dominant models of culture and the economy mandate.

One thing is certain: the distance between dominant discourses of biodiversity conservation and the political ecology of social movements is great and perhaps growing. We hope that, in the spaces of encounter and debate provided by the biodiversity network, academics, scientists, NGOs, and intellectuals can find ways to reflect seriously on, learn from, and support the alternative frameworks that developing-world social movements are crafting with a greater or lesser degree of explicitness and sophistication. Then we can address in a more grounded way the following question at the root of political ecology: can the world be redefined and reconstructed from the perspective of the multiple cultural, economic, and ecological practices that continue to exist among its many communities? This is above all a political question, but one that entails serious epistemological, cultural, and ecological considerations. It speaks of the utopia of reconstructing the world in an ecologically sustainable, socially just, and culturally pluralistic manner.

NOTES

1. Susan Paulson drafted this chapter in conversation with Arturo Escobar and using material drawn from previous publications (Escobar 1999b, 1998; see the latter for a more extended discussion and references). Both collaborators have spent decades researching and participating with local people and social movements in South American rainforests and mountain communities. Thanks to members of the Proceso de Comunidades Negras for their dialogic work and countless conversations and to Enrique Leff for his inspiring work and interest in this piece.

2. The Scientific Committee on Problems of the Environment (SCOPE) Program on Ecosystem Functioning of Biodiversity and the United Nations Environment Program's Global Biodiversity Assessment Program, for instance, follow this approach. See SCOPE's technical volumes, particularly Mooney et al. (1995).

3. Key empirical questions concern to what extent specific knowledges enable practices that are environmentally sustainable. Dahl (1993) makes clear that not all local practices of nature are environmentally benign and not all social relations that articulate them are nonexploitative:

    All people of necessity maintain ideas about, and of necessity act on, their natural environment. This does not necessarily mean that those who live as direct producers have great systematic insights, although on the whole subsistence producers have detailed knowledge about the working of many small aspects of their biological environment. Much of this knowledge has from experience proved to be true and efficient, some is misconceived and counterproductive, and some is incorrect but still functions well enough. (6)

4. This brief presentation of the social movement of black communities is taken from a much longer text (Grueso et al. 1998; also see Escobar 1997). It is based on ongoing

ethnographic research with movement activists that Escobar has been conducting since 1993. The social movement discussed here (PCN's ethnocultural proposal) is largely restricted to the central-southern part of the Pacific region.

5. This presentation of PCN's political ecology framework is based chiefly on conversations and in-depth interviews with key PCN activists, particularly Libia Grueso, Carlos Rosero, and Yellen Aguilar (conducted in 1995, 1996, 1997). It is also based on an intensive eight-day workshop on riverbasin ecological design, which Escobar conducted with Libia Grueso and environmental planner Camila Moreno. Held in Buenaventura in August 1988, the workshop was attended by twenty-five activists and river community leaders. It proved to be extremely useful to both the movement and Escobar since some of the notions discussed here emerged as a collective articulation chiefly by activists and leaders.

REFERENCES

Alvarez, Sonia, Evelina Dagnino, and Arturo Escobar, eds. 1998. *Cultures of Politics/Politics of Cultures: Revisioning Latin American Social Movements*. Boulder, Colo.: Westview.

Asher, Kiran. 1998. "The Politics of Gender and Ethnicity in the Pacific Coast of Colombia." Ph.D. diss., Department of Political Science, University of Florida at Gainesville.

Brush, Stephen. 1998. "Prospecting the Public Domain." Paper presented at the Globalization Project, Center for Latin American Studies, University of Chicago, February 12.

Camacho, Juana. 1996. "Black Women and Biodiversity in the Tribugá Golf, Chocó, Colombia." Final report presented to the MacArthur Foundation, Bogotá.

Dahl, Gudrun, ed. 1993. *Green Arguments for Local Subsistence*. Stockholm: Stockholm Studies in Social Anthropology.

Del Valle, Jorge I., and Eduardo Restrepo, eds. *Renacientes del Guandal*. Bogotá: Proyecto Biopacífico/Universidad Nacional.

Descola, Philippe, and Gísli Pálsson, eds. 1996. *Nature and Society: Anthropological Perspectives*. London: Routledge.

Escobar, Arturo. 1997. "Cultural Politics and Biological Diversity: State, Capital and Social Movements in the Pacific Coast of Colombia." In *Between Resistance and Revolution*, edited by R. Fox and O. Starn. New Brunswick, N.J.: Rutgers University Press.

———. 1998. "Whose Knowledge? Whose Nature? Biodiversity Conservation and the Political Ecology of Social Movements." *Journal of Political Ecology* 5: 53–82.

———. 1999a. "After Nature: Steps to an Anti-Essentialist Political Ecology." *Current Anthropology* 40, no. 1: 1–30.

———. 1999b. "Biodiversity, a Perspective from Within." *Seedling* 16, no. 2: 24–32.

———. 1999c. "Gender, Place, and Networks. A Political Ecology of Cyberculture." In *Women@Internet: Creating New Cultures in Cyberspace*, edited by Wendy Harcourt. London: Zed.

———. 2003. "Displacement and Development in the Colombian Pacific." *International Social Science Journal* 175: 157–67.

Escobar, Arturo, and Alvaro Pedrosa, eds. 1996. *Pacífico: Desarrollo o diversidad? Estado, capital y movimientos sociales en el Pacífico Colombiano*. Bogotá: CEREC/Ecofondo.

Foucault, Michel. 1980. *The History of Sexuality*, translated by Robert Hurley. Vol. 1. New York: Pantheon.

Global Environment Facility/United Nations Development Program (GEF/PNUD). 1993. *Conservación de la biodiversidad del Chocó biogeográfico: Proyecto Biopacífico*. Bogotá: DNP/Biopacífico.

Grueso, Libia, Carlos Rosero, and Arturo Escobar. 1998. "The Process of Black Community Organizing in the Southern Pacific Coast of Colombia." In *Cultures of Politics/Politics of Cultures: Revisioning Latin American Social Movements*, edited by Sonia Alvarez, Evelina Dagnino, and Arturo Escobar. Boulder, Colo.: Westview.

Guattari, Félix. 1995. *Chaosophy*, translated by Paul Bains and Julian Pefanis. New York: Semiotext[e].

Gudeman, Stephen, and Alberto Rivera. 1990. *Conversations in Colombia: The Domestic Economy in Life and Text*. Cambridge: Cambridge University Press.

Hobart, Mark. 1993. "Introduction: The Growth of Ignorance?" In *An Anthropological Critique of Development: The Growth of Ignorance*, edited by Mark Hobart, 1–30. London: Routledge.

Ingold, Tim. 1995. "Building, Dwelling, Living: How Animals and People Make Themselves at Home in the World." In *Shifting Contexts: Transformations in Anthropological Knowledge*, edited by M. Strathern. London: Routledge.

———. 1996. "The Optimal Forager and Economic Man." In *Nature and Society*, edited by Philippe Descola and Gísli Pálsson, 25–44. London: Routledge.

Janzen, Daniel, and H. Hallwachs. 1993. *All Taxa Biodiversity Inventory*. Philadelphia: University of Pennsylvania. Internet document.

King, Mary. 2001. "Translating Risk and Safety through the Transnational Biodiversity Network." Paper presented at the annual meeting of the American Association of Anthropologists, Washington, D.C., November 28–December 2.

Leff, Enrique. 1992. "La dimensión cultural y el manejo integrado, sustentable y sostenido de los recursos naturales." In *Cultura y manejo sustentable de los recursos naturales*, edited by Enrique Leff and Julia Carabias. México, D.F.: CIICH/UNAM.

———. 1995a. *Green Production: Toward an Environmental Rationality*. New York: Guilford.

———. 1995b. "De quién es la naturaleza? Sobre la reapropiación social de los recursos naturales." *Gaceta Ecológica* 37: 58–64.

———. 1997. "Epistemología política, apropiación de saberes etnobotánicos y manejo sustentable de la diversidad vegetal." Paper presented at the Second International Congress of Ethnobotany, Mérida, Mexico, October 16–17.

Lozano, Betty Ruth. 1996. "Mujer y desarrollo." In *Pacífico: Desarrollo o diversidad? Estado, capital y movimientos sociales en el Pacífico Colombiano*, edited by Arturo Escobar and Alvaro Pedrosa. Bogotá: CEREC/Ecofondo.

Mackay, David. 1996. "Agents of Empire: The Banksian Collectors and Evaluation of New Lands." In *Visions of Empire: Voyages, Botany, and Representations of Nature*, edited by David Miller and P. H. Reill. Cambridge: Cambridge University Press.

Martínez-Alier, Joan. 1995. "Political Ecology, Distributional Conflicts, and Ecological Incommensurability." *New Left Review* 211: 70–88.

Melucci, Alberto. 1989. *Nomads of the Present*. Philadelphia: Temple University Press.

Miller, David, and P. H. Reill, eds. 1996. *Visions of Empire: Voyages, Botany, and Representations of Nature*. Cambridge: Cambridge University Press.

Mooney, H. A., J. Lubchenko, R. Dirzo, and O. E. Sala, eds. 1995. "Biodiversity and Ecosystem Functioning." In *Global Biodiversity Assessment*. Cambridge: Cambridge University Press/United Nations Environment Program.

Ribeiro, Gustavo Lins. 1997. "Transnational Virtual Community? Exploring Implications for Culture, Power, and Language." *Organization* 4, no. 4: 496–505.

———. 1998. "Cybercultural Politics: Political Activism at a Distance in a Transnational World." In *Cultures of Politics/Politics of Cultures: Revisioning Latin American Social Movements*, edited by Sonia Alvarez, Evelina Dagnino, and Arturo Escobar, 325–52. Boulder, Colo.: Westview.

Richards, Paul. 1993. "Cultivation: Knowledge or Performance?" In *An Anthropological Critique of Development*, edited by Mark Hobart, 61–78. London: Routledge.

Rojas, Jeannette. 1996. "Las mujeres en movimiento: Crónicas de otras miradas." In *Pacífico: Desarrollo o diversidad? Estado, capital y movimientos sociales en el Pacifico Colombiano*, edited by Arturo Escobar and Alvaro Pedrosa, 205–19. Bogotá: CEREC/Ecofondo.

Sánchez, Enrique, and Claudia Leal. 1995. "Elementos para una evaluación de sistemas productivos adaptativos en el Pacífico Colombiano." In *Economías de las comunides rurales en el Pacífico Colombiano*, edited by Claudia Leal, 73–88. Bogotá: Proyecto Biopacífico.

Shiva, Vandana. 1993. *Monocultures of the Mind*. London: Zed.

———. 1997. *Biopiracy*. Boston: South End.

Strathern, Marilyn. 1980. "No Nature, No Culture: The Hagen Case." In *Nature, Culture, and Gender*, edited by C. McCormick and Marilyn Strathern, 174–222. Cambridge: Cambridge University Press.

Takacs, David. 1996. *The Idea of Biodiversity*. Baltimore: Johns Hopkins University Press.

Wilson, Edward O. 1993. *Naturalist*. Washington, D.C.: Island.

World Resources Institute, International Union for the Conservation of Nature, United Nations Environment Program (WRI/IUCN/UNEP). 1992. *Global Biodiversity Strategy*. Washington, D.C.: WRI.

NOTES ON CONTRIBUTORS

METTE J. BROGDEN is an anthropologist and public issues mediator and practitioner in the field of environmental and public policy conflict resolution. She manages the Udall Center for Public Policy's Environmental Conflict Resolution program and has worked on multistakeholder policy development from local to national levels. She uses political ecology approaches to understand complexity and system transformation.

BILL DERMAN is a professor of anthropology at Michigan State University and Professor II at the Institute for Environment and Development Studies at the Agricultural University of Norway (Noragric). He has been carrying out research in Zimbabwe since 1987, after a long period of research in West Africa. His interests include environment and change, planned rural development, analyses of development projects, and, more recently, decentralization of natural resource management institutions. Derman has published a series of papers on decentralization, human rights, development, and water reform.

MICHAEL R. DOVE is the Margaret K. Musser Professor of Social Ecology in Yale University's School of Forestry and Environmental Studies. An anthropologist, he has studied relations between society and environment in Asia for three decades. Twelve of those years were spent in-country (mostly in Indonesia and Pakistan) carrying out collaborative teaching and research with indigenous groups, local universities, international NGOs, and U.S. foundations. His research focuses on the links between the resource-use systems of local communities and wider societies—between urban and rural, rich and poor, and less- and more-developed countries.

ARTURO ESCOBAR is a professor of anthropology at the University of North Carolina in Chapel Hill. He has been working for the past ten years in the Colombian Pacific, chiefly in conjunction with activists from the region's social movement of black communities and biodiversity projects. Escobar is currently completing a book on the subject. Previous books include *Encountering Development* (1994) and a co-edited volume called *Spaces of Neoliberalism: Land, Place, and Family in Latin America* (2002).

ANNE FERGUSON is an associate professor and director of the Women and International Development Program at Michigan State University. She researches and teaches in the areas of development studies, gender, and agricultural and environmental change. Currently, her research centers on the gender dimensions of Malawi's new water reform policies. In 2000, she received a Fulbright Hays Faculty Research Abroad Program grant to study the gender dimensions of Malawi's and Zimbabwe's water reforms.

ANDREW GARDNER is a Ph.D. candidate in the Department of Anthropology at the University of Arizona. He is currently working on a study of transnational labor in the petroleum-rich nations of the Arabian Gulf. He received the Society for Applied Anthropology's Peter K. New annual student paper award in 2000.

LISA L. GEZON is an associate professor and chair of the Department of Anthropology at the State University of West Georgia. Her current projects include a study of a sense of place among sustainable and conventional farmers in Georgia and a commodity-chain approach to a study of land use and urban consumption in northern Madagascar. The project in Madagascar has been funded by the National Geographic Society, a Fulbright-Hays Faculty Research Abroad Fellowship, and the National Science Foundation.

JAMES B. GREENBERG is associate director of the Bureau of Applied Research in Anthropology and professor in the Department of Anthropology at the University of Arizona. He is the co-editor of the *Journal of Political Ecology*. He received his Ph.D. from the University of Michigan in 1978. His areas of specialization include political ecology, law and development, economic anthropology, applied anthropology, Mexico, and the borderlands.

JOSIAH McC. HEYMAN is a professor of anthropology and chair of the Department of Sociology and Anthropology at the University of Texas at El Paso. A long-time student of the U.S.-Mexico border, he is the author or editor of three books and thirty articles on border culture, states, migration, labor, and consumption. He was honored by the Royal Anthropological Institute of Great Britain and Ireland with the 1999 Curl Essay Prize for an article on the moral debate over Mexico-U.S. immigration. His recent essay, "The Inverse of Power," published in *Anthropological Theory*, addresses political-ethical issues in the anthropological study of power.

ALF HORNBORG is an anthropologist and professor of human ecology at the University of Lund, Sweden. He is author of *The Power of the Machine: Global Inequalities of Economy, Technology, and Environment* (2001) and co-editor of *Voices of the Land: Identity and Ecology in the Margins* (1998) and *Negotiating Nature: Culture, Power, and Environmental Argument* (2000).

A. FIONA D. MACKENZIE is a professor in the Department of Geography and Environmental Studies at Carleton University, Ottawa, Canada. Among her publications on Kenya is the monograph *Land, Ecology, and Resistance in Kenya, 1880–1952*, published in 1998 by the University of Edinburgh Press and co-published by Heinemann in the United States. Her current research concerns identity, community, and the environment in the highlands and islands of Scotland.

SUSAN PAULSON began to explore Andean and Amazonian life in 1985 and soon moved to South America, where she spent twelve years working and researching in many intriguing contexts. Her work, published in ten countries, strives to better understand processes through which class, race, ethnic, and gender systems interact with environment and health. She currently serves as the director of Latin American Studies at Miami University.

CHARLES J. STEVENS teaches American and International Studies at Miami University in Oxford, Ohio. He completed his Ph.D. in anthropology at the University of Arizona. Stevens has conducted fieldwork on agricultural practices in the kingdom of Tonga, the midwestern United States, and the Pima-Maricopa Indian community in Arizona. His research interests include agro-ecology, sustainable agriculture, small farming families, and the ethnography of rural communities.

HANNE SVARSTAD is a sociologist and a senior research fellow at the Norwegian Institute for Nature Research, Unit for Human-Environment Studies. She has carried out mono- and interdisciplinary studies on biodiversity management and bioprospecting as well as other human-environment issues in Africa and Norway. Svarstad has edited or co-edited several Norwegian and Nordic volumes on social science, environment, and economic development. Her research encompasses aspects of epistemology, qualitative methodology, discourse analysis, grounded theory, and political ecology.

MICHAEL WATTS has taught at the University of California at Berkeley for twenty-five years and is currently director of the Institute of International Studies and the Chancellor's Professor of Geography. He has written on political ecology, food and mines, political Islam, and oil politics and has co-edited numerous volumes, including *Liberation Ecologies* (1996) and *Violent Environments* (2001).

INDEX

abstraction, 197

activism, 27, 31, 56, 62, 113, 197, 208–209, 245, 265, 270–271

adaptation, 20

Adger, W. Neil, 251

Adorno, Theodor, 24

advertising, 121

agency, 4, 11, 147–149, 243

agriculture: and industrialization, 162, 164; and modernization, 182, 184–185

agroforestry, 5, 154–155, 161–162, 220

Agua Prieta, 113–132

Ahearn, Laura M., 148

Althusser, Louis, 92n5

Andes Mountains, 174–195

Antrosio, Jason, 119

Appadurai, Arjun, 9

applied anthropology, 18, 61

Arce, Alberto, 61

Arizona, land use, 3, 12, 41–60

authenticity, 205–206

Ayurveda, 229

babul (*Acacia nilotica (L.) Willd. ex Del.*), 227

Balick, Michael, J., 244

Baluchistan, 223

bands, 199

Barrett, Christopher B., 140

Bastidas, Elena, 130n11

Bateson, Gregory, 20, 23

Beakhurst, Grahame, 17

Beanlands, Gordon, 203

Bedouin nomads, 4, 14, 26, 76–93

beef consumption, 114

Bell, Janet, 246

Berkeley, University of California at, 21

Berry, Sara S., 149

biodemocracy, 261

biodiversity, 4, 7, 87, 94–112, 164, 176, 185–187, 240, 257–258, 273; definitions of, 259, 269; discourse, 259; networks, 259

bioimperialism, 261

biopiracy, 7, 245–246

bioprospecting, 6–7, 239–256, 257

Blaikie, Piers, 2, 18, 27, 29, 61, 95, 174, 217, 239

blue jeans, 122

Bolivia, 5, 21, 174–195

borders: in Saudi Arabia, 26, 82–83; between U.S. and Mexico, 4, 27, 113–132

Border Environmental Cooperation Commission, 129n9

Bourdieu, Pierre, 263

Bourque, Susan, 186

Brazil, 25–26

Brookfield, Harold, 2, 27, 29, 61, 95, 217, 239

Brundtland Report, 189

Brush, Stephen, 190, 260

Bryant, Raymond, L., 231

buffering, 85

Burawoy, Michael, 14, 95, 109, 137

Burkina Faso, 105

Butler, Judith, 28

Canadian Indian policy, 197

capabilities, 127

Cape Breton. *See* Nova Scotia

capitalism, 7, 30, 63, 135, 209, 211–212, 266; and time/space, 120; capitalization of nature, 97

Carney, Judith, 101, 103

Carter, Simon E., 105
causation, 12, 46, 77–80, 88–91; and
    overdetermination, 90 and proximate
    causes, 7, 160; and structural factors, 7
Champion, Daryl, 91n4
Chatty, Dawn, 87
class, 13, 26, 99, 222–223; in Saudi Arabia,
    80, 83–84
Cleaver, Frances, 106
climate information, 78, 88–89
Coalition Against Biopiracy, 245
Cockburn, Alexander, 17, 25
coffee, 102
Cole, Donald P., 77, 87
collaborative interdisciplinary research,
    174–195, 239, 257–277
collective consumption, 126
collective ethnic identities, 257–277
Colombia, 7, 21, 257–277
colonialism, 8, 20, 23, 99, 138–139, 146, 154,
    183–184, 198, 240
Columbia University, 20
commodification, 3, 43, 51, 71, 209, 211, 241
commodity fetishism, 121–122
common property, 106
community, 1, 22
community-based collaborative groups,
    43, 52–53, 57
conceptual encompassment, 206–208
conflict, 12
conservation, 5, 139–141, 250, 257–258;
    and development plans, 270
consumption, 4, 27; literature on, 128n1;
    perspective on, 113–115; political ecol-
    ogy of, 115–123; politics of, 124–126;
    social inequality and, 129n7; status imi-
    tation and, 129n7
Convention on Biological Diversity, 241,
    259, 261
cooperatives, 102
Cowling, Wendy, 163
credit, 121
Crowley, Eve L., 105
Crumley, Carole L., 30
cultural autonomy, 261
cultural ecology, 3
cultural geography, 21, 25
cultural politics, 264, 273
customary law, 99–100, 149

deep ecology, 6, 210
deforestation, 8, 185, 190
degradation, environmental, 1–2, 5, 174; in
    Latin America, 175
democratization, 157, 163, 169
Denevan, William M., 21
Department of Indian Affairs, 199, 205
dependency theory, 23, 187
Derrida, Jacques, 218
Descola, Philippe, 30
desertification, 4
development, 6; and counter-develop-
    ment, 72–73
disaster studies, 22–23
discourse, 29, 64, 72, 95–96, 196–197,
    202–209, 232, 239, 242–252, 274; and
    globalization, 258
disembeddedness, 209–210
Dolan, Catherine S., 103, 105
Dominican Republic, 9
drought, 26, 72–73
Dublin Principles, 63–64
Duinker, Peter, 203–204
Durning, Alan, 113

Earth Summit, 244, 259
ecological anthropology, 3, 20, 25; "new"
    ecological anthropology, 30
ecological capital, 97
education, 207–208
Eisner, Thomas, 244
electric lighting, 120
Ellen, Roy F., 211
emergence theory, 50
Endangered Species Act, 53
environmental conflict resolution, 41, 51
environmental impact assessment, 201
environmentalism, 196
environmental justice, 26–27, 197
Epstein, A. L., 138
Escobar, Arturo, 17, 148
ethnicity, 1, 26, 86–87, 175, 196, 204–205,
    222–223, 257–258, 263, 269
ethnography: institutional, 223. See also
    methods
Evans, Mike, 163–164
event ecology, 77, 89–91

Fairhead, James, 8, 107

farinaceous crops, 155
feasts, 156–160
Food and Agriculture Organization, 64
Forde, C. Daryll, 19
Fordism, 129n3
foresters, 219; dynamics with farmers, 223
Forestry Planning and Development Project, 217–238
Foucault, Michel, 243, 259
Fourth World, 197
Frank, André Gunder, 242
Frankfurt School, 24
Friedman, Jonathan, 20, 25
fuel sources, 119
fuelwood, 220, 233n6
fur trade, 198–199

Gambia, 101
Geertz, Clifford, 154
gemeinschaft, 199
gender, 1, 26, 97, 125, 174, 177, 189–190, 266; analysis, 177–182; and landscapes, 179, 182; and politics, 179
generational differences, 125
Genetic Resources Action International, 245
germplasm management, 182
Giddens, Anthony, 205
Gifford, James, 160
Gleick, Peter, 64
global and the local, 14, 61, 85, 95—97, 174, 182, 196–197, 206–209, 212, 219; as one domain, 136, 158; and fieldwork, 248–250; and scales of analysis, 9–10; and water reform, 65–66.
Global Biodiversity Strategy, 259
globalization, 8, 43, 91, 135–136, 154, 160, 168, 174, 196, 239; and abstraction, 197–198; and degradation, 57; and ethnography, 137; and grassroots movements, 142; and pastoralism, 84–85; and political ecology, 2, 8, 90–91, 239–256
globalocentric, 261
Glooscap. See Kluskap
Gramsci, Antonio, 243
granite quarry, 196–214
grassroots movements, 27, 142
Gray, Leslie C., 105

Great Britain, 161
Greenberg, James, 13, 129n4
greenhouse gases, 130n10
Grifo, Francesca, 244
Grove-White, Robin, 209–210
Guattari, Félix, 271
Guha, Ramachandra, 9
Guinea, Republic of, 107
Gulf War (1991), 14, 26, 78
Guyer, Jane, 105

Haenn, Nora, 232
Hardin, Garrett, 44
Harper, Janice, 10
Harvey, David, 30
Hecht, Susanna, 25
hegemony, 147, 243
Heidegger, Martin, 263
Hellum, Anne, 64
Hewitt, Adrian, 140
Hewitt, Kenneth, 22
hierarchical relations, 156
Hill, Sarah, 127
Hirschman, A. O., 209
holism, 79–80, 203–204
Horkheimer, Max, 24
Hornborg, Alf, 148, 174, 187
households, 22, 129n8, 155, 163–164, 169, 221
housework, 115
Houston, 10
human ecology, 27, 217
human rights, 64

identity, 149, 155, 196–197, 202–205, 211–212, 265, 273; collective, 257
India, 130n10
Indian jujube (*zizyphus Mauritania Lam.*), 227
indigenous, 136, 233n3
Ingold, Tim, 263
institutions, 3; ethnography of, 223
integrated conservation and development projects (ICDPs), 139
intellectual property rights, 241, 258, 261–263
intercropping, 181

Janzen, Daniel, 260

Jarosz, Lucy, 8
Johnston, Barbara, 11, 31
Juma, Calestous, 240

Kandeh, H.B.S., 105
Kauffman, Stuart A., 50
Kenya, 4, 94–112
Kevane, Michael, 105
Khor, Martin, 246
Kingdom of Saudi Arabia. See Saudi Arabia
Kingdom of Tonga. See Tonga
Kluskap, 200
Kroeber, Alfred, 19, 21
Kurin, Richard, 230
Kuwait, 78

labor, 25, 101
land, commodification of, 43, 51
land managers, 26
landscape, 2, 21, 76, 135, 137, 174, 176, 184,
    189, 196; social construction of, 5
land tenure, 4, 86–87, 94–112, 143, 145–146,
    155, 161, 169, 179; and privatization, 163;
    in sub-Saharan Africa, 98–101
Latin America, 175
Latukefu, Sione, 160
Law of Popular Participation, in Bolivia,
    190–191
Leach, Melissa, 8, 107
Lee, Richard B., 211
Leff, Enrique, 31, 272
Lévi-Strauss, Claude, 229
life world, 196
livestock, 6
local and global. See global and local
local knowledge, 7, 96–97, 258, 262, 273
Long, Norman, 61

Madagascar, 5, 8, 135–153
maquiladoras, 114
Marcus, George, 14, 137
marginality, 2
market, 6, 87
Martinez-Alier, Joan, 9, 73
Marxism, 13, 23–24, 27, 118, 121, 187, 217;
    feminist, 23, 118; and proletarianiza-
    tion, 118; structural, 23
mass media, 121
Matose, Frank M., 107

McGregor, Joann, 107
McKean, Margaret A., 106
meanings, 196
Meggers, Betty, 21
Merchant, Carolyn, 24
mesquite (Prosopis juliflora (Swartz) DC),
    227
metis. See local knowledge
methods, 14–15, 20, 56, 116–117, 135–138,
    155, 174, 177, 198, 220–224; appliance
    histories, 116–117; case method, 138;
    event ecology, 77; participant observa-
    tion, 137; participatory, 179; transect
    walks, 179
Mexico, 113–132; economy of, 113–114; and
    peso devaluation, 113–114; purchasing
    power, 113–114
Michigan State University, 61
Mies, Maria, 188
migration, 6, 82–84, 102, 117, 121, 162–164,
    169, 175–178, 187
Mi'kmaq Indians, 196–214; the Grand
    Council, 200; Warriors, 200–201
missionaries, 161
modernity, 72, 196–214, 266
modernization, 6, 87–88, 91, 183
Morgan, Lewis H., 19
mudir syndrome, 91n4

National Conference of Black Communi-
    ties, 265
National Environmental Action Plan
    (Madagascar), 140–141, 143
nature, concepts of, 4; cultural construc-
    tions of, 262
Nature Conservancy, 54
neem tree (Azadirachta indica A. Juss.),
    227
neoliberalism, 7, 146
Netting, Robert McC., 105, 154
New Zealand, 162
Nietschmann, Bernard, 21
Nigeria, 105
non-governmental organizations (NGOs),
    136, 139–140, 176, 184, 187, 189, 245,
    257, 259–261, 270–271
Northwest Frontier (Pakistan), 218, 223
Nova Scotia, 6, 12, 196–214
Nova Scotia Human Rights Act, 204

nutrition and environment, 182, 185

objectification, 206–208
Okoth-Ogendo, H.W.O., 98
Orlove, Benjamin S., 190
Ortner, Sherry, 24, 137–138, 146
overdetermination, 92n5
overgrazing, 47, 76–93
OXFAM, 185

Pakistan, 6, 217–238
Pakistan Forest Service, 217–238
PAN (*Partido de Accion Nacional, Mexico*), 124–125
Park, Thomas K., 13
Parsons, Elsie Clews, 200
Parsons, Howard L., 24
Parsons, James J., 21
participatory research methods, 177–179. See *also* methods
pastoralism, 76–77
patents, and biopiracy, 249–252
peasant studies, 23
Peet, Richard, 11
Peluso, Nancy, 30
People's Global Action against Free Trade, 267
Pierce, Jennifer, 218–219
place, 25–26, 136, 168, 211
plant diversity, 162–163
Pliny, 234n21
poison tree, 235n30
policy, 22, 62–63, 66, 85, 114–115; and moral suasion, 114; and price incentives, 114-115; and public participation, 115
political capital, 224
political ecology: and action, 11; and ethnography, 14, 79, 90–91, 106, 115–117, 137, 154, 223, 262, 273 (*see also* methods); and consumption, 4, 116; critiques of, 77; and culture, 13, 18–19, 109, 140–141, 218, 262; definition of, 2, 17, 62, 239, 257, 268, 274; and discourse, 242; and feminism, 28, 95; and gender analyses, 11, 174–195; and history, 90–91, 117, 160, 169, 189; and materialism, 13, 18, 19–20, 24, 109; and "the political," 27–28, 98, 177, 217, 219, 230,

232, 240, 263; and poststructuralism, 95, 108–109; and practice theory, 28, 273; and social movements, 258, 263; and space, 120–121; and time, 120; in urban contexts, 4, 9
political economy, 3, 17, 90, 104, 106, 117, 155, 161, 239, 262; and cultural meaning, 218; genealogy of, 23–25; of global practice, 240–242; and Marxist social relations, 27
political organization, 156, 161
Polynesian social structure, 160
population change, 164
postcolonial, 95
postmodernism, 29, 97, 205, 210
poststructuralism, 28, 231, 251, 259
Potter, L. M., 166
power, 4, 11–12, 95, 135, 174, 198, 205, 217, 231, 260; and conceptual encompassment, 206–208; defining, 28; and the discourse of biodiversity, 262–263; as the focus of political ecology, 62; as the political, 137–138
practical knowledge of the environment, 263
Price, Lisa Leimar, 107, 108
Price protests, and effects on politics, 124–125
primitive, 211
Proceso de Comunidades Negras, 258, 265
processualism, 77, 80, 90–91, 135–136, 147–149, 189
production, 8, 24, 272
productivity, 5
progressive contextualization, 77, 90–91
proletarianization. See Marxism
property rights, 94
protected areas, 142
pruning, 230
public land, 48, 86–87
public policy. See policy
Punjab, 218, 223

quarry. See granite quarry

race, 1, 69, 72, 99
Raffles, Hugh, 9
ranching, 12, 47–49
rapid appraisal, 26, 77

Rapp, Reyna, 118
Rappaport, Roy, 20, 22
reflexivity, 211–212
Reid, Walter V., 245
religious celebrations, 156
research methods. *See* methods
reserves, 199
resistance, 4, 12, 99, 102, 135, 212
reterritorialization, 45, 54, 57
Richards, Paul, 22, 105, 263
rights, 155, 245, 258, 264–265
Rio Summit (1992), 260
risk, 4, 197
ritual, 5, 156–160
Rocheleau, Dianne, 9, 17, 97–98, 109
Roe, Emery, 247
Roseberry, William, 154
Rosenthal, Joshua, 244
Rural Advancement Foundation International, 245

Sacred Mountain Society, 200–201
Sahlins, Marshall, 160
Sassen, Saskia, 9
satellite image analysis, 136
Satterfield, Terre, 136
Saudi Arabia, 4, 14, 26, 76–93
saudiization, 83–84
Sauer, Carl, 21
scale, 7–8, 11–12, 14, 25–26, 135–137,
    147–149, 174, 222–223, 239, 258
Schmink, Marianne, 130n11
Schroeder, Richard, 103, 235n28
Scott, James, 96, 229, 231
sexual status, 179
shade, 217–238
Shiva, Vandana, 188, 246, 262, 271
shopping, 115–116
Silverblatt, Irene, 182
sissoo (*Dalbergia sisoo Roxb.*), 226
Small, Cathy A., 163
smallholder farmers, 160, 224–225
social capital, 190, 207
social differentiation, 3
social inequality, in Latin America, 175
social justice, 18, 26, 62
social movements, 7, 196, 257–258,
    261–266, 273
social organization, 160

social system, 156
soil degradation, 164, 174
soil erosion, 176, 185, 190
soil fertility, 155, 165–168, 175, 228
Southeast Asia Regional Institute for
    Community Education, 245
sovereignty, 261
space, 7, 168, 175, 180, 211, 239, 258, 265,
    270; regional space, 121, 269; urban
    space, 121
Special Places Protection Act, 204
spirituality, 197, 203–204, 208–210, 212
sprawl, 48, 50–51
stakeholder participation, 67–69
state, 3, 43–44, 57, 80–82, 90, 145, 206, 217,
    223, 258
Steward, Julian, 8, 19–20
Stone, M. Priscilla, 105
Stott, Philip, 30
stoves, 118–119, 176
structural adjustment, 102, 140
structure, and agency, 163
sustainability, 17, 97, 155, 161–162, 189, 201,
    210, 244, 250, 270; and allocation, 57;
    and economics, 42
symbolic anthropology, 24, 95, 155, 159
systems ecology, 21

Tanzania, 7, 239–256
technology, 87–88, 197
technoscientific networks, 260
television, 121
territorialization, 3, 43, 57, 269
Thailand, 107
Third World Network, 245
Thompson, E. P., 119
time: and wage labor, 120; and school,
    120
Tonga, 5, 154–173
traditional knowledge, 251
traditionalism, 205
tragedy of the commons, 44, 56–57, 82,
    86–87, 143
transportation, 120–121
trees, 141–142, 176, 218; and shade, 6,
    217–238
tribes, 82
Tsing, Anna L., 14, 135–136, 147
Turner, Matt, 29

Unani Tibb, 229, 231
Union of Nova Scotia Indians (UNSI), 202
United Nations, 207, 259; Convention on Biological Diversity, 94; Statistical Commission, 189; Working Group on Indigenous Populations, 267
University of Michigan, 22
University of Zimbabwe, 61
urban services. *See* utilities
U.S. Agency for International Development (USAID), 139–140, 217–238
utilities, 126

Vayda, Andrew, 13–14, 20, 77, 89, 217
vulnerability, 85

Walters, Bradley, 13–14, 89
Warren, Kay, 186
water resources, 11, 61–75, 86–87; and user-pays principle, 70–71

Watts, Michael, 11
Wilk, Richard, 128n1
Wilson, Edward O., 259
Wissler, Clark, 19
Wittgenstein, Ludwig, 230
Wolf, Eric, 8, 17, 24, 28, 154
women, and the environment, 5, 11, 97, 188, 249
World Bank, 63, 102, 105, 139–140, 143, 261
World Conference on Sustainable Development, 61
World Conservation Union, 244
World Resources Institute, 244
world system theory, 8, 23, 187, 197
World Wildlife Fund for Nature, 244

youth culture, 122–123

Zimbabwe, 11, 61–75, 106, 107
Zimmerer, Karl S., 11, 29, 177, 187